Perspectives on Human Dignity: A Conversation

Perspectives on Human Dignity: A Conversation

Edited by

Jeff Malpas
University of Tasmania
Australia

and

Norelle Lickiss
University of Tasmania and University of Sydney
Australia

Springer

A C.I.P. Catalogue record for this book is available from the Library of Congress.

ISBN 978-90-481-7594-9
ISBN 978-1-4020-6281-0 (e-book)

Published by Springer,
P.O. Box 17, 3300 AA Dordrecht, The Netherlands.

www.springer.com

Printed on acid-free paper

Foreword

The Honourable William Cox AC RFD ED,
Governor of Tasmania

The issue of human dignity was given a new impetus at the end of the Second World War as a reaction to the horrors of the Jewish holocaust and other Nazi atrocities. The immediate consequence was its recognition in such international documents as the Charter of the United Nations (1945) and the Universal Declaration of Human Rights (1948). Several new national constitutions likewise gave it recognition. Though undefined, it was seen as a supreme value possessed by all human beings and one giving rise to rights and obligations in and upon them. In recent decades the existence of these rights has led to acceptance of procedures whereby they may be enforced, and to the overthrow of such doctrines constraining them as that of Sovereign Immunity.

In domestic law, too, there have been ramifications, while advances in medical science have raised ethical issues in respect of genetics, human cloning, and the termination or officious prolongation of life. It was timely then that consideration should be given to human dignity by a wide range of researchers and practitioners in disciplines such as law, philosophy, history, political science, medicine, the arts, and theology at the Colloquium in Hobart in 2004 organized by the editors of this volume.

Depending upon one's view of what constitutes human dignity, some meaningful attempt can be made at defining the nature and extent of human rights and obligations. For the Christian, human dignity derives from God's creative love. Genesis records that at each stage of creation God saw what He had created and found it to be good. In the case of mankind He bestowed a special gift—participation in His own life cycle. He made humanity in His image, that is to say, human beings became part of His perception of Himself, a perception so intense that it is personified in the Word or Logos. Because human beings are the object of God's love they have a special dignity which demands universal respect. Even when a person turns from God in favour of self, God's love for that person never wanes nor is that dignity lost. Humanists on the other hand see the source of human dignity in humanity's intellect and free will—that unique capacity to reason and to make moral choices. Whatever be the *raison d'être* of human dignity as a characteristic possessed by human beings by virtue of their humanity alone, its centrality and importance in our world is now being increasingly recognized, and scholars from a multitude of disciplines are seeking to analyse its nature and to determine its consequences for, and application to, their fields of endeavour. This series of essays is presented as a conversation between international and national exponents of these disciplines, exchanging views each from his or her own perspective. As Norelle Lickiss says in her contribution, 'There are so many prisms through which the gaze may pass! It is obvious that the sciences concerning the human necessarily interpenetrate, with permeable boundaries.'

This volume is a most worthwhile channel through which to launch further analysis and reflection upon a subject which is of vital importance to our increasingly materialistic and utilitarian world in its daily intercourse and which, in view of our common mortality, inevitably affects us all.

Acknowledgements

This volume would not have been possible without the collaboration and support, not only of the participants included here, but also those who were part of the Hobart Interdisciplinary Colloquium that took place in Hobart, Tasmania in November 2004. Among those who were not able to be represented in this volume, the editors would particularly like to acknowledge Donna Marwick, Geoff Parr, and John Tooth. Thanks are also due to Mundipharma Australia for its generous support of the activities of the Colloquium, as well as to Amanda Wojtowicz and the University of Tasmania. The editors would also like to thank Fritz Schmuhl for his advice and encouragement, and to Eilidh Campbell St John for her invaluable assistance in the preparation of the final typescript.

Contents

1
Introduction to a Conversation

Jeff Malpas and Norelle Lickiss

This book has its origins in an unusual meeting in Hobart, Tasmania, in November 2004. Over two days, some 25 historians, physicians, and others gathered together to participate in a single conversation on the subject of human dignity. The conversational character of the meeting was quite deliberate: although each participant came with some prepared material to present to the others, the aim was to encourage a true interdisciplinary engagement, and to encourage a dialogue between individuals that would allow new perspectives and ideas to emerge. Most of the participants had not met one another previously, and the only point in common was a shared contact with the two organizers.

It seems hardly possible that the idea of dignity that was the focus for that meeting, and the focus for this volume, could be approached adequately other than in such a multidisciplinary and 'conversational' manner—the idea does not fit easily into any particular disciplinary framework, it is called upon by lawyers, physicians, philosophers, and historians, it arises as a key concept in different contexts and with different intentions, and yet it is also a concept that remains in common usage even if sometimes imbued with varying meanings and connotations. It is also an idea that seems increasingly under threat from a number of directions: the treatment of refugees and so-called illegal immigrants in Australia and overseas; the use of torture in places such as Guantanamo Bay and Abu Graib; the continuing debate over voluntary euthanasia; new medical technologies from cloning to stem cell research; even changes in industrial legislation and the new face of contemporary work. As the world becomes a more stressful, demanding, and challenging place, so questions concerning the nature and worth of human being become all the more pressing, and it is to these latter questions that the concept of human dignity directs us. Moreover, just as the questions at issue here are large and complex and do not always admit of easy or clear-cut answers, so too does the concept of human dignity present itself as equally complex and multifaceted.

Far from being an indication of its uselessness or irrelevance, the breadth of the concept, its ubiquity, especially in legal and biomedical contexts, and the difficulty in giving of it a clear and unambiguous definition, all point towards its absolutely fundamental character. Dignity connects up with too many other concepts, and in too many ways, for it to be amenable to any simple rendering—it has to be seen as part of a network of concepts from which it cannot easily be

J. Malpas and N. Lickiss (eds.), Perspectives on Human Dignity: A Conversation, 1–5.

disentangled. Ruth Macklin's well-known and provocative claim (also briefly discussed by Daniel Sulmasy in his contribution to this volume) that 'dignity is a useless concept… and can be eliminated without any loss of content',[1] seems not only to lack any clear argument or substantiation in Macklin's own presentation (the importance of the claim seems at odds with the paucity of argument provided to support it), but it seems also to neglect the simple but crucial point that almost no key concept is amenable to the sort of definition that Macklin appears to demand—indeed, the more important the concept, the less likely it is that we can expect to be able to define it in an clear and unambiguous fashion. Dignity is, in this respect, no different from other foundational concepts. As the philosopher Donald Davidson has noted:

> For the most part, the concepts philosophers single out for attention, like truth, knowledge, belief, action, cause, the good and the right, are the most elementary concepts we have, concepts without which (I am inclined to say) we would have no concepts at all. Why then should we expect to be able to reduce these concepts definitionally to other concepts that are simpler, clearer, and more basic? We should accept the fact that what makes these concepts so important must also foreclose on the possibility of finding a foundation for them that reaches deeper into bedrock.[2]

The essays contained in this collection deal with the idea of dignity, and more specifically, human dignity, from a wide range of different perspectives, and with respect to a variety of interests and approaches. The volume is organized into two parts. The first deals with the concept of dignity as such, with its nature and some of its history. With one exception, these essays are primarily philosophical in their orientation, and they attempt various explorations of the nature and significance of dignity in the broadest of senses. Although philosophical, many of these essays are also attuned, *pace* Macklin, to the role of dignity in medicine and medical practice, and yet they also go beyond the usual rather limited engagement of philosophy with medicine that goes under the name of 'bioethics'. In this regard, a number of the essays in this first section of the volume can be viewed as attempting something of that wider engagement between the medical and the philosophical that Henk Ten Have has forcefully advocated elsewhere.[3] Daniel Sulmasy's essay begins the volume

---

[1] 'Dignity is a Useless Concept', *British Medical Journal*, 327 (2003), p.1420. Admittedly, Macklin includes here the qualification 'in medical ethics', although it is not clear what force this qualification actually carries—does Macklin accept that the concept has content in what she views as its original context of religious or human rights discourse? The tone and direction of her comments suggest that she does not. On a more charitable reading of Macklin's argument, one might take her to be pointing to the difficulty in giving an account of dignity that can adequately be operationalized within medical contexts, but this is probably more indicative of the shortcomings in the demand for operationalization than in the concept of dignity.

[2] Donald Davidson, 'The Folly of Trying to Define Truth', *Truth, Language and History* (Oxford: Clarendon Press, 2005), p.20.

[3] See Henk Ten Have, 'From Synthesis and System to Morals and Procedure: The Development of Philosophy of Medicine', in R. A. Carson and C. R. Burns (eds), *Philosophy of Medicine and Bioethics* (Dordrecht, The Netherland: Kluwer, 1997), pp.105–123.

with a general overview of the concept of dignity and its contemporary deployment; the essays by Malpas and Lickiss both explore, in different ways, the connections between dignity and our conception of human being; drawing on Confucian thought, Brennan and Lo discuss the way dignity is tied up with notions of honour and self-determination; Hursthouse looks at the way dignity is implicated with the idea of charity; Schultziner takes a more directly analytic approach, charting the roles and meanings associated with the concept, while, finally, Lewis provides us with an introduction to its conceptual history. The essays that comprise the second part of the volume treat of dignity in more specific terms, with respect to particular aspects or applications, or its appearance within particular contexts, including the literary, the legal, the biomedical, and the historical. Mason's and Brady's contributions both consider the way dignity appears within particular literary contexts—in Mason, the focus is on Forster's *A Passage to India* and Ishiguro's *Remains of the Day* and in Brady, Patrick White's *Tree of Man*; St John and Blackler take up the exploration of dignity with reference to a specifically Christian religious context; Dening and Tarling, both historians, examine the way dignity figures within certain historical and social contexts; Green, Chalmers and Ida, Davis, and Tate, all explore aspects of the way dignity currently figures within national and international legal theory and practice; and the final four essays, from Tattersall, Hacker, Christakis, and Coulehan, all take different approaches to dignity as it arises in medicine and medical practice.

Running across many of these essays is one clear line of debate: the relation between dignity and autonomy, or, as it sometimes also appears, between dignity and equality. Dignity is often understood, especially in contemporary legal and medical discourse, as best articulated in terms of these two concepts, such that human dignity is respected and upheld only when the autonomy of human decision-making is itself respected and upheld, and when human beings are treated in ways that are non-hierarchical and non-discriminatory. There are, of course, good reasons for understanding the concept of dignity in just this way—those individuals, societies, and governments that have acted in ways that tend to undermine human dignity have very often been individuals, societies, and governments that have also tended to act in ways that are corrosive of ideas of human autonomy and equality. Yet it nevertheless remains a question whether dignity can indeed be explicated in just those terms. One possibility, as a number of papers in this collection argue, is that dignity is best understood in terms of notions of mutuality, reciprocity, and relationality (implying a notion of the self akin, for instance, to Charles Taylor's, such that the self exists, as Taylor puts it, 'only within… "webs of interlocution" '[4]),

[4] 'I am a self only in relation to certain interlocutors: in relation to those conversation partners who were essential to my achieving self definition. … A self exists only within what call "webs of interlocution" ', Charles Taylor, *Sources of the Self* (Cambridge, MA: Harvard University Press, 1989), p.36. Taylor writes further, 'To ask what a person is, in abstraction, from his or her self-interpretations, is to ask a fundamentally misguided question, one to which there couldn't, in principle, be an answer. … We are only selves insofar as we move in a certain space of questions, as we seek and find an orientation to the good', Taylor, ibid., p.34.

and not only does this temper any emphasis on autonomy alone, but it also forces one to recognize that, on some occasions, dignity may be possible precisely through the way in which human beings are able to find a place for themselves, and a sense of who they are, within what may otherwise appear to be unequal or hierarchical forms of social organization. That does not imply any simple endorsement of inequality, but it does suggest that the maintenance of dignity and the denial of inequality cannot be construed as simply identical.

While there are certainly differences that separate some of these essays—the issue of the relation between dignity and autonomy being the most notable—there are many more points of commonality that draw these essays together. The most obvious, perhaps, is indeed the shared recognition of the importance, even the urgency, that accompanies the question of dignity as it arises in the world today—an importance that clearly derives from the centrality of the concept of dignity to any attempt to think about, and respond to, our human situatedness. Yet what many of the contributions collected here also share is a view of the human, and of the dignity of the human, that is essentially 'humanistic' in the sense of looking to the humanities and the arts as providing essential insight into the issues at stake here. A sense of human dignity is perhaps most profoundly encountered, then, in poetry and story (both the story of history as well as literature), in art and music, and certainly not only in philosophical or legal analysis. The sense of human dignity that is at issue here involves, one might say, a feeling of and for the human—although this should not be taken to mean that it is in some way exclusionary of that which is other than the human, that it involves a lack of feeling for, as one might put it, the wider world. If the humanities and the arts can be seen to open up a proper sense of dignity through opening up a space for human being in which the human appears as human, then what must also appear there is the world within which such humanity is itself possible. A proper sense of the dignity of the human might thus be taken to imply also a proper sense of the dignity of the world—although to fully explore this line of thinking would require more pages than are available here.

In emphasizing the essays that make up this volume as constituting a conversation, the point is not merely to draw attention to the actual genesis of those essays in the Hobart Colloquium of 2004, nor is it merely to bring to the fore a dialogic conception of philosophical inquiry; more than this, it indicates a certain essential connection between dignity and conversation. True conversation is a mode of engagement that enables participation from different perspectives within a single ongoing movement. To engage in conversation is thus to recognize and allow for the worth of the other, and what they might contribute, through allowing the other a space in which to speak, be heard, and be responded to. In this way, true conversation can be seen to depend upon, and so also to embody a commitment to, the recognition of the dignity of conversational partners. Moreover, inasmuch as conversation is itself a mode of engagement into which we enter only inasmuch as we allow a space to those with whom we converse (conversation thus always involves a certain reciprocity), so the realm in which human dignity appears is surely also a realm that is similarly 'conversational' in structure. Dignity is surely not a matter of the assertion or affirmation of the individual alone, but rather of a certain form of response to ourselves and to others that affirms and acknowledges our common worth, our shared humanity, that attends to it, and acts upon it.

Of course, the conversation that takes place in these pages neither can include, nor can it properly do justice to, all of those forms of indignity that constantly threaten; nor can it encompass the voices of all of those for whom the loss of dignity constitutes a real and immediate threat—the voices, for instance, of asylum seekers in leaky boats or in detention centres, persons in situations of destitution, individuals whose lives and communities have been uprooted by the cataclysms of nature, those in captivity , those on death row, women trafficked as commodities, mothers watching children dying of hunger, abused child soldiers, those who are the victims of malice or culpable ineptitude, those deemed disposable or unworthy of life, those whose powerlessness leaves them prey to the strong. Yet these voices cannot be absent here either, since the experience out of which they come provides the essential human background against which this conversation is set. If these voices are not heard directly in these pages, then, their echoes nevertheless resonate through each and every essay. Dignity remains a vital and significant concept if for no other reason than that it directs our attention to just these voices, insisting that they be heard, that they be recognized and that they be responded to.

This volume does not provide any definitive or complete account of human dignity, nor does it aim to do so. Rather the aim is to assist in opening up a conversation about human dignity, and about human worth, that will go beyond these pages. Where that conversation may lead cannot be wholly known in advance, although that it can and must continue is clear—just as we cannot cease the exploration of our own humanity, so we cannot cease the exploration of the meaning of human dignity. It is to be hoped that such an exploration, such a conversation, will not remain restricted merely to the exchange of ideas, but that it will also have some greater effect on the way we think, and, perhaps more importantly, on the way we act. Dignity is not an idea abstracted from human action, but has life only in the actual relations between human beings. Dignity is, in the end, evident only in the concreteness of human life and practice, and the extent to which our life and practice can be seen as enabling of human dignity is perhaps the best measure of its humanity.

I
The Concept of Human Dignity

2
Human Dignity and Human Worth*

Daniel P. Sulmasy

Dignity appears to be an important concept in ethics. The word is used frequently in international documents such as the Universal Declaration of Human Rights of the United Nations[1] and the European Convention on Human Rights and Biomedicine.[2] As Ronald Dworkin has noted, the very idea of human rights depends upon 'the vague but powerful idea of human dignity'.[3]

The invocation of dignity in bioethical argumentation, however, has provoked a spate of recent, vituperative criticism. Ruth Macklin has called dignity a 'useless concept', alleging that any meaning it has can be reduced to respect for autonomy.[4] Similarly, Harris and Sulston have argued that dignity can be reduced to a Benthamite belief in human equity, 'the idea that each is entitled to the same concern, respect, and protection as is accorded to any other'.[5]

The conclusion, however, that the concept of dignity has no moral relevance seems hasty. These critics have cast aside thousands of years of philosophical writing, dismissed the contemporary bioethical discourse of continental Europeans, and swept away a whole body of international law. The critics have offered no substantive arguments or logical or linguistic 'proofs' that dignity can be reduced to respect for autonomy or to equity. They have reached these conclusions merely by begging the question. If one defines a word completely in terms of another concept more to one's liking, it will always follow that the word in question adds nothing to the

---

* This chapter is based on a presentation to the US President's Council on Bioethics, Washington, DC, 2 February 2006.

[1] *Universal Declaration of Human Rights* (http://www.un.org/Overview/rights.html).

[2] 'Convention for the Protection of Human Rights and Dignity of the Human Being with Regard to the Application of Biology and Medicine: Convention on Human Rights and Biomedicine', ETS no.164 (http://conventions.coe.int/Treaty/EN/CadreListeTraites.htm).

[3] Ronald Dworkin, *Taking Rights Seriously* (Cambridge, MA: Harvard University Press, 1977), pp.198–199.

[4] Ruth Macklin, 'Dignity is a Useless Concept', *British Medical Journal* 327 (2003), pp.1419–1420.

[5] John Harris and John Sulston, 'Genetic Equity', *Nature Reviews Genetics* 5 (2004), pp.796–800.

J. Malpas and N. Lickiss (eds.), Perspectives on Human Dignity: A Conversation, 9–18.

concept one already endorses. While shrouded in rhetoric, this is precisely the structure of both of these discussions of dignity. Premise: dignity means nothing more than 'respect for autonomy/human equity'. Conclusion: therefore dignity means nothing more than 'respect for autonomy/human equity' and (corollary) therefore dignity adds nothing to bioethical discourse.

The fact that one critic can see fit to reduce dignity to respect for autonomy while the other critics have reduced dignity to equity also suggests that something is amiss. At the very least, the existence of multiple competing claims provides evidence that contemporary Anglo-American philosophy has no obviously 'correct' interpretation of the meaning of dignity to offer. The opposition between the claims of these critics also highlights what seems to be a major problem with both projects. The concept of dignity offers a deeper ground for ethics than the critics seem willing to consider. Dignity, I shall argue, is not *either* respect for autonomy *or* equity, but the *ground* of both concepts. Dignity is the answer to the more fundamental questions: 'Why *should* I respect people's autonomy?' and 'Why *should* I treat people with equity?' Dignity is the ground of rights, not a synonym for rights.

Given that the meaning and importance of the notion of dignity has been challenged so vehemently, however, and that no contemporary exposition of the notion of dignity has been sufficiently clear to satisfy the critics, a careful treatment of the topic is in order. In this brief chapter, I hope to supply the outlines of such an exploration of the concept of dignity. I will (1) say something about the history of the concept of dignity, (2) present an argument about the meaning of dignity on the basis of consistency, (3) present an argument about the meaning of dignity based on 'axiology' or the theory of value, and (4) gesture towards the relevance of this understanding of dignity for bioethics.

History

The word 'dignity' has an interesting history in Western thought. While it is often assumed that the idea of dignity is essentially religious, it is hard to make this case from the Jewish and Christian Scriptures.[6] The Hebrew word translated as 'dignity', *gedula*, occurs rarely in the Hebrew Scriptures and means something more like nobility of character or personal standing in the community. The Greek σεμνοτης (*semnotes*) is sometimes rendered in English as 'dignity'. It occurs, however, only three times in the Christian Scriptures and is probably better translated as 'seriousness'. The word best translated today as 'dignity', αξιοπρέπεια (*aksioprepeia*), is not used in the New Testament at all.

[6] see Daniel P. Sulmasy, 'Death and Human Dignity', *Linacre Quarterly* 61 (November 1994), pp.27–36; 'Death With Dignity: What Does It Mean?' *Josephinum Journal of Theology* 4 (1997), pp.13–23.

Aquinas uses *dignitas* and its cognates 185 times in the *Summa Theologiae* and it tends to mean the value something has proper to its place in the great chain of being; for example, plants have more dignity than rocks; angels more dignity than human beings. In a nutshell, as one observer has put it, while Christians may have always had some concept of human dignity, until very recently 'it had not been developed into either a clearly defined literary form or an internally consistent set of ideas'.[7]

Nor does the Western notion of dignity come from the ancient Greek philosophers. Aristotle does not use the word *aksioprepeia* in his ethical writing. He uses the word *semnotes* only three times, and not at all in the *Nichomachean Ethics*. In the *Eudemian Ethics* he defines *semnotes* as a virtue, 'the mean between servility and unaccomodatingness'.[8] This hardly seems the way we use the word dignity today.

Roman stoics, particularly Cicero and Seneca, made copious use of the word. Recent translators note that for the Romans, this Latin word literally meant 'worthiness' and that in its common political sense, it meant a person's 'reputation or standing'.[9]

Renaissance writer Pico della Mirandola is credited with being the first to make a connection between human freedom and human dignity.[10] By contrast, Hobbes tied dignity to power. He wrote that 'The value or worth of a man, is as of all other things, his Price; that is to say so much as he would be given for the use of his power.'[11] In turn, he offered this definition of dignity: 'The publique worth of a man, which is the value set on him by the Commonwealth, is that which men commonly call DIGNITY.'[12]

Although he never cites him, Kant's notion of dignity seems to be a response to Hobbes. Kant writes:

> The respect I bear others or which another can claim from me (*osservantia aliis praestanda*) is the acknowledgement of the dignity (*dignitas*) of another man, i.e., a worth which has no price, no equivalent for which the object of valuation (*aestimii*) could be exchanged.[13]

Kant connects this to human freedom—as the capacity for moral agency that is intrinsic to the nature of human beings.[14] He insists elsewhere that 'Humanity itself is a dignity.'[15]

---

[7] Charles Trinkaus, 'The Renaissance Idea of the Dignity of Man', in: Philip P. Weiner, ed., *Dictionary of the History of Ideas*, vol. IV (New York: Charles Scribner's, 1973), pp.136–147.

[8] Aristotle, *Eudemian Ethics*, 2nd edn., 1221a.8, trans. Michael Woods (New York: Oxford University Press, 1991), p.17.

[9] M.T. Griffin and E.M. Atkins, 'Notes on Translation', in *Cicero: On Duties* (New York: Cambridge University Press, 1991), pp.xlvi–xlvii.

[10] Giovanni Pico della Mirandola, 'Oration on the Dignity of Man', in: Ernst Cassirer (ed.), *The Renaissance Philosophy of Man*, trans. Elizabeth L. Forbes (Chicago, IL: University of Chicago Press, 1948), pp.224–225.

[11] Thomas Hobbes, *Leviathan*, X., Richard Tuck, ed. (Cambridge: Cambridge University Press, 1991), p.63.

[12] Ibid., pp.63–64.

[13] Immanuel Kant, 'The Metaphysics of Morals, Part II: The Metaphysical Principles of Virtue', Ak462, in *Ethical Philosophy*, transl. James W. Ellington (Indianapolis, IN: Hackett, 1983), p.127.

[14] Ibid., Ak419–420, pp.80–81.

[15] Ibid., Ak462, p.127.

The Kantian notion has a familiar ring. In another very long story, one can trace how this Kantian idea of dignity was married to the notion of human beings having been created in the image and likeness of God by a Kantian theologian named Antonio Rosmini and how this subsequently made its way into Catholic theology, and was first explicitly used in the social encyclical *Rerum Novarum*,[16] in which Pope Leo XIII defended the dignity of workers in the late 19th century.[17] Thus, it is by the retroactive baptism of a Kantian idea that dignity became an important word in theology.

Given the history I have outlined, it is clear that many people have used the word 'dignity' to mean different things. I suggest that one convenient way to classify these uses is to distinguish between *attributed*, *intrinsic*, and *inflorescent* conceptions of human dignity.[18]

By *attributed* dignity, I mean that worth or value that human beings confer upon others by acts of attribution. The act of conferring this worth or value may be accomplished individually or communally, but it always involves a choice. Attributed dignity is, in a sense, created. It constitutes a *conventional* form of value. Thus, we attribute worth or value to those we consider to be dignitaries, those we admire, those who carry themselves in a particular way, or those who have certain talents, skills, or powers. We can even attribute worth or value to ourselves using this word. The Hobbesian notion of dignity is attributed.

By *intrinsic* dignity, I mean that worth or value that people have simply because they are human, not by virtue of any social standing, ability to evoke admiration, or any particular set of talents, skills, or powers. Intrinsic value is the value something has by virtue of being the kind of thing that it is. Intrinsic dignity is the value that human beings have by virtue of the fact that they are human beings. This value is thus not conferred or created by human choices, individual or collective, but is prior to human attribution. Kant's notion of dignity is intrinsic.

By *inflorescent* dignity, I mean the way people use the word to describe how a process or state of affairs is congruent with the intrinsic dignity of a human being. Thus, dignity is sometimes used to refer to a virtue—a state of affairs in which a human being habitually acts in a way that expresses the intrinsic value of the human. This use of the word is not purely attributed, since it depends upon some objective conception of the human. Nonetheless the value itself to which this use of the word refers is not intrinsic, since it derives from the intrinsic value of the human. Aristotle's use of the word is *inflorescent*, as are some of the Stoic usages.

---

[16] Pope Leo XIII, *Rerum Novarum: On Capital and Labor Encyclical*, 15 May 1891, http://www.papalencyclicals.net/Leo13/l13rerum.htm

[17] Sulmasy, 'Death with Dignity: What does It Mean?' op. cit.

[18] Ibid. The notion of derivative dignity is a later development of this theory and is presented at greater length in Daniel P. Sulmasy, 'Dignity and the Human as a Natural Kind', in: C.R. Taylor and R. Dell'Oro (eds), *Health and Human Flourishing* (Washington, DC: Georgetown University Press, 2006).

These conceptions of human dignity are by no means mutually exclusive. Attributed, intrinsic, and inflorescent conceptions of dignity are often at play in the same situation. Yet each has been taken as the central basis for particular moral claims in bioethics.

The Argument from Consistency

I next want to sketch out an argument that to be consistent in our use of moral words; to do the kind of moral work that Dworkin wants the word 'dignity' to do; to make good use of the word in bioethics, the notion of *intrinsic* dignity is foundational.

The argument is simple in its form. Consistency is at least a necessary condition of a valid moral argument, even if one would quickly add that consistency is not sufficient. In discussions about its fundamental moral meaning, the word 'dignity' can be defined as the value or worth that a human being has either: (a) in terms of some property, or (b) in terms of simply being human. I will show, however, that defining the fundamental moral meaning of dignity as the value human beings have by virtue of their possession of any particular candidate property leads to gross inconsistencies in our universally shared, settled moral positions. Therefore, one is led to the alternative: that dignity, in its fundamental moral sense, is defined in terms of simply being human. This kind of argument depends on the exhaustiveness of the list of candidate properties and is not decisive. But at least it puts the burden of proof on those who oppose assigning moral priority to the intrinsic sense of dignity to come up with an alternative property (such as age, size, or IQ) to define fundamental human worth or value.

What sorts of candidate human properties have been proposed? Some have argued that human dignity, in its most fundamental moral sense, depends upon the amount of pleasure and pain in a human life. Certainly, however, most of us are able to tell stories about the extraordinary lessons in human dignity we have learned from persons whose lives have been racked by pain, and most of us also know undignified human beings who have spent their whole lives in the pursuit of pleasure. Basing morality squarely on a balance between pleasure and pain has seemed, since the time of Aristotle, to be an *anaemic* account of morality and human dignity, and one that most persons would reject.

Some might think that Hobbes was right—human dignity depends upon social worth. But there are problems with such a conception of human dignity. The unemployed, the severely handicapped, the mentally ill, and all others who cannot contribute to the economic well-being of society would then have no dignity. Yet our society has gone to great lengths to recognise the dignity of such persons. If we did not believe that human dignity remains even if people are handicapped and lose their economic value to society, then we would not be making access ramps for them!

Some might think that human dignity depends upon freedom. But this view is also hard to sustain consistently. One would have to hold that those who have lost control of certain human functions or have lost or never had the freedom to make choices, have lost or never had dignity. This would mean that infants, the retarded, the severely mentally ill, prisoners, the comatose, and perhaps even the sleeping would have no human dignity. This seems wrong.

Some might suggest that what counts is the *capacity* for control and freedom, and not the *exercise* of control and freedom. One might suggest that some individuals without full control and freedom nevertheless deserve to be treated with dignity either because they have a *potential* for such a capacity (so that children, for instance, come to be regarded as placeholders for actual persons with dignity), or they have a *history* of having exercised such a capacity (so that the demented, for instance, come to be regarded as remnants of persons with dignity). But these arguments are quite tenuous. Who would feel dignified and secure as a placeholder or a remnant? Further, these arguments still cannot answer why those who never could and never will make free, rational choices (such as the severely mentally retarded) are worthy of human dignity. The most fundamental meaning of human dignity is not human freedom and control. The famous photograph of the Rev. Martin Luther King, Jr. sitting in an Alabama prison cell is a portrait of human dignity in the face of lost freedom and control. Prison bars and the attitudes of others did not erase his dignity.

Some might think that human dignity is something individuals are free to define as they choose, according to their own inner lights. One might anticipate hearing the ultimate 'conversation stopper': 'You can't impose your views of human dignity on me.' But this view also leads to inconsistencies. First, the concept of a moral term implies that it has universal meaning, a position acknowledged both by Kant[19] and by Utilitarians such as R.M. Hare.[20] Second, one cannot make an objective argument that morality is subjective. It is self-contradictory to make an objective moral claim that morality is subjective. Third, to say that human dignity is subjective is to claim that one person can never reliably recognise the dignity of another person, because one can never know exactly what the other thinks dignity is at any given moment. But morality seems to depend upon our mutual commitment to knowing that each of us has dignity before we open our mouths and explain our notions of dignity to each other. Human dignity cannot be a purely subjective concept.

Thus, the argument from consistency claims that fundamental human dignity must therefore be something each of us has simply because we are human. It is the notion of dignity that drove the civil rights movement. It is the notion the Rev. Dr. Martin Luther King, Jr. says he learned from his grandmother. 'Martin, don't let anyone ever tell you that you're not a somebody.'[21] No matter what value others

[19] Immanuel Kant, *Grounding for the Metaphysics of Morals*, Ak 421, trans. James W. Ellington (Indianapolis, IN: Hackett, 1981), p.30.

[20] R.M. Hare, *Moral Thinking: Its Levels, Methods, and Point* (New York: Oxford University Press, 1981), pp.107–116.

[21] Garth Baker-Fletcher, *Somebodyness: Martin Luther King, Jr. and the Theory of Dignity*, Harvard dissertations in divinity, No. 31 (Minneapolis, MN: Fortress Press, 1993), p.23.

may attribute to persons because of properties such as skin colour, or how free they are to do as they would like, they have dignity because they are *somebodies*—human beings. Being somebody; being a human being, is the foundation of the notion of human dignity. The argument from consistency says that if this is what dignity means in civil rights, this is what dignity must mean in bioethics.

The Axiological Argument

I will very briefly outline another way to arrive at this conclusion that depends on the theory of value or axiology.[22] Classically, axiology distinguishes between intrinsic and instrumental values. Instrumental values, however, are a subclass of attributed values. The primary distinction in axiology is between intrinsic values and attributed values.

Intrinsic value is the value something has of itself—the value it has by virtue of its being the kind of thing that it is. It is valuable independent of any valuer's purposes, beliefs, desires, interests, or expectations. Truly intrinsic values, according to environmental ethicist Holmes Rolston, 'are objectively there—discovered, not generated by the valuer'.[23]

Attributed values are those conveyed by a valuer. Attributed values depend completely upon the purposes, beliefs, desires, interests, or expectations of a valuer or group of valuers. That is why I argue that instrumental values are a class of attributed values. An instrumental value is one that is attributed to some entity because it serves a purpose for a valuer. The instrumental value of the entity consists in its serving as a means by which the valuer achieves some purpose. But there can be non-instrumental attributed values as well, for example, the value of humour may serve no clear instrumental purpose.

The next step in the argument is that if there are intrinsic values in the world, the recognition of the intrinsic value depends upon one's ability to discern what kind of thing it is. This brings me to the notion of natural kinds, a relatively new concept in analytic philosophy.[24] The fundamental idea behind natural kinds is

---

[22] These ideas are developed at greater length in Daniel P. Sulmasy, 'Death, Dignity, and the Theory of Value', *Ethical Perspectives*, 9 (2003), pp.103–118 (reprinted in: P., Schotsmans and T. Meulenbergs (eds), *Euthanasia and Palliative Care in the Low Countries* (Leuven, Belgium: Peeters, 2005), pp.95–119; also in Daniel P. Sulmasy, 'Dignity and the Human as a Natural Kind', n. 14, above.

[23] Holmes Rolston III, *Environmental Ethics* (Philadelphia, PA: Temple University Press, 1988), p.116.

[24] Credit for initiation of the discussion of natural kinds is usually given to Saul Kripke, in his two essays, 'Identity and Necessity', in: Milton K. Munitz, ed., *Identity and Individuation* (New York: New York University Press, 1971), pp.135–164 and 'Naming and Necessity', in: Gilbert Harman and Donald Davidson (eds), *Semantics of Natural Language* (Dordrecht, The Netherlands: D. Reidel, 1972), pp.253–355. For a good contemporary approach to the concept of natural kinds, see David Wiggins, *Sameness and Substance* (Cambridge, MA: Harvard University Press, 1980), pp.77–101 and his *Sameness and Substance Renewed* (Cambridge: Cambridge University Press, 2001).

that to pick something out from the rest of the universe, one must pick it out as a something. This leads to what its proponents call a 'modest essentialism'—that the essence of something is that by which one picks it out from the rest of reality as anything at all—its being a member of a kind. The alternative seems inconceivable—that reality is actually completely undifferentiated and that human beings carve up this amorphous stuff for their own purposes. It seems bizarre to suggest that there really are no actual kinds of things in the world independent of human classification—no such things, *de re*, as stars, slugs, or human beings. Thus, the intrinsic value of a natural entity—the value it has by virtue of being the kind of thing that it is—depends upon one's ability to pick that entity out as a member of a natural kind.

I would then define intrinsic dignity as the intrinsic value of entities that are members of a natural kind that is, as a kind, capable of language, rationality, love, free will, moral agency, creativity, and aesthetic sensibility. This definition is decidedly anti-speciesist. If there are other kinds of entities in the universe besides human beings that have, as a kind, these capacities, they would also have intrinsic dignity—whether angels or extraterrestrials.

I agree with Dworkin that intrinsic dignity is the foundation of all human rights.[25] We respect rights because we recognise intrinsic dignity. We do not bestow dignity to the extent that we bestow rights. Human beings have rights that must be respected because of the value they have by virtue of being the kinds of things that they are.

Importantly, the logic of natural kinds suggests that one picks individuals out as members of the kind not because they express all the necessary and sufficient predicates to be classified as a member of the species, but by virtue of their inclusion under the extension of the natural kind that, *as a kind*, has those capacities. The logic of natural kinds is extensional, not intensional. Very few bananas in the bin in the supermarket express all the necessary and sufficient conditions for being classified as bananas. We might define a banana as a yellow fruit of a certain shape, etc. Yet some specimens in the bin are yellow, some are green, some are spotted, and some are brown. Nonetheless, they are all bananas. Health care depends profoundly upon this kind of extensional logic. It is not the *expression* of rationality that makes us human, but our belonging to a kind that is capable of rationality that makes us human. When a human being is comatose or mentally ill, we first pick the individual out as a human being, then we note the disparity between the characteristics of the afflicted individual and the paradigmatic features and typical development and history of members of the human natural kind. This is how we come to the judgement that the individual is sick; and because that individual is a member of the human natural kind, we recognise an intrinsic value that we call dignity. In recognition of

---

[25] Daniel P. Sulmasy, 'Dignity, Rights, Health Care, and Human Flourishing', in: G. Diaz Pintos and David N. Weisstub (eds), *Human Rights and Health Care*(Dordrecht, The Netherlands: Springer, 2006).

that worth we have established the healing professions as a moral response to our fellow humans suffering from disease and injury. The plight of the sick rarely serves the purposes, beliefs, desires, interests, or expectations of any of us as individuals. Rather, it is because of the intrinsic value of the sick that we serve them. Thus I would argue that intrinsic human dignity is the foundation of health care. The bottom line is that every patient is a somebody. We lose our grip on that notion to our common peril.

Relevance to Bioethics

Accordingly, understanding these differing conceptions of dignity and the centrality of the intrinsic notion of dignity *does* make a difference in bioethics. It should be obvious that this conceptual richness cannot be reduced to respect for autonomy or equity.

At the very least, this conceptual analysis helps us better to understand arguments in bioethics that invoke the word 'dignity'. For example, arguments both for and against the morality of euthanasia invoke the word 'dignity'. The conceptual analysis I have offered helps to make sense of this. It would appear that those who invoke 'dignity' in arguing for the legalisation of euthanasia are using the word in an attributed sense, and appear to be ignoring (or perhaps denying) the notion of an intrinsic sense. One might hear someone say, 'I will have lost all my dignity if I am in diapers. If that happens, please do the merciful thing for me and put me out of my misery.' Those who invoke 'dignity' in opposition to the legalisation of euthanasia appear to be using the word in an intrinsic sense. Sometimes these critics appear to be denying the existence of an attributed sense of the word, but all they really need to do is to argue, as I have above, that the attributed depends upon the intrinsic. Those who say, 'Killing a human being, even out of a sense of mercy, is an offence against human dignity', are arguing that there is a sense of dignity that is not lost when a person becomes dependent, unproductive, disfigured, or shunned by others. This notion is intrinsic, since it depends not upon any state of affairs but upon the person's belonging to a natural kind that has, as a kind, the value I have called intrinsic dignity. Finally, some who oppose euthanasia appear to invoke an inflorescent notion of dignity in their arguments, suggesting, for instance, that to ask to be killed in the face of death or because of the loss of independence or productivity that sometimes precedes death, is an undignified way to face one's end—unworthy behaviour for a creature that has intrinsic dignity.

Understanding bioethical arguments in light of these different notions of dignity can thus illuminate the bases for differences of opinion between the interlocutors. Further, if it is correct that intrinsic dignity is the most fundamental of the three notions of dignity, then this taxonomy can also help to resolve a question such as whether euthanasia ought to be morally permissible.

Conclusions

In this brief chapter, I have shown how three concepts of dignity emerge from the history of Western thought—the attributed, the intrinsic, and the inflorescent. I have defended the notion of the intrinsic sense of dignity, and demonstrated why it is the most fundamental. I have then shown very briefly how these three notions of dignity function in arguments about euthanasia as a way of demonstrating the importance of the concept of dignity to bioethics. Much work remains to be done in developing the importance of this notion for bioethics.

3
Human Dignity and Human Being

Jeff Malpas

The question of human dignity is surely inseparable from the question of what it is to be human. This seems to be most obviously so inasmuch as the concept of human *dignity* is closely related to the idea of human *worth*—to attend to human dignity is to attend to the *value* or *significance* that belongs to human being (this alone is a reason why the concept of human dignity cannot be discarded), but to attend to this is already to presuppose an understanding of the *nature* of human being, of what human being *is*. Yet few discussions of human dignity make this connection a focus for discussion in itself—rather than probe the question of human dignity as a question about human being, the question is treated in a way that often seems to imply a severance from such 'ontological' concerns.

That human dignity is often approached as if it were indeed a concept that stood somewhat independently of other more ontologically based notions partly reflects a tendency within the ethical and political thinking that derives from Western liberalism to eschew ontological questioning as inherently problematic, and to look instead to more procedurally oriented conceptions. It probably also reflects a more general contemporary discomfort with notions of human being or human nature as such—whether because such notions are thought to be unduly universalist, incapable of satisfactory elucidation, or because of a rejection, within those modes of thinking influenced by deconstructionist or postmodern thinking, of the 'humanism' with which they are associated. The clear implication here, of course, is that the very connection I have asserted as so obvious and self-evident is itself a contentious one—perhaps the question of dignity has nothing whatsoever to do either with the nature of what it is to be human or with the specifically human at all.

In respect of this latter claim—the denial that dignity has any to do with the specifically human as such—it is certainly true that there is a sense of dignity that is broader than just that which is applicable to the human, and some might even want to claim that some sense of dignity might extend beyond the animal as well (as one might talk, for instance, of the dignity of nature). Yet in asserting a connection between the question of human dignity and the question of human being, I am not asserting any necessary restriction on the idea of dignity as such, but instead wish to direct attention to a fairly simple and straightforward point: how we think about the dignity that is ours (whoever 'we' may be) depends very much

J. Malpas and N. Lickiss (eds.), Perspectives on Human Dignity: A Conversation, 19–25.

on our conception of ourselves. In this respect, my own assertion of the necessary implication of the ontological here can be seen as simply an assertion of the interconnectedness of our concepts and of our thinking.

The most common way in which the idea of human dignity is currently articulated, in fact, is in terms that correspond to a very specific understanding of human being—in terms of dignity as a matter of individual, rational autonomy, and of the human being as an autonomous, rational individual—and this is so in spite of the fact that dignity and autonomy sometimes appear as distinct terms (for instance, in the UNESCO *Universal Declaration on Bioethics and Human Rights*[1]). Indeed, this way of thinking about dignity is evident, prima facie, in a number of the essays in this volume. From this perspective, broadly characterised, what counts as a diminution in human autonomy—a diminution in the capacity of human beings rationally to make their own decisions and to determine their own lives—is ipso facto a diminution in human dignity and in human being.

Although the notion of autonomy has become such an integral part of contemporary discourse, its historical origins are often forgotten or overlooked. Yet the focus on autonomy arises largely out of the thinking associated with the Enlightenment, and the paradigmatic instance of this conception of the human, and of human dignity, is to be found in the work of Immanuel Kant, in works such as *What is Enlightenment* and the *Groundwork of the Metaphysics of Morals*. Kant had no qualms, however, about connecting the ethical with the ontological,[2] or the practical with the theoretical, and his understanding of human being as essentially configured in relation to the rational will is a determining element in his ethical thought. In contemporary discussion, however, the ontological assumptions that may underlie the understanding of human dignity in terms of autonomy are not so clear, neither are they typically made so explicit—and the idea that human dignity is a matter of human autonomy has become so commonplace that the fact that it is married to a specific conception of human being is often not remarked upon or discussed. Yet the conception of human being in terms of individual autonomy carries important implications, not least of which is the tendency for it to prioritise the individual, and individual capacities and attributes, over the social, cultural, and historical situatedness of human being.

It is not that autonomy has no relevance to an understanding of human being, but rather that too great an emphasis on autonomy alone threatens to deliver a distorted picture of that in which human being actually consists. Who and what we are is not determined solely by our existence as independent beings, but is instead intertwined with the being of those others in relation to whom our lives are shaped, as well as with respect to the wider world in which our lives are played out. This is not merely a point that derives from the pragmatic reliance on others that is a part of our socialised mode of existence—the fact that, practically speaking, human life depends on

[1] In this document, 'human dignity and human rights' are the subject of Article 3, while 'autonomy and individual responsibility' are dealt with under Article 5.

[2] Although it is worth noting that Kant's Critical Philosophy also sets clear limits on the nature and extent of the ontological or metaphysical claims that might be relevant here.

cooperative relations with other human beings in order to satisfy basic needs of food, shelter, and security—but rather reflects the way in which, at an even more fundamental level, the very possibility of grasping one's own individual being, and so of understanding oneself as having a life of one's own (something that is itself an essential element in the possibility of autonomous choice), itself depends on grasping the being of others and the being of things around one. In the work of the American philosopher Donald Davidson, this point is put in terms of the idea that there are three 'kinds' of knowledge that are mutually implicated with one another: knowledge of self, knowledge of others, and knowledge of the world.[3] It is Davidson's contention that no one of these is possible without the others—knowledge of self, for instance, of one's own attitudes, feelings, and so on, is thus interdependent with knowledge of others and with knowledge of the world. Moreover, while Davidson appears to couch this in epistemic terms, what is actually at issue goes beyond the merely epistemic—since who and what we are is so much bound up with our knowledge of ourselves, and since our knowledge of ourselves is interdependent with our knowledge of others and the world, so who and what we are is itself bound up with our knowledge of others and of the world.

The picture Davidson presents here is one that I have developed elsewhere in terms of the essentially 'topographical' character of human, since one way of understanding the interrelatedness that is at issue here is precisely in terms of a certain form of complex situatedness.[4] Rather than being somehow self-enclosed and separate, human being has to be understood in terms of his/her particular *topos*—in terms of the place in which he/she finds himself/herself—a topos or place that is formed through the interrelations between individuals and groups of individuals, between individuals and the environments and things that surround them, and between individuals and themselves. If we take such topographical interrelation seriously then not only must it be seen as determining the structure of our epistemic lives, but also our ethical lives. Indeed, we might say our ethical relations play out across the same three dimensions that Davidson also identifies—relation to self, to others, and to the world—and that these three dimensions of relation are also interdependent with one another.

It might be said, of course, that this is already to assume a relational conception of ethics, when such a conception remains contentious. Yet this relational conception of *ethics* follows more or less directly from the relational conception of *meaning* and *knowledge* that is present in Davidson, and that can be seen to entail a relational conception of *human being* as such. Moreover, there are, in any case, independent reasons for thinking that ethics is itself essentially relational. At a very ordinary level, most key ethical notions—of honesty, trust, respect, and so on—have their primary application only in a relational, or more specifically, an interpersonal context, and this is perhaps reflected in a common tendency to think of ethics

[3] Davidson, 'Three Varieties of Knowledge', in *Subjective, Intersubjective, Objective* (Oxford: Clarendon Press, 2001), pp.205–220.

[4] See my *Place and Experience: A Philosophical Topography* (Cambridge: Cambridge University Press, 1999).

as concerning our actions and judgements inasmuch as they affect others as well as ourselves. At a more philosophical level, the idea of a certain universality that attaches to ethical judgement, so that what I judge right for me ought to be consistent with the judgements I make about what is right for others (the idea given a very particular expression in Kant's famous Categorical Imperative—'act only in accordance with that maxim through which you can at the same time will that it become a universal law'[5]), can be seen to imply an interdependence of ethical judgment that mirrors the interdependence that obtains at, for instance, the level of knowledge. One might object that the relationality that appears here is a relationality that derives primarily from the need for consistency, but even if that were to be admitted, it would be a form of relationality nonetheless.

If we think of ethics, and so also human being, in these interdependent, relational terms, then ethical thinking and acting will always involve thinking and acting in ways that are attentive to the complex set of relations in the midst of which our own human lives are constituted. The idea of autonomy is not rendered irrelevant by such an account, since the importance of autonomy can be seen to derive from the importance of the relation we have to ourselves as one of the three dimensions of human being, knowledge, and judgement, and also from the very topographical character of the tripartite structure that is at issue here. Indeed, one way of thinking of autonomy is in terms of the self-determination that occurs when an entity or structure operates according to the principles that belong to it as such. If the principles that determine human being are indeed principles of relationality that place human thinking and acting in an ever-present relation of interdependence with others and with the world, then to think and act autonomously will not be to think and act in separation from others and the world, but to think and act in a way that is attentive to them. There is, then, a sense of autonomy that is quite consistent with relationality—but this only becomes evident when we recognise the way in which the very notion of autonomy itself has to be understood against a certain 'ontological' background. The nature of the autonomy that belongs to human being depends upon the nature of the human being that is autonomous.

The conception of ethical and human life that emerges here is an especially interesting one when we return to the focus on human dignity. For if human being is indeed relational in the way that I have sketched, then human dignity will, in turn, be similarly relational in character. What this means, first of all, is that dignity will play out across the three dimensions of relationship that are at issue here: there is a sense of dignity that obtains in terms of the sense of worth that we have in relation to ourselves, a sense of dignity that we have of ourselves in relation to others, and so also a sense of the worth of others in relation to ourselves, a sense of the worth of ourselves in relation to the wider world, and of that wider world as it stands in relation to us. That dignity is expressed here in terms of a 'relation to' should not be taken to suggest that the dignity at issue does not belong to anything 'in itself', but rather that dignity always and only appears as something standing within a wider structure of relations since only then does something even appear.

[5] Immanuel Kant, *The Groundwork of the Metaphysics of Morals*, 4:421.

While this relational conception of dignity means that dignity plays out across a number of different dimensions, it also means that no one dimension is completely determining either in affirming dignity or denying it. Dignity may be maintained even in cases where others deny or demean one's dignity simply because one's own dignity or worth is not solely dependent on what any other person, or group of persons, may think, judge, or do in relation to oneself. The dignity that one can maintain in one's self, and through one's own sense of the dignity of others, can resist the indignity that others may attempt to impose—as we know from the experiences to be found within, for instance, the concentration camp and the prison. Dignity can thus be retained even in the face of the fiercest assault. Indeed, one might argue that no human being can ever be said to lose *all* dignity just as no human being can ever be said to lose their *humanity*. What can be lost is the capacity or willingness to recognise and express one's own or another's dignity, or for others to do so, and we may say, in this regard, that what is lost is only ever the capacity for *respect*, and never dignity as such (although since the two are closely entwined, the failure of respect may well appear as itself a loss of dignity).

Inasmuch as human dignity is tied to human being, then one's own dignity cannot be separated from the dignity that belongs to others. While it may well be possible to retain a high level of self-esteem even in the face of one's devaluation of others (and recent studies suggest that, contrary to common belief, individuals who value themselves too highly may well be more likely to devalue those around them[6]), there nevertheless seems to be a sense in which the denial of the dignity of others also involves a certain diminution of one's own dignity. To treat one human being as without dignity is potentially to deny the dignity of every human being, even one's own, and so one may even say that an assault on the dignity of one is an assault on the dignity at all. This is perhaps part of the reason why it is so hard to think of dignity as attaching to the great evildoers of history—Hitler, Stalin, or even Martin Bryant (the man who shot dead 35 people in Port Arthur, Tasmania, in 1996). Dignity, in this respect, is automatically tied neither to the capacity for action or decision, nor to the ability to exercise any kind of power or authority. Indeed, in many cases, incapacity or forbearance may serve to bring dignity to light in a way that action or decision could not, and may do so precisely because of the way in which they illuminate the vulnerability and fragility of human life. In this respect, dignity and power, or the exercise of power, may turn out to be somewhat opposed—something that may be thought to be given a very specific exemplification in the life and work of Mahatma Gandhi.

Inasmuch as human dignity concerns human worth, then so it must have an especially significant role within the structure of ethical life. Ethics surely begins with it the recognition that there is a question that can be asked about the propriety of action (or of certain attitudes or modes of comportment) that goes beyond mere issues of prudence or practicality. The difficulty is in understanding the nature of the question that could be at issue here. I want to suggest that what marks out the questions of

---

[6] See Roy F. Baumeister, 'Violent Pride', *Scientific American*, 284 (2001), pp.96–101.

ethics is that they are just those questions that concern the propriety of actions inasmuch as those actions affect our own worth as human beings or as persons. I say 'worth' here rather than, for instance, 'welfare' or 'well-being', since for welfare or well-being alone, in the ordinary sense of these terms, to be made primary would be to render obscure the distinction of the ethical from, for instance, the prudential. Inasmuch as the ethical is a distinct realm, then the ethical concerns our actions and judgements inasmuch as those actions and judgements affirm or deny the worth of ourselves, of others and of the wider world. The affirmation and maintenance of dignity can thus be understood as one crucial way of expressing that which must lie at the very heart of an *ethical*, which is to say also, a *human* life.

To the extent that human lives are lives whose meaning, indeed, whose very character as human, derives from their relational character, then so the greatest threats to human dignity derive from those actions and circumstances that strip human lives of their relational connection—that disable the sense of relatedness to self, of relatedness to others and of relatedness to world. Such a stripping away of relations can occur through a loss of certain capacities to engage with others and with the world—through a loss of bodily capacities as well as of cognitive—but perhaps the greatest threat to the maintenance of a sense of human dignity is the experience of pain and suffering, and the humiliations, large and small, that may accompany such experience. Elaine Scarry has explored, in great detail, the way in which pain, particularly extreme or chronic pain, not only shatters our normal communicative relatedness with others, but also dissolves the ordinary distinctions of public and private, inner and outer, self and world, thereby threatening our capacity to maintain the relational structure of our lives. While such a threat to dignity may arise as a result of the contingencies of human life (as a result, for instance, whether directly or indirectly, of trauma or disease), it may also be deliberately inflicted, and in such cases the threat to dignity that operates through the dissolving of the relations in which an individual life is lived is itself closely tied to the attempt to exercise coercion or control. Thus, to take just two examples: the operation of slavery in the 18th and 19th centuries (and still today) depended on destroying the ordinary relationships that make for meaningful human life and turning a human being into a mere commodity, a body to be used, traded, disposed of; the use of torture, whether through physical or psychological violence, whether in Guantanamo Bay or elsewhere, involves a similar denial of the dignity of the individual, operating through the destruction of the ordinary relations that form the individual life, reforming those relations according to the desires of the interrogator, dissolving the world and the individual along with it.[7]

In one sense, human dignity is preserved just so long as human life is preserved (although, even in death, of course, the body can retain a dignity of its own). The dignity that belongs to a human life is not to be accounted in terms of the possession of any single capacity or characteristic, but refers us instead to the worth of a

[7] See Elaine Scarry's account of the structure of torture in *The Body in Pain: The Making and Unmaking of the World* (New York: Oxford University Press, 1985), pp.27–59.

human life which is given only through the articulation of that life in relation to self, others and world. Dignity involves more than just autonomy, therefore, and we can readily identify instances (Jack Coulehan's essay in this volume provides two excellent examples here) in which a form of autonomy can be maintained and yet dignity can be compromised, while dignity can be maintained even though autonomy can be lost. Dignity is thus no less complex and multifaceted than is human life itself, and one cannot understand one without an understanding of the other. While human dignity may come to the forefront for those of us who find ourselves in situations in which the threat to human dignity is to the fore—in situations of human suffering and distress, pain, debility, or hardship—human dignity is also at the centre of ethical life and so at the centre of our everyday ethical practice. The reason for this is simple: it is precisely the need to be attentive to human worth that is at the centre of ethical thought and action. Moreover, to be attentive to human worth is to be attentive to the complex relatedness in which all human life consists; a relatedness that encompasses ourselves, the others with whom we live, and the wider world.

4
On Human Dignity: Fragments of an Exploration

Norelle Lickiss

> What counts in the things said by men is not so much what they may have thought or the extent to which these things represent their thoughts, as that which systematizes them from the outset, thus making them thereafter endlessly accessible to new discourses and open to the task of transforming them.[1]

How should we begin to think about human dignity? Rodney Hall, the Australian writer, wrote a fascinating novel called *The Island in the Mind*. He wrote, at one level, about the postulated southern land in the mind of 17th-century Europeans (an 'island in the mind').[2] Maybe the idea of human dignity is an 'island in the mind': it is there, we are aware of it, it is present to us in the substratum of our discourse, it gets into our writings, it is in the background of all sorts of debates, and, as in Rodney Hall's book, it is a *terra incognita*. There is an island there, a mysterious island indeed, and I propose to try to explore this notion or terrain as if one were exploring an island which beckons for exploration: images of childhood here!

How does one get to an island? We have several possible routes, and many options. If we had a lifetime, we could consider many streams of human archaeology: what do the traces of the human tell us—especially about the symbolic life? The resources are too rich: even a fragment is fascinating to a non-professional inquisitive explorer. For example, the ancient Upper Paleolithic images in the Lascaux caves in France are considered to reflect sophisticated shamanic activities,[3] and aboriginal rock paintings in Australia may well reflect similar thought worlds[4]: Parr, a Tasmanian artist, gave attention to these considerations in the 2004 Hobart Interdisciplinary Colloquium.[5] We certainly learn from even a glimpse of archaeological richness that, as Walt Whitman wrote, 'I am not contained between my hat

[1] M. Foucault, *The Birth of the Clinic: The Archaeology of Medical Practice* (New York: Vintage, 1993).

[2] R. Hall, *The Island in the Mind* (Sydney: Pan Macmillan, 1996).

[3] D. Lewis-Williams, *The Mind in the Cave* (London: Thames & Hudson, 2002).

[4] G. Chaloupka, *Journey in Time* (Sydney: New Holland Publishers, 1999).

[5] G. Parr, 'Time Past, Time Future: Mutuality with the Natural World' unpublished paper presented in Hobart 2004.

J. Malpas and N. Lickiss (eds.), Perspectives on Human Dignity: A Conversation, 27–41.

and my boots,[6] and neither can the concept of human dignity be so contained. The awareness of the social world and symbolic universe immediately appear to be generated within, not outside human consciousness, albeit in response to other realities.

There is an interesting connection here with debates concerning the origin of religious practices and ideas, usually based in major traditions on some revelatory event. Gillman discusses this usefully for the modern inquirer[7]; he notes that for Kaplan,

> The experience of revelation is very much akin to other forms of human creativity. When we experience within our social order, or in humanity at large, a striving for ever-growing levels of perfection, when we devise means to reach those levels, and when we are personally impelled to put these means into effect, we have experienced revelation.

Gillman notes further that 'salvation' for Kaplan 'denotes the actualization of all our values and the elimination of all evils that come in the way of personal and social fulfilment', and the word 'God' denotes not a 'personal' being but a 'certain kind of activity … salvational activity'. Could these ideas take forward an exploration of current, possibly difficult, notions of 'human dignity' as: (a) conferred from outside (for example, by a creative or revelatory event—man as the image of God, or others (politicians, lawmakers, physicians)), or (b) restricted to the notion of autonomy (after Kant) or, (c) even, as in a recent literature review concerning the illness experience of older adults as 'an individually defined construct involving self-esteem, respect, well-being, and pride?'[8] Extensive medical practice induces restlessness with conventional ideas of human dignity such as mentioned: the notion of 'God' may be obscure in a secular culture (especially contemporary clinical subculture), the limits of autonomy as a basis of or defining human dignity become more and more obvious, and even the 'individually defined construct' appears inadequate in the face of the complexity of the human condition. Relationality (or, as we may also refer to it, mutuality) must somehow be recognized as primary in any exploration of human dignity.

Alternatively, we could engage with philology—and semiotics to try to grasp the notion of the human and human dignity which can be appreciated by an adequate understanding of human language and symbols—over time and space, in diverse cultures. We quickly recognize that dignity was closely related to status (*dignitas*) in the Greco-Roman period, but in more recent times, for example, since the French Revolution, other notions are included: this touches the realm of the historian.[9] Extensive studies of contemporary language in diverse cultures could yield a rich harvest of how men, women, and children understand human dignity, meaning, and

---

[6] W. Whitman, 'Song of Myself', no.7, *Leaves of Grass*, 1855. Edited with an introduction by Malcolm Cowley (Harmondsworth: Penguin Books, 1976, ca.1959).

[7] N. Gillman, *Sacred Fragments: Recovering Theology for the Modern Jew* (Philadelphia, PA: The Jewish Publication Society, 1990), pp.18–24.

[8] D.A. Gruenwald and E.J. White, 'The Illness Experience of Older Adults Near the End of Life: A Systematic Review', *Anaesthesiology Clinics of North America*, 24 (2006), pp.163–180.

[9] See Milton Lewis, 'A Brief History of Human Dignity: Idea and Application', Chapter 8, this volume.

circumstances which threaten dignity and modes of restoration. Any such exploration would at least touch on human rituals for recognition of and restoration of respect for dignity, with the actions themselves pointing beyond language.

As another option, we could ponder the physical universe, to try to comprehend more of the meaning, place, and possibility of man: we would be within a long tradition if we did so, especially if we can accept that the sacred concepts and writings of most people appear to have been a response to such reflection, as in, in the Hebrew scriptures, for example.[10] But even some of these writers considered that a search for wisdom is 'chasing of the wind'![11] One of the matters, which can frustrate, especially the young seeker after the 'meaning of man' and by inference 'our dignity', is the enigma of our place in the universe. The physicists no longer cut us down to size, but in their best moments (like the poets) they seem to help us cope with the size we are, a speck, but a precious speck, even immortal diamond.[12] We do participate in the matter of the universe; and, even as matter, we share in whatever immortality (or not) the physical universe has, being maybe, each of us, a unique but passing pattern, rendered coherent for a time (or forever) by or whatever spirit is, came from, or means.

Cultural anthropology (obviously cognate with linguistics and semiotics) offers another route to this island of the mind. What is understood by human dignity in one culture may be considered indignity in another; or we could examine formally the historical dimensions of the idea of human dignity, even in one culture or place, over time, and in relation to other events, trends, or pressures. Or sociologists could be consulted: what do we know of the social dimensions, origins, implications, or the idea of human dignity, in our time and in past times? And how do political scientists and legislators view human dignity?

There are so many prisms through which the gaze may pass! It is obvious that the sciences concerning the human necessarily interpenetrate, with permeable boundaries. The situation is like the story of many men feeling part of an elephant and each trying to describe first (easy), then interpret (harder), what they have felt or experienced. Dilthey, in his introduction to the human sciences (as distinct from natural science), stressed the historical dimension in any approach to understanding the human, since man is a historical being, in evolution.[13] It can be contended that medicine is fundamentally a human science, however a significant place the natural sciences hold in the study and practice of medicine: there is much to learn from the consideration of the writings of Dilthey who was, as a philosopher, 'totally consumed with that most universal of beings in the universe, man himself, all his manifestations... and Dilthey's pursuit of man took him in all the directions that

[10] For example, Gen. 1, Psalm 104, Job.

[11] Ecclesiastes 2: 17.

[12] G.M. Hopkins, *That Nature is a Heraclitean Fire and of the Comfort of the Resurrection*, *Poems of Gerard Manley Hopkins* edited with notes by Robert Bridges (London: Humphrey Milford, 1918.)

[13] W. Dilthey, *Introduction to the Human Sciences* (1923), trans. R.J. Betzanos (Detroit: Wayne University Press, 1988).

man himself has taken'.[14] It may be said that the entire philosophical tradition has been obsessed by the human seeking understanding,[15] with the ill-defined idea of the dignity of the human, as a driving force, continuing to press the search for knowledge if not comprehensive understanding of man.[16]

In addition to sociology, philosophy, and anthropology, where the idea of human dignity is if not often articulated, nevertheless always implicit, conventional theological and religious studies often specifically focus on 'human dignity' as explicitly linked with the thought or reality of a supreme being, however, named. I have already alluded to Kaplan's notions, which might not find much acceptance in more conventional religious cultures, but on the other hand, may prove to be a useful bridge. The Second Vatican Council (notably in the document *The Church in the Modern World*, in the writing of which the late Pope John Paul II, as Bishop Carol Wojtyla was much involved) devoted a chapter to 'The Dignity of the Human Person', detailing the concept that man is made in the image of God, with dignity lying in observing the law 'in his heart', in response to conscience, and that dignity 'rests above all in communion with God'.[17] Pannenberg, a Protestant Professor of Theology, nearly 20 years after the Vatican Council, sought to examine the disciplines concerning the human (the 'anthropological disciplines') with reference to such themes. The result is a weighty tome and Pannenberg may well have considered that 'human dignity' is part of its *raison d'être*, but he does not analyse 'human dignity', nor include it in the index.[18]

Contemporary literature in ethics, especially but not only, emanating from continental Europe in relation to medicine, frequently explicitly attends to the concept of human dignity.[19] Weisstub and Thomasma ask the question: 'Why then has dignity become so central to our moral-liberal thinking at the beginning of this (21st) century?', and respond,

> It is incontestable that the western preoccupation with dignity was accelerated after the degrading experiences of the Holocaust, that shocked democratic observers who previously had come to the naïve conclusion that enlightened values were our best protection against evil. In the years after World War 2 and in view of widespread cynicism with regard to

[14] B.J. Betzanos, 'Wilhelm Dilthey: An Introduction', in W. Dilthey, *Introduction to the Human Sciences*, p.16.

[15] R. Tarnas, *The Passion of the Western Mind: Understanding the Ideas that have Shaped our World View* (New York: Ballantyne Books, 1991).

[16] P.H. Rhinelander, *Is Man Comprehensible to Man?* (Stanford, CA: Stanford University Press, 1973).

[17] A Flannery (ed.), *The Church in the Modern World (1965), Vatican Council II: The Conciliar and Post Conciliar Documents* (Dublin: Dominican Publications, 1975), p.903.

[18] W. Pannenberg, *Anthropology in Theological Perspective*, trans. M.J. O'Connell (Edinburgh: Clark, 1985).

[19] L. Nordenfeldt, 'Dignity and the Care of the Elderly', *Medicine, Health Care and Philosophy*, 6 (2003), pp.103–106. D. Beyleveld and R. Brownsword, *Human Dignity in Bioethics and Biolaw* (Oxford: Oxford University Press, 2001). (See also review by M.E. Sokalska, *European Journal of Health Law*, 9 (2002), 413–421.) L. Gormally, *Euthanasia, Clinical Practice and the Law* (London: Linacre Centre, 1994).

> transcendental metaphysical assertions about absolute values, many democrats, in order to avoid the punishing consequences of radical relativism, turned to human dignity as the one arching protector value.

These writers went on to note: 'It is no accident that the German constitutional system fashioned human dignity as the basic and absolute value of the entire constitutional structure.'[20] Reference to human dignity is frequent in other European writings, and is explicit in documents of the Council of Europe: the history of indignity on European soil has surely compelled the highlighting of dignity. The German Basic Law, after specifically stating that 'the dignity of man is inviolable', continues by linking it clearly with human rights, and articulates that universality of the concept as a systematizing idea: The German people therefore uphold human rights as inviolable and inalienable and as the basis of every community, of peace and justice in the world.[21]

What can be added to this treasure of scholarship by the experience and musings of a practising clinician? I take as my standpoint the here and now, the everyday experience of men and women often in limit situations, articulating in their actions if not in speech or writing (though empirical research can yield rich results) what is implied by 'human dignity'. What, do we as clinicians, experience about the human condition—and what, of that which we experience and know, could be a resource for philosophy?[22] What can be a starting point?

Those at the coalface of the care of fellow citizens experiencing grave illness and/or frailty do speak, and sometimes write about human dignity?[23] and undertake research which explicitly mentions human dignity.[24] In addition, there is the voluminous research which though not explicitly referring to dignity, is highly relevant, for example, the vast corpus of research on pain, suffering, abuse, and so on.[25] Human dignity as a concept is there in the depths of the mind, and its violation causes distress to staff, especially nursing staff. But, those same staff do have difficulty in defining any measure of dignity, as was found in a small study which focused on retained (not lost) capacities in the last three days of life. It was also found however, that staff can identify matters they regard as of high rank with

---

[20] 'The Dignity of Man is Inviolable. To respect and Protect It Shall be the Duty of all Public Authority', *Basic Law of Federal Republic of Germany* (1949).

[21] D.C. Thomasma, D.N. Weisstub, and C. Herve (eds), *Personhood and Health Care* (Dordrecht, The Netherlands: Kluwer, 2001).

[22] K.W.M. Fulford, 'The Potential of Medicine as a Resource for Philosophy', *Theoretical Medicine*, 12 (1991), pp.81–85.

[23] A. Street and D. Kissane, 'Constructions of Dignity in End-of-life Care', *Journal of Palliative Care*, 17 (2001) pp.93–101.

[24] K. Turner, R. Chye, and G. Aggawal et al., 'Dignity in Dying : A Preliminary Study of Patients in the Last Three Days of Life', *Journal of Palliative Care*, 12 (1996), pp.7–13. T.F. Hack, H.M. Chochinov, T. Hassard, L. Kristjanson, S. McClement, and M. Harlos, 'Defining Dignity in Terminally Ill Cancer Patients: A Factor Analytic Approach', *Psycho-Oncology*, 13 (2004), pp.700–708.

[25] D. Doyle, G.W. Hanks, N. Cherney, and K. Calman (eds), *Oxford Textbook of Palliative Medicine* (Oxford: Oxford University Press, 3rd edn., 2004).

regard to human dignity. It was noted that two 'retained capacities' (continence and cognitive) rate at the top in the minds of experienced professionals—and at least offer a challenge to contemporary medicine. Patients' lists may be statistically analysed, but for the individual patient the elements in a concept of dignity may be unexpected, unpredictable, and indeed change from time to time as experience, loss, and wisdom concurrently accumulate: serious illness or the last phase of life may be a period of rapid personal growth. But items on lists are not portraits—just impressions giving teasing glimpses of the underlying reality, worth pondering, and exploring to try to find some coherence in the emerging portrait(s) of human dignity.

What *is* human dignity? What is that underlying complex reality which seems to clinical staff to be manifest sometimes in observable, even recordable, appearances, or sensed intuitively (as something threatened, lost, maintained, or regained) in contexts of deep individual or communal distress? What is it that we name, when we use the words 'human dignity?' What do we mean by 'human dignity?'

There may still be value in considering, through the prism of clinical practice, some further notions relevant to the idea of human dignity, to try to find structures on which a coherent frame can be built. What is the shape of the image, the schema, the symbolic frame, the construct, the idea, the place in the mind, underlying all? It seems that, even to approach this place, we need to explore many matters including what we mean by 'person', what is 'suffering' in relation to dignity, and a way of considering human dignity, however understood, in the processes of clinical decision-making.

Towards an Adequate View of a Person for Purposes of Clinical Practice

Jacob Needleman famously remarked: 'What medicine lacks is an adequate view of the person. ...'[26] Continental philosophers, notably Ten Have,[27] are taking up that challenge. Experience in seeking to understand some health aspects of indigenous people in Sydney in the late 1960s led this author to develop a schema, a frame to support the thinking of a clinician.[28] This frame, slightly modified, served as an instrument for both thinking and teaching in the ensuing decades. It could be styled as an ecological view of a person, and is, hopefully, in accord with some fundamental contemporary philosophical insights (Fig. 1).

---

[26] J. Needleman, 'The Perception of Mortality', *Annals of the New York Academy of Sciences*, 164(3) (1969), pp.733–738.

[27] Henk Ten Have, 'Images of Man in Philosophy of Medicine', *Advances in Bioethics*, 4 (1998), pp.173–193.

[28] J.N. Lickiss, *The Aboriginal People of Sydney: A Study of Human Ecology*, MD thesis (Sydney: University of Sydney, 1972).

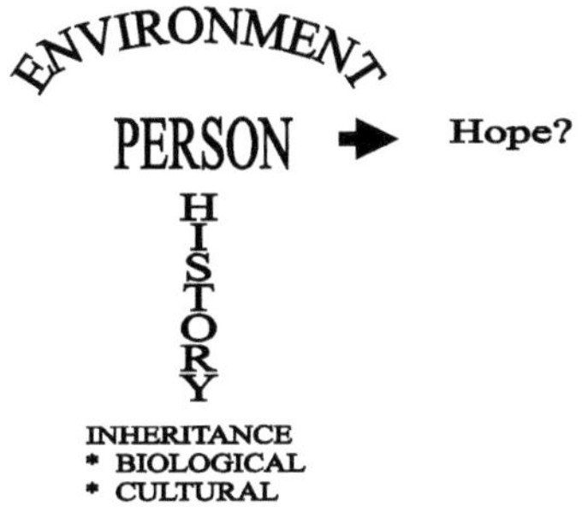

Fig. 1 An Ecological View of Person

Fundamental to the schema or frame is the conviction that a person is a relational reality. Initially, the relation is recognized to exist with the current environment, personal and non-personal, in a continuous dialectic. Taylor[29] among others has stressed that personal identity is:

> [D]efined by the commitments and identifications which provide the frame or horizon. … I am a self only in relation to certain interlocutors: in relation to those conversation partners who were essential to my achieving self-definition. … A self exists only within 'webs of interlocution'.

Taylor writes further,

> To ask what a person is, in abstraction, from his or her self-interpretations, is to ask a fundamentally misguided question, one to which there couldn't in principle be an answer. … We are only selves insofar as we move in a certain space of questions, as we seek and find an orientation to the good.

The place of language in all this is critical,—and its presence for cognition, even if not articulation in speech needs to be recognized. We may have difficulty in expressing the critical importance of retaining language (comprehension or expression) for human dignity—but it is clear that a capacity for language (not necessarily speech) must be close to the core of the dignity of being human (an immense subject for consideration).[30]

A person is a relational reality with respect to present *sitz im leben*, but also in relation to a personal past: the essential historicity of a person stressed so profoundly by 20th-century philosophers such as Heidegger, is a practical consideration for medical staff. Not only the facts of the past (medical, social, psychological) but also the manner in which the patient understands, incorporates, and interprets the past, is of immediate importance to the clinician seeking to understand, in order

---

[29] C. Taylor, *The Sources of the Self: The Making of Modern Identity* (Cambridge, MA: Harvard University Press, 1989), p.36

[30] J.N. Lickiss, 'Speech and Community', *Proceedings of Annual Convention of Australian Association for Speech and Hearing* (1978), pp.4–12.

to restore, rehabilitate, or to continue to care for a patient even in situations of predictable deterioration even approaching death. 'Narrative medicine', currently being recognized again[31] as a strand of clinical endeavour, is that perspective on clinical medicine which emphasizes that the patient understands himself or herself as narrative—and the substance of this needs to be grasped by listening, especially (rather than providing boxes to tick!), in addition to judicious questioning and prompting; and the telling of the narrative, especially if received attentively, is itself a healing process. Neglect of the historicity of the patient, with so many dimensions, inevitably will reduce the possibility of, for example, relieving suffering—a goal which is core business for medicine.[32]

The inheritance of a person, the platform so to speak on which and within which one's personal history is constructed, may be considered to have two dimensions: (a) biological (obviously relevant for genetic influences on disease development, but also for much of personal significance, even stature or musical ability or social significance (so often tied to ethnicity) and (b) cultural. Volumes have been written on the former, and there will be no further comment here save to note that in medical circles, an emphasis on eugenics proved a tragic disaster in the early 20th century, and the present emphasis on genetics in medical education, research, and converse needs to be balanced by a regard for persons adequately understood (influenced but not determined by genetics); the humanities are a crucially necessary companion for medical lore, and their relative absence is of grave moment.

Culture is a complex reality and has been variously defined. The cultural matrix in which a child is born, and continues to be embedded, includes not only, what has been termed the 'womb of language' but also much else which will not only influence what happens to this developing person, but also how this person will interpret what happens—and all this includes disease and illness and treatment, and health care, and this has been widely researched.

Thus far, the frame in Fig. 1 might be seen as a closed system, with an internal dynamic as the parts, current environment, history, inheritance and the medical state (health or illness), continually interact in describable ways. It has seemed, in my clinical experience, that the person can move out of such a closed system by means of hope. One can call hope a strategy of transcendence, but we need to be aware of the complexity of that term (and facile aberrations) and some sensitive philosophical literature.[33] One of the most painful questions one can ask (gently) of a person in a limit situation is, 'Can you tell me what you most hope for now?' and the answer is unpredictable. Hope has been given attention by countless writers, poets, novelists, playwrights theologians, and philosophers, but also (formally) by

---

[31] T. Greenhalgh and B. Hurwitz (eds), *Narrative Medicine* (London: British Medical Journal Books, 1998). B. Hurwitz, 'Narrative and the Practice of Medicine', *The Lancet*, 356 (2000), pp.2086–2089.

[32] E. Cassell, 'The Goal of Medicine and the Relief of Suffering', *New England Journal of Medicine*, 306 (1982), pp.639–646.

[33] F. Kerr, *Immortal Longings* (London: SPCK, 1997).

nurse researchers,[34] and physicians (to a lesser extent).[35] For present purposes in our consideration of what we mean by 'person', it may simply be noted that hope,[36] the arrow as it were, which leads out of the possibly closed relational system appears to be closely related to human dignity, at least to the awareness of self-worth (as the last vestige of hope), even *in extremis*. Articulated hope for an ill person may be for recognizable things (and even measurable things): to be cured, to be out of pain, to get home again, to walk, to sleep, to see a particular person again, to be reconciled, to observe some ritual, or, as one man said to me, 'to see Halley's comet'. But the hope may be anchored in other domains: the hope may be for immortality, or that I mean something to you, to others, to an Absolute, to God (however understood), or have significance in the universe. The fostering of such hope is a very deep facet in a clinical care relationship, where there is responsibility to assist the patient (and those in the 'web of interlocution' in which she/he is constituted and lives) to fix hope on things or personal fidelity which will not fail, lest the fostering of false hope engender death in despair. It is worth recalling that in Erikson's schema of personal development[37] the choice of the last phase of life is between 'integrity' (a sense of the wholeness of life) and despair; clinicians or others bent on giving hope need to be aware, then, of the tragic consequences of falsely orientated hope.

The 'going out' to the other, however conceived, even simply by the awareness or articulation of hope, appears to be part of human dignity-as-process, as a dynamic construct, as a living, evolving idea in the mind. Human dignity, the living idea, may be manifest in action, but that action is not, in the last analysis, directed inwards, but outwards, in relationship, even in surrender. Absolute autonomy may the antithesis of dignity, the self-locked in (truly no exit). Human dignity, therefore, maybe incorrectly conceived as a static entity, or property, but rather as process, always a becoming and moving to what is not yet… as is life. Dignity is embedded in life's dynamism.

In sum, after recognition of the complexity of person as a relational reality, it can be conceded that to consider patients in a bed or a clinic chair as 'contained within their hat and their boots', is gross, radical error—and impoverishment. Some glimmer of the role of the personal (and place) relationships, which not only contain, restrain, but also constitute what a particular person is needs to be appreciated by a physician and nurse—however busy.

---

34 J.M. Morse and B. Doberneck, 'Delineating the Concept of Hope', *Sigma Theta Tau International*, 27 (1995), pp.277–285. J.R. Cutcliffe and K. Herth, 'The Concept of Hope in Nursing 1: Its origins, Background and Nature', *British Journal of Nursing*, 11 (2002), pp.832–840.

35 C.L. Nekolaichuk and E. Bruera, 'On the Nature of Hope in Palliative Care', *Journal of Palliative Care*, 14 (1998), pp.36–42.

36 J. Hockley, 'The Concept of Hope and the Will to Live', *Palliative Medicine*, 7 (1993), pp.181–186.

37 E.H. Erikson, *Identity and the Life Cycle*. Psychological issues monograph (New York: International Universities Press, 1969). E.H. Erikson, *The Life Cycle Completed: A Review* (New York: Norton, 1982).

Understanding 'Suffering' and Its Relation to Dignity

Human suffering is a core activity, and deserves mention: consideration of current concepts of suffering may throw light on human dignity.

Clinical experience forces the conclusion that dignity is not to be equated with comfort or absence of fear, pain, or suffering, however much these human experiences may threaten or even impinge on dignity. Emotions are core experiences in human life—and in the lives of other animals. Contemporary philosophers such as Nussbaum[38] have stressed the value of emotional intelligence and the place of emotions in the totality of personal life: we are not just rational animals. We can simply attest to the role of human emotional responses in response to powerful stimuli—and to the complex cognitive, processes concerned with self-interpretation and critical decision-making in times of personal crises, with profound effects on personal development, as emphasized in Erikson's corpus. As previously mentioned, Erikson portrays the last developmental phase of life as characterized by either a movement/choice towards a sense of 'integrity' (by which he means wholeness of life)—or despair: Erikson does not imply that what he deems the negative choices at critical points of personal development equate with loss of dignity. Health professionals indeed can observe individuals with seriously flawed personal development, even with seriously identifiable psychopathology, who retain in the midst of it, human dignity, not merely intrinsic because they remain fully human, but even a stance expressing that dignity… this, even in despair, even in face of approaching death as well as in the midst of life. Serious psychopathology may threaten but not negate even the observable expression of human dignity.

Similarly, doctors and nurses and others closely involved in the care of very ill and distressed persons can and do distinguish human dignity from 'suffering': human dignity, even as observable, is not necessarily negated or depleted by suffering. Many seek to define suffering in a clinical context,[39] but world literature is replete with images. Job suffered from the withdrawal of persons and goods, from what appeared to be constitutive of who he was. In the drama (it is surely a drama) the pursuit of meaning follows several well-worn paths, ending with the bursting in of absolute transcendence and the forceful statement that merely human effort cannot construct meaning, or the reason why, in the midst of such suffering. But there is no hint of Job losing 'dignity', even as he lost his bearings—'footing', so to speak. Food for thought!

---

[38] M. Nussbaum, *Upheavals of Thought: The Intelligence of the Emotions* (Cambridge: Cambridge University Press, 2001).

[39] J.M. Morse, 'Toward a Praxis Theory of Suffering', *Advances in Nursing Science*, 24 (2001) pp. 47–59. N. I. Cherny, 'The Problem of Suffering', D. Doyle G. Hanks, N. Cherny and K. Calman (eds.), *Oxford Textbook of Palliative Medicine* (Oxford: Oxford University Press, 3rd edn., 2004), pp.7–14.

Cassell, in his landmark paper[40] offered an operational definition of suffering: a sense of impending personal disintegration. It is to be noted that the suffering is in the sensing of a possibility of, in common parlance, 'going to pieces'. Patients can attest to ever having felt like this in the course of a serious illness and, if so, can define the 'trigger' (McCosker, Best, Lickiss, unpublished study). May the 'sense' of impending personal disintegration imply also a fear of loss of dignity, as if dignity is dependent on radical cohesiveness, or even a statement of it? It appears that one of the 'triggers' named may be very close to this: for example, one woman could cope with everything (a poor prognosis, pain, stress of complex investigations, side effects of arduous treatment) but she said that a bout of faecal incontinence made her feel like going to pieces. ... Sometimes the comment is 'broke my spirit'. We are close to the human core here. Patients may be conscious of an interior cohesiveness, which may, in limit situations, be threatened. For others the 'cohesiveness' stopping disintegration is related to the presence of others (the webs of interlocution of Taylor) maintaining their structural integrity. This idea appears close to the 'general resistance resource' critical to well-being when health is under threat, described (on the basis of major fundamental research) by Antonovsky[41]: he wrote about the role of the general resistance resource in maintaining 'a sense of coherence'. He, from a sociological perspective, may have been throwing light on factors such as supportive relationships which assist the person to cohere: the impending sense of personal disintegration (Cassell's 'suffering') may be relieved, if not prevented, by relationships, as well as or in concert with individual cognitive processes. It appears that personal integrity/integration/non-disintegration is not equated with 'human dignity', but the concepts appear to inhabit the same space, so to speak, and a threat to personal coherence can certainly be interpreted, if not experienced by a patient—as a threat to dignity. Human dignity is, like a person, intrinsically relational, and may be intimately concerned with the cohesiveness of relationships, which constitute the person. Antonovsky later wrote also of salutogenesis (restoration of health) and the significance of others[42]: very recent work indicates that outcomes for women with breast cancer are more influenced by friendship networks than many other apparently more obviously relevant factors.[43]

Two other related comments arise from clinical experience. A patient who has lost a sense of self-worth (a far more telling state than a psychiatric diagnosis of depression) and articulated by such words as, 'I am not worth bothering about', is a challenge for the clinician—who, merely by staying in the same space (on a hospital chair) for a time may assist the return of self-affirmation. Similarly, the patient

---

[40] E. Cassell, 'The goal of medicine and the relief of suffering', *New England Journal of Medicine*, 306 (1982), pp.636–639.

[41] A. Antonovsky, *Health Stress and Coping* (San Francisco, CA: Jossey-Bass, 1979).

[42] A. Antonovsky, *Unravelling the Mystery of Health: How People Manage to Stay Well* (San Francisco, CA: Jossey-Bass, 1987).

[43] C.H. Kroeke, L.D. Kubansky, E.S. Schernhammer, M.D. Holmes, and I. Kawachi, 'Social Networks, Social Support, and Survival After Breast Cancer Diagnosis', *Journal of Clinical Oncology*, 24 (2006), p.1105.

who has no sense of continuing control over medical interventions, however benevolent (so-called battered-patient syndrome),[44] expressed in the statement, 'I do not know what they will do to me next', offers a challenge to create an opportunity not merely for respite but also decision-making. These two scenarios from real life, rare in good circumstances, but unforgettable, appear to be in the same conceptual space as 'suffering' and 'dignity'. There appears to be a layer of human reality far beneath (or deep within) that which is the readily visible, and articulated, stuff of everyday: it is this that a physician is privileged to know, touch and feel—and ponder on.

Philosophers will be able to articulate, place in an intellectual frame, and trace even the traditions of thought, to which such instances and articulations relate: clinicians must experience them, be sensitive to them, and respond basically through the instrumentation of one's own humanity to the other, face to face, not merely physically but in the sense Levinas identifies as interpersonal encounter with the other.[45] The Levinasian corpus points to the philosophical basis for the duty of care as not being, law, social, or individual contract, but the call of the other.[46] Dr. Rieux in *The Plague*, the allegorical novel by Camus, comments at the close of the book, after a harrowing experience of plague in the city, that there is more good in men to admire than evil to despise.[47] What the experienced physician, even battered and bruised by decades of privileged concourse with fellow citizens in difficult circumstances, often notes is that human dignity may be threatened but is not negated by fear, pain, suffering, passivity, powerlessness, or dying—and that, in all circumstances, there is the imperative for the physician to be the unfailing advocate of the weak.[48] This unfailing commitment to radical human worth, which we might term 'dignity', should be considered part of that which 'systematizes' (in Foucault's terms)[49] the thought worlds of clinical practice and discourse.

The debate about whether or not dignity in dying is facilitated by deliberately accelerating death by physician assisted suicide, or by euthanasia will not be entered into here, but the comments of Callaghan[50] should be remembered as a background to this difficult discussion: our dignity should not rest on the actions of others asked to put us to death. If one accepts the traditional Jewish ethic that a

---

[44] J.N. Lickiss, 'Care of the Patient Close to Death', in: J. Klastersky, S. Schimpff, and H.J. Senn (eds), *Supportive Care for Oncologists: A Handbook for Oncologists* (New York: Dekker, 2nd edn., 1999), pp.677–692.

[45] E. Levinas, *Basic Philosophical Writings*, A. Peperzak, S. Critchley and R. Bernasconi (eds.) (Bloomington, IN: Indiana University Press, 1996), p.8.

[46] D. Manderson, 'Philosophical basis of the duty of care', unpublished lecture, Annual Symposium, Sydney Institute of Palliative Medicine (2001).

[47] A. Camus, *The Plague* (New York: Vintage International, 1947, reissued 1991).

[48] J.N. Lickiss, 'On the Care of our Aged: Privilege and Responsibility', *Australian Rehabilitation Review*, 2(6) (1982), pp.51–57.

[49] See quotation at the beginning of this chapter.

[50] D. Callaghan, *The Troubled Dream of Life: In Search of a Peaceful Death* (New York: Touchstone, 1993).

physician should strive to affirm life, but not obstruct death,[51] then there is much room for scrutinizing carefully the circumstances, even in great hospitals, where dying is sometimes apparently occasionally 'obstructed'.

Human Dignity as a Value in the Context of Clinical Decision-making

Human dignity as an idea, with its appreciation as a value, is part (or should always be part) of the matrix of clinical decision-making. The decision will usually involve a choice of options, made in the light of: (a) the fact base, (b) recognition of the relevant values in the cultural environment where the health care is occurring, and (c) respect for the traditional ethical principles: autonomy, beneficence, non-maleficence, justice (individual and social). Awareness of values is part of the adequate consideration of beneficence, and the perspective should include matters considered by the patient as pertaining to his/her dignity; this may of course include issues related to the body, for example, care, comfort, respect, having life prolonged at reasonable cost, or being allowed to die, with death not being obstructed, but also freedom for the spirit to express relationships, to move towards another, even the Absolute other in prayer. Decision-making in this perspective justifies extended consideration elsewhere.

What are the implications for medical education in the 21st century? Memories of the ghastly failures of the medical profession in the 20th century haunt the mind: actions especially and specifically with respect to all aspects of human dignity, in the form of unspeakable aberrations and grossly unethical experimentation on the relatively powerless, (citizens in camps, prisoners, the elderly, handicapped children, not only in Europe) considered as means not ends, even in the land walked by Kant who declared how unethical is would be to do so. The most massive moral collapse of medical authorities (including senior academics) began apparently with ostensibly slight misjudgements, a salutary point for today, outlined in the conclusion of Alexander, medical observer at the Nuremburg trials[52]:

> The beginnings at first were merely a subtle shift in emphasis in the basic attitude of the physicians. It started with the acceptance of the attitude, that there is such a thing as a life not worthy to be lived. This attitude in its early stages concerned itself merely with the severely and chronically sick. Gradually the sphere of those to be included in this category was enlarged to encompass the socially unproductive, the ideologically unwanted, the racially unwanted and finally all non-Germans. But it is important to realise the infinitely small wedged–in lever from which this entire trend of mind received its impetus was the attitude toward the non-rehabilitatable sick.

Palliative medicine, the branch of clinical science and practice concerned especially with the subjectivity of the patient and the care of the 'non rehabilitatable sick', needs

[51] A.L. Mackler, *Jewish and Catholic Bioethics: A Comparative Analysis* (Georgetown University Press, 2003).

[52] L. Alexander, 'Medical Science Under Dictatorship', *New England Journal of Medicine*, 241 (1949), pp.39–47.

to be seen not as marginal but central to medical practice, indeed as core business: the touchstone of the quality of a health service or hospital, as well as the practice of an individual clinician. Disregard by doctors of the dignity of the powerless is a grave omen: involvement in torture of prisoners falls under the same condemnation.[53]

In mainstream health care practice, there is need to recognize the danger of the conjunction of: (a) absorbing intellectual interest in what is genetically possible (even designer babies), (b) almost fixation or adulation on what is physically perfect (models, sports heroes), (c) a near obsession to remove from society, render invisible, or prevent the occurrence of marred human beings, and (d) excessive respect for efficiency in administration/business/health care[54]: all four being understandable, but complex and ethically risky approaches to thought and action. Any idea of creating humans to serve solely for the survival of others (for example, as source of organs for transplantation) jars a sense of fittingness in relation to human dignity, the social as well as personal implications require deep reflection, not only by novelists.[55] If such currents of thought (and even medical enthusiasms) are not combined with well-founded moral principles, unfailing respect for the dignity of persons more adequately understood, and sound medical academic leadership, a repeat of the moral collapse of the medical profession in the West could occur. 'Never again' applies to the medical profession, with its oldest contemporary members still reeling from the shocks of what happened in Europe in 1930–1945, and many of its youngest members totally oblivious to the events—and therefore vulnerable to be deflected gradually into ways of practice, which should be unthinkable.

Medical education involves leading out (from *educere*) and nourishing (from *educare*)—a stretching and nourishing, not only with concepts of the natural sciences, but also in humanness: and this must not fail in the West (or anywhere) again. Can we educate the medical profession to recognize human dignity as inhering in the life of every man, woman, and child, to be respected during life and after death; that this dignity and awareness of it may be increased or jeopardized (though not destroyed) by the actions of others. Further can we inculcate the idea that respect is due not only to the body, but also relationships with other persons, personal history, place, and cultural context, and finally, with whatever is perceived as the absolute other (and personal rituals expressing this relationship)? In addition, it needs to be imparted that deliberate non-recognition or disrespect of the dignity of another (by humiliation, torture, or violence) is never fitting for a physician. How can we teach that physicians, as advocates of the weak and the ultimate guardians of human dignity should be trustworthy (even if the structures of society are in ruins and all else has failed)—and that there is no greater privilege, nor more onerous responsibility? Is this the radical charge to medical education for the 21st century, so that what happened in the 20th century at the hands of physicians will never happen again?

---

[53] R. Farberman, 'A Stain on Medical Ethics', *The Lancet*, 366 (2005), p.712.

[54] J.N. Lickiss, 'Late Lessons from Auschwitz: Is There Anything More to Learn for the 21st Century?', letter, *Journal of Medical Ethics*, 27 (2001), pp.137–138.

[55] K. Ishiguro, *Never Let Me Go* (London: Faber & Faber, 2003).

This chapter began with a statement from Foucault. It could as easily be a challenge: 'What counts in the things said by men? What systematizes their thoughts, "making them endlessly accessible to new discourses and open to the task of transforming them?"'[56] Perhaps the answer is the idea of human dignity, 'the island in the mind', if it is allowed to expand to its fullness, and become firmly rooted in the depths of the mind it may restore and refresh the heart (even of a burned-out physician)[57] and sustain the humanity of the physicians of the future, helping them to justify the trust their fellows need to place in them. And an island, even in the mind, has its beauty, as noted in the words of an anonymous Australian poet responding to Rodney Hall's novel, *The Island in the Mind*:

O there are
islands in the mind !
clouds of unremembered dreams,
cliffs, crevasses, waterways
of spent tears sea seeking,
and a forest clearing, charred wood
of past fire, and caves
still lantern lit, flaming
the lost fire still,
and the sound of a day breaking on a quiet shore.
And you are there !

If it be said that the idea of human dignity is, after all, merely poetry, how much do we need poets to 'redress' the balance of our times?[58] Macklin has noted the vagueness of the notion of human dignity and questions its usefulness,[59] but vague ideas, even rumours, can begin fires!

What if health services, or individual hospitals, or medical schools were dedicated to 'Human Dignity'? Dedication to 'The Glory of God' is commonplace in some cultures, but it is to be noted that Irenaeus, Bishop of Lyons in the 2nd century wrote that 'the glory of God is man fully alive', not too far from a paean to human dignity! We may have run full circle. We may arrive at a radical humanism, after all. It has been said, by a professor of anatomy, that 'the task of medicine is to emancipate man's interior splendour'[60]. It may be a lifetime's task to understand what this means, but it is surely something to do with the dignity, however obscured, of every man, woman, and child everywhere.

---

[56] M. Foucault, *The Birth of the Clinic: The Archaeology of Medical Practice* (New York: Vintage, 1993).

[57] D.E. Meier, A.L. Back, S. Morrison, 'The Inner Life of Physicians and the Care of the Seriously Ill' *Journal of the American Medical Association*, 286 (2001), pp.3007–3014.

[58] S. Heaney, *The Redress of Poetry* (London: Faber & Faber, 1995).

[59] R. Macklin, 'Reflections on the Human Dignity Symposium: Is Dignity a Useless Concept?' *Journal of Palliative Care*, 20 (2004), pp.212–216.

[60] K. Mortimer, 'The Impossible Profession: The Doctor–Priest Relationship', *Proceedings of the Australian Association of Gerontology*, 2 (1974), pp.81–82.

5
Two Conceptions of Dignity: Honour and Self-Determination

Andrew Brennan and Y. S. Lo

Meritocratic Dignity

In Bernardo Bertolucci's film *The Last Emperor* (1987), Pu Yi, the last of the Qing emperors is 're-educated' by the Communist regime through having to share a prison cell with his former servant, making his own bed and working at menial tasks. The valet endures enormous conflict as he is 'liberated' from the role of servant while still clinging to that very role. Although the film may be unreliable as history, it is enlightening on the topic of dignity. Pu Yi has been brought up to behave with the kind of dignity and demeanour of one who controls a vast empire, yet he is treated by a succession of manipulators as little more than a puppet to be used for political ends of which he is often unconscious. He is repeatedly shamed as it becomes clear that he has no real power over his own life. The valet has spent his life in thrall to his master, yet is re-educated to take a new view of himself and the master as equals. While the dignity of Pu Yi is reduced by the people who imprison him, the valet's is enlarged. Here we see some of the multiform nature of dignity: it seems to be something an individual can possess, cultivate, and feel. Yet it also seems to be at the disposal of others, to give or take away from us.

As far as cultivation of dignity is concerned, there are few better sources than the traditional writings of the Confucian canon. The 'gentleman' (君子) in these writings is someone who has a grave deportment, eats carefully without conversing, acknowledges others according to their rank and circumstances, and takes care over fine details such as the proper adjustment of his garments and how they fall during his movements.[1] According to one disciple, Kongzi (Confucius) himself was

[1] Book 10 of the *Analects* contains many instances of dignified, gentlemanly behaviour, for example, '(10.3) When summoned by his ruler to receive a guest, his countenance would become severe and he would quicken his steps. When he bowed to those in attendance beside him—stretching out his hands to the left or to the right, as their position required—his robes remained perfectly arrayed….(10.25) When passing someone dressed in funeral garb, he would bow down and grasp the crossbar of his carriage' (P.J. Ivanhoe and B. van Norden, *Readings in Classical Chinese Philosophy*, Indianapolis, IN: Hackett, 2001, Chapter 1, pp.27–29, trans. E.G. Slingerland). All other translations of Kongzi in the main text are taken from D.C. Lau, *Confucius: The Analects* (Hong Kong: The Chinese University Press, 1992).

J. Malpas and N. Lickiss (eds.), Perspectives on Human Dignity: A Conversation, 43–58.

'cordial, well-behaved, respectful, frugal and deferential'.[2] 'A gentleman who lacks gravity does not inspire awe', says Kongzi.[3] Clearly, dignity involves a special *feeling*—a feeling of importance or worth—felt both by the person who is important and also by others who perceive this worth. When felt by others, it is admiration, veneration, or in Kongzi's term, 'awe'. When felt by oneself, it is self-esteem, self-respect, or *amour propre*, which is often manifested or projected in one's demeanour. The sense of the term 'dignity', as used in the West, probably draws on the meaning of the Latin original. *Dignitas* was the status that dignitaries had—a quality that demanded reverence from the ordinary common person—the *vulgar*, in the original meaning of that term.

As other contributors have shown in detail,[4] the classical notion of dignity fits well with a hierarchical conception of human being and human society, according to which some people have more dignity, or are more dignified, than others, and therefore deserve higher esteem and more privileges. In many hierarchies, higher positions often come at the expense of stringent and demanding duties. For example, knighthood in medieval Europe was at the same time an honour, a set of privileges, and a set of duties and rules of conduct. Even people who did not earn, but were born into, high positions were expected to take on wider public responsibilities, from which people lower in the hierarchy were immune. Implicit in such conventions was the demand of justification for hierarchical privileges or rights.[5]

Ideally, the feeling of dignity as esteem (or self-esteem) would flow from the esteemed person being honourable or having some worthy quality. In real life, however, the feeling of esteem is often induced not by the genuine possession of worthy qualities, but by mere external appearances that are often associated with it. Dignity frauds, as we might call them, lack genuinely worthy qualities, but project the feeling of greatness by mere imitation of (some characteristic aspects of) the demeanour of people who possess such qualities. Discrepancies between projection and reality are often comic. A top quality professional cycling outfit would look funny on a learner riding a tricycle. The same kind of facial tension and bodily movements as displayed by Kung Wah Chung would look ridiculous if displayed by someone whose playing is completely out of tune. Such comic effects involve a feeling of absurdity (discrepancy between expectation and reality), and they rely on our expectation that admiration (especially, self-admiration) needs to be *justified* by some genuine merits.

---

[2] *Analects*, 1.10.

[3] *Ibid.*, 1.8.

[4] See for example, Milton Lewis, 'A Brief History of Human Dignity: Idea and Application', Chapter 8, this volume.

[5] In medieval Europe, examples of the reward and responsibilities of dignity abounded—for example, in the selection of high officials in the early days of the Venetian Republic (based on merit, integrity, and previous service to the republic). Compare this with the widespread practice in 15th-century Italy of purchasing public office, see Jacob Burkhardt, 'The Greater Dynasties', *The Civilization of the Renaissance in Italy*, 1.5 (Oxford: Phaidon, 1945).

In Pico's famous oration of 1486, dignity itself is identified as an ability internal to the person, one which, when properly exercised, enabled humans to aspire to great moral heights. But at the same time, Pico recognized the incompleteness and hesitancy of the human being when confronted with the choice of what to be and what to do. He wrote:

> Thou, like a judge appointed for being honourable, art the moulder and maker of thyself; thou mayest sculpt thyself into whatever shape thou dost prefer. Thou canst grow downward into the lower natures which are brutes. Thou canst again grow upwards from thy soul's reason into the higher natures which are divine.[6]

There is a suggestion here, as in the Confucian canon of self-cultivation, that dignity amounts to more than just feelings and behaviour of a certain kind. Instead, the cultivation of dignity is the cultivation of certain abilities and character traits, both involving dispositions to feel, as well as to behave, in certain ways under certain circumstances. In particular, dignity is partly constituted by the disposition to feel self-esteem and to induce esteem from others. This affective disposition is the first component of dignity. It is justified by the second component of dignity, namely the behavioural disposition to honour the duties and rules of conduct that are rightfully expected of a person of dignity. Without such behavioural disposition to act honourably, the affective disposition to induce self-esteem or esteem from others would be unjustified.

Like the cultivation of all other skills and abilities, Confucian self-cultivation cannot be detached from the notion of hierarchy or from the idea that there are gradations of human excellence and merits. If dignity relies on the possession of certain worthwhile abilities (dignity-relevant merits), and if such merits vary from person to person, then some important questions arise:

1. Does dignity vary from person to person according to the extent to which they possess those dignity-relevant merits?
2. If dignity does vary across individuals, then how differently (if at all) should we treat people with different degrees of dignity?
3. What merits or qualities are dignity-relevant?

From the meritocratic perspective, the answer to the first question is positive: the more dignity-relevant merits one has (either in terms of the number of such merits or in terms of the extent to which one has them), the more dignified and honourable one becomes. From the same perspective the answer to the second question is that people who have more dignity deserve higher esteem and should be rewarded with privileges. It is important, however, to point out that not all entitlements or rights are privileges rewarded for merits. The right not to be tortured, for example, is not a privilege earned by merits. On the other hand, the right of retired Federal politicians in Australia to free domestic air travel is. The meritocratic perspective does not disallow the right not to be tortured, and only becomes

[6] Quoted from 'On the Dignity of Man' in E. Cassirer, P.O. Kristeller, and H.H. Randall, Jr., *The Renaissance Philosophy of Man* (Chicago, IL: University of Chicago Press, 1948), pp.224–225.

problematic if all rights are treated as privileges. Finally, for Kongzi virtues (both moral and intellectual) are qualities that add to a person's dignity and honour, whereas qualities such as material wealth, fame, popularity, social, and political power are not dignity-relevant. The Confucian gentleman who seeks virtues and conducts himself according to duties and principles has much more honour and dignity than the 'small [petty minded] person' (小 人) who seeks only personal gains and favours, and has no sense of standard, shame or dishonour. Likewise, Cicero would agree that a farmer who earns his living by honest physical labour is more dignified and honourable than a corrupt government official, tyrant, or businessman who profits by exploiting the poor or the weak.[7] Just as dignity can be acquired via cultivation of virtues, it can be lost via neglect and degeneration of character. Just as virtues give rise to honour, vices bring about indignity, dishonour, and shame. That is why the Confucian gentleman is supposed to be 'on his guard [against degeneration] when he is on his own', i.e. even when he is not being watched, examined, or judged by others.[8] The meritocratic notion of dignity is often associated with things larger than the individual as Jack Coulehan emphasizes in his chapter.[9] To be associated with, or part of, some larger cause, group, or locus of meaning, can be integral to the cultivation of dignity. In losing oneself in, or even sacrificing oneself for, some greater cause, one attains a greater worth for oneself. On the other side of the same coin, being part of, and benefiting from, a larger entity which pursues horrific and wicked causes brings disgrace and indignity to the individual.

Language and culture carry the resonances, associations, and senses of terms from their past uses into the present. One of the problems with theorizing dignity and associated notions is that our speculations cannot break free from the accumulated meanings that words carry. Within the depth and multiplicity of the term, there is clearly a sense of 'dignity' that is hierarchical, elitist, and closely associated with notions such as reverence, honour, and esteem, all of which are essentially restricted to the few. Not everyone has the same greatness of character. Kongzi claimed that he could never dare to think of himself as the most cultivated and dignified of people—a sage.[10] As David Hume once remarked, the term 'dignity', like 'beauty', and 'wisdom', is reserved for a property that is rare.[11] If we marvel at the dignity of

---

[7] For his views on the joys of farming, and on the importance of earning respect in old age by means of deeds carried out when younger, see Cicero's 'On Old Age', *Cicero: Selected Works*, trans. Michael Grant (Harmondsworth, Middlesex: Penguin, 1960).

[8] In *The Great Learning*, one of the 'four classics' of Confucianism, it is recommended that in order to avoid self-deception, and so that 'what truly is within will be manifested without', therefore 'the gentleman must be watchful over himself when alone'. By contrast, the petty-minded or unscrupulous man knows no restraint in private.

[9] see Jack Coulehan, 'Dying with Dignity: The Story Reveals Its Meaning', Chapter 21, this volume.

[10] *Analects*, 7.34.

[11] David Hume, 'On the Dignity or Meanness of Human Nature', in S. Copley and A. Edgar (eds.), *David Hume—Selected Essays* (Oxford: Oxford University Press, 1996).

Gandhi or Nelson Mandela, at the greatness and nobility exemplified by their capacity to uphold convictions in face of brutalities, and the strength with which they bore sufferings for a greater cause, then we are drawing on the meritocratic idea of dignity, a rare quality but one expressed in a concept that would have made sense to Kongzi, Cicero, and Pico. This kind of dignity is fragile, subject to loss in an instant, and retained by its possessors as much by luck and circumstance as through their own efforts.

Democratized Dignity

What we call the *modern* notion of dignity drops the hierarchical elements implicit in the meaning of *dignitas*, and uses the term so that *all* human beings must have *equal* dignity, regardless of their virtues, merits, actual social and political status, or any other contingent features. Closely associated with the modern notion of dignity are those of *universal human rights,* and the *intrinsic value* or *sanctity* of human life. These rights, and the associated dignity, are no longer fragile, but are guaranteed to all who are born human.

Obviously, there is an immediate tension between that older (but still present) classical notion we discussed in the previous section and the modern notion of dignity. In the classical picture dignity is meritocratic, hierarchical, and can be lost, whereas in the modern picture dignity is democratic, egalitarian, and guaranteed. What *prima facie* reasons does the classical picture provide for thinking that dignity is hierarchical and contingent? As we have seen, a person's dignity (on the classical view) is a direct function of certain worthwhile personal qualities, such as virtues. It is clear both that not all human beings are equal in merit or virtue and that such qualities are contingent and can be lost or damaged. Therefore, the hierarchical and contingent characters of the classical notion of dignity are well founded on its meritocratic character. Can the same be said for the modern democratized picture of dignity? What *prima facie* reasons does it provide for thinking that dignity is equal and guaranteed for all human beings? If people's dignity is a function of certain of their qualities, then in order for people to have dignity to an equal extent, they must also have those dignity-relevant qualities to an equal extent. Furthermore, in order for their equal dignity to be guaranteed immune from loss or damage, the dignity-relevant qualities must share this immunity. What exactly are these qualities?

An immediate response is that dignity is not something that people can earn by merit, and that to assume that dignity has to be earned is uncritically to presuppose or smuggle in the classical notion. If that is true, then from what does human dignity originate such that it is universal, egalitarian, and necessary? The Christian answer is that human dignity comes from God's grace. The Kantian and existentialist answer is that it comes from humanity understood as rational agency, autonomy, or radical freedom. The key response is the religious one, which can be summarized in the form of the following argument:

G1. God is all-knowing and all-good (the Judaeo-Christian definition of 'God').
G2. God believes something if and only if that thing is true (from G1 and definition of 'all-knowing').
G3. God loves X if and only if God believes that X has value (from G1 and definition of 'all-good'[12]).
G4. X has value if and only if God loves X (Judaeo-Christian metaethical analysis of 'value', from G2 and G3).
G5. God *unconditionally loves* all human beings *equally*, in that:

(a) God *non-instrumentally* loves all human beings equally (i.e. equally loves them independently of their usefulness).
(b) God *intrinsically* loves all human beings equally (i.e., equally loves them for their intrinsic qualities, especially for their origin, i.e. their being God's creations).
(c) God *necessarily* loves all human beings equally (Why necessarily? Because, God's love for human beings is independent of all contingent factors in the universe. This means that God's love for human beings is necessary.).

G6. All human beings have an *equal unconditional value* which is:

(a) Non-instrumental (i.e. independent of their usefulness)
(b) Intrinsic (i.e. dependent on their intrinsic qualities)
(c) Necessary (from G4 and G5)[13]

In short, G4 states that God's love is the origin of all value, and the inference from G4 and G5 to G6 seeks to show that it is God's equal and unconditional love for all human beings that confers equal and unconditional worth on all human beings. Human dignity, according to the modern democratized notion, is nothing but this God-given worth, which is the sole foundation for universal human rights. Since God's love, approval, and commands are traditionally the source and foundation of all values and moral principles, the modern secular notion of moral dignity, value, standing, or right as absolute and unconditional inherits the notions of necessity and universality from Christian theorizing. However, for those who lack the faith in the existence of such a loving and powerful God, what rational grounds are there for thinking that all human beings have equal and necessary dignity, which in turn generates equal, universal, and absolutely inviolate human rights? What, apart from such a powerful theoretical device as God's equal and unconditional love for all human beings, can legimitize the demanding modern democratized conception of dignity?

In order to provide a secular foundation for the inherent worth or dignity of the human being, some philosophers have tried to replace 'God' with various versions of

---

[12] The idea here is Aristotelian: the virtuous person not only knows the good but loves the good. It follows that a good person at least loves what he believes to be good.

[13] A hidden premise in the argument is that God necessarily exists. Without this hidden assumption, there would be possible worlds in which God does not exist, and therefore possible worlds in which human beings are not loved by God, and therefore possible worlds in which human beings have no value. Thus, without, the worth of human beings is not *necessary*.

'ideal agents' (e.g. fully rational agents). For example, consider the Kantian argument for human dignity, the structure of which is very similar to the religious one:

K1. Something has value if and only if all rational agents value it.
K2. All rational agents value all rational agents equally and necessarily for their rational agency.
K3. Rational agency is humanity (the essence of being human).
K4. All human beings have equal intrinsic and necessary value (from K1, K2, K3)[14]

There are serious problems with using this style of argument to support the modern democratized conception of human dignity. For one thing, it is arguably not true that rationality is necessarily self-appreciative. There are good reasons for thinking that rational agency in the Kantian sense (i.e., autonomy, the capacity to reflect, to will, to make choice for oneself) is not always a good thing. In some tight situations, for example, instinct is sometimes a better response than Kantian reason. For another and much more serious reason, the modern moral democrats (who endorse the *Universal Declaration of Human Rights*) are concerned with beings who are biologically human. It is clear that not all biological human beings are rational agents in the Kantian or any other sense of the term. Many have pointed out the empirical fact of human inequality in rationality, and argued that it follows from the Kantian perspective that beings who lack rationality are excluded from the Kantian kingdom of ends (i.e., the kingdom in which all members are always to be treated as ends in themselves and never as mere means). One commentator writes:

> One serious objection raised against Kant's ethical theory is that in claiming that only rational beings are ends in themselves deserving of respect, it licenses treating all things which aren't persons as mere means to the ends of rational beings, and so it supports morally abhorrent attitudes of domination and exploitation toward all nonpersons and toward our natural environment.[15]

Most (if not all) nonhuman beings on Earth are not persons (i.e. not rational beings). Likewise, many people who suffer from a large range of diseases and injuries are not persons either. Furthermore, no typical human beings (whoever we take them to be!) are equally rational all the time in the Kantian sense. If rational agency is the necessary and sufficient condition for dignity, then given that rational agency comes in gradations in human beings, the Kantian picture for human dignity is meritocratic and hierarchical, rather than democratic and egalitarian. In short, without the foundation of some dignity-relevant quality genuinely, equally shared by all human beings, the modern secular democratized conception of equal human dignity is free floating, and would seem to be nothing more than an ethical residue of the traditional religious world view.

Consider again the idea central to Pico's oration—that humans all have a similar capacity, but that the exercise of that capacity varies widely from person to person.

---

[14] Christine M. Korsgaard, *The Sources of Normativity* (Cambridge: Cambridge University Press, 1996).

[15] Robin S. Dillon, 'Respect', in: E. Zalta (ed.), *Stanford Encyclopedia of Philosophy* (2003) (http://plato.stanford.edu/entries/respect/).

Two important things flow from Pico's idea, one, widely recognized, the other, not. We have just commented on the first, namely the subsequent attempt to secularize an essentially Christian ethic by appeal to features—reflexive rationality, freedom, the will to power, and so on—that are supposedly unique to human beings. The second feature in Pico is far less often noted but we regard it as significant: this is the distinction he makes between capacities on the one had, and their exercise on the other. Can we make sense of some of the Kantian and post-Kantian ideas about dignity by distinguishing what is true of our capacities from what is true of our exercise of them?

In Kant's own account of dignity, and in the work of many of those who follow him, there is a close association between dignity and something we might call *autonomy*. In the sense we are using it here, autonomy involves more than the term's literal meaning—the capacity to lay down laws for oneself. We use the term to refer to a capacity to determine one's ends, and make authentic choices. To have autonomy in this way is to be self-legislating, self-governing, to make valuations, to be able to respect both oneself and other beings. Dignity, autonomy, and respect are all locked together in the Kantian claim that all (and only) persons have a special kind of worth—dignity—which requires respect. The respect that is required by this worth is not a feeling, by the way, but rather (as Kant tries to make clear in *The Metaphysics of Morals*) a duty to behave in a certain way towards others, a way in which we limit 'our self-esteem by the dignity of humanity in another person, and so as to respect in the practical sense'.[16] This dignity of persons is, for Kant, something absolute and incomparable. Not everyone lives up to their dignity, of course, but simply through possessing it everyone has an equal worth.

What we suggest is that dignity, as understood in contemporary post-Kantian debates, relies on two different elements, which can be regarded as conditions of having dignity (and that the absence of either condition can be taken as contributing to indignity). If autonomy—as a capacity—is the ground, or basis, of the absolute worth of all human beings, then people will retain this worth even when unable to exercise that capacity. While imprisoned, or under the influence of drugs or disease, for example, people may be unable to be *autonomous* (freely exercising their capacities) while yet possessing these capacities in a relatively intact way.[17] Once released from the confines of the prison, the drugs or the disease, they can return to the exercise of their capacities. So we can make sense of the idea that people can have autonomy, and henceforth, even where they are prevented from freely exercising that autonomy. Indeed, if autonomy is what underpins the claim that people have a special moral status, then certain offences against people—unjust detention, for example,—are objectionable not because they interfere directly with the capacities

---

[16] Immanuel Kant, *The Metaphysics of Morals* (1797), trans. M. Gregor (Cambridge: Cambridge University Press, 1991) 6: 449.

[17] The distinction between autonomy as capacity and autonomousness as exercise is described in detail in Y.S. Lo, 'Natural and Artifactual: Restored Nature as Subject', *Environmental Ethics* 21 (1999), pp.247–66. In that paper, the distinction is used to distinguish different levels of impact made by human interference on animals and on the natural world.

that we have, but because they interfere with the exercise of such capacities. For the modern conception, then, it seems that the possession (or loss) of dignity relies both on having (or lacking) a capacity of certain sort, and also on being able (or unable) to exercise that capacity.

Our suggestion enables us, for example, to distinguish two different ways in which dignity can be lost or in which people may be exposed to indignity. Consider, to begin with, what we might call 'dignity-preserving practices' in, for example, medical and legal contexts. If the exercise of autonomy is an important aspect of our behaviour, then practices can be established to help us continue to exercise as much autonomy as possible in difficult circumstances. Hospital regimes can be more or less free, for example, according to the degree of importance given to the importance of keeping patients active in as many of their everyday roles as possible. As other contributors to the present volume have noted, finding ways to help compromised patients exercise autonomy faces many challenges, even when the illness or disability in question does not itself undermine, reduce, or destroy their capacities for self-determination. Limitations on staffing, and institutional requirements will inevitably result in some loss of the ability to exercise capacities, even where the exercising of these capacities would not in principle interfere with regimes of appropriate treatment. These ways in which dignity is compromised, however, are rather different from a second case, namely one where—for example,—disease and increasing incapacity start to undermine the ability even to undertake or fulfill everyday roles (including basic functions such as moving around, controlling bodily functions, and feeding oneself). In such cases, there is direct interference with the capacities in which autonomy itself consists, and dignity is doubly prejudiced.

The balance between dignity-preserving and dignity-diminishing practices is a big subject, and one on which we will not dwell long. 'Dignity-diminishing practices' may be built into legal, medical, and other institutions. Such practices enforce—in an unjustifiable way—certain behaviours on people who would otherwise be able to exercise normal autonomy. For example, subjecting patients to regimes of examination by students, or public exposure, can be an imposition that limits the exercise of normal autonomy and thus may count as dignity-diminishing. In dealings with the law, detention without being charged, and without access to legal advice, intrusive body searches, and so on, could be seen as forms of action that unduly limit the exercise of personal autonomy, and hence would be classified as *prima facie* dignity-diminishing. As we consider further practices that make yet more serious incursions on the individual's exercise of autonomy, we encounter the extreme cases such as torture. Torture itself need not immediately destroy the capacity for self-determination (although in the long term it may very well do so). But at a minimum, physical torture always removes from the victims the basic exercise of control over their bodies—which are instead at the disposal of the torturer. Torture always involves therefore a gross limitation on the exercise of autonomy of the most intimate kind. When torture is prolonged, then there is also the possibility that it may destroy much of the victim's capacity for self-determination. If dignity relies both on autonomy as a capacity and on the ability to exercise that capacity, then torture, like brain cancer, can doubly undermine dignity. By contrast with this case, it should be noted that the presumption of innocence until proof of guilt has been established, and the tradition of habeas corpus, are ways of minimizing the state's interference with the exercise of autonomy. Of course, presumptively innocent people are still subject to periods of detention, and bail is only available to some people in some circumstances. So if the loss of the ability to exercise autonomy involves a reduction in dignity, then even the best of current legal systems subject those accused of criminal acts to some indignity, in the sense that the exercise of their capacities for self-determination is limited.

Loss of dignity, then, comes not only in degrees, but also in a number of forms. Our account draws attention to the complexity of the modern view, combining as it does a doctrine of capacities with a doctrine about the exercise of these. How, then, can we make sense of the idea that human beings are universally worthy of respect, and that such respect is grounded in the capacity for self-determination? Although the appeal of universality is tempting, the approach we have adopted so far does not quite do the job of providing a satisfactory gloss on Kant, let alone anything like the universal feature mentioned in the preamble and in Article 1 of the 1948 *Universal Declaration of Human Rights:* 'All human beings are born free and equal in dignity and rights. They are endowed with reason and conscience and should act towards one another in a spirit of brotherhood.' Members of the biological species *Homo sapiens* who are born without fully functional nervous systems, for example, will lack some or all of the very capacities that are constitutive of *autonomy*. Given the fact that Article 1 goes on to mention the endowments of 'reason and conscience', it may be that the declaration is intending to focus on the typical, undamaged, and fully functioning adult human being. But even on this reading, our account of dignity and its degrees does not yield the universality to which the *Declaration* aspires. Consider the way that differences in education level, for example, impact on the amount of information that is available to people in taking decisions about their lives. Someone fortunate enough to be well educated and born into a wealthy family may in fact be able to exercise a well-developed capacity for autonomy to a high degree. By contrast, someone with little education and trapped in poverty may have less of a capacity in the first place and may have fewer opportunities to exercise those capacities. Given dignity's double reliance on both capacity and exercise, it seems we may have to conclude that normal adult human beings differ in dignity—exactly denying what the *Declaration* states.

There is a way, however, of reconciling (at least in a partial way) the *Declaration* and the account of dignity we have so far provided. Let us suppose that as a matter of fact people do differ in their capacities and that there is great variation in the exercise of capacities. The Preamble and Articles of the *Declaration*, however, are not intended as statements of fact. The claim that everyone is born free and equal in dignity is a normative claim, a claim about the opportunities that people should have, not a claim about what capacities they actually have. Read as a normative claim, the *Declaration* insists that everyone should have equal opportunity to exercise their capacities. Consider the fact that different people know different amounts about health and disease. Doctors in the exercise of their profession practise not only the science of medicine, but also the art of empowering their patients in making decisions about their lifestyles and treatment to the extent that such decisions are possible. What limits the patient's involvement in discussions and decisions over such matters as treatment? One important matter will be the degree to which the patient understands what is wrong with him or her, and understands the nature and implications of various treatment regimes. Part of the art of medicine involves not only identifying the patient's limitations, but also extending the patient's capacities for understanding where this is possible and desirable. Such extension would be part of empowering the patient in the clinical setting. But there are limits to the ability of practitioners to engage in such forms of empowerment, so another part of the medical art will involve helping patients reach decisions in the light of their own limitations. A doctor who treats each patient with equal respect, then, does not treat each patient as equal in understanding. Rather, the practitioner will give each patient the opportunity to exercise their capacity for self-determination to whatever degree they have that capacity. Generalizing from this one example, then, we may suggest the following gloss on universally equal dignity: 'everyone has equal dignity' is a normative claim to the effect that everyone should be allowed to exercise their capacities for self-determination to whatever degree they posses such capacities.

Implications of the Complex View

The modern democratic version of Kantianism states that everyone should be regarded as equal in autonomy—the capacity for self-determination. The Christian view that everyone has an immortal soul, and that God loves each person equally, can underpin the normative claim about equality: since God's love is an infallible guide to where worth resides, then since God loves all people equally, they must themselves have equal worth. Without this underpinning, the normative claim that all people should be regarded as equal in worth, and equivalent in dignity, is free-floating and unanchored. Are there any ways to provide a secular anchoring for the modern view? Before approaching this question we want to suggest some implications of the complex view that may be overlooked if we concentrate too much on the exercise of capacities.

The complex view of dignity which we have outlined here allows for two different ways in which to think about equalizing the differences among human beings. As many examples make clear—for example, the tragic consequences of Alzheimer's dementia—capacities themselves can be eroded through illness. This is but a single example of a much broader problem, namely the fact that capacities themselves can be compromised in various ways. Those capacities that are constitutive of autonomy are thus fragile: they may not develop properly in the first place, they can be damaged or destroyed through disease or accident, and they may be eroded by certain forms of dignity-diminishing treatment such as torture, solitary confinement, and the like. The fragility of autonomy poses a challenge for government and other social institutions: how best to nourish, enhance, and preserve individual autonomy. This question is not just a technical one, but rather one that raises a morally urgent matter, as we argue in a moment. By contrast, there is another—and easier—question, this time dealing with the exercise of capacities themselves: are governments and other social institutions able to facilitate equal opportunities for the exercise of capacities for self-choosing and self-determination?

Those countries that have established a focus on human rights have taken considerable steps to address the challenge posed by the latter question. Liberal democracies try, in general, to ensure that citizens can pursue their various conceptions of the good life provided this pursuit does not interfere too much with the similar pursuits of other citizens. The assumption behind liberal democracy conceived in this way is that the state itself is not governed by any comprehensive conception of what is good or valuable in life—one which it enforces through coercion on its citizens. Instead, the liberal state is meant to tolerate a multiplicity of conceptions of how to live well and looks for agreement among all citizens on enforceable principles of justice that will be acceptable across a wide range of different individual viewpoints.[18] The politics of liberalism thus becomes detached from any one comprehensive moral view of what is a—or the—good way to live.

Such a focus on protecting the exercise of various freedoms makes sense, provided the citizens being shielded in this way are one and all capable of choosing ends for themselves, making decisions about the priorities among such ends, and able to plan for ways in which these ends can be achieved. Some theorists argue that we should be permitted to choose ends for ourselves, make decisions about what kind of persons we are going to become, free from government interference and imposition. This focus on individual, radically free choice, contrasts with more cultural—or communitarian—conceptions of the human being, ones that see us as born into structures that are already given, and which are themselves partly constitutive of who we are. The latter conception is well expressed by Sandel when he writes:

> self is not prior to, but rather constituted by, its ends—we cannot distinguish "me" from "my ends" ...our selves are at least partly constituted by ends that we do not choose, but rather *discover* by virtue of our being embedded in some shared social context.[19]

Whether we are radically free, or are already locked in to familial and social settings which partly constitute us, it would seem desirable for us to be able to consider our situations clearly, think about the kinds of values and ends that we might have, and make reasonable decisions about which of these to pursue and to what extent to do so. What is important to note, however, is the assumption on the part of all liberal theories that we are indeed free to make such decisions in virtue of our autonomy. Given that autonomy itself is fragile, this assumption can be disputed in a way that may seem to pose an especially severe problem for the proponents of radical freedom. While the communitarian may rely on the wisdom of tradition to

[18] This kind of view is expressed in many works by political philosophers. See, for example, the first chapter of John Tomasi, *Liberalism Beyond Justice: Citizens, Society, and the Boundaries of Political Theory* (Princeton: Princeton University Press, 2001).

[19] Michael Sandel, quoted in Will Kymlicka, *Contemporary Political Philosophy: An Introduction* (Oxford: Oxford University Press, 1990), p.211.

mould the values and ends to which its members aspire, the theorist of radical freedom has to rely on the capacity of each individual to reflect on, weigh, and make choices among various forms of life—the ends which will constitute that person's choice of deliberate self-creation. Such a capacity is often characterized as *rationality* or *reason*.[20] Yet even the communitarian has to hope that in moments of calm reflection, individuals will themselves endorse the values around which their lives as community members have been built.[21]

There are at least two factors involved in autonomy viewed as capacity—factors which give additional complexity to the view we have been developing. First, there is the ability to decide on ends, and make decisions among several ends, each of which may have its attractions. A further factor involves understanding the means by which our envisaged ends are to be achieved. The anatomy of autonomy needs to take these different capacities into account. As is clear from recent neurological studies, popularized in the work of Antonio Damasio, damage to certain systems in the brain (ones concerned mainly with emotion) can result in a severe impairment in decision-making ability while knowledge and understanding themselves remain largely unaffected.[22] This result shows something of importance: that the different factors involved in autonomy itself are to some degree independent of each other. Good education, for example, may advance the autonomy of children precisely because it helps to equip them with the knowledge of how to achieve various ends. It is much less clear whether, and how, education can help in the cultivation of decision-making capacities.

Education has often been regarded as an important element in helping people develop their understanding of the world. A tacit assumption of such approaches to education has been that knowledge alone is the principal factor in determining our capacity for freedom, self-expression and responsible choice. The moral to be drawn from Damasio's work, however, is that such a goal for education is itself too narrowly focused. Since affect—emotion—is a central component in weighing options and making decisions, it may be that education aimed at developing some

---

[20] For a modern version of Kantianism with the notion of reason at its core, see C.M. Korsgaard, *Creating the Kingdom of Ends* (Cambridge: Cambridge University Press, 1996).

[21] In the case of Kant, the radical freedom of the moral agent culminates in a voluntary choice by the rational subject to place himself or herself under the constraints of the moral law. Since the moral law endorsed by Kant's rational agent is strangely similar to the Protestant ethics of his culture, sceptics may wonder whether Kant's entire theory of the rational will and the moral law is nothing but a rationalization of an existing moral tradition.

[22] One of the best introductions to this idea is Antonio Damasio's description of his patient 'Elliot' in Chapters 3, 4, and 9 of *Descartes' Error* (New York: Harper Collins, 1995). Elliot's incapacity to make sensible choices was invisible on standard tests of reasoning, moral development, and judgement. The gap between his rational, theoretical understanding of situations and his disastrous real-life incapacity to choose was evident to Elliot himself in the following incident: 'At the end of one session, after he had produced an abundant variety of options for action, all of which were valid and implementable, Elliot smiled, apparently satisfied with his rich imagination, but added: And after all this, I still wouldn't know what to do' op. cit., p.49.

kinds of emotional capacities might be effective in increasing the autonomy of some individuals. Such education would not necessarily focus on what is commonly known as 'emotional literacy', although work in that area may have a role to play in enhancing the autonomy of some people.[23]

Conclusion

We have identified two ideas of dignity. The first, classical notion of dignity is plainly meritocratic, suggesting that dignity comes in degrees, that it often attaches to offices of honour and worth, and that it can be cultivated to some extent through individual dedication and practice. The more modern egalitarian and democratized notion is itself a complex of two ingredients that are often not separated in discussions of dignity, respect, and autonomy. First, there is the notion that is found in the great monotheistic religions, and which is given voice in Renaissance thought and reaches its most elaborate philosophical expression in the work of Kant: that dignity is something that every rational being possesses to the same degree, a kind of distinctive moral worth, constituted by and founded on the fact that such beings are ends in themselves, self-choosers and self-legislators. Such worth is based in a number of capacities that are summed up by the word 'autonomy'. This worth and autonomy is supposed to call forth respect from other similar beings, a respect that takes the form of treating rational beings as never merely means to an end, but rather as ends in their own right.

A second ingredient in the complex modern notion of dignity is the idea that because they are possessors of autonomy, rational moral agents should be permitted—as far as practicable—to exercise this autonomy to an equal degree. We have argued that autonomy is not in fact a single capacity but resides in a number of capacities including the capacity for knowledge or understanding and the capacity for taking decisions. We have also argued that much of the literature on dignity, rights, and respect focuses on the equal exercise of autonomy (what we called autonomousness) while ignoring the pressing question of whether the capacities that constitute such autonomy are themselves equally present in all normal human beings. We have shown that contingent upon facts of birth, disease, and social practice, the capacities that constitute autonomy are actually unequally divided among people. Belief in an immortal soul, or in the universal love of an all-powerful creator, may enable some people to ignore the apparent inequalities among people, allowing them to insist that autonomy is indeed a capacity that is shared equally among all humans. In the absence of such supernatural justification, we propose that it is important to face up to the unequal distribution of autonomy, and to be sceptical of founding claims about human rights and respects on the free-floating

---

[23] See, for example, J.D. Mayer and C.D. Cobb, 'Educational Policy on Emotional Intelligence: Does It Make Sense?' *Educational Psychology Review*, 12 (2000), pp.163–183.

doctrine of universal and equal human dignity. In this respect, our account retains an important legacy of the older notion of dignity—its fragility.

If such universalism is given up, our commitments and practices need not be surrendered. In medicine, it is recognized that accident, disease, and aging project people onto trajectories that lead to loss of the opportunity to exercise their capacities, and—tragically and inevitably—to the degeneration and loss of the capacities themselves. Recognition of the inevitable loss of autonomy need not be associated with a reduction in care and respect for patients. Since there are two aspects involved in retaining as much dignity as possible—capacities on the one hand and their exercise on the other—then there will be two dimensions of clinical assessment and treatment. We would contend that many practising physicians and medical staff already recognize the complexities involved in such cases, even if they have not articulated their ideas in the way presented in the present paper.

While the unjust detention of people is an offence against the exercise of their autonomy, we have also suggested that practices such as torture and solitary confinement may take their toll on the capacities that constitute autonomy itself. The detention of children, and policies of mandatory sentencing of juveniles, can also be criticized on the ground that they undermine both autonomousness and autonomy itself. Detention that reduces or inhibits the development of understanding and decision-making capacities can be argued to be more objectionable than simple deprivation of liberty. Social policies and institutions, then, can take their toll both on the exercise of capacities, and also on the capacities themselves.

Language, like culture, is a repository of meaning and of memory. Old meanings seldom disappear entirely, and the modern complex notion dignity—equal capacity and equal exercise of capacities—sits alongside that older notion of *dignitas*, ready to lure us into contradiction, or surprise us with new moral possibilities. What prospects are there for reconciliation between the two? We do not know the answer to this question, and hope that the present paper draws attention to the difficulties we face at present in making sense of dignity. While the older notion underwrote a claim for moral esteem and special privilege by appeal to rank, merit, and social status, the modern notion seems to involve a divorce of the empirical from the normative. If we are right in suggesting that people are not alike in their capacities, and if they do not possess any God-given and necessary equality in this regard, we can still argue for the normative doctrine that we *should* give them all an equal chance to exercise whatever degree of autonomy they have. Once we have argued for that normative position, however, it would seem strange to rest content in the acceptance that there are massive inequalities in people's individual capacities. Some of these inequalities are beyond our control, when accident and disease strike unexpectedly and incurably. Others, however, are controllable. By noting these, by avoiding practices that damage or destroy the capacities that enable autonomy, and by looking for methods by which we are able to enhance those same capacities, we will be taking steps to reduce inequalities of autonomy, not just those of autonomousness. A commitment to equality in the latter regard, then, can be a spur to work towards the ideal of equal autonomy in full awareness that such an ideal can never be fully attained.

A problem of great moment still remains, however. The theological conception of equal autonomy was, if we are right, the spur to the modern idea of equalizing the exercise of human capacities. It was recognition of the inherent dignity of the individual—a common, and equal humanity—that drove forward the idea that all human beings had rights to exercise their freedom to the extent that this did not harm their fellows. Without the religious foundation, however, the notion of equal dignity floats free. Is it really plausible to think that by starting at what came later—the demand for free and equal exercise of our self-choosing capacities—we can work our way back, in a secular way, to the earlier ideal, thus rehabilitating the Renaissance doctrine of the dignity of man if not its Christian foundation? The trouble is that we seem to have no firm anchoring within a secular framework for the key moral ideal that respect, autonomy, and dignity should—and must—be equal across all people. What we have called the complex modern notion of dignity is not a solution to the equality problem: rather it expresses a normative ideal that has wide support in liberal democracies, but which makes good sense only against a religious and spiritual background that is no longer widely accepted by the philosophical, medical, and scientific communities in these same countries. Whether the complex modern notion of dignity and its associated moral ideals can survive within these countries, or will be robust enough to challenge alternative moral ideals prevalent in other societies, are very much open questions.

6
Human Dignity and Charity

Rosalind Hursthouse

Introduction

Most people find it difficult to believe that they do not know what they mean by some of the words and phrases they use. Even philosophers find it difficult, notwithstanding the fact that it is a phenomenon with which we are all too familiar, and one for which—at least in many cases—we have an account. It shows up in the following way. In a certain context, I may assert something confidently, convinced of its truth—for example, 'Every human being has human dignity, just *because* they are human.' But in another context I may say, or find myself agreeing with someone who says, that some human beings lack it or have forfeited it, and thinking that this is true too. Well, on the face of it, they cannot both be true, and yet, in some way, I may think they both are. So what do I mean by each of these conflicting assertions, such that they do not really conflict? It is not easy to say, even though they are my own thoughts in my own words.

Looking the words up in the dictionary is no help, because dictionaries always lag behind changes in use, and the term 'human dignity' is surprisingly modern. If you look up 'dignity' in the *Oxford English Dictionary* (OED), none of the examples illustrating its use contains the phrase 'human dignity'. Moreover, the examples make it fairly clear that if there were any, they would have to say something such as 'Human dignity is often claimed but seldom attained' or 'Human dignity is as rare as roc's eggs.' For 'dignity', the OED. says, means, 'worth, honourableness, excellence, (high) desert'—something that ranks one person (or country or estate or position) above others. In this usage 'human dignity' would have to be rather like 'human goodness' or 'human virtue'. Human goodness is not goodness that every human being has, simply because they are human. Rather, it is the sort of goodness which is *proper* to human beings—to be distinguished from the goodness proper to the gods, or to politicians or to horses; and only some, indeed alas rather few, human beings have it. So, similarly 'human dignity' would be a sort of dignity proper to humans which some had and some did not. The Queen Mother (so the newspapers always said) but not Madonna, for example, or more seriously, Nelson Mandela but not Robert Mugabe. Yet clearly, that is not how 'human dignity' is used nowadays. The Queen and Madonna, Mandela and Mugabe, and all of us and every child, have it, simply because they and we are all *human*.

J. Malpas and N. Lickiss (eds.), Perspectives on Human Dignity: A Conversation, 59–72.

Saying that 'human dignity' is simply ambiguous suggests that my problem will be easily resolved, but it is not. The phrase 'human dignity' is not like 'lead'. When I say 'His heart is lead' and someone asks me 'Towards what?' I can immediately say 'No no, I meant his heart is heavy.' But I cannot say immediately what I meant by either of my two conflicting assertions about human dignity; indeed, I learnt a great deal about what I meant—and did not mean—by both of them at the workshop and am still thinking about it.

The account one gives of a simply ambiguous term such as 'lead' is that its ambiguity is incidental. A rough test for whether we have simple ambiguity is whether we think a language which always translated our one term as two (or more) gave a good translation. If we do, our one word is simply ambiguous; if we do not, but think that, in this area, there is not a good fit between the languages, we have something rather different. The account that philosophers give of this 'rather different' sort of ambiguity is in terms of 'a complicated network of similarities overlapping and criss-crossing'.[1] Wittgenstein also speaks of our extending a concept in the way we spin a thread, twisting fibre on fibre.[2] No one fibre runs through its whole length, but we can speak of *one* concept, *one* term we would want to see preserved in a good translation of our talk about human dignity, because of the overlapping of many fibres. Although she connected a similar image to 'diverse concepts' of human dignity, Norelle Lickiss spoke felicitously of them as 'the residues of strands of thought which became apparent and gained ascendancy in differing times and places in the course of human history'.[3]

So the way to get clear about what we mean, in different contexts, by our different uses of 'human dignity' is to identify at least some of the fibres or strands that have been woven in to it over the centuries.

Some History of Ideas

Long before we had the phrase 'human dignity', there were two intertwined thoughts about human beings' special *status* vis-à-vis the other animals.

The first dates back at least to the ancient Greek philosophers Plato and Aristotle. The thought is that, because we are, uniquely amongst the animals, *rational* (and thereby, moral agents) we are superior to—of more worth, of higher status than, to be ranked above—all the other animals.

Plato and Aristotle both took it that we shared rationality with the gods, and in Christianity, this became the thought that we are superior to all the other animals because we are made in God's image—not, of course, insofar as we suppose God to have two legs and opposing thumbs, but insofar as we are rational and God is

---

[1] L. Wittgenstein, *Philosophical Investigations*, trans. G.E.M. Anscombe, 3rd edn. (Oxford: Blackwell, 2001), §66.

[2] Ibid., §67

[3] Norelle Lickiss, 'On Human Dignity: Fragments of an Exploration', Chapter 4, this volume.

supremely so. In both traditions, this rationality is of a rather special sort. It is not the capacity to do philosophy, mathematics, and science, nor even to figure out means to ends; it is the capacity to set our *own* ends, to choose good rather than evil; hence its connection with being a moral agent and the idea of free will.

What does this claim that the human being is the uniquely rational animal *do*? I mean—what argumentative or justificatory role does it play in philosophical and theological thought? In Plato and Aristotle, it certainly is not put to the purpose of supporting the idea that any and every human being has worth, honourableness, excellence, or high desert. Quite the contrary! In them it plays the role of calling us to the high and difficult road of living in a way suited to our rationality instead of living the way (they thought) most people lived—as little or no better than the other animals. A *human* life, appropriate to our rationality, is the life of virtue, the life in accordance with right reason. Plato and Aristotle both take it that although it is in our nature to be rational, we are all capable of corrupting and eventually destroying this divine element within us and, in effect, changing our nature and becoming no better than animals. Unlike all the other animals, we make our own lives, mould our own nature, for well or ill, and if we do it ill, we are worth no more than any other animal. So for them 'human dignity' would indeed be like 'human goodness'—not at all the sort of thing that anyone had merely in virtue of being human. Mandela would have it, but Mugabe would not, having lost it irrevocably, quite some time back.

Now whether or not that makes the likes of Mugabe *worthless* depends, of course, on what you think about the other animals. Aristotle, famously (and unfortunately) claimed that the other animals existed merely for the sake of human beings and were there for us to use, but some other ancient Greeks held a view more akin to Buddhism, regarding life as sacred in *all* of its manifestations. From the Buddhist perspective, humans are unique in just the same way as they are in the ancient Greek tradition, namely that we, uniquely amongst the many life forms, can choose to act for good or evil. And what follows then is that, given the huge number of life forms that fill the universe, human life is a rare *privilege* with special responsibilities to these other life forms. They, knowing no better, kill and harm each other; we can, and should, choose not to. So in both these ancient traditions, the point of claiming that the human being is the uniquely rational animal, and thereby has a special sort of status, is to call us to moral duties or responsibilities that we have *because* we are human. That is the role that it plays. It plays that role in Christianity too, calling us to the life of virtue. But, in Christianity, it also plays a second role; it grounds the virtue of charity or love.

At least one big difference from Western thought that the development of Christianity made was that however wicked and debased you might have made yourself, you still had not lost irrevocably, the thing that made you, as a human, different from the other animals. *Every* human being is to be loved, is worthy of love, simply because they *are* human, made in God's image—and of course possessed of an immortal soul. Where the ancient Greeks thought that you could, through your own ill-doing, destroy your humanity and become a mere brute, in Christianity you cannot. And so charity requires, as a duty, a concern for the well-being of *all* our fellow humans regardless of their nationality or social status or, indeed of their goodness or wickedness—simply *because* they are human—something that the ancient Greeks would have regarded as quite insane.

So, after Christianity, but long before 'dignity' (or words we translate that way) came to be used in relation to human beings or 'man', the idea that human beings had a special status vis-à-vis the other animals, in virtue of their rationality, could play two quite different roles, thereby creating two strands. The first (which I will call the 'Greek', even though Christianity, as I just noted, shares it) concerns what we human beings owe to ourselves; each of us, because we are human, ought to be living the life of virtue, the life that befits us, as rational creatures. The second, which I will call the 'Christian', concerns what we human beings owe to other human beings; other human beings, because they are human, made in God's image, ought to be treated with Christian love.

It seems to me that the differing 'Greek' and 'Christian' roles for the idea of the special status of human beings are still influencing our modern use of 'human dignity', and well explain some of our conflicting intuitions about it. I will return to these points below, but we need a bit more history of ideas to get to the modern use.

Before my involvement in the Colloquium, I had not known of the existence of Giovanni Pico della Mirandola, and his 1,486 *Oration on the Dignity of Man*,[4] though note that Steve Farmer claims that this was not his original title but the invention of an editor in 1504.[5] This is the earliest use of the phrase 'the dignity of man' I have been able to track down, and it is interesting to note that Pico's *Oration* contains not a hint of the Christian idea that this dignity is something that no man can lose. Man, he says, is unique, with the unique power to make and mould himself—and thereby, not only the power to make himself 'to be reborn into the higher forms [of life], the divine', but also to degenerate 'into the lower forms of life, the beasts'.[6] It might be Plato or Aristotle speaking.

The earliest example of the use that expresses the Christian idea in philosophy that I know of occurs famously, indeed infamously, in the work of Kant in 1785. (He introduces it as a technical expression, 'everything has either a price or a dignity.')[7] If something is exalted above all price and so admits of no equivalent, then it has a dignity, or intrinsic value. Rational beings (humans and God) have dignity; other things do not. Humans are *persons* and must be treated as ends in themselves; everything else (notably, all the other animals) are called *things*, have only relative not intrinsic value, and may be treated merely as a means to our ends.

In Kant, the idea serves the two roles I noted above. Firstly, that I have human dignity is what lands me with the responsibility of living and acting in a certain

[4] Giovanni Pico della Mirandola, *Oration on the Dignity of Man,* http://www.wsu.edu:8080/~dee/REN/ORATION.HTM.

[5] Steve Farmer, *Syncretism in the West*, http://www.safarmer.com/pico/oration.html.

[6] Pico, *Oration,* http://www.wsu.edu:8080/~dee/REN/ORATION.HTM paragraph 3.

[7] Immanuel Kant, *Groundwork of the Metaphysics of Morals 1785*, trans. H.J. Paton (New York: Harper, 1964), pp.102–103.

way, befitting my rationality—in Kant, as one who can will that her maxims should become universal laws. Secondly, that all of you—and Mugabe and Hitler and so on—have human dignity is what lands me with various duties regarding you all.

The earliest example of the use of the term 'human dignity' in official Christian rather than explicitly philosophical writings that I have been able to track down is only in relation to the first role—reminding us of the responsibility we have, *because* we are human, to live in a certain way. It is from a papal encyclical of 1888 on liberty and begins:

> Liberty, the highest of natural endowments, being the portion only of intellectual or rational natures, confers on man this dignity—that he is 'in the hand of his counsel' [1][8] and has power over his actions. But the manner in which such dignity is exercised is of the greatest moment, inasmuch as on the use that is made of liberty the highest good and the greatest evil alike depend.[9]

And then it goes on to speak of 'true liberty', which watches over the dignity of the human person and is *quite* different from the liberty or licence to do what you want without interference. It is *not* that, but the liberty or freedom of Man 'to obey his reason, to seek moral good, and to strive unswervingly after his last end.'[10]

The second one I was able to find is in relation to the second role—reminding us of the duties we have towards certain other people simply because *they* are human. It is from another papal encyclical of 1891,[11] largely about the conditions of the working classes in the industrialised nations. It argues that socialism is a very bad thing but is right in its attack on the way the rich are exploiting the poor. It says that rich employers have a duty 'to respect in *every* man his dignity as a person ennobled by Christian character.'[12]

Later it says that the law should intervene if 'employers laid burdens upon their workmen which were unjust, or degraded them with conditions repugnant to their dignity as human beings'[13] and later again that 'No man may with impunity outrage that human dignity which God Himself treats with great reverence.'[14]

You might notice that the word 'rights' has not yet occurred. Duties yes, rights not yet. Modern writers, reflecting back on this second encyclical say, 'The encyclical calls for a revolution that offers the hope of a new, alternative world in which God's gifts are shared in a just way and where all human rights are respected'[15] but

---

[8] 1. Ecclus., 15:14.

[9] Pope Leo XIII, *Libertas: On the Nature of Human Liberty*, Encyclical (20 June 1888), paragraph 1, http://www.papalencyclicals.net/Leo13/l13liber.htm.

[10] Ibid.

[11] Pope Leo XIII, *Rerum Novarum: On Capital and Labor*, Encyclical (15 May 1891), http://www.papalencyclicals.net/Leo13/l13rerum.htm.

[12] Emphasis added.

[13] Ibid., paragraph 37.

[14] Ibid., paragraph 40.

[15] St. Paul and Minneapolis, Office for Social Justice John Paul II, Papal Encyclical 1991, *Centesimus Annus* in everyday language. http://www.osjspm.org/majordoc_centesimus_annus_everyday_language.aspx

the phrase 'human rights' does not occur anywhere within it; this is a contemporary, interpretive, gloss. The introduction of human rights, as a further strand, is, I think, the move that brings us to the predominant modern usage and before I consider it, I think it is worth reflecting on what else has been woven in so far.

Some Further Strands

Given the 'Greek' strand as I have sketched it, it may seem that Plato and Aristotle would not have been able to make sense of our saying—as in some contexts we do—that human dignity is indestructible. Did I not insist on the point that they thought it was all too easy for human beings to destroy their own humanity and become mere brutes? Yes, I did. But I did not mention their views on the indestructibility of human virtue, which introduces another strand. Neither would have had any difficulty in understanding the point that Mandela's human dignity was indestructible, for Plato claimed, and Aristotle in many contexts echoes him, that the virtuous man *cannot* be harmed. Do to him what you will, his virtue remains intact, and it is in this, his developed, rational soul that his worth, his excellence, his honourableness, his special status, resides, even if his society scorns him and condemns him to death as they did Socrates. So when Christianity, with its rather different idea of the rational human soul, introduced the thought that it could not be destroyed, the strand wove in very easily, overlapping with what had gone before. Although, as I noted, the sort of rationality that is assumed to make human beings unique is not the capacity to do philosophy, neither Plato nor Aristotle was able to resist the temptation to make the study of philosophy the finest end to which human beings could aspire. Thereby, they wove an exaltation of the reflective intellect into the concept of the special status of human beings which, I think, has bedevilled moral philosophy ever since. It is noticeable in Pico, and very apparent in Kant, who, referring to his astonishingly abstract categorical imperative claims:

> Everyone does, in fact, decide by this rule [the categorical imperative] whether actions are morally good or bad. Thus people ask: If one belonged to such an order of things that anyone would allow himself to deceive when he thought it to his advantage ...would he assent of his own will to being a member of such an order of things?[16]

The strand that Kant introduces, overlapping with Plato and Aristotle's intellectualist elitism, was the one that emphasises humans' rational capacity for *autonomy*. This became extremely influential in moral, legal, and political philosophy, but it should be noted that, as this strand has been spun on, although it has retained a fair amount of the intellectualism, it has lost much of Kant's original meaning. Autonomy, in Kant, is very remote from self-rule or self-determination or indeed 'autonomy' as we now understand them, for in Kant, if you act in pursuit of the ends you want you are *not* acting autonomously. (This is because you are not acting

[16] Immanuel Kant, *Critique of Practical Reason* (1788), Chapter 2, 5: 69

free from external constraints. Your own desires, even though they are your own, count as 'external' constraints because they are external to your rational will.)

Another strand dating back to Plato and Aristotle involves ideas about what the state can, and thereby should, do to enable human beings to realise their unique capacity to live the life of virtue. Since this entails not only possessing virtue but also exercising it, they both advocated the state's organising moral education from the earliest age (to enable people to possess it) and also considered how the ideal state might be constructed in such a way that, once the education has laid the foundation, virtue might be best developed and exercised. It seems that their picture of laws against crimes has more to do with the threat of punishment helping to keep people on the straight and narrow, for their own sake (so they do not fall into habits which will lead to them destroying their humanity) than with protecting the innocent from being wronged.

So, bearing these further strands in mind, let us look at what happens when the connection with rights gets woven in. As far as I can determine, the first occurrence of 'human dignity' in connection with human rights is in the preamble to the UN *Declaration of Human Rights* in 1948: 'Whereas recognition of the inherent dignity and of the equal and inalienable rights of all members of the human family is the foundation of freedom, justice, and peace in the world.' Now that *is*, it seems our predominant contemporary usage of 'human dignity'—one that explicitly connects human dignity with human rights. Surfing the web, that is certainly what I found—talk about human dignity nowadays is, mostly, talk about what are, or what ought to be recognised as—human rights—rights that humans have simply *because* they are human. But it is important, I think, to notice several rather disquieting things about this connecting up of the idea of human dignity with that of rights:

1. It has introduced real obscurity which, in my view, can only be clarified by shifting to talk about duties instead. The most well-known human right is the right to life. But what do any of us mean by that? The way to answer that question is to consider, explicitly, what duty or duties we think correspond to the right. One of us may think it is the duty each of us has not to kill another human being, another that it is the duty not to kill another human being *except* in self-defence, and obviously those two people mean significantly different things when they say that we all have a right to life. One of us may think the further duty to save or preserve life is, in some way, entailed by the right to life; another not, and so they mean significantly different things too.
2. Talk about rights—just over the last 30 years or so I think—has become increasingly vague. One can no longer be sure that a right generates any duties at all, since 'I, we, all human beings, have a right to so and so' often amounts to no more than 'It would be an awfully good thing if I, we, all human beings had so and so.' Speakers slide from 'I have a right to do so and so' to 'It is (morally) all right for me to do so and so' and have lost all grasp of what used to be an obvious truth, namely that it can be wrong to exercise a right which I undoubtedly have.
3. The modern concept of a right, the concept that motivated the French and American Revolutions, has, as a paradigm, the human being's right to liberty.

But, far from this being the liberty appropriate to human dignity mentioned in the 1888 encyclical above, *that is* 'to obey his reason, to seek moral good, and to strive unswervingly after his last end', it is the right to do what you want without interference as long as (in some rather vague way) you do not harm other people. So the predominant contemporary usage of 'human dignity' has not only lost its connection with the idea that we owe it to ourselves to live as well as we can, to strive to perfect our rational natures, but also has handed us (from the Greek perspective at least) *carte blanche* to debase ourselves (as long as it does not harm anyone else). Or, one might say, the paradigm is the right to autonomy—and this, as noted above, has undergone the same slippage. The autonomy appropriate to human dignity, extolled by Kant, is now acting as you *want*, not acting in accordance with your rational will, i.e. as you ought to.

4. So in its connection with rights, the idea of human dignity can play only the 'Christian' role identified above. It has lost all connection with the thought that, as human beings endowed with rationality, we ought to live in a way appropriate to that rationality, i.e. to live morally. It is concerned with our rights, not with what we owe to ourselves.
5. Finally—and perhaps this is the most sinister—it plays only a limited version of the 'Christian' role. True, insofar as rights generate duties (though, as noted in (2) they may not), it concerns what we human beings owe to other human beings. We owe it to them to respect their rights. But important as justice is, charity, or love, is equally if not more important, and it is only justice, not charity, that is concerned with rights. It is charity, not justice, that requires that we stop to help the wounded stranger by the roadside and do for him all that the good Samaritan did; we would be 'quite within our rights', if not, perhaps, to pass by on the other side, at least to do a great deal less; and the predominant contemporary usage has lost its connection with Christian charity. So the strand that introduces human rights is in danger of failing to meld with the others and of pulling the concept of human dignity asunder; and I believe that that has started to happen—a point I shall return to below. But good old ideas die hard, and, as I said above, I think the 'Greek' and 'Christian' roles for the idea of the special status of human beings are still influencing our modern usage. As promised, I will now consider how these may explain some of our conflicting intuitions about human dignity.

Conflicting Intuitions

Consider first the case of the French dwarf, Wackenheim (mentioned below in the essays by Don Chalmers and Ryuichi Ida,[17] and by Julia Davis[18]) who wanted to continue to earn his living being tossed, one intuition is that allowing this is somehow

[17] Don Chalmers and Ryuichi Ida, 'On the International Legal Aspects of Human Dignity', Chapter 15, this volume.

[18] Julia Davis, 'Doing Justice to Dignity in the Criminal Law', Chapter 16, this volume.

an affront to human dignity; the other is that it would be an affront to his human dignity to forbid it. Insofar as we incline to the latter, we are most obviously thinking in terms of his right to liberty or autonomy in the modern sense. He is a human being, so he has this human right; it ought to be respected, so he ought to be allowed to pursue his chosen profession, since it harms no one else. If we incline to the former, we are thinking in terms of human dignity as expressed in living a life that befits our rationality—the 'Greek' strand—and as something that we lose if we debase ourselves. It remains unclear, it seems to me, to what extent that second thought is particularly about Wackenheim himself—that *he* is debasing himself—and to what extent it is about those who do the tossing and those who watch and are entertained—that *they* are debasing themselves.

This seems clearer in the case of consensual sadomasochism. Here, again, the modern idea that human dignity involves the right to liberty or autonomy which inclines us to say that human dignity must be respected by not interfering, conflicts with the older intuition that sadomasochistic actions are themselves an affront to human dignity. To my ears, at least, the thought that such activity was an affront to, or inconsistent with human dignity, is precisely the old Greek thought that sexual activity unconstrained by right reason is the paradigm of the 'brutish' and that hence the participants were debasing themselves. Note here too, the influence of the Greek idea that the business of law is not so much to prevent citizens from harming each other but to try to prevent them from debasing themselves and destroying their human dignity.

Don Chalmers' and Ryuichi Ida's discussion of human dignity in terms of empowerment and human dignity as constraint is more difficult. As Chalmers and Ida note, on the one hand we have appeals to human dignity which ground rights, particularly the rights of liberty and autonomy, on the other hand we have appeals to human dignity which ground *constraints* on liberty and autonomy in relation to human cloning—an outright conflict. It is easy here to identify the human-dignity-rights-to-liberty-and-autonomy strand, but which strand is (or strands are) in play with respect to the constraints is not so clear. One aspect of the discussion certainly seems to be the Greek strand again—that we would be debasing ourselves by going in for human cloning, that to think of ourselves or humanity at large, as possibly *benefiting* from human cloning is a corruption. To be tempted by the thought of a 'designer baby' is to stray from the path of virtue that our human dignity calls us to; that is just not the right—the morally right—way to think about one's prospective children. However, there are obviously other factors at work—it is surely no accident how often the phrase 'playing God' occurs, and it looks to me as though the idea that we have human dignity because we are made in God's image, whereas a cloned baby would be an image of ourselves is having an influence, even amongst the secular.

I want to conclude by returning to the conflict between two very general intuitions about human dignity with which I started—that every human being has it, and that some human beings lack it or have forfeited it. The area where the different 'Greek' and 'Christian' strands conflict most strongly—and where, I believe, the recognition of them is most clarifying—is over the issue of whether human beings can lose or forfeit their human dignity through evildoing. There is a strong inclination to say ‘Yes’, which comes from the Greek strand, and a strong inclination to say ‘No’ which comes from the Christian. The case of Martin Bryant (the man who murdered 35 people at Port Arthur in Tasmania in 1996) is well known to Tasmanians and the case also gained notoriety worldwide. But what of Bryant? Had he lost or forfeited his human dignity or is it indestructible?

I came to this conversation in favour of the Greek strand but, for a number of reasons I shall try to make clear in these concluding remarks, came away from it in favour of the Christian one. What was I thinking of when I thought that a human being could lose human dignity? Well, I was indeed thinking of people like Bryant, and some of the notorious concentration camp commanders—of people I was willing to call wicked. And this was in part because I think of such people that they have, through their evil deeds, forfeited a fair number of their rights, that I see no reason to respect rather than to despise them, that I think their autonomy, given the way they exercised it, is a thoroughly bad thing not something of intrinsic value. In certain contexts I would not flinch from saying that I thought such people were worthless. But, I hasten to add, I was not thinking of them as people that it was all right to treat in any old way at all, and there are no contexts in which I would have said that they were. However, looking back, I don’t think I had *noticed* this. It was the enlightening and heartening prevalence of the ‘Christian’ strand in the conversation, insisting on the indestructibility of human dignity, that made me realise it.

What are we thinking of when we say ‘Human dignity is indestructible’? Well, at the irreducible minimum, we are insisting that, no matter what evil someone such as Bryant has done, and no matter how evil, perhaps, he is, this does not license our doing *anything* to him. We might express that by saying that he still has some rights—equal treatment in accordance with the law, for example,—which we must respect, or, without mentioning rights, by saying simply that we still must not treat him in certain ways.

This is something it is important to stress, given the extremes that hatred and righteous rage prompt people to and something that devotees of the Greek strand, such as me, need to be reminded of. It is really no more than the old truism that two wrongs do not make a right, but it is startling and frightening to realise how readily one can lapse into willing wrongdoing with the thought that the recipient—having forfeited his human dignity—cannot be wronged. And the obvious corrective to that is the thought that he has not, and cannot, forfeit his human dignity.

It is also the obvious corrective to the Greek thought that human beings lack human dignity when they are children or childlike, lacking adult rationality. Although the ancient Greeks did not, of course, think that children could be treated any old way, and had ideas of filial piety that required care for one’s parents, no matter how demented, it does seem that you were not expected to do anything for the mentally incapacitated if they were not your parents—you could treat them any old way.

But of course the Christian strand brings in more than an insistence of an irreducible minimum of decent treatment. At the maximum when we say human dignity is indestructible, we are saying that no human being is irredeemably evil, or lacking, and that *any* human being is, as such, a proper object of love, the ideal of charity expressed, for instance, in *Dead Man Walking* and in the account John Tooth gave us of the work at the Adards Nursing Home in which staff strive to provide for patients suffering from Alzheimer's and related disorders something that resembles a 'normal' home so that behavioural disturbance is decreased and dignity retained.[19]

---

[19] As Dr. Tooth explains in his written comments at the Colloquium on Human Dignity, Hobart, 2004:

> The Adards Nursing Home (ADARDS is the acronym for Alzheimer's Disease and Related Disorders Society which initially administered the facility). This Special Care Unit in Hobart, Tasmania was designed to replace the dementia ward of the State Psychiatric Hospital to which ambulant people with dementia were consigned when behavioural difficulties precluded their remaining at home. At that institution the stark surroundings and loss of dignity of patients appeared to engender considerably more behavioural disturbance. Terror appeared to be the most common emotion and this resulted in aggression and consequent further loss of dignity when inappropriately managed. It was postulated that if a building could be designed to resemble a 'normal' home, with homelike furnishings, single bedroom privacy, home cooked food and gardens of beauty, together with dogs, cats, chickens and birds, and with appropriately selected and well-trained staff, behavioural disturbance would significantly decrease and dignity would be retained. The result was the Adards Nursing Home which opened in 1991 and now contains 36 ambulant residents with dementia and behaviour so difficult that no other facility could manage them. Adards is owned and administered by a charitable not-for-profit organization and it is probably unique in this as normally those with the most difficult behaviour are accommodated in Government facilities (in Australia, the State Governments). These have the significant advantage over Adards in that the resources of government stand behind them. For instance should a resident with extremely disruptive and aggressive behaviour be admitted it may be desirable for extra staff to be 'called in' for some days or even weeks and this can be done without calling into question the financial viability of the facility. Not so with Adards; on a few occasions in the 14 years since opening extra staff have been called in for a few days but budgetary constraints have precluded this happening often. On the other hand Adards has other advantages over Government facilities, especially in the flexibility of its administration. This flexibility is particularly noteworthy when it comes to the selection of new staff. The Director of Nursing can choose staff according to their personality characteristics and his decision cannot be challenged by somebody with better 'book' qualifications. New care staff at Adards may often have had no training at all but provided they have the necessary personality attributes we have found that it is relatively easy and quick to train them. The result has been an amazingly happy and competent care staff amongst whom there has not been one case of 'burn out' in the 14 years. The DON can also do away with unnecessary rules—such as the requirement for residents to get up or go to bed at a stated hour. Adards certainly has not solved all the difficulties that can occur amongst bewildered, potentially anxious and incontinent people with dementia but the care staff always respond to these challenges with good humour, compassion and a friendly smile on their faces. They also constantly strive to maintain the dignity of the resident no matter how difficult the behaviour.

– Taken from the written version of Dr. Tooth's comments at the Colloquium on Human Dignity, Hobart, 2004.

Concluding Remarks

The expression of this ideal that emerged in so many of the papers at the workshop, not only forced me to abandon the 'Greek' strand, but also reinforced my implacable hostility to the modern rights one. As noted above, I had realised before that connecting human dignity to rights was in danger of pulling the concept asunder; indeed, part of my reason for favouring the 'Greek' strand was that the prevailing rights-connected usage—with its unmoralised conception of 'rationality', and its vaunting of liberty and autonomy as licence—was becoming something morally rather lightweight. But the papers that expressed the ideal of charity have led me to believe that by far the most dangerous thing about it is (point 5 earlier) that it has lost the connection with the ideal of Christian love or charity.

There are some philosophers who argue to a greater or lesser degree that foetuses and infants do not have the right to life (basically, since they lack rationality and autonomy).[20] In common with a frighteningly large number of other people, such philosophers have forgotten about charity. Charity, as Philippa Foot reminded philosophers in her paper on euthanasia almost thirty years ago, is 'the virtue which attaches us to the good of others' and, where life is a good to its possessor, 'an unjustified act of killing' (except in cases where life is no longer a good to its possessor) is contrary to charity.[21] If the one killed has the right to life, it is contrary to justice too, but the prohibition from charity is as strong and as absolute as the prohibition from justice.

The danger I see in the modern usage, is that it is all too easy to argue in the way this unnamed author does and to maintain that certain sorts of human beings—the very young, the very old, the mentally deranged, the unconscious—cannot be the bearers of rights, be they legal, moral or human. Political philosophy, for centuries, not only ignored the existence of women, but also all those other human beings who, because of their lack of rationality, were not engaged in the political process. Thereby, it developed a whole host of rights for the actively, actually, *rational*, that is, a whole host of things the state (or the ideal state) is required to allow or prohibit or enforce or provide regarding *them*, many of which are quite inappropriate if applied to babies, children, the unconscious, and the deranged. Of course the writers did not say explicitly that this was what they were doing, because they did not *notice*; they said they were talking about natural rights or the rights of man. Many of their ideas have passed into moral and legal philosophy and into common currency. The upshot is that, ironically, the modern

---

[20] Michael Tooley, *Abortion and Infanticide* (Oxford: Clarendon Press, 1983); Mary Anne Warren, 'On the Moral and Legal Status of Abortion', in *Biomedical Ethics*, pp.417–423; James Rachels, *The End of Life* (Oxford: Oxford University Press, 1986); Virginia Ramey Mollenkott, 'Reproductive Choice: Basic to Justice for Women', *Christian Scholar's Review*, 17 (March 1988), pp.286–293.

[21] Philippa Foot, 'Euthanasia', *Philosophy and Public Affairs*, 6 (Winter 1977), pp.85–112.

usage of 'human dignity', connected to 'human rights', far from upholding the view to which I ascribed it at the outset, namely that everyone has it simply because they are human, is moving dangerously towards the view that only some human beings have it—the rational, autonomous ones, the only ones that can be said to have rights.

Several contributors to the conference noted the dangers of concentrating on autonomy. Autonomy is supposedly a human right, something everyone has a right to *because* they are human and have human dignity. But how do we set about respecting the autonomy of a baby or a toddler, a schizophrenic, someone in delirium or with dementia? Not in the way we respect the autonomy of an ordinary adult human being that is for sure. It seemed to me that some people at the workshop were inclined to describe their admirable treatment of those in their care in terms of respect for autonomy, but I believe myself that this is showing too much deference to the modern usage of 'human dignity'. Rather than accepting the prevailing connection with rights, and thereby justice, we should insist on the importance of charity, the original 'Christian' contribution to the concept of human dignity.

Charity, I am inclined to say, is greater than justice. It is possible to treat some human beings vilely in the name of justice, much harder to do it in the name of charity or love, and charity, unlike justice, 'thinketh no evil and hopeth all things'.[22] It is not, first and foremost about their rights that we should think when considering what we should—and should not do—regarding our fellow humans, but, directing the required loving gaze upon them, about what they need and what they might achieve and about how we could help them. And, if we do so, we find that charity not only forbids all the serious things that justice forbids, but suggests a great deal more that can be done. Killing one's fellow human beings, torturing them, mutilating them, treating them they way they were, and are, treated in concentration and refugee camps, are forbidden by charity every bit as strongly as they are forbidden by justice. But it is charity, not justice that directs one's attention to the particularities of the individual before one, to find the perhaps unique thing you can do, just for them, here and now. I see this loving concentration on the particular in all the accounts of the hospice workers, in Greg Dening's[23] approach to history, in much of the discussion, and for me, most memorably, in Tooth's provision of a municipal bus shelter in the grounds of his nursing home.[24] (It would be absurd to speak of one human being's 'human right' to an old bus shelter. But it was exactly what she needed).

---

[22] 1 Corinthians, 13:4.

[23] Greg Dening, 'Giving the Past its Dignity', Chapter 12, this volume.

[24] One of his patients continually worked herself into a state of miserable panic because she feared to 'miss the bus'. So he persuaded the council to give him an abandoned bus shelter, and when she started to fret, she was taken to it, and would sit there happily for hours, until someone came to tell her that the bus was not coming today after all, but she would be able to catch it tomorrow, which she accepted without question.

Postscript

In my original contribution to the workshop, I laid some stress on the important difference between the Western and Eastern traditions concerning the idea that human beings are unique in virtue of their rationality. I wanted to emphasise an unfortunate aspect of the ancient Greek, Christian tradition, as contrasted with, for example, the Buddhist, namely the idea that we have duties not to behave in certain ways to other humans *because* they are human—rather than *because* it is cruel, or a failure of charity or compassion or irresponsible or self-indulgent or arrogant or....

For look at the difference between 'You shouldn't do such and such to this being *because* it would be cruel' and 'You shouldn't do such and such to this being *because* it is a human being.' The latter suggests, as the former does not, that it would be OK to do whatever it is to something that was not human, such as another sort of animal. 'You shouldn't kill or torture or exploit this because it's a human being'—'that? Oh that's just an animal'—'go ahead'. Or, if there is a reason why you should not just go ahead, it will not be because the animal has worth or dignity of some sort, but for some other reason. (Kant, infamously, claims that the only reason it is wrong to be cruel to animals is that it makes you more likely to be cruel to humans, which is not only false but quite beside the point.)

After the Colloquium, I wanted to write much more about charity, and so the above point about our tendency to ignore the other animals when talking about human dignity no longer fitted in neatly. But we should not, I think, forget it, for charity is (once again unlike justice), kind and not necessarily limited to human beings.

Boundless compassion for all living things is the firmest and surest guarantee of our moral conduct.... Tastes differ, but I know of no finer prayer than the one that ends old Indian dramas.... It runs 'May all living things remain free from pain'.

7
Human Dignity: Functions and Meanings[1]

Doron Shultziner

What is Human Dignity?

The concept of human dignity has several possible linguistic functions, which imply different and quite distinct meanings in various contexts. As Wittgenstein notes in his *Philosophical Investigations*, in order to understand the meaning of a word or a concept 'one cannot guess how a word functions. One has to *look at* its use and learn from that.'[2] By applying a Wittgensteinian methodology in this paper, I seek to identify and depict different language spheres in which the concept of human dignity has different meanings, which may, at times, be contradictory. The main reason for conflicts regarding the essence of human dignity derives from the fact that changing the context of a word may generate a misunderstanding of its meaning: 'Of course, what confuses us is the uniform appearance of words when we hear them spoken or meet them in script and print. For their *application* is not presented to us so clearly. Especially when we are doing philosophy!'[3] Furthermore, following Nathan Rotenstreich,[4] I contend that human dignity is a rather eclectic and ambiguous notion that cannot be precisely defined. However, I do believe that a better understanding of the meanings of this term is possible by outlining and mapping the main linguistic functions of human dignity, an undertaking that will help clarify both the ambiguity concerning human dignity and the recurrent political use of this term.

Hence, this paper aims at outlining a model for the concept of human dignity in a philosophical–linguistic analysis. I intend to specify the main functions and normative meanings ascribed to the concept of human dignity (a) as a justification for various rights and duties in legal instruments, (b) as containing a *thick* meaning

---

[1] This chapter is reprinted with permission from the Berkeley Electronic Press. The original paper can be found online in the journal *Global Jurist Topics* at http://www.bepress.com/gj/topics/vol3/iss3/art3/.

[2] L. Wittgenstein, *Philosophical Investigations*, trans. G.E.M. Anscombe, 3rd edn. (Oxford: Blackwell, 2001), §340 (original emphasis).

[3] Ibid., §11.

[4] N. Rotenstreich, *Man and His Dignity* Jerusalem: Magnes Press, 1983.

J. Malpas and N. Lickiss (eds.), Perspectives on Human Dignity: A Conversation, 73–92.

which can be compared to a world view that encapsulates the following, (c) rights and duties, (d) honour, and (e) a *thin* meaning defined by a degrading attitude or humiliation of human worth.[5] These functions will be analysed below.

Human Dignity as a Justification for Rights and Duties

The first main function of human dignity is primarily prevalent in legal instruments, both national and international. Put simply, this function is assigned to serve as a justification for the specific contents detailed in the legal document. The contents obviously vary between legal documents, but the *cause* for their enactment is attributed to human dignity. Let us look at some examples for this prevalent linguistic use in international and national legal instruments.

One of the first applications of human dignity in international documents is found in the preamble of the *Charter of the United Nations* (1945), where it is stated that:

> We the people of the United Nations determined to save succeeding generations from the scourge of war, which twice in our lifetime has brought untold sorrow to mankind, and to reaffirm faith in fundamental human rights, in the dignity and worth of the human person, in the equal rights of men and women and of nations large and small.

A similar reference is mentioned in the preamble of the *Universal Declaration of Human Rights* (1948):

> Whereas recognition of the inherent dignity and of the equal and inalienable rights of all members of the human family is the foundation of freedom, justice and peace in the world, Whereas disregard and contempt for human rights have resulted in barbarous acts which have outraged the conscience of mankind, and the advent of a world in which human beings shall enjoy freedom of speech and belief and freedom from fear and want has been proclaimed as the highest aspiration of the common people.

One can discern that *human dignity* and *human rights* are two separate and interdependent concepts, although this interdependence is not yet explained in its hierarchical and explicit formulation. Two further conventions of the UN clarify the affinity between these concepts in the following wording:

> Considering that, in accordance with the principles proclaimed in the Charter of the United Nations, recognition of the inherent dignity and of the equal and inalienable rights of all members of the human family is the foundation of freedom, justice and peace in the world, *Recognizing that these rights derive from the inherent dignity of the human person.*[6]

[5] In using the Thick and Thin concepts in this paper I have relied on Michael Walzer's useful distinction in his *Thick and Thin: Moral Argument at Home and Abroad* (Notre Dame: University of Notre Dame Press, 1994). The strong linguistic and conceptual relations between human dignity and humiliation are found in Daniel Statman, 'Two Concepts of Dignity', *Iyyuney Mishpat* 24 (2001), pp.541–603 [in Hebrew] and 'Humiliation, Dignity and Self-Respect', in: D. Kretzmer and E. Klein (eds.), *The Concept of Human Dignity in Human Rights Discourse* (The Hague: Kluwer Law International, 2002).

[6] United Nations Covenant on Economic, Social and Cultural Rights, adopted by GA Res. 2200A (XXI) of 16 December 1966; United Nations Covenant on Civil and Political Rights, adopted by

That is to say, in these UN documents, human dignity is regarded as a supreme value that not only stands separated from human rights but also supersedes them. Human rights are derived from human dignity while the later encompasses the essential characteristics of human beings. Legal instruments do not specify what these traits are or what exactly human dignity consists of: these are taken to be, as Teresa Iglesias puts it, 'bedrock truths'.[7]

The linguistic function of human dignity as a justification for rights and duties is found in other international documents. For instance, the *American Declaration of the Rights and Duties of Man* (1948) declares that 'the American peoples have acknowledged the dignity of the individual' and from this follows their recognition that 'the essential rights of man are not derived from the fact he is a national of a certain state, but are based upon attributes of his human personality.'[8] Similarly, the *Final Act of the Helsinki Conference* acknowledges that 'they [the states] will promote and encourage the effective exercise of civil, political, economic, social, cultural, and other rights and freedoms all of which derive from the inherent dignity of the human person.'[9] To conclude this point, it is apparent that human dignity in international instruments is the foundation and justification for rights and duties legislation: because of human dignity, human beings have rights and duties.[10]

After the examination of some international legal documents, we shall now examine some national constitutions. Actually, since the end of World War II and the inception of the *Universal Declaration of Human Rights*, the linguistic application of human dignity in national constitutions has become very prevalent in comparison to the period before that war.[11] It was the scourges of the war that yielded the increase of the linguistic application of human dignity.[12] For instance, in the *Basic Law of*

GA Res. 2200A of 16 December 1966, Preamble (emphasis added). All the covenants mentioned in this paper are conveniently collected in: Ian Brownlie (ed.), *Basic Documents on Human Rights* (Oxford: Clarendon Press, 1994).

[7] 'To be a human being is not a status conferred upon me by anyone. Nor is this a status that I, nor anybody else, can confer upon others. ... These are facts of recognition, of acknowledgment, constituting the very beings we are, and that we take for granted in what we do. We are not 'instructed' in these truths, they become part of us in the process of being alive and aware as human beings. Let me acknowledge these facts as bedrock truths.' Teresa Iglesias, 'Bedrock Truths and the Dignity of the Individual', *Logos* 4 (2001), p.114.

[8] *American Declaration of the Rights and Duties of Man*, Final Act of the Ninth International Conference of American States, 1948.

[9] Final Act of the Helsinki Conference, adopted on August 1975, article VII.

[10] Cf.: 'human dignity is the source from which human rights and liberties are derived. ... It is human dignity that provides the causa, as well as the ratio, for all human rights legislation.' H. Cohn, 'On the Meaning of Human Dignity' (original emphasis), *Israel Yearbook on Human Rights*, 13 (1981), pp.231–232.

[11] There are about four constitutions (Mexico, Finland, Ireland, and Cuba) that refer to Human Dignity in the period of 1900–1945 (before the end of the war); and more than 37 from 1945–1997, see Iglesias, 'Bedrock Truths and the Dignity of the Individual'.

[12] Y. Arieli, 'On the Necessary and Sufficient Conditions for the Emergence of the Doctrine of the Dignity of Man and His Rights', in: D. Kretzmer and E. Klein (eds.), *The Concept of Human Dignity in Human Rights Discourse*, pp.11–17.

Spain it is said: 'The Spanish State proclaims as a guiding principle of its acts, respect for the dignity, integrity and freedom of the human person'[13]; The *Constitution of India* seeks 'to promote among them all [India's citizens]; Fraternity assuring the dignity of the individual and the unity and integrity of the nation'[14]; the *Constitution of Portugal* establishes that 'Portugal is a sovereign Republic, based on the dignity of the human person and the will of the people'.[15] In these examples and many more, human dignity is mentioned alongside other supreme values such as 'freedom', 'integrity of the nation', 'just society', 'solidarity', 'God'.[16] Human dignity is taken, then, as a supreme value that bestows moral justification upon the concrete instructions specified in the document. In other words, the articles in a constitution are meant to articulate and specify the belief in human dignity and what it requires.

I know of only three unusual linguistic functions in national constitutions regarding the concept of human dignity. Their distinction lies in determining human dignity as a discrete *human right*. The first, in chronological order, is to be found in the *Constitution of Hungary*, where it is stated that 'In the Republic of Hungary everyone has the inherent right to life and to human dignity. No one shall be arbitrarily denied of these rights.'[17] Second is the Israeli *Basic Law: Human Dignity and Liberty,* where the right to human dignity is implied in article 4: 'Everyone is entitled to protection of his life, body and dignity.'[18] The third unusual function is to be found in the new *Constitution of South Africa,* where human dignity is mentioned as the first supreme value upon which South Africa is founded.[19] Moreover, article 7(1) establishes a similar relation between human dignity and human rights to the one we have observed in the international instruments, i.e. where human rights are derived from human dignity and affirmed by it: 'This Bill of Rights is a cornerstone of democracy in South Africa. It enshrines the rights of all people in our country and affirms the democratic values of human dignity, equality and freedom.' Nevertheless, article 10 declares that, 'everyone has inherent

---

[13] *Basic Law of Spain*, 1945, article 24.

[14] *Constitution of India*, 1949, Preamble.

[15] *The Constitution of Portugal*, 2 April 1976, article 1.

[16] 'In the name of the Most Holy Trinity, from Whom is all authority and to Whom, as our final end, all actions both of men and States must be referred, We, the people of Ireland, humbly acknowledging all our obligations to our Divine Lord, Jesus Christ, Who sustained our fathers through centuries of trial, Gratefully remembering their heroic and unremitting struggle to regain the rightful independence of our Nation, And seeking to promote the common good, with due observance of Prudence, Justice and Charity, so that the dignity and freedom of the individual may be assured, true social order attained, the unity of our country restored, and concord established with other nations, Do hereby adopt, enact, and give to ourselves this Constitution.' *Constitution of Ireland*, 1937, Preamble.

[17] *The Constitution of Hungary*, 20 August 1949, article 54(1).

[18] *Israeli Basic Law: Human Dignity and Liberty*, 25 March 1992 (revised at 10 March 1994).

[19] 'The Republic of South Africa is one, sovereign, democratic state founded on the following values: a. Human dignity, the achievement of equality and the advancement of human rights and freedoms.' *The Constitution of South Africa* (1993), article 1.

dignity and the right to have their dignity respected and protected'. This assumption is strengthened in light of article 37(5), which confirms that human dignity is a right that cannot be restricted under any circumstances.[20]

These last three examples, however, are the exception and do not constitute the rule. As has been said with regard to most constitutions, human dignity is regarded as the source or the supreme value upon which all rights and duties, and all state actions depend. Because human beings have dignity they *should* be given certain treatment and human dignity *must not* be degraded or humiliated.

Symbolic Representation and the Lack of a Fixed Content

One is bound to inquire, however, about the legal essence of human dignity, and wonder about what exactly it means by required treatment (the *should*) and by humiliating actions (the *must not*). This leads to observing a twofold feature of human dignity as it is used as a justification for rights and duties in legal documents: symbolic representation and a lack of a fixed content.

First, let us examine what is meant by symbolic representation. In the preambles of documents that specify rights and duties, there seems to be some sort of a priori bedrock-truth justification, which is usually articulated as human dignity. This approach enables an accepted starting point for legislation, because as for itself, human dignity does not determine what *the* reason or rationale among possible reasons and rationales for the existence and protection of certain norms in a legal document is, but, rather, leaves the philosophical debate undecided.[21] There is a major advantage to this approach, for the abstention from a *philosophical* decision regarding the source and cause for rights and duties paves the way for a *political* consent concerning the specific rights and duties that *ought* to be legislated and enforced *in practice* without waiving or compromising basic principles of belief.[22] Thus, the different parties that take part in a constitutive act can conceive human

[20] It is worth noting that the Supreme Justice of South Africa, Arthur Chaskalson, realises that such a linguistic usage is rare and explains this in the following way: 'The reluctance to give dignity the status of a discrete right in human rights instruments may be due to the breadth of its meanings and the difficulty of defining its limits… where this has been done, the entrenchment or implication of a residual right of dignity might be thought to have an open-ended quality which would be unmanageable.' Chaskalson, 'Human Dignity as a Constitutional Value', in: D. Kretzmer and E. Klein (eds.), *The Concept of Human Dignity in Human Rights Discourse*, pp.135–136.

[21] Cf.: 'The Universal Declaration of Human Rights, striving for a pronouncement that would appeal to diverse political systems governing diverse peoples, built on that faith and eschewed philosophical exploration.... There is no agreed theory justifying "human dignity" as the source of right, and we are not told how the needs of human dignity are determined.' L. Henkin, 'International Human Rights as "Rights"', in: M. Winston (ed.), *The Philosophy of Human Rights* (Belmont: Wadsworth Publishing Company, 1989), pp.134–135.

[22] This was, in fact, the approach taken by the drafters of the *Universal Declaration of Human Rights*. See: 'Maritain restated the question before the committee. Instead of, "How can such disparate intellectual positions be reconciled?", he asked, "How much agreement can we reach

dignity as representing their particular set of values and world view. In other words, human dignity is used as a linguistic symbol that can represent different outlooks, thereby justifying a concrete political agreement on a seemingly shared ground.

This leads to the second aspect: *the lack of a fixed content*. The very fact that various world views and ideologies are strongly related to the concept of human dignity produces a paradoxical situation in that human dignity *as for itself* does not contain any concrete content or meaning. Because human dignity anchors different world views, it cannot represent any particular set of values or meaning that 'naturally' stem out of it. There is no fixed and universal content that spouts out of human dignity and, hence, *its content and meanings are determined separately in each legal document in accordance with the political agreement achieved at the time*. This is mainly why recognition in human dignity yields different legal documents, as is evident when comparing the overarching duties in the *African Charter on Human and People's Rights*[23] and the *American Declaration of the Rights and Duties of Man*[24] to the liberal rights emphasis in the *International Covenant on Civil and Political Rights*[25] and to the limited scope of rights enumerated in the Israeli *Basic Law: Human Dignity and Liberty*,[26] all of which recognize human dignity as a supreme value. Therefore, the content of human dignity is a corollary of a political agreement and compromise set in each legal document by the cultural, political, constitutional, and other conditions, which can evolve and change in the course of history.[27]

The Thick Meaning of Human Dignity

So far, we have observed the linguistic usages of human dignity functioning as a justification for rights and duties in legal instruments. Yet, human dignity is not merely a legal concept that is expressed by specified norms. Rather, it is primarily

regarding practices even while remaining incurably divided regarding the underlying theory for such practices?" .... This distinction—taken over from the UNESCO experience by those working on the Universal Declaration—allows people to stand firm on all points of principle, avoiding the trap of moral indifferentism or relativism. A Muslim need not surrender one iota of Muslim faith, or a Christian of Christian faith. Nor need a Communist abandon Communist theory. Maritain's approach was to ask one question only: Do you agree that the support of this practice and the prohibition of that other practice is a worthy criterion for the world community? Do you agree to declare that your nation will live under this code of practices? (original emphasis).' M. Novak, 'Human Dignity, Human Rights', *First Things*, 97 (1999), p.42.

[23] *African Charter on Human and People's Rights* (17 June 1981), Chapter II (Duties), articles 27–29.

[24] *American Declaration of the Rights and Duties of Man* (1948), Chapter II (Duties).

[25] Cf. footnote no. 2.

[26] Cf. footnote no. 13.

[27] Cf.: 'Developments in the idea and jurisprudence of rights during two hundred years under the Constitution suggest continuing refinement of our society's sense of human dignity and an evolving appreciation of what human dignity requires.' L. Henkin, 'Human Dignity and Constitutional Rights', in: M.J. Meyer and W.A. Parent (eds.), *The Constitution of Rights: Human Dignity and American Values* (Ithaca, NY: Cornell University Press, 1992), p.227.

a moral–philosophical term, which, like other moral concepts, has different levels of meanings depending on its context and linguistic function. Michael Walzer, on whom I have relied in using the *thick* and *thin* terminology, states this argument clearly: 'Moral terms have minimal and maximal meanings; we can standardly give thick and thin accounts of them, and the two accounts are appropriate to different contexts, serve different purposes'.[28] Specifically, the main difference between the linguistic functions that will be analysed hereafter reflect discrete moral meanings intertwined with the concept of human dignity.

As a moral concept taken in the thick meaning, human dignity embraces two fundamental and interrelated premises: human and dignity. In fact, our understanding of *human dignity* is deeply inherent in our way of perceiving the world and its dwellers. The word *human* relates to basic assumptions in our consciousness, or rather subconsciousness, about human nature, worth, place in the cosmos, attributes, and character, and inseparably of *human*, we have a strong understanding of *dignity*: human dignified or natural existence, human normative behaviour that best reflects their good nature, and human positive and negative attributes. Put differently, the thick meaning of human dignity encapsulates a whole moral world view.

Our world views are 'a complex, often unarticulated (and perhaps not fully articulable) set of deeply held and highly cherished beliefs about the nature and organization of the universe and one's place in it'.[29] A world view is formulated (and changes) in the course of our lives together with the process of forming our consciences. Our world view encapsulates the recognition about the 'nature and organization of the universe' and one's place in it'.[30] Therefore, the extensive meanings associated with human dignity overlap those inherent in a world view, a moral world view to say the least. Both are composed of general principles that are not lucid or fully verbalized. Namely, the thick meaning of human dignity is a maximal moral meaning that encapsulates both the convictions in human moral worth and the variety of desirable moral conducts that are commensurable with human essential worth, as also their reverse.

The thick meaning of human dignity is brought up in diverse contexts of moral parlance: for example, when an attitude is taken regarding the issue of whether certain conduct towards children—like compulsory education or their lack of freedom in various issues—is commensurate with their human dignity or opposes it; when

[28] Michael Walzer, *Thick and Thin: Moral Argument at Home and Abroad*, p.2.

[29] M. Benjamin, *Splitting the Difference: Compromise and Integrity in Ethics and Politics* (Kansas: University Press of Kansas, 1990), p.88.

[30] Compare Benjamin's definition to Herbert Spiegelberg's saying: 'The search for grounds of human dignity presupposes a full pledged philosophical anthropology, showing not only man's essential nature, its ingredients, its structure and its place in the cosmos, but also his values, rights and responsibilities. Only on such basis will it be adequate survey of the possible grounds for his dignity.' H. Spiegelberg, 'Human Dignity: A Challenge to Contemporary Philosophy', in: R. Gotesky and E. Laszlo (eds.), *Human Dignity: This Century and the Next* (New York: Gordon & Breach, 1970), p.61. See also, N. Rotenstreich, *Man and His Dignity*, Chapter III.

establishing a principle (or principles) of distributive justice that embody the dignity of a the human being and the values of a just society[31]; when debating a policy that encroaches on citizens' privacy in favour of national security; when establishing a military moral code for soldiers and to soldiers in the military apparatus that is becoming of human dignity[32]; when debating important issues such as the death penalty or abortions on the grounds of respecting or degrading human dignity. The linguistic function of human dignity in these linguistic spheres is embedded in a particular cultural or ideological understanding of what human dignity entails, which is a thick, stratified and all-embracing understanding, and which is not confined to only one area of human action or to one form of life. To put it in Wittgenstein's words: 'to imagine a language means to imagine a form of life'.[33] In our context, one can say that the different linguistic functions of human dignity reflect our diverse forms of life.

Moreover, although the thick meaning of human dignity is discernible in a particular culture, it is even more apparent in a cross-cultural perspective. It is a well-known fact that there are quite heterogeneous premises about human nature and human dignified conduct towards his fellow human beings. Therefore, human dignity has various thick meanings based on cultural and subcultural contexts.[34] Our thick perception of human dignity is shaped in a particular social and cultural climate, which dictates the way we learn to recognize and evaluate other human beings.[35] Nevertheless, it goes (almost) without saying that our particular thick conception of human dignity is far from being objective or universal.

A citizen of a liberal democracy, for instance, will find traditional Islamic conceptions of human dignity to be different and even incompatible with his own. 'The Islamic tradition', says Abdul Aziz Said, 'does not provide an explicit model for growth as understood in the West. Islam views materialism as detrimental to human dignity, undermining the nobility of the human species.'[36] Furthermore, the notion of freedom in traditional Islam might also seem to be in conflict with a thick liberal

---

[31] For conceptions of distributive justice as reflecting a thick meaning of morality, see the second chapter in Walzer *Thick and Thin: Moral Argument at Home and Abroad* and on the historical and conceptual connection between human dignity, economics and religion see M. Novak, 'The Judeo-Christian Foundation of Human Dignity, Personal Liberty, and the Concept of the Person', *Journal of Markets and Morality*, 1 (1998), pp.107–21.

[32] See *Human Dignity in the Israel Defence Forces* (Israel Democracy Institute, 2001).

[33] L. Wittgenstein, *Philosophical Investigations*, §19.

[34] See also Tom Bryder, 'Patterns for Future Research on Self-Esteem and Human Dignity in Mass Society', *Political Psychology* 15(3) (1994), pp.401–414.

[35] Yuval Luria explains that 'concepts of dignity, by which we observe our life and others around us, are like psychological-glue through which social values that guide our life are attached to us and shape our conduct. They are the initial and fundamental dress that embody humane cultural values'. Y. Luria, 'A Matter of Dignity', in: A. Nemdar (ed.), *Virtues and Feelings* (Ramat Gan: Hoshen Le Mishpat, 1994), p.179.

[36] Abdul, Aziz Said, 'Human Rights in Islamic Perspectives', in: A. Pollis and P. Schwab (eds.), *Human Rights: Cultural and Ideological Perspectives* (New York: Praeger. 1979), p.90.

conception of human dignity that is identified with rights and lack of restraints. In Islam, 'human rights exist only in relation to human obligations. Individuals possess certain obligations towards God, fellow humans, and nature, all of which are defined by the Shariah' and 'those who do accept these obligations have no rights, and any claims of freedom that they make upon society lack justification'.[37] In addition, the dignified existence of *man* in traditional Islam and his appropriate posture in the social order is remarkably different from that of a (or 'his') *woman*. In Islam, this difference between man and woman within the thick meaning of human dignity is due to the basic assumptions regarding their appropriate place in the cosmic and social order, which are considerably different from Western assumptions and practices.

In a similar manner, there are other thick traditional–cultural world views of human dignity that express human dignity in a way not parallel or committed to human rights. These thick meanings of human dignity emphasize the entitlements of society over those of the individual and the duties of the latter to his community, which imparts his human value.[38] These cultural differences also project on the way in which political relations and regimes are organized. Societies whose historical and cultural heritage is founded upon the centrality of the individual have regimes and constitutive arrangements that emphasize and assure the rights of individuals counter to state power and society, while societies whose heritage is founded upon conformity, uniformity, and adherence to a (more or less) defined set of values and norms have regimes and constitutive arrangements that emphasize the duties of the individual to his or her community.[39]

To conclude this point, the thick meaning of human dignity is a particular cultural understanding of what it means to be human and have a dignified life with fellow human beings. In the thick meaning of human dignity, the emphasis is on the particular and subjective, not on the universal and objective. For this reason, Rhoda Howard's definition is very precise for the thick meaning: 'I define human dignity *as the particular cultural understandings of the inner moral worth of the human person and his or her proper political relations with society*'.[40] Howard's definition enables the inclusion of a variety of existing particular cultural understandings of human dignity and, hence, to recognize that there is more than one true meaning of human dignity, and by so to fit the cultural heterogeneous reality.[41]

So far, we have seen the similarity between the thick meaning of human dignity and that of a moral world view, and further argued that various cultural

---

[37] Ibid., 92.

[38] Jack Donnelly, 'Human Rights and Human Dignity: An Analytic Critique of Non-Western Conceptions of Human Rights', *American Political Science Review*, 76 (1982), pp.303–316.

[39] R. Howard and J. Donnelly, 'Human Dignity, Human Rights and Political Regimes', *American Political Science Review*, 80 (1986).

[40] R. Howard, 'Dignity, Community, and Human Rights', in: A.A. An-Na'im (ed.), *Human Rights in Cross-Cultural Perspective; A Request for Consensus* (Philadelphia, PA: University of Pennsylvania Press, 1992), p.83 (original emphasis).

[41] Consult also: A. Pollis and P. Schwab, *Human Rights: Cultural and Ideological Perspectives* (New York: Praeger, 1979).

understandings of human dignity exist. We shall now turn to examine three main components of the thick meaning of human dignity. These additional components are not alternative moral conceptions with lesser moral significance in comparison to the thick meaning of human dignity. Rather, they are contained and encapsulated within the thick meaning. The three other components of human dignity consist of a twofold function: first, they embody three distinct moral language spheres in which human dignity plays a central role and where its meanings are formed; and second, each of these meanings corresponds to a distinct moral echelon that is part and parcel of the thick meaning.

Rights and Duties

The first component is rights and duties that are integral to a thick conception of human dignity. Actually, many people, especially in the West, use the term *human rights* as a synonym for human dignity,[42] and when they speak of human dignity, they refer to a certain list of rights. But human dignity is not expressed and assured in every world view by human rights alone, and there are world views that dictate more duties than rights or rights only in subjection to duties. While the Western world identifies human dignity especially with human rights, other cultural and ideological world views depict human dignity in regard to individual duties to his society, state, God, constitution, the duties of women to their husbands, and the like.[43]

Rights and duties are the main echelon in creating an affinity between a human's basic worth and his dignified existence, and they stem from the basic premises regarding human essential worth according to a particular cultural understanding. Rights and duties are enumerated in constitutional documents, which usually give voice to the central (or mainstream) values of society. For instance, the constitutions of Germany, Greece, Portugal, Spain, Belgium, Sweden, Switzerland, and other liberal-democratic states voice a strong affinity between human dignity and human rights, since the former is taken to be the justification of the latter, as has been shown previously. But one can notice that human dignity is defined in a special way within societies and cultures that are not liberal in character.

For example, the preamble of the constitution of China establishes that the people, organizations and political parties of China 'must take the Constitution as the basic norm of conduct, and they have the duty to uphold the dignity of the Constitution and ensure its implementation' and on top of that, article 5(1) states that 'the state upholds the uniformity and dignity of the socialist legal system'.[44] A similar

---

[42] For a similar claim see R. Howard and J. Donnelly, 'Human Dignity, Human Rights and Political Regimes', p.801.

[43] Jack Donnelly, 'Human Rights and Human Dignity' (1982).

[44] And compare: 'The personal dignity of citizens of the People's Republic of China is inviolable. Insult, libel, false charge, or frame-up directed against citizens by any means is prohibited.' Article 38, *Constitution of China*, adopted 4 December 1982. I have relied on the translation of the constitutions mentioned hereinafter found in: www.oefre.unibe.ch/law/icl/home.html.

duty to uphold and dignify the constitution of the state as part of society's goals is to be found in the constitution of Iran, which is founded on the belief in Allah and Shiite Islam: 'It is incumbent on all to adhere to the principles of this Constitution, for it regards as its highest aim the freedom and dignity of the human race and provides for the growth and development of the human being.' [Mass Communication Media (Article)][45] Moreover, it is worth mentioning that the Iranian Constitution emphasizes the special elements of woman's essential worth, and in accordance with this special worth, she is destined and honoured to be responsible for the basic unit of society, that is the family, while helping to foster and promote her man [Woman in the Constitution (Article)]. A different cultural emphasis can be found in the constitution of Thailand, which recognizes the dignity and rights of the individual, but first and foremost, recognizes the duty of every citizen to dignify the King, who is the first among citizens[46] and who must not be exposed to an accusation of any sort.[47] That is to say, human dignity in the meaning of rights and duties is defined upon concepts that pertain to the rights and duties' parlance and sometimes as synonyms for rights and duties themselves. Yet, the precise balance between them is a consequence of cultural and ideological factors.

Honour and Dignity

Apart from rights and duties, other norms that are related to human dignified existence are derived from the basic premises about human moral worth and are grasped within a wide moral view. Among these norms, *honour* is included. In Hebrew, the word *Kavod* entails three meanings: dignity, honour, and respect.[48] But English also has the connotation of dignity in the meaning of respect and honour, as when using the expression *to dignify* or *dignified* to describe certain acts and practices. This linguistic semblance stresses the strong connection between honour and dignity and it can be traced back as to the word *Dignitas* in ancient Rome, where and when it

[45] See also: 'The Islamic Republic is a system based on belief in: '6) the exalted dignity and value of man, and his freedom coupled with responsibility before God; in which equity, justice, political, economic, social, and cultural independence, and national solidarity are secured by recourse to: a) continuous leadership of the holy persons, possessing necessary qualifications, exercised on the basis of the Koran and the Sunnah, upon all of whom be peace...' article 2, *Constitution of Iran*, adopted 24 October 1979.

[46] 'May the Thai people unite in observing, protecting and upholding the Constitution of the Kingdom of Thailand in order to maintain the democratic regime of government and the sovereign power derived from the Thai people, and to bring about happiness, prosperity, and dignity to His Majesty's subjects throughout the Kingdom according to the will of His Majesty in every respect.' *Constitution of Thailand* (1997), Preamble.

[47] 'No person shall expose the King to any sort of accusation or action', article 8, ibid.

[48] See also Orit Kmir's recent linguistic and conceptual analysis in her 'Honor and Dignity Cultures: The Case of Kavod and Kvod Ha-Adam in Israeli Society and Law', D. Kretzmer and E. Klein, *The Concept of Human Dignity in Human Rights Discourse*.

'connotes a certain position in the social context', worthiness for an office of counsel *(dignitas consularis)*, suitability or fame.[49] With the downfall of the old social hierarchies, a linguistic change occurred in the linguistic function of the concept of dignity and it was separated from its old hierarchical meanings in favour of more universalistic meanings.[50]

Honour is a *social-appreciation* given to moral conducts, achievements, and characteristics that are considered worthy by the relevant group, and this appreciation is expressed and *conditioned* by a certain *attitude* of society.[51] For example, a young man or woman who makes room for an old person in a public bus will probably gain recognition (whether explicit or implicit) from other passengers on that bus; otherwise, they might be condemned for refusing to do so themselves. A successful firm manager will gain appreciation (in different possible ways) for his traits and achievements that have brought him to this social status; an excellent sportswoman will earn appreciation on sports achievements in her field by granting her medals and trophies; an artist will be appreciated when her works of art are displayed in public; and a minister or parliament member will be admired for holding a high social and political rank.[52] In other words, honour is another echelon that dictates what is a dignified and undignified, a moral and immoral conduct within the thick meaning of human dignity. Honour is constructed upon the rights and duties echelon by the latter being more fundamental to human existence than the former. However, this distinction is not meant to separate sharply between the two interrelated echelons, since an affront to one's honour is usually expressed in rights and duties parlance. For example, insulting a person in public has been compared in Judaism to the spilling of his blood. Rather, it marks two distinct areas of morals that are contained within the thick meaning of human dignity.

Honour is comprehended differently in a cross-cultural or chronological perspective, just as we have seen in the case of rights and duties. A person married to several women in a particular culture and takes care of their needs might gain

---

[49] Rotenstreich, *Man and his Dignity*, pp.11–12.

[50] Charles Taylor, 'The Politics of Recognition', in: A. Gutmann (ed.), *Multiculturalism and the Politics of Recognition: An Essay*, (Princeton, NJ: Princeton University Press, 1992), pp.25–51.

[51] Honour requires social relations between humans, because without the attitude of the public towards the honourable man or woman, without this honour demonstrated in some way, honour does not exist—namely, honour is fully conditioned by appraisals of others to the honourable (Luria, 1994: 166); and compare: 'The Value, or Worth of a man is, as of all other things, his Price; that is to say, so much as would be given for the use of his Power: and therefore is not absolute; but a thing dependent on the need and judgement of another. An able conductor of Souldiers, is of great Price in time of War present, or imminent; but in Peace not so. A learned and uncorrupt Judge, is much Worth in time of Peace, but not so much in war. And as in other things, so in men, not the seller, but the buyer determines the Price. For let a man (as most men do) rate themselves at the highest Value they can; yet their true Value is no more than it is esteemed by others' (original emphasis). T. Hobbes, in: R. Tuck (ed.), *Leviathan* (Cambridge: Cambridge University Press, 1996), p.63.

[52] Also compare: 'The publique worth of a man, which is the Value set on him by the Commonwealth, is that which men commonly call DIGNITY. And this Value of him by the Commonwealth is understood, by offices of Command, Judicature, publique Employment; or by Names and Titles, introduced for distinction of such Value.' Hobbes (1996), pp.63–64.

great honour in a society that recognizes and values polygamy, but not necessarily (and sometimes necessarily not) in other societies and cultures. Alternatively, a society that once valued polygamy or approved of the slavery institution might very well condemn them at some other point in time. Furthermore, a society that esteems the value of individual autonomy will honour certain actions that promote this value: material aid, education for one's rights, and fighting for them. Yet in another aspect, religious and traditional societies might think that certain material aids (e.g. television), education for woman's rights and boisterously demanding religious freedom, are actions without honour and even as a real insult to human dignity according to their world view.[53] In other words, honour is culturally relative since it is defined by the thick meaning of human dignity, which stems from different cultural contexts.

The Wide Moral View

The two meanings of human dignity just described, rights and duties, and honour, are contained in a wide moral view that is destined to create harmony between the particular cultural understanding regarding human inherent moral worth and his or her proper social relations with fellow humans.[54] This is an upward ambitious moral view (metaphorically and positively speaking), for its *end* (telos), to use an Aristotelian manner of speaking, is to create harmony between the fact that the human being is a social animal in nature and the social–political order that will assist in epitomizing the good virtue in the most optimal way, just as physical and climatic conditions are required for the end of making a seed become a blossoming and fruitful tree.[55] The wide moral view stems from basic assumptions about human

[53] For the possible contradiction between claiming rights and human dignity see: 'However, every time a person claims his rights this activity is not expressive of his dignity. Claiming one's rights might be unrelated to expressing dignity or even, in extreme cases, antithetical to the expression of human dignity. Someone might conceivably claim his rights in a very undignified way. He might be too pushy about his rights or he might claim some rights insincerely, not really believing that they were his but still hoping to get the benefit of the display.' M.J. Meyer, 'Dignity, Rights and Self-Control', *Ethics*, 99 (1989), p.524.

[54] Daniel Statman defines the wide moral outlook as 'dignity as a moral attitude'. According to Statman, every immoral behaviour is contained within dignity as a moral attitude. D. Statman, 'Two Concepts of Dignity', p.544.

[55] Aristotle in his *Nicomachean Ethics* distinguishes between the ultimate end (telos), that is happiness, and honour. Aristotle claims that some people confuse honour—which is what politicians strive for and is conditioned by those honouring the honoured—with the quality of the person whose virtue is not conditioned by others, but is inherent in him. Compare: 'People of quality, for their part, those who tend towards a life of action, go for honour; for pretty much this is the end of the political life. But it appears more superficial than what we are looking for, as it seems to be located in those doing the honouring rather than in the person receiving it, and our hunch is that the good is something that belongs to a person and is difficult to take away from him... so it is clear, at any rate according to them, that excellence is of greater value. In fact, perhaps one might suppose that this is even more the end of the political life than honour is' (1095b21–1095b31).

moral worth, and aims at promoting humans towards a state of harmony between these basic assumptions and the proper social–political relations that ought to exist. Yet, as the wide moral view is directed upwards, there is a third element within the thick meaning of human dignity that is included in a narrow moral view that is directed downwards, and this will be discussed in the following analysis.

The Thin Meaning of Human Dignity

The thin meaning of human dignity is a third discrete component of the thick meaning of human dignity. This component corresponds to a prevalent linguistic function with the concept of human dignity that connotes a meaning related to humiliation and lowering of human worth. The use of human dignity within the thin linguistic sphere indicates a behaviour that is not in line with the premises about human worth. Such behaviour is comprehended in terms of humiliation and as a conduct that is blatantly incommensurate with the basic assumption about human moral worth.[56] Whereas rights and duties, and honour, are contained within the upward wide moral view that is meant to harmonize human moral worth and his proper social–political relation with other human beings, the thin meaning is contained within a thin moral view that is focused on the crude violation of that basic moral worth. In other words, with regard to behaviour that is not honourable or that bounds rights and duties, the thin meaning of human dignity is revealed in behaviour and situations that embody a breach and debasement of the very human moral foundations.

The thin meaning of human dignity is not susceptible to a precise definition by a list of concrete immoral conducts; yet, when such a humiliating or degrading conduct occurs, it is intuitively perceived by the humiliated person and those who share his feelings.[57] In this way, for example, Victor Frankl in his *Man's Search for Meaning* describes the humiliations that he has endured in the concentration camps during the Holocaust:

> The pain he caused me was not from any insults or any blows. That guard did not think it worth his while to say anything, not even a swear word, to the ragged, emaciated figure standing before him, which probably reminded him only vaguely of a human form. Instead, he playfully picked up a stone and threw it at me. That, to me, seemed the way to attract the attention of a beast, to call a domestic animal back to its job, a creature with which you have so little in common that you do not even punish it.[58]

---

[56] The thin meaning of human dignity with relation to humiliation is demonstrated both linguistically and conceptually in Statman's articles (2001, 2002).

[57] 'Its [human dignity] intrinsic meaning has been left to intuitive understanding, conditioned in large measures by cultural factors. When it has been evoked in concrete situations, it has been generally assumed that a violation of human dignity can be recognised even if the abstract term cannot be defined' (emphasis mine). Oscar Schachter, 'Human Dignity as a Normative Concept', *American Journal of International Law*, 77(4) (1983), pp.848–854.

[58] Victor Frankl, *Man's Search for Meaning* (New York: Simon & Schuster, 1984), p.36.

> The majority of prisoners suffered from a kind of inferiority complexes. We had all once been or had fancied ourselves to be "somebody". Now we were treated like complete nonentities (The consciousness of one's inner value is anchored in higher, more spiritual things, and cannot be shaken by camp life. But how many free men, let alone prisoners, possess it?) Without consciously thinking about it, the average prisoner felt himself utterly degraded.[59]

We perceive the humiliating and degrading situations that Frankl suffered intuitively and, hence, immediately understand the blatant lack of morality they are imbedded in due to the sharp contradiction between the humiliating situation and the most fundamental human values on which we were educated and brought up. Not in every event that a person throws a stone at another person do we perceive this to be an offence to the latter most basic human existence; yet, when this action is accompanied by an attitude that is not even appropriate to animals, we regard this as an offence to human dignity, as we refer to the thin meaning of the term.[60]

Similarly to the thick meaning of human dignity, the thin meaning is neither static nor universal. Certain behaviour and conducts that were customary in the past are subjected to historical and cultural changes and, therefore, are weighted differently in different places and points in time. The slavery institution, to take a salient example, was widespread throughout the centuries, starting with the ancient civilizations of Mesopotamia, India, China, Greece, through the black slaves in Africa and the white slaves (Mamluks) in medieval Islam and ending with the slaves brought to North and South America. Only in the 19th century was there a substantial effective resistance to the established slavery institution and it was gradually perceived as not moral.[61] This understanding culminated in the 20th century to be regarded as

---

[59] Ibid., p.72.

[60] Frankl's feelings that he has been treated like an animal lacking human dignity is a recurring theme in his book: 'A man's character became involved to the point that he was caught in a mental turmoil which threatened all the values he held and threw them into doubt. Under the influence of a world which no longer recognised the value of human life and human dignity, which had robbed man of his will and had made him an object to be exterminated (having planned, however, to make full use of him first—to the last ounce of his physical resources) —under this influence the personal ego finally suffered a loss of values. If the man in the concentration camp did not struggle against this in the last effort to save his self-respect, he lost the feeling of being an individual, a being with a mind, with inner freedom and personal value. He thought of himself then as only a part of an enormous mass of people; his existence descended to the level of animal life. The men were herded—sometimes to one place then to another; sometimes driven together, then apart—like a flock of sheep without thought or a will of their own.' V. Frankl, *Man's Search for Meaning*, p.60.

[61] Although slavery still exists in some parts of the world (like in parts of Africa). Compare: 'Mindful that the peoples of the United Nations reaffirmed in the Charter their faith in the dignity and worth of the human person; Considering that the Universal Declaration of Human Rights...states that no one shall be held in slavery or servitude and that slavery and the slave trade shall be prohibited in all their forms; .... Being aware, however, that slavery, the slave trade and institutions and practices similar to slavery have not yet been eliminated in all parts of the world; Having decided, therefore, that the Convention of 1926, which remains operative, should now be augmented by the conclusion of a supplementary convention designed to intensify national as well as international efforts towards the abolition of slavery, the slave trade and institutions and practices similar to slavery' (emphasis added). Preamble to *Supplementary Convention on the Abolition of Slavery*, the Slave Trade and Institutions and Practices Similar to Slavery, adopted on 7 September 1956.

a severe breach of human dignity and concrete national and international measures were taken for its abolition.[62] A further moral development can be seen in the case of suffrage. Despite the lack of an equal and general democratic voting right in most places in the world until the mid-20th century, this was not necessarily perceived as a humiliation or degrading conduct of the citizens lacking this right such as women, blacks in America and minorities; yet nowadays, in liberal-democratic states at least, the denial of equal suffrage on the basis of sex, race, religion, or any other distinction not based on good enough reasons is considered a substantial offence to human dignity.

The reason for the thin meaning of human dignity is subjected to change or, put differently, for humiliation not being static or universal, is due to the fact that the thin meaning is dictated and encapsulated by the thick meaning of human dignity.[63] Hence, changes in the thick meaning will probably involve changes in our understanding of the thin meaning, namely, our conception of what humiliation means. The social and historical developments emphasize how world views have gradually changed from a point in which a certain norm, to take slavery again, that was considered permitted and even perceived as a sign of honour by slave owners, has become a conduct without honour, until it was finally regarded as an immoral, degrading, and humiliating conduct forbidden by national and international law.

As a result of the change in the moral outlook of people in particular and societies at large concerning the required moral behaviour that stem from human dignity, social–political conflicts arise between societies or between different groups that comprise the same society. Such conflicts occur when changes in the moral consciousness of one group generate tensions with the moral consciousness of another group. This change can be formed, for instance, when social and historical processes cause one group to perceive (or to strengthen their perception of) the existing social order as a blatant injustice lacking moral justification, until the point they perceive this social order as inflicting severe humiliation of their most basic human worth.

A significant example for the last point is the Civil Rights Movement struggle in the USA under the leadership of Martin Luther King. The blacks in America were probably never satisfied with their political, social, and economic status, yet only in the mid-20th century did a critical mass of black citizens start seeing this status as intolerable and as an insult to their equal worth and dignity as humans. Their rights prescribed by law were not respected and they suffered severe daily humiliations upon their dignity as described in King's 'Letter from Birmingham City Jail'.

---

[62] Jochen Frowein, 2002, 'Human Dignity in International Law', in: D. Kretzmer and E. Klein (eds.), *The Concept of Human Dignity in Human Rights Discourse*, p.122.

[63] Compare: 'minimalist meanings are embedded in the maximal morality, expressed in the same idiom, sharing the same historical/cultural/religious/political) orientation. Minimalism is liberated from its embeddedness and appears independent, in varying degrees of thinness, only in the course of a personal or social crisis or a political confrontation....' Walzer, *Thick and Thin: Moral Argument at Home and Abroad*, p.3.

> [W]hen you take a cross-county drive and find it necessary to sleep night after night in the uncomfortable corners of your automobile because no motel will accept you; when you are *humiliated* day in and day out by nagging signs reading "white" and "colored"; when your first name becomes "nigger", your middle name becomes "boy" (however old you are) and your last name becomes "John", and your wife and mother are *never given the respected title* "Mrs."; when you are harried by day and haunted by night by the fact that you are a Negro, living constantly at tiptoe stance, never quite knowing what to expect next, and are plagued with inner fears and outer resentments; when you no [*sic*] forever fighting a degenerating *sense of nobodiness* then you will understand why we find it difficult to wait.[64]
>
> I had hoped that the white moderate would understand that the present tension in the South is a necessary phase of the transition from an obnoxious negative peace, in which the Negro passively accepted his unjust plight, to a substantive and positive peace, in which all men *will respect the dignity and worth of human personality.*[65]

King described the humiliating attitude towards the blacks as distorting their human personalities by instilling in them a sense of 'nobodiness' similar to Frankl's feeling that he and his prisoner friends were treated like 'nonentities'. This attitude towards the blacks was not worse in comparison to their conditions in previous centuries in America, yet it was due to some improvement in their conditions and social status that the blacks could now see the salient contradiction between their wretched social conditions and the American values of freedom, equality, and justice. In other words, the blacks now saw the racial separation in public transportation, restaurants, education (and much more) not only as a lack of due social respect or honour, but as concrete humiliation to their human dignity. Of course, not all Americans saw eye to eye with the blacks' struggle for basic human recognition at that time; and, unfortunately, there were some who probably did not see anything wrong with that situation. But nowadays, it is perfectly clear that the sort of segregation and attitude under which blacks were until the 1960s of the 20th century were morally defective and stood in contrast to human dignity in a most fundamental way. Changes in the moral outlook in the USA (in general) have turned legitimate conducts of the past to evidently immoral conducts at present and the very thought of them upsets our moral conscience today.[66]

Unlike the case of the Civil Rights Movement in America, other moral conflicts are not that clear and easy to resolve. As aforesaid, the thick meaning of human dignity as a moral world view dictates what the thin meaning is. Hence, in a comparative perspective, one can observe that a part of one society's cultural heritage can seem to another as an offence and humiliation to human dignity. For example, a female might loose her life for violating the honour of the family in light of the high value ascribed to the honour of the family in some Bedouin and Moslem societies. Moreover, in large parts of Africa and in small communities in other parts of the world, a large number of little girls are circumcised (sometimes forcefully) by their families and it is estimated that more than 135 million girls

---

[64] Martin Luther King, 'Letter from Birmingham Jail', 1963 (emphasis added).

[65] Ibid., p.295 (emphasis added).

[66] Compare also to Henkin, 'Human Dignity and Constitutional Rights', at n.27 above.

and women around the world have had female genital mutilation.[67] These unfortunate examples stem first and foremost from traditional, religious, and cultural world views that assume hierarchal relations between woman and man. Of course, there is no wrong in sticking to our moral convictions that these practices should be prohibited; yet, one should acknowledge that their motive is not pure evil or a deliberate offence to human dignity, but an outcome of a different cultural perspective. Things get even more complicated once the conflict concerning human dignity is among groups that comprise the same society. Heterogeneous societies might find themselves in confrontation regarding different conceptions of human dignity and what it requires. What seems to one group to express human worth and dignity—like in the case of polygamy, abortion, euthanasia, and more—is an affront in the eyes of the other.

Conclusion

Human dignity is a moral–philosophical term that has several levels of meanings, which correspond to different linguistic functions. The thick meaning of human dignity is a moral world view that contains a particular cultural understanding of human moral worth and his proper relations with society. The kernel of the thick meaning is composed of basic assumptions about human worth that one is brought up on and they become basic moral premises in one's conscience. Out of this kernel sprouts a narrow moral view that embraces and defines the thin meaning of human dignity, which can be compared to roots planted deep in the soil. The parlance about conducts and attitudes that endanger these roots of humanity are bound with terms of humiliating and degrading human worth and dignity. Furthermore, from these very basic assumptions about human worth emerges a wide moral view that embraces and defines two more components of human dignity: rights and duties, and honour. Rights and duties stem from the moral kernel and unite into a solid trunk of a tree that is the main echelon in creating harmony between a human's basic worth and proper relations with society. Honour is like normative branches that grow parallel to the making of the trunk and on top of it, while in the process of growing, some branches thicken and become an integral part of the trunk.

The three parts of the tree resemble the normative hierarchy between the three meanings of human dignity inside the thick meaning: the thick meaning is the whole tree. This becomes clear by mapping the damage onto each echelon. When one offends one of the tree branches, the honour, the tree is naturally hurt. Yet, this does not endanger the existence of the whole tree. When the trunk of the tree, the rights and duties, is hurt, this entails a severe damage to the tree, since there is not much point in honour when more basic elements of human existence (that support

[67] For the different reasons for this practice and its scope see Amnesty International's *Female Genital Mutilation: A Human Rights Information Pack* (AI Index: ACT 77/05/97), http://www.amnesty.org/ailib/intcam/femgen/fgm1.htm#a7.

honour) are jeopardized. However, when the roots of the tree, that is, the thin meaning of human dignity, are hurt or threatened, the whole existence of the tree as a tree and the human as a human is in danger.

This distinction is not a dichotomic one, for rights and duties are not absolute and they should frequently be balanced with one another and with other important values, and also because an offence to honour in a certain situation can be equivalent to an offence in the thin meaning of human dignity, that is, as a humiliation to his basic human worth. In other words, identifying an offence to human dignity on the different levels that were presented is context dependent and requires the examination of cultural and subcultural aspects, and in any case, the model is not meant to separate these interrelated components. But in any event, whereas many conflicts and offences are uttered in different language spheres as offences to human dignity, the analysis in this paper, I believe, helps to identify and clarify the relevant normative echelon that is referred to.

There is great beauty in the fact that human dignity has become so prevalent in modern moral discourse. Yet, as Nathan Rotenstreich argues, 'precisely because the idea has become so current, the justification behind it and its particular meaning has become rather blurred, vague, or even ambiguous'.[68] Rotenstreich's conclusion is that the notion of human dignity is 'rather eclectic' and that it entails 'different types of justification and presentation which have evolved in the course of philosophical and the history of man's self-reflection, of self-evaluation'.[69] The purpose of this chapter has been to provide a conceptual map for the eclectic idea of human dignity. But following Wittgenstein's warning of assuming there is a 'final analysis of our forms of language' and 'a *single* completely resolved form of every expression',[70] I do not argue this to be a final model for this ambiguous notion, but rather a flexible one that helps to discern the different linguistic functions of the concept and its interrelated meanings for this present time.

The recurrent linguistic use of human dignity in moral, political, philosophical, and other discourses stresses our refined moral sense concerning human behaviour. Especially in liberal democracies, human dignity is inseparably understood as granting all citizens equal rights without any sort of discrimination. It seems apparent at this point in time, however, that liberal democracies have transcended this understanding of human dignity. Charles Taylor in his *Politics of Recognition* has observed that 'with the move from honour to dignity has come a politics of universalism, emphasizing the equal dignity of all citizens, and the contents of this politics has been the equalization of rights and entitlements.'[71] This social–historical move has generated two tendencies in politics: the politics of equal dignity and the politics of difference. 'With the politics of equal dignity, what is established is meant to be universally the same, an identical basket of rights and immunities; with the politics

---

[68] Rotenstreich, *Man and his Dignity*, p.9.

[69] Ibid.

[70] L. Wittgenstein, *Philosophical Investigations*, §91 (original emphasis).

[71] Charles Taylor, "The Politics of Recognition", p.37.

of difference, what we are asked to recognize is the unique identity of this individual or group, their distinctness from everyone else.'[72] In fact, the politics of difference are themselves part of the politics of dignity, only instead of demanding equal rights and treatment, they demand recognition in their distinctness and specific identity. Thus, we paradoxically have a modern Roman version of *Dignitas* today, whereby dignity means treating me not like an equal but, rather, recognizing my unique particular worth in the social order.

It is interesting to note that nowadays it is simply not enough to give an identical treatment and the same parcel of rights to all people. Not recognizing someone's particular identity or culture might be regarded as 'a form of oppression, imprisoning someone in a false, distorted, and reduced mode of being.'[73] Remarkably, this type of misrecognition of others is voiced today similarly to the way King talked about his sense of 'nobodiness' and Frankl's sense of 'nonentity'. Of course, these situations differ considerably and cannot be compared; nevertheless, one can observe that nowadays, a lack of due recognition is also seen and uttered in the thin meaning of human dignity.

These demands are probably not just empty words in many cases: they reflect authentic feelings of underprivileged groups; but it should be noted that not every lack of recognition is an insult or humiliation to human dignity in its thin meaning. Most of the conflicts inside liberal-democratic societies today are indeed between equal people who consider each other as such. Yet, it seems that too many conflicts in politics, which find their way into the justice halls, are actually about (social) *honour*—although what some contenders seem to argue for is an offence to their basic dignity. People and representatives of minority groups want not only to be symbolically recognized as equal in dignity and worth by the dead letter of written law; they want to be actually and vividly recognized as special humans with a particular worth by their fellow human beings, especially those who speak their language and share their history. I hope this chapter helps to clarify the vagueness surrounding the concept of human dignity and the recurrent appeals to it, and by so doing to enable human dignity to remain a unifying concept rather than letting it become a controversial one.

[72] Ibid., p.38.

[73] Ibid., p.25.

8
A Brief History of Human Dignity: Idea and Application

Milton Lewis

The Roots of the Idea in the West

Although the explicit application of the idea of human dignity in international politics and law is very recent, its roots stretch back to the early stages of Western civilization. Two characteristics of the West are important as preconditions for the development of the idea: the West's belief in the universal validity of its norms and its eventual basing of its norms in secular principles.

Both Judeo-Christian monotheism and the Graeco-Roman world's understanding of humankind underpinned a universalistic view of man's unique place in the cosmos. Historical sociologist, Max Weber looked to the dual heritage of Christianity and Roman law for the origins of what he famously saw as the unique rationalistic character of Western social, economic, and political relations that ultimately led to modern capitalism and the bureaucratic nation-state.

In Rome, the concept of dignity had moral, political, legal, and social meanings; the first referred to integrity or indifference to profit; the second in the Republican era was associated with those in high public offices like the various magistracies, the *dignitates*; it had another meaning, associated with high social rank; and in law it was applied strictly as 'greater' or 'lesser' in relation to rank and social condition. It is clear that in Rome dignity was not equally distributed.

Roman law was a rational system of secular law, based on the authority of the collective will, the res publica, not on divine authority as interpreted from sacred texts. As Rome became the ruler of the known, civilized world, it adopted the stoic idea of a universal law of nature offering justice and order to all. Through reason, man is part of a rationally organized universe. Reason and nature are congruent. The law of nature is identified with reason and so society, too, is based on the rule of reason.

Since all men were moved by 'right reason,' as Cicero and the Roman jurists who came after him saw it, there existed an ontological equality of humankind. This equality entailed a universal republic and the state was a moral enterprise devoted to the common good of citizens; not merely a framework for the pursuit of interests or for the exercise of an absolute sovereign will.[1]

---

[1] C.R. Miguel, 'Human Dignity: History of an Idea', http://search.netscape.com/ns/boomframe.jsp?query = human±dignity = history = idea = miguel&page = 1&0ffset = 0&, 20 January 2005,

J. Malpas and N. Lickiss (eds.), Perspectives on Human Dignity: A Conversation, 93–105.

Christian theology constructed the idea of dignity, and among the Church Fathers, St. Leo the Great (died 461) is said to have contributed greatly to the construction in two ways: his proposition that baptism confers dignity on Christians; and that because humans are made in the image of God and God became human, all humans have dignity. Being born having dignity, all humans have equal dignity. Dignity is an ontological category from this theological perspective.

Two works of St. Augustine (354–430) were significant for the theological tradition concerning the dignity of man. In *De Genesi ad litteram*, Augustine sees the Fall as seriously corrupting God's image in man and his/her ability to be virtuous is only restored with the Atonement. In *De Trinitate*, man's triune soul, composed of memory, intellect, and will, corresponds to the Holy Trinity which created him. Even intellect and will could be good or evil depending on how they were exercised; good if directed to divinity and evil if directed elsewhere.

St. Thomas Aquinas (1225–1274) differed from Leo in that he saw human dignity rooted in nature, not theology. As a person, a human being is naturally free. Dignity is lost when sin is committed. The rational human then assumes the status of a nonrational beast. Dignity, then, is an ethical, not an ontological category.

The humanist philosophers of the Renaissance proceeded further down the path opened by Aquinas's concern with the natural roots of human dignity and came to celebrate the glory, not condemn the sinfulness of humankind. Giannozzo Manetti (1396–1459) in his *De dignitate et excellentia hominis* (1452) advanced both theological and naturalistic arguments: humans are creatures of God but much superior to the rest of creation and their natures are related to the divine one; indeed such is the perfection of their bodies and souls that we are getting close to seeing God as the image of man. Humans are born having dignity and have it in equal measure. Giovanni Pico della Mirandola (1463–1494) wrote perhaps the best-known Renaissance piece on the concept, *De hominis dignitate* (1486). All creation is strictly governed by God's laws except humans to whom God has given free will to determine their own natures. Dignity comes from this freedom to be what you will. Like Manetti, Pico sees humans as being born possessing dignity and having it in equal amount. But where Manetti sees dignity arising from human excellence, Pico sees it in the freedom to attain such excellence.

The Renaissance humanists had begun to advance nontheological arguments for dignity, but they also remained attached to Christianity's transcendental realm. The empiricism of David Hume's (1711–1776) essay on the dignity or meanness of human nature means a naturalistic approach to dignity has prevailed: not metaphysics but empirical facts show that a human being may behave in a worthy way; humans are naturally inclined to behave worthily (although it is not certain they will always do so); when he/she has a self-image of being worthy, a person will try to act up to it; finally, while not born having dignity, all humans tend to become worthy.

---

pp.2–3; Y. Arieli, 'On the Necessary and Sufficient Conditions for the Emergence of the Doctrine of the Dignity of Man and His Rights', in: D. Kretzmer and E. Klein (eds.), *The Concept of Human Dignity in Human Rights Discourse* (The Hague: Kluwer Law International, 2002), pp.9–17.

For Immanuel Kant (1724–1804), dignity is grounded in human autonomy; the human being is always an end, not a means, in actions directed to other rational beings as well as to himself. Dignity is an ethical category. All humans are born having dignity and are equal in dignity. With Kant, we have arrived at an ethical understanding of dignity which the framers of the Universal Declaration of Human Rights shared.[2]

In laying the foundations, as it were, for the mid-20th-century application of the concept of human dignity in international law and politics, Roman law, significantly, recognized the autonomy of the *sacrum* (man's relations to the divine) and of the *saeculum* (the sphere of social relations). Catholic Christianity accepted the legitimacy of the secular sphere so that after the establishment of Christianity as the state church, the *imperium* and *sacerdotium* recognized the legitimacy of each other's authority. It proved a tensionful coexistence, but neither succeeded in totally subordinating the other until the Reformation split the Church and belief in Christianity waned with the humanism of the Renaissance and the advent of science in the age of Enlightenment. The Reformation promoted the idea of freedom of conscience and individual opinion, and led to the characteristic Western coexistence of church and state.

The unique Western recognition of the legitimacy of the two loci of authority was thus established at the birth of European civilization. The very existence of a separate realm of the sacred allowed a deepening of the realm of the secular. There was room for legitimate growth of political, social, legal, and philosophical ideas. The res publica or the 'commonwealth' (in the older English sense) was recognized as the legitimate framework for community life.[3]

In contrast, Islam has a theologically based concept of human dignity. It does not allow for the autonomy of the secular; for the autonomy of civil and political society. Its ideal state is one governed by a 'theocracy,' not in the sense of the rule of a priesthood (because it has no priesthood as such) but the rule of God. Only God makes the law and He occupies the same sovereign position as the polis, the crown or the people in the Western political tradition. Far from creating the law, the state is created by the Holy law and the ruler's role is to defend the law by which he too is bound.[4]

Both Hinduism and Buddhism put community before the egoism pervasive in the contemporary West. But the centrality of the hierarchical caste system in Hinduism makes for fatalism about social rights and social justice and, logically,

---

[2] C.R. Miguel, 'Human Dignity: History of an Idea', pp.3–14; 'Renaissance Idea of the Dignity of Man', *Dictionary of the History of Ideas*, http://etext.lib.virginia.edu/cgi-local/DHI/dhi.cgi?id = dv4–20, 28 September 2004, pp.5–6, 12–23.

[3] Y. Arieli, 'On the Necessary and Sufficient Conditions for the Emergence of the Doctrine of the Dignity of Man and His Rights', pp.11–17.

[4] B. Lewis, *The Political Language of Islam* (Chicago, IL: University of Chicago Press, 1988), pp.30–31.

for support for the existing ruling group. Buddhism focuses on the release of the individual from suffering and it rejects caste. Both religions value human dignity. Thus, Hinduism casts some gods in human form, and Buddhism believes in the intellectual and spiritual capacity of humankind to achieve superhuman wisdom and so release from the world.[5]

Some modern scholars of Chinese culture have identified in Confucianism ideas of human dignity and equality. They see these as points in the culture at which human rights may be nurtured.[6] Yet, they face the problem of the centrality of social and political hierarchy (and the low status afforded women) in Confucianism. Further, it is noteworthy that contemporary Chinese political dissidents and human rights activists do not look to Confucianism in their struggle with the Communist Government, implying any relationship for them between rights and Confucianism is irrelevant and academic.[7]

The daughter of Xu Wenli, one of the leaders of the 1978 'democracy wall' movement (gaoled for 12 years for this 'crime') recently pointed out that Pen-Chung Chang, who played a significant role in the drawing up of the Universal Declaration of Human Rights, 'believed that rights are for everyone, not just westerners.' She continued: 'When the Chinese people have spoken—PC Chang in 1948, Wei Jinsheng, Xu Wenli...in 1978, Tiananmen worker and student demonstrators in 1989, and Xu Wenli again this year—they have claimed their right to all of the universally acknowledged human liberties, not just to a list impoverished by some supposed peculiarity of culture.'[8]

The Growing Inclusiveness of the Idea

In the West prior to the Enlightenment, the exercise of the right to a full measure of dignity and self-determination was restricted to upper class and high-status groups: in Ancient Greece, only the male citizen of the polis, not the woman, noncitizen, slave, or non-Hellene; in Rome, male members of the upper orders, not noncitizens, male members of the lower orders, women, or slaves; in medieval Europe, male members of the nobility and highly placed prelates (and, perhaps, wealthy burghers), not women, serfs, members of the urban lower orders, and non-Christians.

Since the Enlightenment and the great Revolutions of the 17th and 18th centuries (English, American, and French), democratization and universalization of the right to

---

[5] 'Hinduism and Buddhism. A Comparison', http://sc.essortment.com/hinduismandbud_rtqs.htm, 13 October 2004, pp.1–2.

[6] Q. Zhang, 'The Idea of Human Dignity in Classical Chinese Philosophy: A Reconstruction of Confucianism', *Journal of Chinese Philosophy*, 27 (2000), pp.299–323.

[7] M. Svensson, 'Review of Confucianism and Human Rights', *Journal of Asian Studies*, 58 (1999), pp.1–2.

[8] Quoted in M.A. Glendon, *A World Made New. Eleanor Roosevelt and the Universal Declaration of Human Rights* (New York: Random House, 2001), p.221.

dignity has proceeded. Indeed, central to modernity is the rejection of political and moral hierarchies as normative ideals. Western societies over the last three centuries have come to give full political and moral status to non-noble and propertyless men, non-Christians, women, and nonwhites. This process culminated in the Universal Declaration of 1948 when equal moral status was accorded all human beings.[9]

Realizing the Idea in the 1940s

The UN Charter, 1946 and the Universal Declaration of Human Rights, 1948 introduced the concept of human dignity into international law. The latter is the first document in the history of declarations of rights to identify human dignity as the basis of human rights.[10]

The Preamble of the Charter pledges the UN to save humankind from war and reaffirms 'faith… in the dignity and worth of the human person…' The Universal Declaration commences, ' Whereas recognition of the inherent dignity and of the equal and inalienable rights of all members of the human family is the foundation of freedom, justice and peace in the world.' The first article begins, 'All human beings are born free and equal in dignity and rights.' Article 22 states that a person's 'economic, social and cultural rights [are] indispensable for his dignity.' Article 23(3) states that he should receive a remuneration sufficient to provide 'an existence worthy of human dignity.'[11]

Why the Idea is Explicit in the Founding Documents of the UN

There is a significant difference between the Covenant of the League of Nations and the UN Charter that reflects the different historical circumstances out of which each emerged. The Covenant did not use ideals or norms to describe its aims

[9] Y. Arieli, 'On the Necessary and Sufficient Conditions for the Emergence of the Doctrine of the Dignity of Man and His Rights', in: D. Kretzmer and E. Klein (eds.), *The Concept of Human Dignity in Human Rights Discourse*, p.5; M.J. Meyer, 'Dignity as a (Modern) Virtue', in: D. Kretzmer and E. Klein (eds.), *The Concept of Human Dignity in Human Rights Discourse*, p.202; R. Ammicht-Quinn, 'Whose Dignity is Inviolable? Human Beings, Machines and the Discourse of Dignity', in: R. Ammicht-Quinn, M. Junker-Kenny, and E. Tamez (eds.), *The Discourse of Human Dignity* (London: SCM Press, 2003), p.38.

[10] K. Dicke, 'The Founding Function of Human Dignity in the Universal Declaration of Human Rights', in: D. Kretzmer and E. Klein (eds.), *The Concept of Human Dignity in Human Rights Discourse*, pp.111–112.

[11] Quoted in H. Spiegelberg, 'Human Dignity: A Challenge to Contemporary Philosophy', in: R. Gotesky and E. Laszlo (eds.), *Human Dignity. This Century and the Next* (New York: Gordon & Breach, Science Publishers, 1970), p.40.

(although the League was obliged to protect the rights of minorities). But the Charter Preamble expressed its purposes in normative terms.

The differences between the threats to which they were responses help explain this basic contrast. World War I was a struggle between sovereign states having comparable societies, polities, and value systems. Neither side feared defeat would mean utter subjugation of its way of life. However, the traditional balance-of-power system of international relations had resulted in a conflict of unprecedented destructiveness for European civilization so an effort had to be made to ensure it never happened again. That would be through a transcendence of the offending principle of national sovereignty in a supranational global body functioning along quasi-parliamentary lines. But, the victors in World War II had faced an enemy bent on permanent world domination and using military conquest as well as enslavement and genocide of 'racially inferior' peoples to this end. The UN was not to be just a means of resolving international conflicts peacefully, but a tool for realizing in international relations the highest ideals concerning humankind that had evolved in Western thought and practice, especially from the Enlightenment onwards. The Universal Declaration states those ideals and norms. It is, from one perspective, the liberal-democratic world's counterideology to the ideology of the Axis powers.[12]

Among delegates to the 1945 San Francisco conference to discuss establishment of a United Nations organization were some who took seriously the Allied Great Powers' wartime statements of purpose such as Franklin Roosevelt's 1941 ' Four Freedoms' speech that tied peace and security to respect for freedom of speech and of worship, and freedom from want and from fear; and the Allies' 1942 declaration that the purpose of victory was 'to defend life, liberty, independence and religious freedom and to preserve human rights and justice in their own lands as well as in other lands.'[13]

Carlos Romulo of the Philippines, who was a wartime aide to General Douglas MacArthur and had won a Pulitzer Prize in 1941 for newspaper articles arguing colonialism in Asia would soon end, was one who worked hard to have the interests of smaller nations recognized by the Great Powers who were intent only on furthering their own interests. Supported by the Soviet Union, he managed to have included in the Preamble of the UN Charter as a purpose of the UN the 'self-determination of peoples.' Romulo and representatives of Brazil, Egypt, India, Panama, Uruguay, Mexico, the Dominican Republic, Cuba, and Venezuala pushed for inclusion of anti-discrimination statements. Supported by China, France, and the Soviet Union, they had included in the Charter the statement that all should enjoy human rights 'without distinction as to race, sex, language, or religion.'[14]

Australia's Minister for External Affairs, Herbert Vere Evatt was another who argued for the interests of the small powers. With widespread support, he proposed to

[12] Y. Arieli, 'On the Necessary and Sufficient Conditions for the Emergence of the Doctrine of the Dignity of Man and His Rights', pp.1–3.

[13] Quoted in M.A. Glendon, *A World Made New*, pp.10–11.

[14] Ibid., p.13.

limit the individual veto power of the five permanent members of the Security Council—Britain, China, France, the US and the Soviet Union. The Great Powers would simply not countenance such a limit on their individual freedom of action, and President Truman privately asked the Australian Prime Minister to restrain his Minister. Evatt, however, was more successful in arguing security could only be preserved if there was an effort to promote economic and social justice, and especially full employment. Again with wide support, he was able to have included in the Charter provision for an Economic and Social Council, which was to be a principal organ of the UN.

Another delegate of the same outlook was Charles Malik of the new Republic of Lebanon. He argued that peace and security could only be reliably based on genuine justice within and between nations.

Support was forthcoming from delegates of the Latin American nations. Just prior to the San Francisco conference, 25 had agreed to call for a declaration of rights to be included in the Charter. Panama proposed a bill and was supported by Cuba, Chile, and Mexico. While accepting inclusion of rights in the statement of the UN's concerns, the US would not support the Latin American proposal to include a bill in the Charter and also provision for a commission on education, culture, and rights.

Over 40 nongovernmental organizations—mainly American—were in San Francisco as observers and consultants. They included legal associations, labor and peace organizations, and Catholic, Protestant, and Jewish groups. They too pressed for recognition of rights. Some of the American bodies met Edward Stettinius, the US Secretary of State. The representative of the Joint Committee for Religious Liberty called for America to follow its best traditions; the representative of the American Jewish Committee pointed to the strength of support for rights among American voters; the representative of the Congress of Industrial Organizations stressed labor's support; Walter White of the National Association for the Advancement of Colored People wanted the colonial peoples included in protection of rights; Clark Eichelberger of the American Association for the United Nations asked for a commission on human rights.

Critically, the US agreed to a Human Rights Commission, and the Soviet Union, knowing the Charter protected it from intervention in domestic matters, did not oppose it.

Brazil, Canada, Chile, Cuba, the Dominican Republic, Egypt, France, Haiti, India, Mexico, New Zealand, Panama, and Uruguay pressed for even more recognition of rights in the Charter, and the first shocking photographs from German concentration camps heightened the feeling in support of this. Speaking at the signing of the Charter, President Truman said he looked forward to the construction of an international bill of rights.[15]

As one scholar has recently noted, the idea of human dignity was 'in the air' at this time.[16] One view of human dignity drew on the Christian, onto-theological

---

[15] Ibid., pp.11–19.

[16] Quoted in K. Dicke, 'The Founding Function of Human Dignity in the Universal Declaration of Human Rights', p.112.

concept of a 'person' developed by Aquinas. The draft Bill of Rights produced by the Catholic Bishops of America thus stated that human dignity is 'a synonym for human worth, the inherent excellence of the human person as distinguished from any other living creature.'[17] A similar concept is embodied in a draft Bill drawn up by the American Jewish Committee: ' the individual human being is the cornerstone of our culture and our civilization. All that we cherish must rest on the dignity and inviolability of the person, of his sacred right to live and to develop under God, in whose image he was created.'[18] There also existed the then more marginal concept, best known in France and Germany, from the natural law, legal tradition stretching back to the stoics of the equality of humans based on their individual capacity to reason.

German scholar, Klaus Dicke argues that a set of principles are needed to regulate the relationship between dignity and rights. In Locke they are 'life, liberty, property'; in the American Declaration of Independence, 'life, liberty and the pursuit of happiness'; and in the French Revolution, 'liberty, equality, fraternity.' He sees 'freedom, equality and participation in a political, social and international order' as the regulative principles of the Universal Declaration. They are goods essential to a life of dignity. He concludes that the Universal Declaration highlights the ethical unity of humankind underneath the cultural and religious differences and the conflicts of national interests.[19]

Other commentators see conceptions of dignity deeply influenced by culture and religion. Societies that historically and culturally make the individual central have political regimes which emphasize individual rights against state power and society. Those that have a history of conformity and acceptance of a defined body of values and norms emphasize the individual's duties to the community, God, or the state. In the Islamic tradition, 'human rights exist only in relation to human obligations. Individuals possess certain obligations toward God, fellow humans, and nature, all of which are defined by the Shariah.'[20]

In the constitutions of many liberal democratic, European states such as Germany, Belgium, Sweden, and Switzerland, not only are dignity and rights closely connected but also the first justifies the second. In nonliberal states like China and Iran, dignity is discussed in terms of duties to the collective. The Chinese Constitution says the people of China ' have the duty to uphold the dignity of the Constitution and ensure its implementation' and 'the state upholds the uniformity and dignity of the socialist legal system.' The Iranian Constitution based on faith in Allah and Shiite Islam says that, 'It is incumbent on all to adhere to the principles of this Constitution, for it regards as its highest aim the freedom and dignity of the

---

[17] Ibid., p.113.

[18] Ibid., p.113.

[19] K. Dicke, 'The Founding Function of Human Dignity in the Universal Declaration of Human Rights', pp.118–120.

[20] Quoted in D. Shultziner, 'Human Dignity—Functions and Meanings', *Global Jurist Topics*, 3 (2003), p.7.

human race and provides for the growth and development of the human being.' The Islamic Republic is:

> a system based on belief in: the exalted dignity and value of man, and his freedom coupled with responsibility before God; in which equity, justice, political, economic, social and cultural independence, and national solidarity are secured by recourse to: (a) continuous leadership of the holy persons, possessing necessary qualifications, exercised on the basis of the Koran and the Sunnah, upon all of whom be peace.[21]

The Thai Constitution reveals another culturally different interpretation of dignity. The dignity and rights of individuals are recognized, but so also is the citizen's duty to dignify the King who must not be exposed to any sort of accusation or action:

> May the Thai people unite in...upholding the Constitution...to maintain the democratic regime of government and sovereign power derived from the Thai people, and to bring about happiness, prosperity, and dignity to His Majesty's subjects... according to the will of His Majesty in every respect.[22]

What the Draftsmen of the Universal Declaration Appear to have Hoped for

On 10 December 1948, the day the UN adopted the Universal Declaration, the chair of the human rights commission, Eleanor Roosevelt, told the General Assembly:

> This Declaration may well become the international Magna Carta of all men everywhere. We hope its proclamation... will be an event comparable to the proclamation of the Declaration of the Rights of Man by the French people of 1789, the adoption of the Bill of Rights by the people of the United States, and the adoption of comparable declarations at different times in other countries.[23]

Three scholars had assisted her with the drafting—Chinese philosopher and diplomat, Pen-Chung Chang; Lebanese philosopher, Ambassador to the US, and rapporteur of the Human Rights Commission, Charles Malik; and French legal scholar and adviser to De Gaulle during the War, Rene Cassin.

Already in 1946, a number of philosophers including Jacques Maritain of France and Richard McKeon of England had been asked by UNESCO to explore the idea of rights cross-culturally. They reported a consensus across cultures concerning some basic rights. In 1947–1948, the tortuous process of drafting the Universal Declaration took place. John Humphrey, Canadian lawyer and Director of the Human Rights Division of the UN Secretariat, and his team used input from various sources including the philosophers, various nongovernmental organizations, the International Labour Organization and some Catholic and Jewish bodies to produce

---

[21] Ibid., p.9.

[22] Ibid., p.9.

[23] Quoted in M.R. Ishay, *The History of Human Rights. From Ancient Times to the Globalization Era* (Berkeley: University of California Press, 2004), p.218.

a first draft of the Declaration. But the document of 400 pages was too unwieldy and Rene Cassin was given the task of drafting what was then called the International Bill of Rights. He drew on the French Declaration of the Rights of Man, the Magna Carta and writs of habeas corpus. Cassin's preamble was voted down. The rest of the document was analyzed article by article by members of the UN General assembly's third committee chaired by Charles Malik.

Malik was asked by Roosevelt to draft the preamble to the Declaration and appears to have made four significant contributions to the overall document:

(a) The preamble (with some stylistic changes by Cassin) which was accepted unanimously.
(b) To article 18, Malik (a Christian Arab) added the right to change one's religion and to worship in public and in private. Although under Sharia law, conversion from Islam is punishable by death, the Pakistani representative, Zafrullah Khan, persuaded Islamic countries to abstain and the amended article was passed unanimously; South Africa also abstained as it was potentially at odds with its apartheid policy.
(c) Malik reinforced the document against selective observance of rights through article 28 that stated all rights were available to everyone.
(d) Malik masterfully pushed the draft Declaration through 85 meetings of the committee (and against the delaying tactics of the Soviets), knowing that the speedily emerging cold war conflict would destroy the project unless a final text went to an Assembly vote before the close of 1948.[24]

Concerning the cross-cultural relevance of the Declaration, it is worth noting that besides the European and North American members of the third committee, six Asian countries were members—China, India, Pakistan, Burma, the Philippines, and Thailand; nine members were predominantly Islamic in culture—Afghanistan, Egypt, Iran, Iraq, Pakistan, Saudi Arabia, Syria, Turkey, and Yemen; three had considerable Buddhist populations—Burma, China, and Thailand; there was a large and vocal group of Latin American nations; and there were two black African members—Ethiopia and Liberia. Moreover, six of the European members were allies of the Soviet Union. It might be argued the dignitarian rights tradition of continental Europe and Latin America with its emphasis on the family and community was as influential in the drafting of the Declaration as the Anglo-American, individualistic rights tradition.

The universality of the Declaration has been subsequently reinforced by the fact that it has guided the rights sections of ninety odd constitutions of nations created after its formulation; and by the fact that by mid-2000, 144 nations had seen fit to sign the International Covenant on Civil and political Rights, and 142 the Covenant on Economic, Social, and Cultural Rights.[25]

---

[24] 'A Conversation with Habib Malik', http://usinfo.state.gov/journals/itdhr/1098/ijdp/habib.htm.

[25] Quoted in M.A. Glendon, *A World Made New*, pp.227–228.

How International Politics Shaped the Response to the Declaration

Fifty of the 58 UN members voted for the (nonbinding) Declaration. The eight abstaining were Byelorussia, Czechoslovakia, Poland, Saudi Arabia, South Africa, Ukraine, the Soviet Union, and Yugoslavia. They saw it as too individualistic and feared it would conflict with domestic law and custom.

The cold war was developing, and the Soviet Union put the emphasis on social and economic rights while the US put it on political and civil rights. Indeed, Roosevelt had had a struggle to persuade President Truman that socioeconomic clauses should be included in the Universal Declaration. She had argued that they flowed logically from President Roosevelt's 'Four Freedoms.' But, the US made clear it did not see them as implying 'an obligation on governments to assure the enjoyment of these rights by direct government action.'[26]

There was continuing conflict within the commission about the relationship between the two sets of rights and it was only resolved by a decision to embody each set in a separate covenant. Roosevelt endorsed a General Assembly resolution put forward by India stating that while just as basic, economic, social, and cultural rights formed a separate category of rights from the civil and political rights because they were justiciable rights and their method of implementation was different.

Developing nations like India and Egypt supported the Soviet's advocacy of social and economic rights, but as poor countries, they did not want to be forced into premature implementation of such rights.

Two covenants relating to the Declaration were adopted by the General Assembly in 1966. They have had legal force from 1976. The first concerned civil and political rights, omitting the right to property at the insistence of the Soviet Union, and the second concerned economic, social, and cultural rights. The first required its rights to be implemented straightaway; the second, progressively, so allowing for capacity to realize such rights.[27]

Globalization and Human Dignity

Globalization in the sense of increasing interconnectedness and transnational flows of people, goods, and services, and capital can be identified by any number of indicators: for example, in 1960 there were 70-million international tourists, in 1995, almost 500 million; in 1900, there were 176 nongovernmental organizations with international concerns, in the early 1990s, almost 29,000; and in the later 1990s, more than $1 trillion a day moved through foreign exchange markets across the world, representing over 50 times the value of world trade.

[26] Quoted in M.A. Glendon, *A World Made New*, p.186.

[27] M.R. Ishay, *The History of Human Rights*, pp.218–224.

Globalization is eroding the boundaries of the modern nation-state, historically one of its key-defining characteristics. It is also eroding the capacity of the state to meet its responsibilities for human rights, especially social and economic rights. At the same time, regional and global machinery for implementing human rights remains weak. The irony is that human rights have been elevated to a global ideology (although a contested one) and nongovernmental organizations pursue the politics of rights to an unprecedented extent just when the conditions for realization of rights have become more problematic as the economic pressures of globalization and the end of the cold war have undermined the case for 'big government.' The gap between the universalization of the idea of rights —at the 1993 World Conference on Human Rights representatives of international nongovernmental organizations almost outnumbered those of states—and the political, economic, and social conditions required for realization has widened.

Acceptance of the idea of rights and the international monitoring of them have, thus, grown greatly. Yet rights abuses in East Timor, Somalia, Rwanda, Sudan, and the former Yugoslavia have been on an appalling scale. Unlike the 19th-century nationalism that promoted democracy and rights, contemporary 'tribal' nationalism manifest in these abuses has been hostile to rights. Further, the intense economic competition inherent in globalization is threatening economic and social rights.

Human rights, and the concomitant concept of human dignity, developed internationally within the postwar environment of sovereign states committed to providing welfare. Now, even in the wealthiest of countries the capacity of the state to sustain high levels of welfare is constrained by the fear of migration of capital and jobs to lower-wage and lower-taxing countries. But a new global politics of rights has emerged, and along with it has, arguably, come an embryonic, global civil society that seeks empowerment of citizens, not state power.[28] On the other hand, globalization has evoked fundamentalist reactions that call on religious and other 'local,' cultural traditions, which challenge the universalist, liberal notions of rights and dignity. Thus, the politics of global human rights encourages both cooperation and conflict.

There has been a great deal of discussion of the tension between universalism and particularism and between cosmopolitanism and local communitarianism in contemporary human rights. And it is true that while abstract systems of economics and communications bind us together globally, we are certainly not integrated in normative terms. There is no single, global, moral community; rather, diversity of values and ways of life are the order of the day. This was well illustrated at the 1993 World Conference on Human Rights in Vienna where Islamic and Asian countries criticized the universalist claims of the Universal Declaration on Human Rights and other UN rights documents as too much based on Western individualism. Yet, significantly, they did not go so far as to reject them altogether. Indeed,

[28] For a trenchant criticism of the unrepresentativeness of the global civil society being created by international nongovernmental organizations, and a defence of the accountable, democratic nation state against the 'transnational progressives' obsession with the human rights of individuals, see J. Fonte, 'Democracy's Trojan Horse', *The National Interest*, Summer 2004, <www.findarticles.co/p/articles/mi_2751/is_76/ai_n6127318>, 20 January 2005, p.1–3.

the representatives of 171 countries reaffirmed their 'commitment to the purposes and principles contained in the Charter of the United Nations and the Universal Declaration of Human Rights.'[29]

The issue goes beyond 'culture wars,' especially between Western and non-Western traditions, or even commitment to particular cultural traditions. A global order based on unrestrained free-market principles produces international and intra-national economic and social inequities that when large enough make it impossible for many people to live a dignified life. They destroy the conditions necessary to the flourishing of human dignity among those at the lower end of the socioeconomic hierarchy, whether national or international.

Moreover, the normative discourse of rights is now largely linked to an international society of states, not individuals. But as we have already noted, even in states which display goodwill toward human rights, capacity of governments to deliver social, economic, and welfare rights in the face of the economic pressures of globalization may be quite limited. The future of human rights seems to need to be grounded in new political and ethical concepts. The idea of global citizenship or some other way of establishing global democracy and political participation will have to be realized, but quite how is still unclear. Similarly, a new global ethics based on the concept of human dignity (or of a duty of 'care') will have to be realized in a less state-centred world.[30] For all its problems of definition, and its strong historical association with Western ethical and political thought, the concept of human dignity may be able to play a significant, transcendental, guiding role of an ethical sort as we inch toward a new global, ethical, and political order.

---

[29] Quoted in M.A. Glendon, *A World Made New*, p.228.

[30] A.G. McGrew, 'Human Rights in a Global Age: Coming to Terms with Globalization' in: T. Evans (ed.), *Human Rights Fifty Years On. A Reappraisal* (Manchester: Manchester University Press, 1998), pp.189–206; T. Evans, 'Introduction: Power, Hegemony and the Universalization of Human Rights' in: T. Evans (ed.), *Human Rights Fifty Years On*, pp.16–20.

II
Human Dignity in Context

9
A Journey Towards Understanding: True and False Dignity

Christina Mason

Before proceeding with any discussion of dignity, I need to say a little about the work I do in London, which clearly has an influence on my understanding of the subject. My place of work is St. Joseph's Hospice in the East End of London. We offer a service of palliative care to several London boroughs, particularly Tower Hamlets, Hackney and City, and Newham. From the point of view of economic indicators, these boroughs are amongst the poorest in the whole UK, but in terms of cultural, ethnic, and religious variation they are wonderfully rich and vibrant. As I write, St. Joseph's is in the midst of celebrating the centenary of its foundation. During the first years of the 20th century, a small group of nuns, from the Irish Sisters of Charity, came from Dublin to London's East End to minister to the sick and poor. On 15 January 1905, the hospice took care of its first inpatient.

I came to work at St. Joseph's on 1 April 1996 as Director of Social Work and, from this time until early in 2004, I worked with a team of social workers, counsellors, and psychotherapists to provide social and psychological care to patients and their families and friends. In January 2004, I was offered the post of Director of Research at St. Joseph's and although the main focus of my work has changed, I maintain a clinical presence in my role as supervisor of the counselling work of five staff, and in offering counselling support to people who have been bereaved.

Working as I do in this large hospice, I am well used to the word dignity being used. Indeed, the pursuance of dignity is one of the central tenets of St. Joseph's Mission statement. 'Dignity is Respect for the uniqueness of each person, created in the image of God, listening with an open ear and ensuring effective communication at all time.'[1] So the idea of dignity is central to my everyday work. My particular contribution to this volume, however, is to provide some brief consideration of dignity in literature, and what I will aim to do here is to start from that point, and the attempt to relate what I have learnt from literature to clinical practice.

I am going to concentrate on two works of literature and examine some of the different ideas that were provoked when I began to explore this topic. The first work is *A Passage to India*, by E.M. Forster and the second is *The Remains of the Day* by Kazuo Ishiguro. I chose these two books for the following reasons: both have been

[1] St. Joseph's Hospice, *Mission Statement* (ca.1980).

J. Malpas and N. Lickiss (eds.), Perspectives on Human Dignity: A Conversation, 109–118.

made into films; both have had a fairly wide readership; both are extraordinary as works of literature; both are books that have made an enormous impression on me personally; both involve journeys; both have something important to say about dignity itself—in *The Remains of the Day*, explicitly, in *A Passage to India*, covertly.

A Passage to India was completed in 1924 and is set, for the most part, in India at the time of the British Raj. There are a number of prominent characters but I only want to mention four: Adela Quested, Mrs. Moore, Ronny Heaslop, and Dr. Aziz. Adela Quested is a young woman who is accompanying her friend and future mother in law, Mrs. Moore, to Chandrapore where the two women will meet with Mrs. Moore's son, Ronny Heaslop. Ronny and Adela have met in Britain and the primary purpose of the visit to India is to confirm the engagement between the couple. Not long after their arrival, Mrs. Moore meets an Indian doctor called Dr. Aziz, while she is taking an evening walk by herself near and in a mosque. Dr. Aziz is in an angry mood. He had just had his evening ruined by the ill-mannered demands of his boss, an Englishman called Major Callender and he also had been snubbed by the major's wife, Mrs. Callender. He is taking rest in the mosque. He is then disturbed by Mrs. Moore and is initially hostile towards her. He challenges her about her footwear. But, to his surprise, she has taken her shoes off and thus respected the culture and traditions of the mosque. Dr. Aziz is disarmed. He and Mrs. Moore find an affinity and begin to speak of children, domestic concerns, and his grievances as he accompanies her back to the English club that he is not allowed to enter.

One of the important themes in this book and indeed in all E.M. Forster's writing is the theme of connection. *Only connect* is a phrase found in several of Forster's works.[2] E.M. Forster tried to reconcile conflict in all aspects of human life. In his writing the most successful connections between individuals are those unplanned moments of grace and it is one of these moments that occurs between Dr. Aziz and Mrs. Moore in the mosque. The word dignity is not used. But it seems to me that in acknowledging the integrity of the Islamic culture, and being obedient to its rules of conduct in the mosque, Mrs. Moore reaches across the racial divisions and the conflict between the rulers and the ruled. By the simple act of removing her shoes she demonstrates her respect for the inherent dignity of all human beings, whatever their colour, ethnicity, religion, or culture.

Dr. Aziz, when he discovers the way in which Mrs. Moore affirms his dignity and treats him with respect, pays her a great compliment. 'You are an Oriental'[3] he says; and later in the book Mrs. Moore is imbued with almost mystical powers by the Indian population. They chant 'Esmiss Esmoor, Esmiss Esmoor'.[4] Although she herself dies on the way back to Britain and is buried at sea, her spirit lives on in the person of another of her sons, Ralph, and he is an important point of connection and healing in the last section of the book.

---

[2] E.M. Forster, *A Passage to India* (London: Penguin, 1979) and *Howard's End* (London: Penguin, 1910).

[3] Forster, *A Passage to India*, p.41.

[4] Ibid., Chapter 24.

Now I want to turn away from Forster's book and discuss *The Remains of the Day*. This book is about many things, one of them, a central one in fact, is a fascinating discourse on the subject of dignity. The four characters that I mention are father and son, Stevens senior and Stevens junior who are both butlers, Miss Kenton, and Lord Darlington, one time owner of Darlington Hall.

The Remains of the Day was first published in 1989. The novel is centred primarily around a motoring trip that Stevens junior makes in 1956. Stevens has been a butler for the whole of his adult life and quite a lot of it has been spent in the service of Lord Darlington at Darlington Hall. At the time of Stevens' journey, Lord Darlington has died and an American has bought the Hall. In contrast to the Hall in the 1930s, Stevens is now operating with a skeleton staff and the purpose of his motoring journey is to visit Miss Kenton, to see if she again might be free to work at Darlington Hall.

The whole book is structured and framed by this motoring trip to Cornwall, which is a metaphor for a psychological journey. Stevens is the narrator and as he proceeds on his motoring and psychological journey, he reminisces on his life as a butler in Darlington Hall, covering the time period of 1922 into the 1930s. The narrative moves from present to past and back again. Stevens, as he remembers the past begins to face facts and emotions that he had shut out for years. Central to his reminiscences and his process of self discovery is the question Stevens asks himself, and discusses with others, what constitutes a 'great' butler. Indeed, it is as if he is obsessed with this question and it is only later that we begin to understand why. At the heart of his thinking about what constitutes a great butler is his concept of dignity.

Stevens cites his own father, Stevens senior, as an example of a great butler who demonstrated a dignity in keeping with his position. He gives examples of dignity that reveal that a butler must be able to remain in the role of butler no matter what the circumstances. Stevens concludes that the very best butlers wear their professionalism as decent gentlemen wear their suits. But, he seems to mean even more than that as the reader discovers on the fourth day of Stevens' journey. He is discussing the idea of dignity with one of the people he meets, and he puts forward the notion that dignity is about 'not removing one's clothing in Public'. In other words, he believes that a butler must become a butler rather than merely acting like one. Dignity has to do crucially with the butler's ability *not* to abandon the professional being he inhabits. To achieve *dignity and its crucial link with greatness* it seems that Stevens believes he must even separate himself from himself. Stevens uses very formal language. He seldom uses the personal pronoun 'I', almost always using 'one' when describing his own actions and thoughts. He gives pedantic attention to correctness and to detail.

Stevens links dignity with detachment and restraint. Indeed, so great is his emotional restraint that he continues to work and serve at table while his father is dying in a room close by. His view of appropriate detachment will not allow him to look closely at what his employer really thinks or does. He denies his own opinions on the Nazi sympathies Lord Darlington expresses. He shuts himself and his own humanity away, and distances himself from his feelings of love for the housekeeper, Miss Kenton, from anger at the firing of two Jewish maids by his employer, from sadness at the decline and death of his father.

As his journey proceeds, Stevens travels closer to acknowledging what he has made of his life. He comes face to face with himself, with his life, and sees it for its waste and emptiness and desolation. At the end of the book he makes the discovery that there is a universe of difference between the dignity he has sought as a butler and the dignity associated with being simply a human being. He says:

> Lord Darlington wasn't a bad man—And at least he had the privilege of being able to say at the end of his life that he made his own mistakes—He chose a certain path in life, it proved to be a misguided one, but there, he chose it, he can say that at least. As for myself, I cannot even claim that—I can't even say I made my own mistakes. Really—one has to ask oneself—what dignity is there in that?[5]

It is the end of the book and nearly the end of his journey. Stevens meets a man who by coincidence is a retired butler. They sit in drizzly rain and have an honest straightforward conversation. Stevens cries. He pours out his feelings, admitting that he blindly followed Lord Darlington and that he has no real dignity. He has set a butler's dignity above human dignity, and realises that human dignity must always come first. Stevens for the first time is deeply and movingly in touch with his feelings. This overall exchange shows that Stevens has attained dignity even though he does not yet realise it. Stevens has thrown off the false dignity of role and reached the core of his dignity as a human being, aware of his own thoughts, feelings, and vulnerabilities.

I turn now to what I see in these books that highlights my understanding of dignity, and that I can take forward into my work as well as my life. So Mrs. Moore and Stevens, what are you saying to us, today in 2005?

Mrs. Moore in *A Passage to India* wears no uniform. She has no role to play. She is an older woman with a lifetime of experience behind her who has come on a journey to India to meet her son. She approaches the people she meets as herself and without any of the expectations or trappings of a role. She meets people as they are. She listens to them. She makes contact that is effective, and she connects. By contrast, Stevens in *The Remains of the Day*, sees the nature of dignity as part of the role that he puts on. That role is low in social status but it gives him a place and a sense of worth in the hierarchical scheme of things. He is not aware until right at the end of the book that in becoming so attached to his role, he has discarded the dignity that lies at the centre of his humanity. Indeed he fears that if he takes off his role or clothes he will lose his dignity. Mrs. Moore reached out, listened, made contact, connected. Stevens hid behind his role; he distanced himself. He made no real, effective contact, and ended not only a disappointed man, but also a man who from the depths cried out about his wasted life. In my work I meet many people who are like Stevens, afraid to make connections as sentient human beings, and who hide behind the uniform of their professional roles. How did they (and Stevens) become like this?

A great deal of work, consisting of empirical observation of children, theorising about developmental processes, and, more recently, experiments in neurophysiology has indicated that the very earliest days of babyhood and later of childhood are vital for their future development as adults. The way babies are held, fed, changed, touched, smiled at, and so on, can give that child a sense of worth—in other words,

---

[5] K. Ishiguro, *The Remains of the Day* (London: Faber &Faber, 1996). p.243.

a sense of dignity. A useful metaphor for this process is the phrase of an early American sociologist, 'the looking glass self'.[6] This is the idea that a person's sense of self develops as parents, siblings, teachers, friends, and so on, reflect and indeed help to create a person's self-image which is then taken into adult life.

John Bowlby[7] in Britain and Daniel Stern[8] in America are among the many psychologists and psychotherapists who have shown how difficulties in forming attachments with others, as well as other psychological and social difficulties can start developing as a result of deleterious childhood experiences.

At this point, I want to refer to a theme that has appeared in a number of the essays in this volume, the theme of mutuality. Jeff Malpas[9] illustrated mutuality as a triangle of self–others–world; Sir Guy Green[10] used the picture of the overlapping circles in a Venn diagram to describe the same idea. Our dignity, our sense of worth is tied to others, and those with low self worth will find great difficulty in affirming the worth of others. That often quoted expression, you cannot love or care for others until you are able to love or care for yourself is in part an expression of this. And I do also wonder if the seeming absence of empathy that leads to the most horrendous acts of cruelty and destruction finds its roots in the kind of developmental deficiencies that I have been describing.

But to return to the professional role, the 18th-century surgeon anatomist William Hunter urged his students to gain what he called *a necessary inhumanity* by dissecting the dead.[11] Perhaps this kind of rite of passage into a profession might have been necessary when anaesthesia was not available. For decades following, however, there seems to have been a tendency in the education of health professionals to train out the personal and emotional responses of practitioners to the suffering they were witnessing.

Recognising some of these difficulties, at least as they relate to doctors, the British General Medical Committee in 1993 suggested a major change of curriculum with 30% of the timetable to be allocated to special study modules in, amongst other things, medical humanities.[12]

There appear to be three purposes to the study of humanities:

- To enable students to understand the experience and perspectives of patients
- To examine motivations underlying professional practice
- To connect through a shared humanity with individuals coming for care[13]

---

[6] C. Cooley, *Human Nature and the Social Order* (New York: Scribner, 1902).

[7] J. Bowlby, *Attachment* (London: Hogarth, 1969); J. Bowlby, *Separation* (London: Hogarth, 1973); J. Bowlby, *Loss Sadness and Depression* (London: Hogarth, 1980).

[8] D. Stern, *The Interpersonal World of the Human Infant* (New York: Basic Books, 1984).

[9] Jeff Malpas, 'Human Dignity and Human Being', Chapter 3, this volume.

[10] Guy Green, 'Human Dignity and the Law', Chapter 14, this volume.

[11] W. Hunter, *Introductory Lectures to Students*, St. Thomas' Hospital Manuscript, 55(182) (c1. 780).

[12] General Medical Council, *Tomorrow's Doctors: Recommendations on Undergraduate Medical Education* (London: General Medical Council, 1993).

[13] D. Kirklin and R. Richardson (eds.), *Medical Humanities: A Practical Introduction* (London: Royal College of Physicians, 2001).

The recommendations of the GMC also bring to the forefront the long-term recognition that one of the most important aspects of healing is the relationship that exists between the healer and the one who is requiring to be healed. And absolutely central to the relationship is the person, the actual self, the unique person of the practitioner or healer. Rather than being a neutral and objective agent, the health professional is seen as central to the work of healing. Yalom, a prominent existential therapist has written that, *the effective therapist cannot remain detached, passive and hidden.*[14]

Stevens, the butler needed to make a journey to discover the self behind the *mask*, the *uniform*, and the *role*. Professionals often too need to make journeys, not in a car to Cornwall, but through the process of reflective practice to discover what might lie behind the mask, the uniform, and the professional role. Practitioners begin to recognise that their own psychological processes, including the ones they would prefer to remain hidden, may sometimes be a liability, but may also be an asset. One of the things that came over strongly from the group of medical doctors who were attending the colloquium, was the potential to become vulnerable in their work with people who are facing serious illnesses and end-of-life care. Unfortunately depression, physical and psychosomatic illnesses, total burn out, and even suicide amongst health care professionals are not uncommon. This may be linked to the observation that one of the most common experiences in health care practice is the experience of loss and disappointment. Yet most of this loss remains unacknowledged. Practitioners rarely fully grieve the losses experienced in their work. An American paediatrician called Ruth Remen[15] had been working for several years during which many of the children she had cared for had died. She had grieved for none of these children. Many years later she began to experience a series of dreams, disturbing in their content. With help she began to realise that the very real care and concern she had felt for these children, and the great sadness she felt when they had died, had never been acknowledged. She wrote of this experience, 'the expectation that we can be immersed in suffering and loss daily and not be touched by it is as unrealistic as expecting to be able to walk through water without getting wet'.[16]

Professional work is emotionally costly and sometimes very difficult indeed. The way we deal with loss can shape our capacity to be present in life and be present to clients in their pain. Reflecting on our feelings of loss in whatever way is personally and culturally appropriate is extremely important. Maybe all that will be needed is to speak with a colleague. But sometimes clients will impact at a very deep level and on occasions such as these, professional supervision or techniques like creative writing can be very helpful.

I have been arguing that one of the very important aspects of healing, whatever the location or context in which it takes place, is the way in which the self of the

[14] I. Yalom, *Existential Psychotherapy* (New York: Basic Books, 1980), p.411.

[15] R. Remen, *Kitchen Table Wisdom* (New York: Riverhead Books, 1996)

[16] Ibid., p.52.

practitioner is brought into the process. I believe profoundly in relationship and the potential of relationship to both hurt and to heal. There are many avenues of such healing. Here I identify six.

1. *Listening* – I suspect that the most basic and powerful way to connect to another person is to listen fully and deeply to what he or she is saying. Mrs. Moore listened, was in touch with her own basic humanity and through it was able to affirm the dignity of others. Stevens, misguided Stevens, who thought that dignity was about hiding within the anonymity of his uniform, was trapped in his role and unable to listen. In the process of listening attention is given fully to the other. It sounds so simple. But it is also remarkable. Listening without judgement affirms the validity *and* the dignity of the other. Listening gives the opportunity for the development of wholeness. As Remen notes, *when you listen generously to people, they can hear truth in themselves, often for the first time.*[17] Although it sounds so basic and unproblematic, listening is a demanding skill especially when the risk is taken to allow clients to touch the tender places of the professional's own self.
2. *Sharing our Humanity* – Carl Rogers,[18] an American psychotherapist who was the founder of the person-centred movement, is said to have taken time before every session to remember his humanity; to remember that, above all else, he was a human being like each and every one of the people who came to him for help. I sometimes wonder how hard we work at trying to get away from our humanity. Certainly the butler Stevens tried very hard indeed to remain in the role of the butler and sought complete perfection in that role. Winnicott[19] coined the phrase 'good enough' in relation to parenting. But in the high-aspiring world of the now 21st century, how many of us can accept such a standard? I certainly became convinced in the early stages of my career that it was not enough to be 'good enough' and tried to make myself other than I am.
3. *Living with Uncertainty and Mystery* – Casement[20] writes that one of the losses involved in training is that it is possible to become deaf to the unexpected and blind to what is different and strange. This can come about because in training we learn about theories, of causation, of cure, and of much else. There is nothing wrong with theories as such, provided they are seen for what they are; a way of structuring complex data, or a way of structuring the world so that we are saved from the anxiety that comes from a feeling that all is chaos. In working with people in distress, if we are able to allow the strangeness and newness of *this* person's unique experience to occupy our attention, we can perhaps deal more ably with the immediacy and reality of this person's unhappiness, perplexity or fear.[21]

---

[17] Ibid., p.220.

[18] C. Rogers, *On Becoming a Person: The Therapist's View of Psychotherapy* (London: Constable, 1967).

[19] D. Winnicott, *The Family and Individual Development* (London: Tavistock, 1965).

[20] P. Casement, *On Learning from the Patient* (London: Routledge, 1985).

[21] A. Campbell, *Rediscovering Palliative Care* (London: Darton, Longman and Todd, 1981), p.105.

4. *The Power of Love* – Many practitioners are taught during their training that it is necessary to be objective in working with people and Sir William Osler[22] is used to support this contention. He is said to have advised objectivity. The word used by Osler, however, was the Latin for 'equanimity' and this is much better translated as 'calmness of mind' or 'inner peace' and has nothing to do with objectivity or the sense of emotional distance that is often associated with the word. Rather than objectivity, I would suggest that engagement and involvement are the aspects of relationship that are important in healing. I would even venture further and suggest that love plays a significant part in healing! Here I am referring to the kind of unconditional love which demands nothing in return and wants only the growth and fulfilment of the loved one. It is a strengthening love, a love that, by definition, does not burden or obligate the loved one.[23] Hobson equates love with tenderness and says 'without tenderness the noise of our talk does harm'.[24]
5. *Presence* – Caring presence is a primary principle in healing and refers largely to the non-instrumental aspects of relationship. Because it is so difficult to explain caring presence and its impact, I am going to illustrate it by a story that I think shows it in action. The story is based on a real-life situation; names have been disguised:
   Michelle is a student social worker working in a large English hospice. She has been there for two weeks and has been to the wards to observe her practice teacher and to complete some assessments of new patients. It was Monday morning and her practice teacher said to her, 'I want you to go and be with Margaret. She was unwell yesterday and was calling out a lot. She has no support from relatives and the ward is extremely busy at the moment with new admissions from the weekend.' Michelle asked her teacher what she should say and do. She felt nervous. Margaret was only 24 and Michelle felt it as a terrible tragedy that this young woman should be so ill. Michelle was told that she needed to sit with Margaret and focus on her experience and her needs. Michelle felt even more nervous when she heard this. She thought it was far easier to be doing something practical to help. Michelle went to see Margaret, who looked extremely anxious and had clearly deteriorated over the weekend. Michelle began to speak of all the things she had done over the weekend. Initially Margaret seemed interested but then it was clear that her attention wandered, and she became agitated and restless. After what seemed an interminable silence, Michelle said 'How are you? Is there anything I can do for you? Are you in pain?' Margaret looked at Michelle and said, 'I'm tired of all this, but I am also frightened. I don't know what I want except for all this to be over.' Still feeling uncomfortable, Michelle started to concentrate not on what she could do or say,

[22] W. Osler, *The Principles and Practice of Medicine* (New York: Appleton, 1892).

[23] M. Kahn, *Between Therapist and Client: The New Relationship* (New York: Freeman, 1997), p.39.

[24] R. Hobson, *Forms of Feeling: The Heart of Psychotherapy* (London: Routledge, 1985), p.280.

but on what she could understand of Margaret's situation. She stilled her mind and gave her attention to Margaret. Then she reached out and very gently stroked Margaret's hand and let her mind focus on Margaret and what she might be feeling. There was silence and after she stopped concentrating on what she should say, it became less heavy. Michelle found herself relaxing as she sat and gave her attention to this young woman. Margaret still looked anxious but as Michelle continued to gently touch her on the shoulder and stroke her hand, her face and body became less tense and more relaxed. Michelle remained with Margaret for half an hour, by which time, Margaret was asleep. Michelle now did not mind how long she stayed with Michelle. Her embarrassment and self-consciousness had evaporated.

6. *The Power of Stories* – We are all unique and it is our uniqueness that gives us value and meaning. Yet we also yearn for connection and ways to transcend the isolation that separates us from each other and from ourselves. The butler Stevens yearned for connection and went on his journey to seek it. He did not find the connection he was looking for but in the process of his journey, he reconnected with his self, his feelings, and his true dignity. Telling stories and listening to each other's stories, we learn what makes us similar and what connects us all. This is one of the great strengths of the courses in medical humanities that are springing up. A piece of literature, a poem, a play, can highlight experiences, thoughts, and feelings that can be discussed in a way that does not challenge the defences in the same way as speaking about ourselves without prior preparation. Many of the stories that have fed my personal and professional development come from direct work with patients and their families and networks. Listening to the stories of the clients with whom I work, I discover the heroism of ordinary people living ordinary lives. But professionals also have their own stories of lived trauma, crisis, anxiety, and depression through which they have direct 'user' experience. This is what one of my nursing colleagues at the hospice told me about the death of his adored brother in his early 20s:

> My journey through bereavement and pain has ultimately brought me great gifts. Stephen died and disaster struck my life with nothing but the certainty that no good could ever come from such a tragedy. My certainty was misplaced. The suffering and pain that was a part of my previous life has been the carving of the depth of my life today. It may be confusing for some to talk of the wounded healer as my aim ultimately is not to offer healing per se. It is, however, to offer healing for the moment and that demands understanding and acceptance of whatever the place is in your life where you find yourself today.[25]

Reading wonderful works of literature, the stories that they tell, and then reflecting on what I can learn from them in my own life is a tremendous opportunity and privilege. For me, like Stevens and Mrs. Moore, I have voyaged afar, and travelled on a very special psychological journey. I am enormously grateful to the organisers of the Hobart colloquium for inviting me to take part and I thank them for the

[25] K. Yates, 'The Nursing Perspective: Pain is the Breaking of the Shell that Encases Your Understanding', in: C. Mason (ed.), *Journeys Into Palliative Care: Roots and Reflections* (London: Jessica Kingsley, 2002), p.175.

chance to reflect and to learn. As a result of these reflections, I would like to add something to the way we think about dignity that emerges from my reading of the two works of literature that I have discussed earlier. Firstly there is the 'dignity' of role that, if carried too far can act as a cloak or mask behind which to hide, and which impedes human connectedness. And I would like to add into our understanding of dignity, an emphasis on recognising and accepting our *own* uniqueness and authenticity in order that we might be more able to affirm the dignity of those we meet and with whom we relate each day of our lives.

The colloquium out of which this essay comes was a wonderful opportunity to share in thinking and discuss this enormously important subject. That it was a multidisciplinary meeting added to its richness and it was fascinating to note the different approaches to this one subject. We all listened and learned from each other. The tension that might have been present when a group of people with different academic languages and frames of reference attempt to communicate was thereby diminished. But there is another sort of tension that I believe it is important to highlight. I sense that there will always be a tension in reflecting on these issues, whether we are sitting in the armchair and contemplating the 'meaning of it all' at the end of an evening, or working in the 'thick of it' during the day. What I mean by this is that I see an irreconcilable tension between explanation and understanding in any discipline and the experience of the phenomena about which theories and ideas are elaborated. Problems arise when the findings of various disciplines are seen not for what they are, analyses of phenomena at a particular level, but the whole truth. To take an example from music; the description of the first movement of Bach's Passion according to St. Matthew as simultaneously three different musical forms (ritornello, fugue, and chorale prelude) is an analysis at a particular level—it will never encompass, nor does it intend to encompass the experiential grasp of the piece as a miracle. Another example from paediatric medicine; the isolation of the enzyme deficiency responsible for Tay Sach's disease is a biological finding; it says nothing, since it intends to say nothing about the suffering attendant on that disease. And of course, I am thinking of the subject of the colloquium; dignity. We spoke about it from all our different perspectives but not one of us was able to capture the experience, known throughout time and throughout the world; the experience of suffering that comes to people when they are not accorded the dignity that is, I believe, their right. All of us I think need to stay alive to this tension in our work, whether it is based in a palliative care setting or in any other kind of environment dedicated to the relief of human suffering in the world at large. And here it is that I end with the wish that the colloquium and this book will lead to ongoing reflection and the opportunity that we all will take to consider the ways in which our life experiences, and our unique stories, can be used in new ways.

10
The Question of Dignity: Doubts and Loves and a Whisper from Where the Ruined House Once Stood

Veronica Brady

From the place where we are right
flowers will never grow
in the spring.
The place where we are right
is hard and trampled
like a yard.

But doubts and loves
dig up the world
like a mole, a plough.
And a whisper will be heard in the place
where the ruined house once stood.[1]

(Yehudi Amichai)

The *Oxford English Dictionary* (OED) defines dignity as 'a quality of being worthy or honorable; worthiness, worth ... of high estate, position, or estimation, rank; nobility or befitting elevation of aspect, manner, or style; becoming or fit stateliness, gravity'. It even sets dignity in a cosmic dimension as astronomy defining it as the 'situation of a planet in which its influence is heightened by its position in the zodiac or by its aspects with other planets.' In this definition dignity is a concept associated with a world view which is at odds with what Edward Gibbon called 'the reigning deities of the age'[2] since its scope is cosmological rather than individual and it has overtones which could be dismissed as feudal; is certainly unfashionable and could therefore be said to be a whisper from the place where a ruined house once stood.

I would argue, however, that this whisper may have important things to say to us in the times in which we live which may still be said to resemble the culture which that shrewd observer Alexis de Tocqueville saw coming into in the new USA in the 1830s. Its inhabitants, he wrote,

---

[1] Quoted as the epigraph to Richard Holloway's *Doubts and Loves: What Is Left of Christianity* (Edinburgh: Canongate Books, 2002).

[2] Quoted in Czeslaw Milosz, *The Captive Mind*, trans. from the Polish by Jane Zielonko (Ringwood: Penguin, 1980), p.198.

J. Malpas and N. Lickiss (eds.), Perspectives on Human Dignity: A Conversation, 119–126.

> owe nothing to anyone, they expect nothing from anyone; they acquire the habit of always considering themselves standing alone and are apt to think they have their whole destiny in their own hands … this [not only makes them] forget their ancestors but it hides their descendants and separates them from their contemporaries, throwing them back forever upon themselves alone and threatening to confine them entirely within the solitude of their own hearts.[3]

It is not a culture with much respect for the dignity of those who fail to achieve power or accumulate possessions; are physically, intellectually, or emotionally disabled; or suffer from illness or fail to measure up to the norm. I suggest, however, that this earlier world view, still current in other cultures especially those of indigenous peoples, being less focused on the individual as an end in and for herself/himself has much to offer to us, resting as it does on what Bourdieu has called 'symbolic capital, the accumulation of being', rather than 'having'.

> This kind of capital is available to anyone, regardless of circumstance or social position and presumes that dignity rests on the assumption that every person has a valuable part to play as part of a larger order of things beyond the self and its interests. It also has a more expansive sense of value, implying that this order and every part of it is sacred since this assumption rests on the belief that, in the words of William James, [T]he so-called order of nature which constitutes this world's experience, is only one portion of the total universe … and … [that] there stretches beyond this visible world an unseen world of which we know nothing positive, but in its relation to which the true significance [and thus, I would add, the dignity] of our present mundane life consists.[4]

This is the notion of dignity which Patrick White explores in his novel *The Tree of Man*, the story of a very ordinary Australian man many people would regard as totally insignificant. White drew but for himself this ideal figure of humanity in an attempt to preserve a sense of his own integrity when he returned to Australia in 1948 after many years overseas and service in World War II. He was looking for 'the state of silence, simplicity and humility' which he saw as the 'only proper state' for a human being[5] but despairing of finding it in the ruins of Europe, an 'aching wilderness in which the ghosts of Homer, St Paul and Tolstoy sat waiting for the crash'.[6]

The place to which he returned, however, seemed like one described in Amichai's poem, 'hard and trampled/ like a yard'. Here, he wrote angrily, it seemed as if 'the mind was the least of the possessions … the rich man was the important man' and people were preoccupied with crude material pleasures whereas he had been longing to hear the 'whisper' which had come to him as a child from the land itself. In Stan Parker, however, he created a character who had nothing to do with these values and was in tune with the natural world around him and able to discover in it 'the extraordinary beyond the ordinary, the mystery and poetry which alone could make

[3] Alexis de Tocqueville, *Democracy in America*. Edited and abridged by Richard Heffner (New York: Mentor Books, Times Mirror, 1956), p.194.

[4] William James, *Varieties of Religious Experience* (New York: Random House Modern Library, 1957), p.51.

[5] Patrick White, 'The Prodigal Son', *Australian Letters*, I, 1, pp.15–16.

[6] Patrick White, *The Aunt's Story* (London: Eyre & Spottiswoode, 1948), p.146.

life bearable'.[7] Incidentally also, as he told John Hetherington, he hoped in this way to help the 'people of a half-savage country to become a race possessed of understanding'.[8]

For these reasons it may be useful to explore what this novel has to say about the question of human dignity. But it is also worth pointing out that in effect White was carrying on the task which Mircea Eliade saw as essential for any people if they were to settle properly into a place hitherto unknown to them, the 'transformation of chaos into cosmos'.[9] This transformation, I suggest, may well be necessary if people are to become capable of the essential dignity, as the OED defines it, which comes from knowing one's place in a larger scheme of things.

The title of the novel, *The Tree of Man*, points to this larger order, echoing the mythical image of the universe as a great cosmic tree, a notion which many of the Romantics drew on. In is description of crossing the Alps in Book VI of *The Prelude*, for instance, Wordsworth uses it with dramatic effect:

> The rocks that muttered close upon our ears,
> Black drizzling crags that spake by the wayside
> As if a voice were in them, the sick sight
> And giddy prospect of the raving stream,
> The unfettered clouds and region of the Heavens,
> Tumult and peace were all like workings of one mind, the features
> Of the same face, blossoms upon one tree:
> Characters of the great Apocalypse,
> The types and symbols of eternity,
> Of first and last, and midst, and without end.[10]

From this perspective everyone and everything becomes significant, even someone like Stan Parker who is in his own estimation and that of others 'nothing much', the son of a mother who 'read a lot'.[11] Stan's story is typical of many of his generation, outwardly in no way special. As a young man he sets out into the bush, clears a small farm for himself, marries, has children, battles floods, fire, and drought, goes off to war in France, survives and returns to the farm. Outwardly as he grows older his life seems to diminish. The two children leave home and drift away, the city expands outwards and finally engulfs their farm and he and Amy, his wife, jog along together in mutual loneliness until Stan dies, with little apparently to show for his life. Yet, as we will see, the novel tells us that 'in the end there was no end'.[12] What then is the source of his dignity?

---

[7] 'The Prodigal Son', p.15.

[8] John Hetherington, *Forty-Two Faces* (Melbourne, Cheshire, 1962), p.140; 'The Prodigal Son', p.16.

[9] Mircea Eliade, *The Myth of The Eternal Return: Or Cosmos and History* (Princeton: Princeton University Press, 1974), p.10.

[10] M. H. Abrams et al. (eds.), *The Norton Anthology of English Literature*, II (New York: Norton, 1962), pp.154–155.

[11] Patrick White, *The Tree of Man* (Ringwood: Penguin Books, 1963).

[12] Ibid., p.480.

It is not social. His neighbours pay little attention to him since he is not particularly sociable and to some he seems to have 'gone a bit queer from the war ... [and] began to avoid him' as there is something in him which makes them uneasy: 'He had never been a talkative man, except on direct practical matters. His advice had been good. But they preferred to take their troubles elsewhere, rather than have his eyes discover any cracks in their demeanour. Stan Parker was queer.'[13] What makes him 'queer', I suggest, is that his centre of gravity lies within. He does not seem interested in the opinion of others or in 'getting on'—and this, to refer once more to our original definition of 'dignity', gives him a kind of stateliness or at least a deep confidence as the goals of his life are uncommon but also seem somehow ordained.

His mother had insisted that he be called 'Stanley'—the name of the famous African explorer and throughout his life he lives up to that name. But the continent he explores is not physical but psychic, the 'omnipotence of distance'[14] he senses within himself. Here he is able to discover 'the extraordinary behind the ordinary, the mystery and poetry' of existence which White himself was looking for. As the epigraph to one of White's later novels, *The Solid Mandala*, puts it, for him 'There [was] another world, and it is in this one.'

In effect he is searching for the sacred; the mystery which fills us with awe but also draws us to it, the order which William James believed gives life its true significance. This, of course, does accord with the kind of world view de Tocqueville described since it is not so much concerned with 'getting on' or of making or remaking the visible world to one's own ends but of knowing one's place within this invisible one and behaving accordingly.

Ultimately, it assumes a sense of reality which is cosmological and even ceremonial. That this is where Stan belongs and values is clear in the scene in which a traveller, recently returned from Africa, visits him and Amy and regales them with 'images of gold and ebony'. Stan is not drawn to them, however. His Africa lies here:

> He did not wish to take his hat from the peg and say, "Well, so long, I'm off to see foreign places ...." He had a subtler longing. It was as if the beauty of the world had risen in a sleep, in the crowded wooden room, and he could almost take it in his hands. All words that he had never expressed might suddenly be spoken. He had in him great words of love and beauty, below the surface, if they could be found.[15]

But this is clear from the beginning of Stan's story. The description of him as he sets out into the bush echoes the *Book of Genesis*, presenting Stan as an Adamic figure making his first impact on the world and naming it; taking his axe to a tree to order his place, 'the first time anything like this had happened in that part of the bush.'[16] Then in the light of the fire he kindles this world begins to take shape, giving him 'the first warmth of content' but also making him aware of 'being there'. That particular

---

[13] Ibid., p.221.

[14] Ibid., p.27.

[15] Ibid., p.39.

[16] Ibid., p.9.

part of the bush had been made his by the entwining fire.[17] One is reminded here of the image Heidegger uses to describe the work human consciousness has to do in shaping the world, comparing it to a fire lit in a forest at night which enables one to see that the trees are there. Similarly, the phrase 'being there' recalls his definition of the human state as *Dasein* (*da* being the German for 'there' and *sein* for 'being'), and of being 'thrown into' existence, finite and mortal and of being-towards-death. As we shall see later, Stan's death represents the culmination of his life.

This intuition that, as Shakespeare's Prospero says, 'We are such stuff as dreams are made on and our little lives are rounded with a sleep', remains with Stan throughout his life together with the sense that it is also therefore risky; that, as White's next novel *Voss* says, 'the shell-less oyster is not more vulnerable than man.'[18] This means that life never feels humdrum. In fact, inner events often matter more than external excitements. So, for instance, the climax of a violent storm which hits the farm, destroying sheds, felling trees and threatening stock, occurs not during it but in its aftermath as Stan calmly goes about his evening work:

> He was tired. He was also at peace under the orange sky, events had exhausted him. He had learned not to think far, and in what progress he had made had reached the conclusion he was a prisoner in his human mind, as in the mystery of the natural world. Only sometimes the touch of hands, the lifting of a silence, the sudden shape of a tree or presence of the first star, hinted at eventual release.[19]

Identity for many people is a 'closed circle around sameness'[20] beyond which they are afraid to move and their dignity depends on recognition within it. But Stan has discovered that, in the words of Emmanuel Levinas 'it is in the laying down by the ego of its sovereignty…, that we find ethics and probably also the very spirituality of the soul, but most certainly the question of the meaning of being.'[21] Stan has made this move from the beginning. As if to underline this and the significance of his name, we are told that his mother had originally thought she would call him Ebenezer (which means 'rock of deliverance) but changed it to Stanley because 'she remembered the explorer.'[22] His task, to draw on the comparison Heidegger makes, is not so much to *build on* the world but to learn to *dwell within* it,[23] a task which calls him to be moving continually beyond the 'closed circle around sameness'.

He is at home with the 'doubts and loves/ [which] dog up the world' rather than the 'hard and trampled' yard of present commonsense. So the novel has almost nothing to say about Stan's time at war, dismissing it as a time of 'mud and metal'[24]

---

[17] Ibid.

[18] Patrick White, *Voss* (Ringwood: Penguin, 1971), p.349.

[19] *The Tree of Man*, p.49.

[20] Luiz Carlos Susin, 'A Critique of The Identity Paradigm', *Concilium* (2000/2), p.88.

[21] Sean Hand (ed.), *The Levinas Reader* (Oxford: Blackwell, 1993), p.85.

[22] *The Tree of Man*, p.10.

[23] Martin Heidegger, 'Building Dwelling Thinking', in his *Poetry, Language, Thought* (New York: Harper Colophon Books, 1975), pp143–162.

[24] *The Tree of Man*, p.199.

or about Amy's passing infidelity with a commercial traveller or their children's gradual rejection of them.

They have little to do with love or indeed the doubt which points beyond itself to the mystery of things. For him the 'whispers' he is listening for come from here, disturbing the world within the circle accepted reality. To put it simply, he lives less by matter-of-fact than by the kind of imagination Keats compared to 'Adam's dream—he awoke and found it truth'.[25] In a way this enables him to rehearse his life and even his death. Towards the end, for instance, he and Amy go to see *Hamlet*, and in it, watching Hamlet leap 'radiantly into the presence of death' and realizing that 'the end of Hamlet is too complicated to follow unless lived',[26] he accepts that he too is about to die.

As it is presented, however, this death is the climax of his story and his final achievement. It is winter time and Stan, now old and frail, is sitting in the weak sunshine in the overgrown garden, which is all that is left of their farm. But far from a sense of failure he feels himself 'large, triumphal scheme' and seated at the heart of it:

> From this heart the trees radiated, with grave movements of life, and beyond them the sweep of a vegetable garden.... All was circumference to the centre, and beyond that the worlds of other circles, whether crescent of purple villas or the bare patches of earth.... The last circle but one was the cold and golden bowl of winter, enclosing all that was visible and material.[27]

Though it is much more peaceful, there are echoes here of Wordsworth's vision, quoted earlier, of the 'great Apocalypse' in which all things appear as 'types and symbols of eternity'. But just at this moment a young man, the embodiment of the individual's will to power, a self-appointed evangelist, absorbed in himself hurdles the garden fence and comes towards Stan, 'stepping over beds rather than following paths ... convinced of achieving his mission by 'direct means and approaches'. Once there, he pours out before the old man the story of his life, presenting himself 'in the most complete nakedness' telling of 'drinking and whoring most weekends', reaching a triumphant conclusion when he describes his conversion when he fell on his knees, and grace descended upon him' and then telling the old man that 'This can happen to you too.'[28]

But Stan has always suspected certainty, aware as he is that life is ultimately mysterious. So thinks to himself that if this young man can understand this mystery, 'then it is a miracle' and replies mildly that he is 'not sure whether I am intended to be saved'.[29] As the narrator remarks, however, 'no subtleties would escape the steam-roller' of the young man's faith who babbles on, offering to 'show you books' about God. Stan now feels that he has 'been cornered enough' and spitting on the ground points with his stick at the gob of spittle 'as it lay glittering intensely

---

[25] M.H. Abrams et al. (eds.), *The Norton Anthology of English Literature*, II, p.396.

[26] *The Tree of Man*, p.405.

[27] Ibid., p.474.

[28] Ibid., p.475.

[29] Ibid.

and personally on the ground'. 'That is God,' he said.[30] This puts the evangelist to flight, leaving Stan alone to his contemplation as 'a great tenderness of understanding rose up in his chest. Even the most obscure, the most sickening incidents of his life were clear in that light'[31] as he understands that 'One, and no other figure, is the answer to all sums.'[32]

As William Blake insisted; 'Everything that lives is holy', part of one great pattern, even disappointment and failure, death and disease. As if to affirm this belief, as he gets up to go indoors, he stabs with his stick at a leaf lying on the path, saying 'I believe in this leaf.' But then he is overtaken by a fit of trembling and stands still 'waiting for the flesh to be loosened on him'.[33] Then he collapses and dies. But the novel tells us that his story does not end here. The epilogue returns to the beginning of the story with Stan's grandson walking through the trees and deciding that he will write a poem about life, of all life, of what he did not know, but knew and thus take up his grandfather's work, aware as he was, of a 'greatness' within him, even if it was still his secret.[34]

To conclude then! White presents a picture of dignity which has nothing to do with social position, wealth, or external achievement but consists in knowing one's place in the universe, accepting it and living it to the full, independent of the judgements of others. This is also true of other characters in the novel, notably Amy's friend, the rumbustious Irishwoman Mrs. O'Dowd. Married to a man who 'goes mad and violent with the drink', she manages in her own way to cope and to care for him and others and when she is diagnosed with cancer remarks philosophically, 'I know it is intended that way', declaring at the same time that she 'will give it a tussle as it allus has been'. The contrast White draws between her and Amy at this moment underlines the point that Mrs. O'Dowd's dignity comes from her sense of a larger order of things beyond personal desire or need. So Amy protests against her friend's acceptance of death. 'Holding her own hands that had begun to tremble, for however much love and pity she did truly feel towards her friend, the experience of pain was also hers. She was aghast at her own unreliable relationship to life'[35]—unreliable, it is implied, because she cannot accept this larger order.

In this way the novel accepts that as the Elizabethan divine Richard Hooker argued, 'the obedience of creatures unto the law of Nature is the stay of the whole world'.[36] Before him Dante expressed a similar view:

> The more there are who would say 'ours' so much the greater is the good possessed by each—so much the more love burns in that cloister.[37]

---

[30] Ibid., p.476.

[31] Ibid.

[32] Ibid., p.477.

[33] Ibid.

[34] Ibid., p.480.

[35] Ibid., p.449.

[36] M.H. Abrams et al. (eds.), *The Norton Anthology of English Literature*, p.389.

[37] Dante Alighieri, *The Divine Comedy*,trans. by Allen Mandelbaum (New York: Bantam Books, 1984). Purgatorio, XV: 55–58.

This is not a fashionable view today. As we have suggested, Stan would not fit easily into our present society since there is little that is competitive or go-getting about him. But in his dealings with others he embodies this sense of community, mutual respect, and readiness to care for others, regardless of their social position—as, for example, when he rescues Madeleine, a rich young woman, from her burning mansion, significantly named 'Glastonbury', perhaps to indicate that as a shrine of wealth and power, it is destructive.

I believe that this kind of dignity is the basis of a civilized society since it accords equal value to everyone, rich or poor, old or young, ill, healthy, or even deserving or undeserving. It also involves the kind of respect for the natural world and a readiness to accept its mysterious power which Stan embodies. As Paul Ricoeur observes: 'Cosmos and Psyche are the two poles of the same expressivity; I express myself in expressing the world; I explore my own sacrality in deciphering that of the world'[38] so that it helps him understand the meaning of existence.

Self-centredness, competition, and greed lead to what Thomas Hobbes saw as the 'war of every man against every man'. Suffering and violence will always exist, it is true, and probably is built into the nature of things. But that means that we must learn to deal with it without allowing it to destroy our dignity as human beings and our trust in existence as a whole.

[38] Paul Ricoeur, *The Symbolism of Evil* (Boston: Beacon Books, 1969), p.12.

11
Religion and Dignity: Assent and Dissent

Eilidh Campbell St John and Stuart Blackler

> [E]ach individual human being has the dignity of a person; he or she is not just something, but someone, capable of self-knowledge, self-possession, free self-giving and entering into communion with others.[1]

Given that this definitive statement appears in an address by the supreme pontiff of the Roman Catholic Church it is easy to assume that it provides a religious perspective on human dignity. Alan Falconer, a Christian theologian provides another example of a seemingly religious statement on human dignity. 'Human dignity is the inherent worth or value of a human person from which no one or nothing can detract.'[2]

These statements, as statements, are uninterestingly uncontroversial. It would be a rare human being indeed who could find anything in either statement with which to quibble. Certainly, both statements appear to coincide with humanistic, even atheistic thinking on the subject. Richard Robinson in his ground-breaking lectures first published by Oxford University Press in 1964 and later reissued as *An Atheist's Values* has this to say about human dignity:

> The first article of the Declaration of Human Rights asserts "All human beings are born free and equal in dignity and rights." The word 'dignity' here suggests another kind of demand for equality .... To be a human being is to have a dignity which requires respect from all persons. In virtue of this there ought to be a certain being on equal terms between any two men [*sic*] whatever, no matter how much one is above the other in some special way.[3]

Additionally, neither Falconer's nor Benedict's statement say anything very much about the nature of human dignity per se. Admittedly Benedict seems to be equating dignity with self-knowledge, self-possession, self-giving, and a desire for and freedom of association. Persons possessing a full quotient of the dignity Benedict describes would have much in common with Maslow's fully self-actualized individuals who are

---

[1] Pope Benedict XVI, *The Human Person, The Heart of Peace: Message for the Celebration of the World Day of Peace*, 1 January 2007, para. 2. http://www.vatican.va/holy_father/benedict_xvi/messages/peace/documents/hf_ben-xvi_mes_20061208_xl-world-day-peace_en.html

[2] Alan D. Falconer, 'Human Dignity', in John Macquarrie and James Childers (eds), *A New Dictionary of Christian Ethics* (London: SCM Press, 1986), pp.278–279.

[3] Richard Robinson, *An Atheist's Values* (Oxford: Basil Blackwell, 1975), p.181.

J. Malpas and N. Lickiss (eds.), Perspectives on Human Dignity: A Conversation, 127–134.

accepting of themselves and others, are relatively independent of the culture or society in which they live, are somewhat detached but with very close personal ties to a few other people, and are deeply committed to solving problems that they deem important.[4] Falconer is much less explicit in his description of dignity than is Pope Benedict. He emphasizes the universality of human dignity, which he equates with worth or value and that such worth or value belongs to every person by virtue of their being human.

These apparent uninterestingly uncontroversial statements, therefore, give rise to at least four questions—two which might be seen as primary and two which could be characterized as subsidiary or perhaps consequential, but which are primarily procedural in their nature.

The first is the question of whether the statements of Pope Benedict and Falconer can really be characterized as a religious statements at all, or at the very least, whether the statements can be seen as necessarily concomitant to a religious premise? The second question concerns the meaning of the words in the statement—particularly the words 'human' and 'dignity'.

The statement from Pope Benedict is preceded in his address by these words: 'Sacred Scripture affirms that "God created man in his own image, in the image of God he created them; male and female he created them" (Gen. 1:27).' He then goes on, '*As one created in the image of God, each individual human being has the dignity of a person*; he or she is not just something, but someone, capable of self-knowledge, self-possession, free self-giving, and entering into communion with others.' The emphasizing use of italics is in the original and makes it clear that Benedict's statement is a religious one in that it uses words from Holy Scripture as its foundational basis.

For those who accept this foundational statement as a theological basis for their thinking and action, there is an unavoidable implication, which is that any behaviour which denies a human his or her dignity is a blasphemy, an irreverence towards God. The theological argument could be summarized thus: God is the source of all life, and all life, being God-given is, therefore, sacred. Human beings are made in the 'image' or likeness of God[5] and by sharing in the divine nature, human life also shares in the worth and value (dignity) which is God's. That value (dignity), being of divine origin, cannot be denied and an assault on human dignity is irreverence towards God and is, therefore, a blasphemy.

It is possible to set religious conceptions of human dignity apart from atheistic notions of the dignity of the person and with psychological understandings of the self-actualizing potential of every human being, but it is important to recognize that these leaves sprouted in the heady air of modernity are grafted onto stock which has its roots in the ancient and rich subsoil of religion.

The statement that 'each individual human being has the dignity of a person' gives rise to another foundational question—namely, what does such a statement

---

[4] Abraham H. Maslow, *Motivation and Personality* (New York: Harper & Row, 1970).

[5] A modern French translation of the Bible uses the inviting word *resemblance. Traduction Oecumenique de la Bible* (Alliance Biblique Universelle- Le Cerf. Gen. 1:26, 1990) and Luther used the noun *Bild*—a picture.

actually mean? Language is a great betrayer. This is not a new thought, of course. From 1620 Francis Bacon tells us that 'The ill and unfit choice of words wonderfully obstructs the understanding'[6] and 250 years later the English moral philosopher Herbert Spencer echoes that thought with 'How often misused words generate misleading thoughts.'[7] In the foreword to his lexicon of Greek philosophical terms F.E. Peters had this to say:

> Philosophers have been uneasy about language almost from the beginning. The sculptor may curse his stone or the painter his oils, but neither contemplates suing for divorce. The philosopher, on the other hand, lives constantly in the shadow of infidelity, now suspecting metaphor, now tautology, or occasionally succumbing to the ultimate despair, the fear that he is dealing with *nomina tantum*.[8]

In many ways it would be satisfying to be able to dismiss ideas we find inconvenient or misleading as *nomina tantum*—only words—but once uttered, and especially once repeated and applied, words take on a powerful dynamism of their own which drags us along pathways we might, upon sober reflection, choose not to tread. 'Man acts as if he were the shaper and master of language, while it is language which remains the mistress of man.'[9] Despite the fact that as translated here, they carry an insidious sexist subtext of their own, Heidegger's words need to be taken seriously. Words innocently misused or deliberately and cynically manipulated have the power to shape our thoughts, our actions, and perhaps most importantly our relationships.

> Words have killed images or are concealing them. A civilization of words is a civilization distraught. Words create confusion. Words are not the word.... The fact is that words say nothing, if I may put it that way.... There are no words for the deepest experience. The more I try to explain myself, the less I understand myself. Of course, not everything is unsayable in words, only the living truth.[10]

Language may well be a great betrayer and we are wise to treat it with a great deal of caution, but treat with it we must because it is also 'the most valuable possession of the human race'[11]; it 'makes progress possible'[12]; it is 'the instrument of our distinctively human development, of everything in which we go beyond the other animals'.[13] It is in the words of Martin Heidegger, 'the house of Being',[14] or more

---

[6] Francis Bacon, *Novum Organum*, Aphorism 43 (1620).

[7] Herbert Spencer, *The Principles of Ethics*, 1, Part 2, Ch. 8 (1879).

[8] F.E. Peters, *Greek Philosophical Terms: A Historical Lexicon* (New York: N.Y. University Press, 1967), ix.

[9] Martin Heidegger, Quoted as an epigraph in George Steiner, *After Babel* (Oxford University Press, 1954).

[10] Eugène Ionesco, journal entry, quoted in George Steiner, 'The Retreat from the Word', in: *Language and Silence* (New York: Atheneum, 1977).

[11] Charles F. Hockett, *A Course in Modern Linguistics* (New York: Macmillan, 1958), Ch. 1.

[12] S.I. Hayakawa, *Language in Thought and Action* (New York: Harcourt Brace Jovanovich, 1978), Ch. 1.

[13] I.A. Richards, *The Philosophy of Rhetoric* (New York: Oxford University Press, 1965, c1936), p.131.

[14] Martin Heidegger, *Letter on Humanism* in *Martin Heidegger: Basic Writings*, ed. David Farrell Krell (New York: Harper Collins, 1993), p.217.

poetically perhaps, in the words of Adrienne Rich, 'only where there is language is there world'.[15] We cannot therefore, dismiss the words which displease or perplex us. We can only adopt a philosophical stance to them, recognizing them and engaging with them in the spirit of Wittgenstein's words, 'Philosophy is a battle against the bewitchment of our intelligence by means of our language.'[16]

In his book *In Search of Humanity*, John Macquarrie explores the issue of what it is to be human, with the initial assertion that 'there is, first of all, an ambiguity in the very word "human".'[17] It is not, therefore, just 'human dignity' which needs exploration, but the very concept of 'the human' needs to be examined. How often do we hear those guilty of criminal acts of shocking cruelty described as 'animals' ? 'Two teenage girls jailed for killing a disabled taxi driver were "violent little animals".... "They should be caged".'[18] Similarly, the discourse in reaction to terrorism has described the perpetrators as 'sub-human' and we have become accustomed to international dictators (the ones we do not like) being described as 'the devil incarnate'. After all, who but 'the devil incarnate' would preside over a country which is part of 'the axis of evil'?[19] The use of language in this way is to describe the essence of a person as a person in terms of behaviour is a very dangerous one for should it prevail it encourages those who do not think, those whose intelligence has been bewitched by words to believe that others can be dehumanized and that, therefore, their dignity is destroyed or compromised.

As insidious as these descriptions are in determining our attitudes to malfeasants, the examples given above are to some extent trivial when compared to the invidious effects of a misappropriation of the term 'human' by infusing it with a culturally specific sense of 'civilized', which in turn is infused with the subtext of 'different from us'. Thus, those who have been described as 'uncivilized' in their social morality, their systems of justice, their art, their skills, their economy, their control of their body politic, their 'difference from us' have by use of language been deprived of their humanity, at least in the eyes of those holding the hegemonic power. This specious interpretation of alterity as lack of humanity and hence with diminished or departed dignity has given rise to the most atrocious crimes against humanity. In the bicentenary year of the abolition of slavery it is important to recall that these atrocities have been condoned and condemned, sustained and eventually abolished by Christian action. The historic slave trade itself was justified by appeal to Scripture and eventually abolished by a similar appeal. Apartheid, a paradigmatic assault on human dignity, was validated by the Dutch Reformed Church with a Bible-based theology. At the same time it was strongly and actively opposed on

---

[15] Adrienne Rich, 'The Demon Lover' in *Leaflets* (New York: W.W. Norton, 1981).

[16] L. Wittgenstein, *Philosophical Investigations*, trans. G.E.M. Anscombe, 3rd edn. (Oxford: Blackwell, 2001), §109, p.2e.

[17] John Macquarrie, *In Search of Humanity* (London: SCM Press, 1982), p.1.

[18] Kim Arlington, 'Fury over term for girl killers', *Mercury* (Hobart, Tasmania, 5 May 2007), p.27.

[19] George W. Bush State of the Union Address, 29 January 2002, http://www.whitehouse.gov/news/releases/2002/01/20020129-11.html

theological grounds by Christian leaders such as Desmond Tutu, Alan Paton, and Trevor Huddleston.

This muddied confusion of 'human' with 'human action' raises the question as to whether one's right to have dignity respected unconditionally can be forfeited by deliberate behaviour. The theological understanding referred to earlier would deny that this is possible—dignity is a given not a merit—the dignity within each person is the presence of the divine, no matter how perverted and distorted the behaviour of the individual. Reactions to the actions of Saddam Hussein's executors with their taunting, in religious terms (in Judaeo-Christian terms to be more specific), were justifiably condemnatory. It is interesting to note, however, that the Christian actions which any champion of the notion of human dignity would reject, have been the outcome not of a definition of 'dignity' but of 'the human'. The nature of this paradox can be seen when we praise 'human endeavour', 'human kindness' and the like, and then rationalize what otherwise would be seen as unworthy behaviour by saying, 'Well, after all, we're only human.' This ambiguity is again the result of muddied and muddled thinking, of intelligence bewitched by words.

In Christianity, of course, the idea of humans being made in God's image is considerably refined. The Gospel According to John claims that 'The Word became flesh.'[20] This is not an understanding of a transcendent divinity taking on the *appearance* of earthly corporeality, so as to be manifested through the semblance of a body in order to reveal a heavenly truth to people in a manner comprehensible to them. The doctrine of the Incarnation means something radically different from such a divine visitation. In the incarnation of the divine Word (*Logos*) in Jesus Christ, God enters into the corporeality, carnality, and materiality of the history of humanity, thus permanently and irrevocably transforming human beings into a different kind of being from the one which had existed previously. This transforming event is commemorated by Christians in the ritual of the Eucharist which in its simplest, most universal understanding reminds participants that they have the capacity for divinity within them. Any violation of the integrity of the human individual is therefore a direct and real attack upon the integrity of God.

Such a theological understanding brings us to the paradox of praxis which Richard Holloway identifies thus: 'the institutions we create have a collective dynamic that often overrides the ethics of the individual.'[21]

The 1998 Lambeth Conference of Anglican Bishops resolved: 'life is God-given and has intrinsic sanctity, significance and worth',[22] nevertheless evidence from the practice of those who profess a religious and Christian orientation on life complicates the issue not only in the behaviour of the religious but in their justification of actions which others (and sometimes they themselves, would condemn as assaults on human dignity but which are justified on religious grounds. For instance,

---

[20] John 1:14.

[21] Richard Holloway, *Doubts and Loves* (Edinburgh: Canongate Books, 2001), p.105.

[22] The Lambeth Conference, Resolutions from 1998, Resolution 1:14 http://www.lambethconference.org/resolutions/1998/1998-1-14.cfm

in *The Book of Common Prayer* (the benchmark for Anglican theology, ecclesiology and pastoralia since its first manifestation in 1549) there is a rubric before the office for the Burial of the Dead[23]:

> Here it is to be noted, that the Office ensuing is not to be used for any that die unbaptized, or for any that are excommunicate, or have laid violent hands upon themselves, or die in the act of committing any grievous crime.[24]

Underpinning this judgemental exclusivism there is an institutional frame of mind with the implication that the right to dignity can be forfeited, not only through individual actions like suicide or the refusal of baptism, but also through no conscious action of the individual as in the case of children 'that die unbaptized'. Thus we have an institution which proclaims the orthodox gospel of Incarnation and Resurrection and its narrative of inherent and universal human dignity engaging in orthopraxis which is in direct contradiction to that gospel. There is probably little doubt that the impetus for this dichotomy was/is the preservation of the gospel and the protection of the institution which proclaims it but the basic truth of the gospel cannot be protected by its contradiction in praxis.

The institutional dynamic which seeks to lay down conditions applicable to the whole at the price of the particular diminishes the dignity of the individual in any given situation but also diminishes the dignity of the agent (and agency) of the institution.

The excluding, discriminatory state of mind encapsulated in the example from *The Book of Common Prayer* is the material of which fundamentalism, and especially religious fundamentalism at its most destructive is made. By fundamentalism we mean the belief that the believer has a purchase on that which is right and any costs to individual human dignity in maintaining the inviolability of their interpretation of a theological or moral principle is 'collateral damage'.

In his important book, *The Dignity of Difference*, Jonathon Sacks, the Chief Rabbi of the United Hebrew Congregations of the Commonwealth, quotes with approval the words of Isaiah Berlin:

> Few things have done more harm than the belief on the part of individuals and groups (or tribes or states or nations or churches) that he or she or they are in *sole* possession of the truth… it is a terrible and dangerous arrogance to believe that you alone are right.[25]

Certainly, the acceptance of the dignity of the human is an existential reality dialogically empowered but not limited by theological insights or moral convictions and given the failures and ever present dangers in the religious position, the final question we want to ask is whether the religious perspective nevertheless has a valuable contribution to make in discussions of the meaning, nature, and consequences of a commitment to the preservation of human dignity as a moral imperative.

---

[23] We bury the living more subtly and without ceremony!

[24] The Prayer Book does not define the expression 'grievous' crime, so in theory at least the rite of burial could be offered to a criminal but not to a new born baby.

[25] Jonathon Sacks, *The Dignity of Difference* (London: Continuum, 2003), p.63.

There is of course a danger when we say such things as 'the Christian attitude to this is…', for the existence of denominationalism and the diversity, and often inconsistency, in Christian thought within churches shows that such consistency cannot be found and certainly cannot be used as a platform from which to argue. This is so in doctrine, in practice and in structure. This is doubly the case in religious institutions like the Anglican Church, for example, where there is no *magisterium*, so that moral teaching is largely left to sacerdotal discretion and in the Unitarian church where all are enjoined to function in the light of informed but individual conscience. Despite the paradoxes and the failures, however, the Christian mind and Christian action have had a considerable role in keeping alive the rumour of human dignity, and in a time when state excesses put the rumour in danger of becoming an underground secret, the role of 'rumour-mongering' has become a call to conscience and to arms to all who in anyway accept the theology of Genesis and of Incarnation. Acceptance of the theology does not, however, imply the implacability and inflexibility criticized above. It is possible to operate from a position of deeply held faith and yet approach issues with a flexibility absent from fundamentalist dogma.

Don Cupitt, an Anglican priest at the time of writing, encapsulated this movement of the theological plates in his words: 'We don't want to privilege anything.'[26] There are many people of faith who are comfortably destabilized by this—who are liberated to explore the essence of biblical precepts rather than be bound by rigid and blinkered adherence to the particularities of text which, essentially, are in themselves both interpretative and interpreted. To adhere to text in such a way is to elevate the words above the meaning of the narrative of the scripture. The possible consequence of such a process is a denial of respect for human dignity and creation of 'collateral damage' in order to hold on to what is perceived as absolute authority under the guise of truth. In such a case, the biblical doctrinal truth of divinely generated human dignity becomes the consequent casualty.

In placing this notion of biblical narrative above scriptural text as the criterion for discovering the meaning of 'human' is to discover the importance of story. Story and stories are a powerful means of meeting and encounter both with the human and the divine whatever that is. In the narrative of scripture there is an implied invitation for those who receive it to enter into it. The supposed 'privilege' of text, structure, institutions, and authority fade away and are replaced by as an ongoing, personal, existential story of the 'here and now'.

A personally, existentialist, responsive approach to human dignity and respect for it in the individual does not, in itself, make the dilemmas and tensions raised in the dignity debate necessarily easier. In many ways it makes it harder and more demanding because there is nowhere to hide from the responsibility which comes from a personal encounter apart from the conviction and respect for the integrity of the other, albeit firmly grounded to one's own satisfaction.

What we discover, though as we enter into the 'here and now' narrative of scripture is that the divine, the sacred, or whatever word might be less packed with the

[26] Don Cupitt (1989), *Radicals and the Future of the Church* (London: SCM Press), p.156.

baggage of superstition—is within the story of which we become a part. 'Your body is the temple of the Holy Spirit', Paul wrote.[27] Human beings are imbued with the divine spark of life—made in the image of God[28] even if we do not take the Genesis myth literally.

All action pursuant to a belief in the inherent dignity to be accorded to, found in others and expected for oneself through nothing more than humanness is wanting the best for the other; and that is as good an understanding as can be found for Paul's word *agape*, which in English is translated as 'love'.

It is not in asserting principles and applying them inflexibly, nor rule-making (which should be seen as nothing more than postulating working propositions), it is in 'being'—both as being' and as 'Being'; Heidegger's *Sein*, Cupitt's *being.*

> Think of Being in a word as ventilating events, as a very light wind, a "gentle gale", or fountain of pure hap that upholds and supports everything that happens.[29]

By Way of Conclusion

There is a distinction between a humanistic and a religious approach to the question of human dignity with the theological bases on which the latter rests, bases which are seen as fundamental and which invest a commitment to human dignity as nothing less than a divine obligation.

Nevertheless, there appears to be no consistency evident in the application of these tenets to practice in Christian history, up to and including the present day. This lack of consistency can be explained by the division in Christendom between those who adopt a textual, doctrinal-based position and those for whom the essential Christian obligation is the acceptance of and desire for the achievement of the best interests of the person: the New Testament understanding of love.

Those who find themselves standing together in their approach to the person-centredness of issues relating to human dignity, despite the perception that they work from apparently differing theoretical bases, may well find merit in considering that the notion of 'Being' establishes a commonality which will strengthen the position of each. In the words of Edwin Markham:

> He drew a circle that shut me out
> Heretic, a rebel, a thing to flout.
> But Love and I had the wit to win:
> We drew a circle that took him in![30]

---

[27] 1 Corinthians 6: 19.

[28] Genesis 1: 27.

[29] Don Cupitt, *The Revelation of Being* (London: SCM Press,1998), p.16.

[30] 'Outwitted', Edwin Markham, *The Shoes of Happiness and Other Poems* (New York: Doubleday: 1916).

12
Giving the Past Its Dignity

Greg Dening

Here I am ending studies that have preoccupied me for 50 years. But in the theatre of history, there is never really an ending. There is only an exit-line that begins another conversation. Fifty years ago I made a discovery that changed my life. I discovered that I wanted to write the history of 'the other side of the beach', of indigenous island and continental peoples with whom I had no cultural bond, of Natives. And on 'this side of the beach', my side as an outsider, as Stranger, I wanted to write the history of people whom the world esteems as 'little'—Not of kings and queens. Not of heroes—'Little people'. Those on whom the forces of the world press most hardly. I wanted to celebrate their humanity, their freedom, their creativity, and—shall we say on this occasion—their dignity?

These years have been years of great pleasure and privilege. By rights I should be a most humble man. Historians must be humbled by living and knowing only vicariously and distantly what their subjects of inquiry have lived and known immediately before them. Anthropologists must be humbled by the difficulty of entering another culture, one so easily known to those who belong to it. History and anthropology are both plagiarisms, replays of others' lives and living. I owe the past and the other the dignity of being able to be their own selves in my representations of them. I owe them all those dignities I expect for myself. It is I who intrude on them, not they on me.[1]

My principal ambition—or the one I have learned to make principle in these 50 years—has been to enter into the believing selves of those whose lives I am replaying.

All humanity is believing—across times—across cultures. All humanity has answers to questions that can never be answered. All humanity has an ultimate metaphor for what is. That metaphor might not be explicit, not easy to see on the surface of things, but it is there. Being cross-cultural in time and space, it seems to me, means entering that ultimate metaphor, translating other's metaphors into my

[1] My writings on encounter history are to be found in such publications as: G. Dening, *Islands and Beaches: Discourse on a Silent Land, Marquesas 1774–1880* (Honolulu: University Press of Hawaii, 1980); G. Dening, *Performances* (Chicago: University of Chicago Press, 1996). *Beach Crossings. Voyaging across Times, Cultures and Self* (Philadelphia: University of Pennsylvania Press, 2004).

J. Malpas and N. Lickiss (eds.), Perspectives on Human Dignity: A Conversation, 135–139.

own metaphor. Hearing the silences of other's metaphors, so that I can hear the silences in mine. It is a very humbling thing to discover that all our ultimate metaphors are equidistant from reality. It is humbling to discover that the location of all our spirituality lies in a question that has no answer other than: 'Here I am. Here is my believing self.'

I have a soul, I think. My soul is my locating, searching self. It is not a soul that is 'saved'. Not an ethereal, wispy, ghost-buster sort that eventually escapes this body and this vale of tears. A soul. A place of reflection where one knows oneself as is—and would be. A place of commitment—and defection; of guilt—and innocence; of love— and hatred; of truth—and lies; of believing—and knowing. My ambition always in writing ethnographical history is to locate others' souls, their searching selves where they find themselves as I do, always on the edge, in-between. Giving others their otherness, giving back the past its own present is how I respect humanity's dignity.

It was a brave new world, this world of the encounter I got involved in 50 years ago. We were engulfed by a dozen disciplines from archaeology to zoology, their internal debates, their lateral pursuits. All the time we thought we were writing history. It was as if life were a permanent Times Literary Crossword Puzzle. It was innocent intellectuality with no responsibility other than to ourselves. In the eyes of many, this history of a Native/Stranger encounter did not have *dignitas*, though. *Gravitas* might be a better word. *Gravitas*, having a seriousness, weightiness, high in cultural estimations. Maybe we will discuss the difference in the days to come. Ancient history and classics had *gravitas*. Renaissance and reformation history, too. Even British History. Australian History was on the edge of being respectful in these years. The history of native peoples in their encounters with the 'civilized' certainly did not. When I told my professor of history that I was off to Harvard to do anthropology so that I could better write encounter history, he said: 'Dening, this is the end of your academic career.' He meant that it was impolitic to engage myself in an area in which my discipline, the university, and society thought to be of little consequence. I venture to say that it is only now at the beginning of the 21st century that the pursuit of knowledge of the otherness of indigenous peoples has the *gravitas* that it must have to seep into our life in Australian history and all its parts. Bennelong, the maverick aboriginal mediator between his people and the convict colonists, has not got the *gravitas* of Ned Kelly, a criminal bushranger and murderer with an Irish spirit of rebellion. A massacre of First People defending their land has not yet got the consequence of Eureka, an armed rising of miners against what they thought of as an unjust taxation. We are a long way from seeing the mutual killings in our past as fratricide. Healing myths will only begin when we really see their brotherhood and sisterhood in death.

For us who reveled in our innocence and looked to the respect that we thought that we were owed by those we studied precisely because we were so beleaguered and unfashionable academically, it was like a kick in the stomach in the 1960s to be told by those whom we studied that we did not treat them with proper dignity, never would, never could. In 1961 Frantz Fanon put it to the world that no one can write two-sided history who in some way benefits by the power of the victors. No one can mediate between the disempowered living and the voiceless dead. It seemed that in an instant the disempowered of the world overheard him. The dignity the disempowered demanded was that they have their own voice to say who they were, where they had been and where they were going.[2]

For me it was the most important lesson of my intellectual life. The past belonged to those on whom it impinged more than to those who had the skills to discover it and tell it. Those on whom it impinged were owed the dignity of being heard with their own voice. Their voice, they immediately told us, was to be found in a myriad of ways—in their dances, their songs, their legends, their myths, their body paint and tattoos, their carvings, their poetry, their very language. It was our responsibility to learn how to listen, they told us. Yes, I agreed with them. It was first our responsibility to listen. But what they did not have the right to say, in my opinion, was that there was no entry into their otherness by those who did not share it. That leads to nihilism, in my opinion. These past decades we have seen claims that the otherness of gender, sexuality, class, age, culture, and race is inaccessible, and that any claim of accessibility is a disempowerment. That is not true. What is true is that accessibility always involves some mutual conferring of human dignity—of white to black, of black to white; of male to female, of female to male; of young to old, of old to young.

Of course it does not end there. The dignity that both Native and Stranger are owed, the dignity that the dead past and living present are owed, is that they be credited with the same responsibility for their actions as I who represent them, as I who re-present them have for mine. The problem of evil is as much a problem for historians as it is for religion, it seems to me. If it is possible for me to find my own bad faith, it must be possible to discover—through a glass darkly—the bad faith of the past.

I am a pragmatist on these issues. We all live with varying degrees of certainty and uncertainty. The only thing impossible for us is absolute certainty and absolute uncertainty. We are always in-between. Our personal global positioning system will always place us there.

My gift to the past is always that in the contingencies that suffuse every part of our being, I discover their true stories with all the strategies of neomodernity and all the tropes of a storyteller. My neomodernity has embraced all the ideals of knowledge—advancement of modernity—perspective, exhaustive research, critical dialogue, disengagement as far as is humanly possible from all that filters that knowledge with prejudice and error. These ideals demand that I sit for hours, days, weeks, months, and years at desks in the archives. My extravagance with time there is rewarded with a sensitivity that comes in no other way. It is an overlaying of images one on the other. It is a realization that knowledge of the past is cumulative and kaleidoscopic, extravagantly wasteful of my energy. This is both the cost and the benefit of my modernity. But my modernity is neo—new. It is in touch at the same time with both the possibilities and the limits of knowing,

---

[2] Frantz Fanon, *The Wretched of the Earth* (Harmondsworth: Penguin Books, 1963).

it is a modernity that is expressive of what is known and how brokenly it is known. It is a modernity that begins with the real and enlarges it with creative imagination. It is a modernity that always acknowledges my authorial presence.

My tropes are the tropes of a storyteller, a teller of true stories. Culture is talk. Living is story. Culture is talk. I hear this talk in all its multivalency, with all its conditions of person and place and occasion. Living is story. I hear these stories in all the tropes with which they are told to me—their metaphors, their metonymies, their ironies. In my turn I tell my true stories as artfully as I can. My true stories will not clone theirs. There will always be part of me as well as part of them in my true stories. My histories will not have the closure of hindsight. There is nothing so undignified and mocking of the past as hindsight. My stories will not freeze them in any one moment of their living. That is what the Terror wants, Jean-François Lyotard has told us, 'to arrest the meaning of words', to put a template on living. The Terror: the terror of fundamentalism, the terror of auto-da-fé; the terror of science in the service of power.[3]

All reification is a process of forgetting is how Herbert Marcuse put his slant on this notion of Terror. 'All reification—the transformation of lived experience into things—is a forgetting.' 'Art fights reification', Marcuse goes on, 'by making the petrified word speak, sing, perhaps dance'. Yes! I give the past the dignity it is owed with my artfulness and my compassion.[4]

In a world, as monstrously without compassion as ours is, it is not surprising that its victims turn to words with the deepest reflective meaning. All over the Pacific, in all the towns and camps and ghettos of Aboriginal Australia, there are poets. An inner dignity demands the intensity of a poem.

Perhaps my true stories to be truly compassionate should be poems. I wish I had the courage to write them. But I have an anthropologist friend, Ivan Brady, who does have the courage. Listen to his ethnographic history and hear the artfulness of his tropes.

GOOD PRISONER
(Yuma, Arizona July 1862)

Guards called him Stupid Indian Prays Too Much.
When they said to put his drinking cup in the door slot,
he did
When they said to leave his shit bucket in the corner,
he did.
When they said to stay silent in the darkness for weeks,
he did.
When they said to dance like a savage Indian on parade,
he did.
When they said he could walk circles in the morning sun,
he did

[3] Jean François Lyotard, *Rudiments Païens* quoted Michel de Certeau, *The Practice of Everyday Life* (Berkeley: University of California Press, 1988), p.165.

[4] Herbert Marcuse quoted Michael T. Taussig, *The Devil and Commodity Fetishism in South America* (Chapel Hill: University of North Carolina Press, 1980), p.154.

When they said the should return to his cell,
he
stabbed a guard
in the eye with
a tortoise shell
knife and broke
for the open
desert.
Soldiers tried to track him
On the endless horizon of nothingness surrounding the prison.
But could not find a trace.
They quit hunting him by noon
Saying that no man could survive without water
in this Hell hole of heat waves and hard times.
Later that afternoon two crows circled over the sun yard.
From that day forward the prisoners called him by the name
Two Crows Runs in Air.[5]

[5] Ivan Brady, *The Time at Darwin's Reef: Poetic Explorations in Anthropology and History* (Walnut Creek: Rowman & Littlefield, 2003).

13
Dignity and Indignity

Nicholas Tarling

Relativities

The meaning of words slips and slides, though rarely perhaps entirely perishing. Is that true particularly of words that describe and generalize about human relationships? Those change restlessly or are changed, in part indeed by the application of words to them. Think for example of 'ethnic', 'gay', 'community', of 'human resources', 'accountability', 'excellence', and 'peer review', of 'mission' and 'services', words with suspiciously military overtones.

Among those the word 'dignity' must be included. Throughout its linguistic life—and some words can be virtually murdered by usage and misusage, though they may retain a capacity to haunt or spook or, ignis fatuus, lead astray—it has retained an association with the concept of human 'worth'. Like other words that seek to describe or determine human relationships, it is not an absolute matter, even at a particular period, but one that relates an individual to other individuals or to a larger 'society' or 'community'. Even a concept of 'self-worth' appears to depend on a relationship with others. Our own estimate of ourselves is surely always comparative: I measure up to, or am better than, others; or I fulfil, or exceed, the norms they have set. They are mistaken about me: there may be an element of assertion, even defiance, or of despair.

'Dignity' was not always associated with equality, as it is now is in the language of rights. 'All human beings are born free and equal in dignity and rights. They are endowed with reason and conscience and should act towards one another in a spirit of brotherhood.'[1] That spirit was presumably not that of Cain and Abel, but rather one designed to challenge patriarchy or hierarchy. It is a political or ideological statement: the second sentence offers a programme for realizing the principle of the first.

Even a cursory perusal of earlier meanings, however, suggests rather that dignity was associated with hierarchy. It was a noun that described the position of the planets in the heavens, and of men (and a few women) of high estate on earth: the 'worthies', though that had or came to have a slightly contemptuous or mocking connotation; the 'quality' in an earlier meaning differentiated from our notions of 'assessment' or

[1] *Universal Declaration of Human Rights*, Article 1 (1948).

J. Malpas and N. Lickiss (eds.), Perspectives on Human Dignity: A Conversation, 141–149.

'fitness for purpose'. It was a matter of rank and honour, of title and office, and, of course, among the various disciplines that engaged the human brain was the 'dignity of philosophical enquiry', no doubt, at least in some cases, marked by 'excellence'.

Indignity, by contrast, covered not only 'unworthiness'—in the sense of our own behaviour—but, more commonly, unworthiness of treatment, slight, administered to us by others. That, too, was related to hierarchy or breach of hierarchy, though it could later apply more or less to worth in the broader sense implied by the UN *Declaration.* The same goes for 'indignation', anger at what is regarded as unworthy.

The shift in meanings seems crucial. Ours relates to a perception of humanity deeply affected by the Enlightenment, the revolutionary thinking of the American and French revolutions, and the Romantic emphasis on the individual. Dignity or indignity is associated with our person—physically, emotionally, mentally—rather than our social standing. We are, or ought to be, 'free and equal in dignity and rights'.

But we cannot assume that what is now is what has been nor that what is true of some is true of all: Japanese prisoners-of-war suffered less 'indignity' than Iraqis have more recently in being stripped, since nakedness was not abhorrent to them. Historians—whatever the 'dignity' of their enquiry—do face a dilemma that is also a challenge, answering which will never be complete but may be productive. We can enquire into the past with our own concerns in mind: perhaps we can do nothing else, however much we attempt objectivity. But we have to do it without assuming that its concerns were necessarily ours: otherwise all claims to objectivity has to be abandoned. The historian must read, but not read into or read back. Historiographical practice is meant to control subjectivity, though it cannot eliminate it. Recognition of that, on the other hand, need not amount to total relativism. If there is a judgement to be made, it should be seen as such. Things are different, but that does not make them equally 'acceptable', 'valid' or 'appropriate', to use our debased currency of praise and blame.

How far can we thus assume that what we see as 'dignity' or 'indignity' had in earlier ages or has in other societies the same parameters or overtones as it has in our usage? It might be, for example, that in a hierarchical society, it was not only the 'quality' that were worthy. Others would, like Ishiguro's butler,[2] find 'dignity' in a recognized place in the hierarchy, rather than positing an 'equality', and suffer indignity, not because of that, but because it was denied or not recognized. In 'service' at Hatfield House in the 1930s, Flo Wadlouv was recently asked on television whether she was happy with the system. 'I felt proud and privileged', she declared. 'I felt elevated as well.'[3] Allow that 'Flo'—as she was called—remembered—as most of us—the sunny days rather than the stormy. But infer that hierarchy gave you not only a wage but a 'place'. Retainers shared in a measure the 'dignity' of their masters. Such positioning might limit rather than enhance arbitrariness. Indeed it imposed some obligation on the masters, the lords, squires, patrons, who

[2] K. Ishiguro, *The Remains of the Day* (London: Faber & Faber, 1996).

[3] BBC Radio 4, 14 August 2004.

might help an able child with a scholarship, or keep a servant on well after he or she could effectively serve. The price of equality might, by contrast, be an insecurity that could lead to 'indignity'.

The Universal Declaration of Human Rights [Art. 4] also, of course, condemns slavery. How far the possible advantages of hierarchy might apply to slaves perhaps depends on the nature of the slavery involved. It is hard not to see 'chattel' slavery as an indignity, though we must be less sure that it was seen, let alone described, by those who suffered it as an 'indignity'. At least in respect of some of its forms in South-east Asia, my own area of expertise, it was seen as an advantage. 'Slavery', like 'piracy', is indeed a term laden with Western associations that make it hard to use in South-east Asian history. The main contrast seems to lie in the continuity between slavery and other forms of dependency, sustained in South-east Asia but not in the West. That tended, too, to muffle the concept of 'freedom', even if in the West itself 'freedom' did and does not imply a total lack of obligation. The words in current use, in general, do not relate to a distinction between slave and free. Only 'merdeka' took on that character in an earlier period. That itself derived, however, from a term used in Sri Vijaya to describe a chief or leader of a group of subjects or bondmen, in turn derived from a Sanskrit description of a person of great spiritual power or wealth.[4]

Traditional South-east Asia

The control of men, rather than of land, was the key to the social systems of traditional South-east Asia, sparsely populated for most of its history: they were, as Europeans used to say, worth their weight in gold. 'The Raja looks to the number of his following as the gauge of his power,' wrote Frank Svvettenham in Malaya in 1875, 'and other Rajas will respect and fear him accordingly. Thus he tries to get men into his service.'[5] What was important to leaders and would-be leaders was the men and women whom they could place in a dependent relationship. 'For the poor and weak, on the other hand, security and opportunity depended upon being bonded to someone strong enough to look after them.'[6] The father of Hang Tuah, the folk-hero of the Malays, 'went in search of a living, [and] presenting himself to the Datuk Bendahara, he made himself *hamba* to him'.[7] The focus was therefore not on the degree of legal freedom a person might possess, but on the object of a person's

---

[4] A. Reid (ed.), with the assistance of Jennifer Brewster. *Slavery, Bondage and Dependency in Southeast Asia* (Brisbane: University of Queensland Press, 1983), p.21.

[5] J. Gullick, *Indigenous Political Systems of Western Malaya* (London: Athlone, 1958), p.98.

[6] A. Reid (ed.), *Slavery, Bondage and Dependency in Southeast Asia*, p.8.

[7] Sullivan, Patrick, *Social Relations of Dependence in a Malay State: Nineteenth-Century Perak.* (The Malaysian Branch of the Royal Asiatic Society, monograph no. 10. Kuala Lumpur: MBRAS. 1982), p.63

obligation, and thus of his or her niche in society. The same terms—*kyun* in Pagan Burma, *phrai* in Siam, *hamba* in the Malay world, *ata* in the Bugis world—were used to cover what in the West would be covered by a range of words, subject, vassal, or slave.

These bonds were transferable, 'and it is this', Anthony Reid suggests, 'that provides the overlap with slavery'. Bondsmen could be 'presented as a marriage gift, donated to a monastery, offered as tribute, given as security for a loan, sold or inherited'. Yet the imagery throughout was 'that of the extended family', and even a slave was 'permitted a level of intimacy with his master which no one who was not a member of the household could dare assume'.[8]

The origin of this system of obligation commonly lay in debt. Meeting ritual obligation was one source of debt, gambling another. 'Sale or commendation of oneself and/or one's wife and children to a wealthier person' was a way out of 'severe hardship'. 'Pawning one's dependants or oneself..., or else entering a very unequal partnership with the creditor who became the patron if not the master, were the common South-east Asian means of obtaining capital.'[9] Theoretically the debt could be redeemed, and that was to enable Europeans to draw a distinction between 'debt' slavery and what they regarded as 'true' slavery. In fact labour was not sufficient to redeem the capital, but only to pay the interest. Of the pre-Spanish Filipinos Antonio de Morga wrote: 'it is to be understood that they made these slaves during their wars and differences: and most frequently on account of loans and usurious contracts, which were current among them, the payment, stock, and debt increasing with delay, until they remained as slaves.'[10] The relationship was not seen in terms of cash return. The term for debtor in 19th-century Perak, for example, was *kawan* or companion, and in Sumatra *pengiring* or follower. 'Nor has the debtor under this system any means of becoming free, unless some relative or friend comes forward to pay for him; and even in this case the creditor might if he so willed, and if were a Rajah in all probability would, under some pretext, refuse the offer of payment.'[11]

That does not, however, mean that these were slave societies, Reid insists, 'since the legal categories of slave and free were not well defined, obligation and fealty were more central to the South-east Asian system than status-as-property, while in certain cases serf seems a more appropriate word than slave'.[12] Even this W.H. Scott doubted. The Visayan *orlpun* and the Tagalog *alipin* were not slaves but, being bound not to the soil but to other men, they were not serfs either.[13] Nor, Reid himself adds, did the distinction between 'savage' slaves, captured or bought from the hill people,

---

[8] A. Reid (ed.), *Slavery, Bondage and Dependency in Southeast Asia*, pp.8–9.

[9] Ibid., pp.9–11.

[10] H. E. J. Stanley (trans.), *The Philippine Islands* (London: Hakluyt Society, 1868), pp.299–300.

[11] P. Sullivan, *Social Relations of Dependence in a Malay State: Nineteenth-Century Perak* (Kuala Lumpur: MBRAS, 1982), p.50.

[12] A. Reid (ed.), *Slavery, Bondage and Dependency in Southeast Asia*, p.12.

[13] Ibid., p.153.

persist after in its initial harshness.[14] The same seems to be true of sea captives. 'A master was liable to neglect a *bangaya* who was remiss in his duties, but their statements and travel accounts of observers reveal that slaves, especially those with knowledge and skills, had good relations with their master and were not easily distinguished among their following.'[15] Harshness certainly existed, but it could be counterproductive. Labour was scarce, and the state administrations were rarely strong enough to enforce a bond challenged by a pull factor as well as a push factor. Debt bondage was indeed preferred to state service in Taung-ngu Burma.

Unable to acquire labour for their new urban centres because the free market was limited, and because they lacked the traditional ties that substituted for it, the early Europeans in South-east Asia resorted to recruiting slaves, preferably from remote areas, India, Madagascar, Arakan, or New Guinea. They fell into South-east Asian ways, however. The tyranny in Batavia, the Dutch Company's capital, was of the domestic sort. Slaves might be badly treated, but that was true of the lower orders more generally. 'The master has all power over the Slave, except that of killing him,' La Loubere wrote of late 17th-century Siam; 'And tho' some may report, that Slaves are severely beaten there (which is very probable in a country where free persons are so rigidly bastinadoed) yet the slavery there is so gentle, or, if you will, the Liberty is so abject, that it is become a Proverb, that the Siamese sell it to eat of a...Durion.[16]

Modern States

While there could be an undue rush of sentiment for the slave-owning Old South—neglecting the violence intermingled with or implicit in or part of the patriarchy—was it better, or felt to be better, to be a 'wage-slave' in an atomized industrializing modernizing, and urbanizing society subject to other forms of violence and degradation? One is reminded—though not quite relevantly—of the redoubtable Tory MP Cal. Sibthorp, who intervened in the debate in which Richard Cobden and John Bright questioned James Brooke's attacks on Dayak 'pirates' in the Borneo of the 1840s. 'There was cruelty enough practised by the free traders at home to those unfortunate persons who were in their employ, and they should begin by putting a stop to that.'[17]

The great economic changes of the 19th and 20th centuries were indeed accompanied by a destruction of old hierarchies and a construction of new forms of association, based on 'nation', race or ethnic, religious affiliation, and employee union, in which individuals sought to find a place, to understand the world, to attain security. In all these changes, it seems clear, there was an increasing sense of

---

[14] Ibid., p.12.

[15] J.F. Warren, *The Sulu Zone* (Singapore: Singapore University Press, 1981), p.219.

[16] A. Reid (ed.), *Slavery, Bondage, and Dependency in Southeast Asia*, p.24.

[17] Hansard, cxi, col. 301.

individual worth and a shifting view of dignity. But they were coupled with a readiness to submit, if not to new hierarchies, to new obligations—in states, societies and 'communities', in unions and churches—as the price of that security, that recognition of human worth which older hierarchies may once have offered. To that the spread of literacy contributed. The risk was that you would lose your autonomy as the price of belonging, have to strike, avoid consuming certain foods or drinks, cover the face, vote as the party said. Those might be indignities, though some seemed and seem positively to enjoy them, finding security in compliance and identity in conformity. If you sought to preserve personal privacy—respect for which Peregrine Worsthorne[18] may not be alone in seeing as contemporarily a prerequisite for dignity—you might only provoke our prurience, stimulate our voyeurism.

The state itself played an ambivalent role. Seeking efficiency, it became more active, made itself better informed about citizens or subjects—indeed defined who qualified or was to be disqualified on the basis of various criteria, residence, 'ethnicity', religion—changed their status and sought to tax them more effectively. At the same time as it grew stronger and brought itself into closer contact with the individual, it offered, often reluctantly but necessarily, greater participation. In that way the state increased its power and capacity to mobilize resources, human and otherwise, beyond anything achieved by the most authoritarian regimes in earlier ages. In counterpoint the discourse of 'rights' was extended in scope and more widely used. And as a world of states was created, that ambivalence was extended. Setting out rights in UN documents was coupled with the full acceptance of state sovereignty. The state was and remains both a potential protector and a potential violator.

The role of the state is ambiguous in another sense. The creation of a world of states may be seen as one kind of 'globalization'. More commonly, it is a word we apply to the changes in the economic and cultural fields and in communications that, at least since the industrialization of the 19th century, appear to have gathered speed and increased scope from the late 20th, though we must also interpret the word as a programme or ideology rather than a description. We could perhaps re-employ Sibthorp's comments on the free traders. Here is another process that destroys old hierarchies and obligations or changes their nature, and one not contained by any formal framework of responsibility or 'accountability' other than a financial bottom line. The state often promotes the process, but it also constrains it. It is the main—though not the only—means by which the impact of economic forces is mediated and either intensified or moderated. Will it prevent our finding other sources of security—and dignity—in association or in isolation—or will it encourage it? Will it act like on old-fashioned patron? Or will it act like the rent-oriented and disobliging landlord that replaced him?

The trends are at best dual, suggesting again that equality and dignity are not necessarily or readily associated. Continental human rights jurisprudence, it has

[18] Peregrine Worsthorne, *In Defence of Aristocracy* (London: HarperCollins, 2004), reviewed by Richard Davenport-Hines, *Times Literary Supplement*, 23 July 2004.

recently been argued, has been and is being shaped by the concept of the right to an honorable image. Fascism diffused traditional marks of dignity to all members of the Volk and passed new laws against insulting ordinary people. Now that notion has extended to all citizens: 'an old aristocratic priority…has traveled into the present via Fascist law.'[19] Contrast the corporate world in its dealings with customers. We are given numbers, like soldiers, and our 'loyalty' is reduced to continuous shopping. We are also at risk of losing our identity and thus our dignity. First names are used as in nursing homes and, I believe, brothels. Am I alone in seeing this as spuriously friendly but actually demeaning? We lose not only our good name, but any name: ignominy indeed. Dropping surnames, as Penelope Lively puts it in one of her novels, suggests not intimacy but a kind of indifference.[20]

Colonial States

Colonial states were even more ambivalent than their Western contemporaries. Imperialism involved an extension to them of the modernization to which their masters were subjecting themselves, but it was necessarily even more incomplete. Once established, their administrations required revenue: they had to create the conditions for and encourage investment, to build up infrastructure, to offer a measure of literacy. But how far could they go without undermining the colonial state? Industrializing was likely to be at odds with metropolitan interests. Extending political participation would lose control, offering at best only a limited extension of tenure to the colonial power. Independence was the only possible basis for a fuller modernization. Securing that became the objective of 'nationalist' movements.

The historian can feel more certain than in respect of earlier hierarchies of the role of 'dignity' in respect of the formation and expansion of such movements. It seems clear that we would resent the 'indignities' of the colonial state and of colonial or pseudocolonial society, especially, but not exclusively, where there were colons, and where 'unacceptable' hierarchies were imposed. We can also be clear that, whether hierarchies were previously acceptable before or not, now they were definitely not—neither the old ones, often turned to account by imperial regimes, nor the new—since they were criticized in language with which we are familiar, the language, indeed, of the imperialists themselves. Much of the education the Spaniards offered in the Philippines was in the liberal arts, law, theology, and medicine. 'Was it at all surprising that education of this sort should produce Filipinos who thought they knew the rights of citizens and the duties of government…and who had the impudence to invoke Rousseau and the Laws of the Indies?'[21]

---

[19] D. Gordon, *Times Literary Supplement*, 13 August 2004, summarizing James Q. Whitman.

[20] Penelope Lively, *Perfect Happiness* (London: Heinemann, 1983), p.105.

[21] OADES, Rizalino Aquino, *The social and Economic Background of Philippine Nationalism, 1830–1892* (Ph.D. thesis, University of Hawaii, 1972 [microfilm]. University of Hawaii, 1974), pp.269–270.

Everyday slights may have been more demeaning than the lack of political participation, though the ambition came to be independence. Certainly that was the basis of the critique the second Raja of Sarawak, Charles Brooke, offered of imperialism in a pamphlet published in 1907 as part of a campaign against British interposition in Brunei. British possessions, he thought, were too much Anglicized. Good and friendly feeling had, he believed, existed in the early part of the 19th century. There had been a falling-off, a separation 'in consequence of the English developing into a higher civilization—as it is termed—among themselves with wives and families, and European luxuries, and so it has happened that though we govern, we only do so by power, and not by friendly intercourse or feeling'. Countries without colonial possessions faced a happier future than those with them. 'My own opinion is that before we reach the middle of this century all nations now holding large Colonial possessions will have met with very severe reverses.'[22]

The forecast was accurate, though what happened did not happen in the way he expected. But if we accept that the downfall of empire was in some part at least the result of the arrogance the Raja criticized, again we may be talking of an elite: how far were these 'indignities' perceived as such not by the 'quality' but by the mass of the people? Who might be used to—or not be aware of—foreign rule? Who were yet to be uprooted by economic and governmental change? Who might be badly treated by their own elites, the newer among whom might indeed be less sensitive to traditional obligations than the old? When they were recruited into nationalist movements, it was often indeed on other more oblique and traditionalist grounds.

China did not, of course, come under control by the Western 'imperialists'. Instead it compromised. The 'unequal' treaties it made in the 19th century came to be seen by later generations as 'national humiliations'. At the time, they were seen differently, and at least before the conflict with Japan of 1894–1895, the Qing Empire was dealing quite successfully with the challenges with which 'imperialism' presented it.[23] The language of 'national humiliation' took hold, however, among the often anti-Manchu intelligentsia and boosted their 'anti-imperialist' nationalism. How far the masses shared it is, however, surely questionable.

The same perhaps applies in respect of nationalist movements developed in face of imperial rule. Indeed the question goes deeper. In the Philippines the great politico Manuel Quezon declared that he would prefer a government 'run like hell by Filipinos to one run like heaven by Americans[24]' Destroying 'national humiliation' surely guaranteed nothing to the masses.

The process is indeed in some cases replicated. The people of West Papua, consigned to Indonesian rule in the 1960s, see themselves as treated like animals, those with jobs kept in low positions. 'Educated Papuans regard common

---

[22] C. Brooke, *Queries: Past, Present and Future* (London, The Planet Office, 1907), pp.13–14.

[23] S. A. M. Adshead, *The End of the Chinese Empire* (Auckland: Heinemann, 1973), pp.11–12.

[24] Aruna Gopinath, *Manuel L. Quezon: The Tutelary Democrat* (Quezon City:New Day Publishers, 1987), p.12.

Indonesian attitudes towards themselves and other Papuans as personal insults, in much the same way as pre-war Indonesian nationalists responded to Dutch prejudices.'[25]

Writing on the rise and fall of British India, Karl de Schweinitz pre-echoed Edward Said.

> If the coercive burden of the old imperialism has become internalized in, and diffused among, many states, who can say that it has become lighter?.... One must hope that in the struggle for equity and justice, the world's states do not in their name impose more appalling restrictions on individuals and groups than did the nineteenth-century imperialists in the maintenance of their rule.[26]

The hope often seems a vain one. But I would not argue, like Michael Hardt and Antonio Negri, that the state is vanishing and ought to vanish.[27] Both in action and restraint it is at least potentially and often actually the best guarantee that we have that the mass of people can live in 'dignity'.

Closing Comment

We have created a world globalized in the sense that it is partitioned among sovereign states and globalizing in the sense that economic and social trends are being powerfully spurred by electronic media. It is one that talks of privacy in the very process of destroying any chance of it. It perversely creates anonymity by the use of first names, and promotes the commodification of people in the practice of 'management'. While it speaks the language of choice, most people on earth have the most limited of options. Their dignity and their rights are endorsed but not effectuated.

The hierarchical societies of the past encompassed oppression, even enslavement. In many cases, however, obligation was mutual, and dignity was not found merely in stoic acceptance of 'fate'. Displacing hierarchy by liberty and equality was to be accompanied by fraternity. At the very least, our societies must recapture a sense of mutuality, and create conditions under which people can find a measure of identity, security, and dignity without resort to damaging others.

[25] R. Chauvel, 'Papua and Indonesia', in: Damien Kingsbury and Harry Aveling (eds), *Autonomy and Disintegration in Indonesia* (London, New York: Routledge Curzon, 2003), pp.120–121.

[26] K. de Schweinitz, *The Rise and Fall of British India* (London: Methuen, 1983), p.256.

[27] M. Hardt and A. Negri, *Empire* (Cambridge, MA: Harvard University Press, 2000), p.336.

14
Human Dignity and the Law

Sir Guy Green

This is a discussion of some aspects of human dignity and the legal system. It includes a discussion of the philosophical roots of the concept and how they are reflected in the law, the ways in which the law upholds human dignity and the circumstances under which and the extent to which it is permissible for the State through its laws to act towards individuals in ways which have the effect of diminishing their dignity as human beings. The discussion deals primarily with Western systems especially those which have their origins in the common law tradition such as Australia, the UK and the USA.

The concept of human dignity has two components: the belief that individual human beings have unique significance and absolute or at least special value and the moral principle which is derived from that belief that those qualities ought to inform how society and other individuals interact with them. In Western culture the concept has several roots. It is fundamental to Christianity. Given the influence which they have had on the development of the secular values of western culture, Christian principles are significant as a major historical source of the belief irrespective of their religious significance. The Christian belief in human dignity does not come so much from explicit passages in the Bible as from necessary implications which can be drawn from much of the New Testament. As well, whatever might be its biblical sources, the belief is influential as a principle which is in fact adhered to by most Christian churches.

A major non-religious source of the concept of the unique value of individuals is the school of thought known as humanism. Humanism comprises a number of concepts but its central emphasis is upon the unique position of human beings in the world. At the same time as denying that they are subject to divine or supernatural forces humanism does assert that humans are not just especially sophisticated animals but are endowed with unique mental and moral characteristics and capacities.

Christianity and humanism share the belief that the special qualities possessed by human beings are intrinsic—that is, individuals possess them solely by virtue of their humanity. In sharp contrast political philosophies such as Utilitarianism and Marxism deny that human rights or qualities are intrinsic and assert that they are relative or contingent and dependent upon the needs of society of which the individual is a

J. Malpas and N. Lickiss (eds.), Perspectives on Human Dignity: A Conversation, 151–156.

member. That characteristic of political philosophies like Utilitarianism and Marxism necessarily entails their according human dignity much less significance than do systems informed by the values of Christianity or humanism.

Utilitarianism defines a moral action as that which produces the greatest good for the greatest number. That can entail a serious assault upon human dignity: for example, an act which does the most good for the majority might also happen to cause appalling harm to the minority.

Marxism too is largely inimical to the concept of human dignity. As a theoretical doctrine its principle of historical determinism and its perception of individuals primarily as economic units diminish both the autonomy and the significance of individuals. And the history of the large-scale denial of human rights in Marxist regimes demonstrates that Marxism as an applied doctrine is equally destructive of human dignity.

In essence, doctrines such as Marxism and Utilitarianism are inimical to human dignity because they regard people as social units rather than as individuals. That distinction was encapsulated by Karl Popper in his classic work *The Open Society and its Enemies*: 'Individualism' he observed 'was part of the old intuitive idea of justice. That justice is not, as Plato would have it, the health and harmony of the state, but rather a certain way of treating individuals, is emphasized by Aristotle, it will be remembered, when he says 'justice is something that pertains to persons.' 'This individualism' Popper continues 'united with altruism, has become the basis of our western civilization…it is the core of all ethical doctrines which have grown from our civilization and stimulated it…there is no other thought which has been so powerful in the moral development of man.'

The differences between those philosophical traditions are relevant to a discussion about human dignity and the law because the dichotomy between those traditions which view the value of individual humans as inherent and those which regard it as a function of the individual's interaction with society can also be found in legal systems and systems of governance. In particular it represents the single most important distinction between democracies where the rule of law prevails and totalitarian regimes.

The concept of humans having intrinsic value was given expression in the Roman law principle that human beings have fundamental natural rights which they possess by virtue of their humanity as opposed to their being conferred upon them by the State or the law. That is also implicit in the 1789 declaration of the Rights of Man and the Citizen made at the beginning of the French Revolution which asserts that 'men are born and remain free and equal in rights' and that 'the aim of every political association is the preservation of the natural and imprescriptible rights of man' and the American Declaration of Independence that 'We hold these Truths to be self-evident, that all Men are created equal, that they are endowed by their Creator with certain unalienable Rights that among these are Life, Liberty, and the Pursuit of Happiness.' Those concepts are reaffirmed in the United Nations Charter and in the Universal Declaration of Human Rights which recognize the 'inherent dignity', 'worth', and 'equal and inalienable rights of the human person'.

Legal systems recognize and seek to protect human dignity by the enactment of Bills of Rights and the like which curtail the power of governments, legislatures, or others to act in ways which impair the exercise of rights which it is thought are especially important for the maintenance of human dignity. But it is not only through legislative or constitutional provisions of that kind that legal systems protect or uphold human dignity. Operational and substantive principles developed by and within those systems themselves are at least as significant. Principles developed within the legal system which directly or indirectly recognize and protect human dignity include: like cases must be treated alike; any curtailment of the freedom of an individual is prima facie unlawful unless justified by positive law; a private person may do anything which is not prohibited or which does not infringe the rights of others; when it is making a decision affecting the interests of individuals a public authority is required to observe procedural fairness or natural justice and various presumptions of statutory interpretation designed to protect individual rights and freedoms.

A powerful contribution made by common law systems has been through the preoccupation of the courts ensuring that a person accused of committing a crime has a fair trial and the consequential emergence of the presumption of innocence—that is that a person may not be convicted of a crime unless proved guilty beyond all reasonable doubt.

The presumption of innocence well epitomizes the difference between the ways in which the two main philosophical perceptions of human value are given expression in different legal systems.

Common law systems find the possibility of an innocent person being wrongly convicted to be so abhorrent that they have imposed upon prosecutors the heavy onus of proof mentioned above which is sometimes expressed in the aphorism that it is better that ten guilty persons should be acquitted than that one innocent person should be convicted. In other words the possibility that sometimes the operation of the presumption of innocence might result in a guilty person being acquitted is regarded as an acceptable price to pay in order to avoid the intolerable possibility of an innocent person being wrongly convicted. But in authoritarian or totalitarian systems where the individual is regarded as expendable in the interests of society as a whole, persons accused of committing crimes are not treated with such tender concern for their rights.

A dramatic example of the contribution made by common law systems to upholding human dignity is provided by its approach to slavery.

Broadly speaking, a slave is a human being who is held as the property of another and as such can be bought, sold, hired out, or inherited. Slavery existed in virtually every society of the ancient world and in some parts of the world it continues right up to the present day. It is an institutionalized denial not only of human dignity but of the individual's very humanity.

Although the institution of slavery has never existed in England, slavery did exist in British colonies in the 18th century; Englishmen engaged in the slave trade and slaves were to be found in England, most of them having been brought from colonies by sea captains or plantation owners. For some time the status of a slave brought to England was uncertain, a number of unsatisfactory and conflicting judicial decisions in the first part of the 18th century leaving the issue unclear. But eventually the question of the legality of slavery was resolved in 1772 in the landmark case of *Somerset v. Stewart*.

James Somerset was a slave who had been brought to England by his master, Charles Stewart of Boston. Somerset escaped, was recaptured, and imprisoned on a ship bound for Jamaica where he was to be sold. A philanthropist and campaigner for the abolition of slavery, Granville Sharp, acting on behalf of Somerset obtained a writ of habeas corpus which required the Captain of the ship, John Knowles, to bring Somerset before the court and show cause, that is demonstrate to the court, that the detention of Somerset was lawful.

The case was significant because, unlike other cases in which the issue of the status of the slave had been incidental to other issues, in Somerset's case it was the only question before the court. The court, presided over by the Chief Justice Lord Mansfield, was under some pressure because the case involved two strongly competing interests: ordering Somerset's release would involve losses of millions of pounds to British citizens while failing to do so would be an affront to the libertarian principles of the common law.

The Chief Justice rejected the claim that the imprisonment was lawful. His reasons were simple: 'The state of slavery' he said 'is of such a nature that it is incapable of being introduced on any reasons, moral or political; but only positive law…it's so odious that nothing can be suffered to support it but positive law. Whatever inconveniences therefore may follow from a decision I cannot say this case is allowed or approved by the law of England…' and he ordered that Somerset be freed. It is instructive to see that this major step in the history of the protection of human dignity did not proceed from the application of the provisions of some grand Declaration of Human Rights or Bill of Rights but was the outcome of the application of underlying principles of the Common Law favouring liberty, the use of a procedural remedy, the writ of habeas corpus, and operational rules of the legal system relating to presumptions and the burden of proof.

A threshold issue in any consideration of human dignity and the legal system is whether humans should be regarded as having absolute value and if not what qualifications to that perception of our humanity are acceptable and by what principles we define those exceptions.

The belief that humans have absolute value presents difficulties when applied to a working legal system. Rigorously applied this entails what might be called the pure pacifist position which holds that under no circumstances should a human be subject to deliberately inflicted harm. Upon analysis of two examples this turns out to be an untenable position.

First, the principle would preclude the use of violence in self-defence or the defence of others. Quite apart from any moral objections to it, such a principle entails a contradiction. Take the case of a person who is threatening to harm another and the only way one can prevent that harm is by taking violent action towards the attacker. The pure pacifist principle forbids your doing so because it would violate the principle that one must never deliberately cause harm to another person; but if you do not take action you are also violating the pure pacifist principle because by your omission you have been instrumental in another person being harmed. It is thus a principle which must be discarded as self-contradictory.

Secondly, a condition of the existence of a society is the rule of law and a condition of the existence of the rule of law is the existence of a power to impose sanctions such as the imposition of a sentence of imprisonment in order to enforce its operation. Thus every society has a system of criminal law that includes a sentencing regime which necessarily entails the taking of measures by the state, which tend to diminish human dignity. Thus if we accept the continued existence of society as an axiom then once again the pure pacifist position is untenable.

It follows that in the legal system of any modern society the value of individuals cannot be regarded as absolute. So at the heart of any discussion of human dignity and the legal system is the issue of the circumstances under which and the extent to which it is permissible for the State through its laws to act towards individuals in ways which may have the effect of diminishing their dignity as human beings.

Leaving aside illegal abuses of individuals by those in authority the action taken by the state which is most calculated to have that effect is the exercise of the power to sentence persons to imprisonment.

The way in which the sentencing power is regulated and exercised provides a crucial indicator of a given society's commitment to the maintenance of human dignity.

While it is accepted that a person may by their criminal acts render themselves liable to penal sanctions such as sentences of imprisonment, it is accepted in the sort of societies being discussed here that there is a point beyond which society should not go in response to those acts no matter what that person may have done. For example, persons sentenced to imprisonment are owed a duty of care and may not lawfully be subject to any penalty or indignity other than that of the imprisonment and its incidents as provided by law; there is an abhorrence of, and in some jurisdictions a constitutional prohibition upon, the imposition of cruel and unusual punishments and the concept of outlawry whereby a person who had committed certain crimes lost the protection of the law has long since disappeared.

A proper regard for human dignity requires that the coercive powers of the criminal law and the sentencing power be exercised parsimoniously and extend no further than is necessary to satisfy the principles which justify their existence. In most cases that is achieved by giving the judiciary a wide discretion as to the appropriate penalty which ought to be imposed upon a person who has been convicted of a crime. This discretion recognizes the great variations which exist in the seriousness of different crimes, in the level of personal culpability of those who commit crimes and in the likelihood of a repetition of the offence. The judicial discretion thus operates as a mechanism for seeing that a sentence both takes into account the individual's characteristics and culpability and recognizes the need for, but goes no further than is necessary for society to be able to protect itself against those who would harm it by committing crimes. In recent years, however, there has been a tendency to curtail the extent of the judicial sentencing discretion or even remove it altogether by legislation requiring that in the case of certain crimes a fixed sentence must be imposed. This tends to negate the careful and principled way in which the law has been able to develop a penal system which is effective but still informed by a regard for human dignity.

An inevitable consequence of the creation of a system of mandatory sentencing is that sooner or later a case will arise when a court is compelled to impose a sentence which even the most punitive minded members of the community are forced to acknowledge is manifestly inappropriate and excessive. This is graphically illustrated by cases arising in those jurisdictions in which even a juvenile who has committed a second property offence is subject to a mandatory sentence of imprisonment no matter how trivial is the offence and no matter how extenuating are the circumstances under which it was committed.

Mandatory sentencing is also in conflict with basic principle. An axiom of all legal or moral systems which recognize the intrinsic worth of each individual is that like cases must be treated alike. A corollary of that axiom is that cases having different relevant characteristics must be treated differently. It follows that a system of mandatory sentencing in which courts are compelled to impose fixed penalties irrespective of the circumstances of the particular offence or the particular offender violates the axiom of consistency.

The only possible justification for creating a system of mandatory sentencing which it is known will violate the axiom of consistency or will inevitably produce manifest injustice in individual cases is that it is the price which must be paid for the larger public benefit, which it is claimed flows from having such a system. But such a rationale is in conflict with the core values of our society which affirm the significance of persons as individuals and reject the doctrine accepted in authoritarian systems that individuals are expendable in the interests of the state.

The example of mandatory sentencing provides a strong illustration of a wider conclusion which can be drawn from the discussion in this essay. Even in a liberal democracy governed by the rule of law the protection which the legal system gives to human dignity can be eroded away and eventually lost if short-term pragmatic considerations in particular situations are allowed to prevail over principles which recognize the intrinsic value of each individual. One needs to be especially conscious of this danger during times when the community feels threatened by, for example, war, terrorism, or an increase in crime.

15
On the International Legal Aspects of Human Dignity

Don Chalmers and Ryuichi Ida

Introduction

Human dignity[1] is a value of great antiquity. Dignity for the classical Roman conveyed the sense of the rank of some citizens of Roman society. Later, in the period of the Renaissance, religious writings expanded the idea of human dignity to a quality enjoyed by all, not simply an elite. The Renaissance fortified the conception of the individual's capacity, through God, to transform themselves.

The second great renaissance in the life of human dignity occurred at the end of World War II. The appalling loss of civilian life during this conflict and the gruesome revelations of the treatment of minorities, most notably the evil treatment of European Jews, revived discussion of human dignity. Human dignity may have waxed and waned in legal and philosophical attention after this time. In the 1970s, one writer suggested that discussion of human dignity 'seems to have suffered the fate of notions such as virtue and honour, by simply fading into the past'.[2] However, human dignity has enjoyed yet another renaissance over the past decades, in debates about dying with dignity and the human cloning debates of the modern Genome Era.

More recently, a number of international conventions dealing with the new genetics and human cloning have revived the use and debate of the value of human cloning as a principled approach to these challenges in human research and the nature of what it is to be human. That the term human dignity is more frequently used is undeniable. The advances in medical science have released a line of argument and discussion about the use of the term at both the beginning and end of life. The expression dying with dignity[3] has become widely used in debates about voluntary

---

[1] For a succinct account of human dignity and its specific implications for bioethics, see J.F. Kilner, 'Human Dignity', *Encyclopaedia of Bioethics* (New York: Macmillan Reference USA, 3rd edn. 2004).

[2] M. Pritchard, 'Human Dignity and Justice', *Ethics*, 82 (1972), p.299.

[3] See Parliament of Victoria, Inquiry into Option for Dying with Dignity. See also cases of *Shorey v. PT Ltd* (2003) 197 ALR 410; Re by Gardner Public Advocate (2003). Unreported Victorian Supreme Court, BC200302640.

J. Malpas and N. Lickiss (eds.), Perspectives on Human Dignity: A Conversation, 157–168.

euthanasia,[4] humane palliative care and advance directives. Equally, the idea of dignity is now more commonly used in professional codes of medical ethics. For example, the Royal Australian and New Zealand College of Psychiatrists Code of Ethics in Principle 1 states that the practitioner should have 'respect for the essential humanity and dignity of each of their patients'. Despite the popular usage of this term it cannot be precisely defined in law. In fact, an internationally recognized bioethicist described the expression 'human dignity' as 'comprehensively vague'.[5] In a similar vein, Ruth Macklin has suggested that '[d]ignity is a fuzzy concept, and appeals to dignity are often used to substitute for empirical evidence that is lacking or sound arguments that cannot be mustered'[6] This paper considers the nature of definitional limits to the concept of human dignity in law. The paper will draw particularly on the recent and influential writings of Professors Beyleveld and Brownsword in the text *Human Dignity in Human Ethics and Biolaw*.[7]

Background to Human Dignity: Romans, Renaissance and Church, and the Dignitarian Alliance

The modern usage of dignity can be traced back to its origins in the Latin word *dignitas*. The classical Roman law recognized the concept of *dignitas*, but made a critical distinction between dignity and rights. In Roman law the concept of *dignitas* encapsulated ideas of the rank and *status* of the individual. Importantly, Roman citizens did not have equal dignity or rank as this depended on their status. This distinction is illustrated in Justinian's Code where it is stated 'a slave does not suffer loss of status by being manumitted, for while a slave…and where the change is one of dignity, rather than of civil rights, there is no loss of status. Loss of status can arise from loss of citizenship or in minor cases, a loss of liberty.'[8] The essential modern idea of the dignity of *all* human beings regardless of rank or status developed later.

The modern idea of human dignity ascribes that quality to all human beings and not only a select group drawn from the upper echelons of a society. The Italian

---

[4] See critical distinction between assisted suicide and voluntary euthanasia in House of Lords, UK, Select Committee on the Assisted Dying for the Terminally Ill Bill Report House of Lords Paper 86-I discussed in 'Assisted Dying for the Terminally Ill: House of Lords Select Committee', *Bulletin of Medical Ethics*, 206 (2005), pp.9–11.

[5] J. Harris, 'Goodbye Dolly? The Ethics of Human Cloning' (1997) 23, *Journal of Medical Ethics* 353. Similarly, John Robertson has commented 'these notions of human dignity, common patrimony of mankind, are no longer applicable because they are too vague' at research.arc2.ucla.edu/pmts/ Germline/Psycho-social%20Dangers/pdcjr2.htm.

[6] Ruth Macklin, 'Cloning and Public Policy', in: J. Burley and J. Harris, *A Companion to Genetics* (Oxford: Blackwell, 2002), pp.206–215 at 212.

[7] D. Beyleveld and R. Brownsword, *Human Dignity in Bioethics and Bio-law* (Oxford: Oxford University Press, 2001).

[8] See Institutes of Justinian Title XVI Book 1 *Of Loss of Status* 1–5 Moyle (Oxford: Oxford University Press, 4th edn., 1906), p.23.

Renaissance philosopher, Giovanni Pico della Mirandola,[9] in his oration on the *Dignity of Man* saw human dignity in all human beings.

> You, with no limit or no bound, may choose for yourself the limits and bounds of your nature. We have placed you at the world's centre so that you may survey everything else in the world. We have made you neither of heavenly nor of earthly stuff, neither mortal nor immortal, so that with free choice and dignity, you may fashion yourself into whatever form you choose. To you is granted the power of degrading yourself into the lower forms of life, the beasts, and to you is granted the power, contained in your intellect and judgment, to be reborn into the higher forms, the divine....[10]

Mirandola viewed this dignity as an individual power to transform oneself, through God and to pursue a freedom of enquiry. The Renaissance fortified the idea of human dignity as intrinsic to all people.

Religious doctrine has always promoted the essential dignity of human being, a dignity that is shared by all, by virtue of being human. Human dignity is, in this sense an intrinsic quality. For example, the Vatican Council II stated that, 'the Church, enlightened by divine relation...can offer a solution...by which the true state of man can be outlined...[and] his dignity and his vocation may be perceived in their true light' and later that man's 'very dignity...required that he should glorify God in his body'.[11] While the Catholic Church is the oldest Christian church with volumes of theological tracts on human dignity, the concept of dignity is not unique to the Catholic nor other Christian faiths. The idea of human dignity is common to the other great world monotheistic religions of Judaism and Islam.[12] The idea of human dignity appears to have been familiar in the development of Japanese society. A recently published study has traced the development of the meaning of *Jinkaku* from the period of the Meiji Restoration.[13] The study concludes that the idea of *Jinkaku* underlies the moral worth of a quality of a person that makes that person respected in society, an idea aligned with the modern conception of human dignity.

Arguably, the most influential account of human dignity is to be found in the works of Immanuel Kant,[14] particularly his *Groundwork of the Metaphysics of Morals*. In his argument, human beings have dignity not by reason of their humanness

---

[9] Pico della Mirandola, interestingly, first studied law at Bologna before deciding to study philosophy.

[10] Pico della Mirandola http://www.wsu.edu:8080/~wldciv/world_civ_reader/world_civ_reader_1/pico.html

[11] See 'Pastoral Constitution on the Church in the Modern World', 7 December 1965, Vatican Council II, pp.913–915 quoted in K. O'Rourke and P. Boyle, *Medical Ethics*, 2nd edn. (Washington, DC: Georgetown University Press, 1993), Chapter 44, 'Sacredness of Human Life'.

[12] Similarly the Buddhist and Hindu faiths have concepts, which embody the spiritual, self-improvement and respect for other human beings as intrinsic ideas of dignity.

[13] Kyoko Inoue, *Individual Dignity in Modern Japanese Thought: The Evolution of the Concept of Jinkaku in Moral and Educational Discourse*, Michigan Monograph Series in Japanese Studies, 35 (Ann Arbor, MI: University of Michigan, 2001).

[14] S. Munzer, 'Property, Patents and Genetic Material' in: J. Burley and J. Harris, *A Companion to Genetics* (Ames, Iowa: Blackwell Publishing, 2002), pp.438–454 at pp.448–450 sets out a brief but helpful account.

but because of the extent to which they are moral. Morality in turn relates to the *autonomy* of the individual and as such, autonomy is the foundation of dignity. 'Every human being has a legitimate claim to respect from his fellow human beings and is in turn bound to respect the other. Humanity itself is a dignity: for a human being cannot be used merely as a means by any human being…but must always be used at the same time as an end. It is just in this that his dignity (personality) consists, by which he raises himself above all other beings in the world that are not human beings and yet can be used, and so overall things. But just as he cannot give himself away for any price (this would conflict with his duty of self-esteem), so neither can he act contrary to the equally necessary self-esteem of others, as human beings, that is, he is under obligation to acknowledge, in a practical way, the dignity of humanity in every other human being. Hence, there rests in him, the duty regarding the respect that must be shown to every other human being.'[15]

In this respect, the guiding principle of autonomy is the Kantian categorical imperative 'never to choose except in such a way that in the same volition the maxims of your choice are also present as universal law'. In this way the fundamental requirement of human dignity requires that human beings should never be treated as a 'means' but 'always also as an end'.[16] The concept of autonomy therefore recognizes the importance of individual choice and responsibility. Autonomy, equally important is the established starting point for any discussion of human dignity. So, human dignity has been explained within the wider philosophic framework of Alan Gewirth's *Principle of Generic Consistency*[17] that uses individual choice and responsibility as the starting point for an analysis of human dignity.[18] Equally importantly, human dignity is the foundation and the fundamental value underlying the principle of respect for others as human beings.

The idea of human dignity has become very influential in recent years, particularly, as stated, in debates about dying with dignity. In the USA, there have been a series of cases dealing with physician-assisted suicide and *dignitarian* harm.[19]

---

[15] Imanuel Kant, *The Metaphysics of Morals*, M.J. Gregor (ed.) (Cambridge: Cambridge University Press, 1996), p.209. See also: D. Beyleveld and R. Brownsword, *Human Dignity in Human Ethics and Bio-law* (Oxford: Oxford University Press, 2001), pp.50–57.

[16] For a succinct account of Kantian ideas on human dignity and its specific implications for bioethics, see J.F. Kilner, 'Human Dignity', *Encyclopaedia of Bioethics* (New York: Macmillan Reference USA, 3rd edn., 2004).

[17] For a discussion of human dignity within the wider philosophic framework of Alan Gewirth's Principle of Generic Consistency, see D. Beyleveld and R. Brownsword, *Human Dignity in Human Ethics and Bio-law* (Oxford: Oxford University Press, 2001).

[18] For a brief but useful review of this book see I. Karpin, Book Review, *Medical Literature Review*, 12 (2004), pp.323–327.

[19] In the *Supreme Court in Vacco v. Quill* 521 US 793 (1997) and *Washington v. Glucksberg* 521 US 702 (1997) the Supreme Court examined the constitutionality of State legislation (in New York and Washington respectively) imposing criminal sanctions on any person aiding or assisting another in committing suicide. The Court considered that the States had the constitutional power to pass such laws. Most American States either common law or in statute prohibit aiding or assisting another to take their life.

The idea of dignity harm has been extended into discussions about a possible duty for medical practitioners to provide pain relief and palliative care to enable a person to have a dignified end of life.[20] Human dignity has been a common theme in debates about human cloning. Brownsword has argued persuasively that the exponents of the human dignity approach can be described as a 'dignitarian alliance'.[21] He also argues that their approach is as influential as the utilitarian analysis of asking '...whether the benefits promised by the practice are outweighed by its possible harms' and the deontological analysis whether the practice in question '...so outrages our sense of justice or of rights or of human decency that it should be prohibited whatever the advantages.'[22] In the USA, the President's Council on Bioethics has invoked the dignitarian approach in its Report on *Human Cloning and Human Dignity: An Ethical Inquiry*.[23] Preceding this report, the Center for Bioethics and Human Dignity[24] had been promoting the idea of human dignity by envisioning a uniquely human future since 1994. The Center aims to discuss the 'pressing bioethical challenges of our day, including managed care, end-of-life treatment, genetic intervention, euthanasia and suicide, and reproductive technologies'.

National Constitutions and International Instruments

After World War II, many national constitutions have included references to human dignity. The period of German post-war reconstruction included the introduction of the *Basic Law for the Federal Republic of Germany* that provides in Article 1: Human dignity shall be inviolable. To respect and protect it shall be the duty of all state authority.

Consistent with many other constitutions that mention human dignity, the *German Basic Law* does not go on to describe any consequence of breach of Article 1 dealing with human dignity. There is no forfeiture of any basic rights or reason of breach of Article 1. By contrast, *the Basic Law* provides for freedom of expression,

---

[20] See B. Rich, 'A Prescription for the Pain: the Emerging Standard of Care for Pain Management', William Mitchell LR26 (1999):1. The Israeli Supreme Court has awarded minimal damages for treatment administered without informed consent on the basis of a breach of dignity. O. Kaplan 'The Development of the Informed Consent Doctrine in the Israeli Courts', 15th World Congress on Medical Law Sydney, 2 August 2004.

[21] See R. Brownsword, 'Bioethics Today, Bioethics Tomorrow, Stem Cell Research and the Dignitarian Alliance', *Notre Dame Journal of Law Ethics and Public Policy*, 17 (2003), p.15.

[22] M. Warnock, 'Philosophy and Ethics' in: C. Cookson et al., *Genetic Engineering: The New Challenge* (European Union Patent Office, 1993), p.67.

[23] *Human Cloning and Human Dignity: An Ethical Inquiry*, Washington, DC, July 2002.

[24] See http://www.cbhd.org/. The Center was launched before the Dolly Experiment but certainly at the height of the death with dignity and reproductive technologies debate. This Center promotes opportunities to discuss human dignity particularly in relation to the new reproductive technologies.

in particular, the freedom of the press (Article 5 para. 1), freedom of teaching (Article 5 para. 3), freedom of assembly and association (Articles 8 and 9), privacy of correspondence, post and telecommunication (Article 10) and rights of property (Article 14) that are, in order to ensure the free democratic basic order, are subject to forfeiture and to the extent declared by the Federal Constitutional Court. In this respect, human dignity as mentioned in the *Basic Law* in Germany can be seen as an underlying principle rather than an operative principle. The concept of human dignity *underlies* the basic human rights, which are set out in the *Basic Law*. Many of the national constitutions promulgated since this time have included references to human dignity.

The post-war period saw idea of human dignity invoked in a number of international conventions. Human dignity was mentioned in the *Universal Declaration of Human Rights* introduced by the United Nations in 1948 after the horrors of the World War II. Article 1 of the *Universal Declaration* states that 'all human beings are born free and equal in dignity and rights.' However, this brief mention was only supplemented with two further references. Article 22 on the *Right to Social Security and the Economic, Social, and Cultural Rights* stated that 'dignity' was indispensable for 'the free development of personality'. Article 23 (3) on the *Right to Just and Favourable Remuneration* was expressed as the basis to ensure an existence worthy of 'human dignity'.

The year of 1966 saw references in both the great support pillars to the *Universal Declaration*, namely the International Covenant on Economic, Social, and Cultural Rights (ICESCR) and the International Covenant on Civil and Political Rights (ICCPR) expressly declare human dignity as a foundational idea. The Preamble of each Covenant provides that 'recognition of the inherent dignity and of the equal and inalienable rights of members of the human family is the foundation of freedom, justice and peace in the world. Both Covenants go on to state 'these rights derive from the inherent dignity of human person'. Thereafter, the Covenants make only modest reference to dignity. Article 13 of the ICESCR provides that education shall be directed to the full development of the human personality for the sense of dignity. Article 10 of the ICCPR provides that old persons deprived of their liberty shall be treated with humanity and with respect for the inherent dignity of the human person. More recently, the *Charter of Fundamental Rights* of the European Union provides in Article 1, that the dignity of the person must be respected and protected.

The idea that human dignity is one of the foundational ideas in human rights conventions, and declarations. Beyleveld and Brownsword stress that human dignity is the underlying principle in the human rights provisions of national constitutions and international conventions.[25] They argue that human dignity, as provided for in these documents, embodies the idea of *empowerment* of the individual against the illegitimate and oppressive exercise of state power. Arguably, human

[25] D. Beyleveld and R. Brownsword, *Human Dignity in Human Ethics and Bio-law*.

dignity in these documents also connotes the idea of empowerment of the individual as an active and competent member of civil society. In these senses, whereas Mirandola saw the transformation of man through God, the modern conception of human dignity relies on the temporal vision of transformation through law.

International Instruments on Biotechnology and Human Cloning

The human dignity argument has become particularly prominent with the rise of biotechnology and, particularly in relation to human cloning. Genetic research into the 'common thread'[26] of DNA has shown remarkable similarities between the DNA of humans, animals, and plants. The capacity of scientists to transfer DNA between species has excited ideas whether man may change his very being, whether *homo sapiens* may become *homo proteus* capable of being altered by genetic intervention.[27] In the late 1990s, there were universal concerns, at the international level, about human cloning expressed by a Papal Encyclicals,[28] the Council of Europe,[29] the World Health Organization.[30] In both the cases of so-called reproductive and therapeutic cloning,[31] the human dignity argument stands squarely against the autonomy approach. The rare supporters of reproductive cloning[32] argue from the standpoint of autonomy but arguments based on human dignity consider that it is simply 'off limits as compromising human dignity'.[33] In essence there are some issues, which cannot be readily reduced to arguments on human rights.

In 1997, the General Assembly of UNESCO introduced a significant statement in relation to genetic research and privacy that also addressed limits to human cloning. The *Declaration on the Human Genome and Human Rights* asserted that the human genome 'underlies the fundamental unity of all members of the human family'. Article 11 of the *Declaration* provides that '[p]ractices which are contrary

[26] J. Sulston and G. Ferry, *The Common Thread* (London: Corgi Books, 2004).

[27] See L. Silver, Re-making Eden (London: Weidenfeld, 1998) and M. Kaku, *Visions*, (Oxford: Oxford University Press, 1998).

[28] See particularly *Veritatis Splendor*, 1993.

[29] The Council of Europe established a Steering Committee on Bioethics which prepared the Protocol on Cloning.

[30] See for instance the Resolution of the 50th World Health Assembly, Geneva, May 1997 affirming that the use of cloning for the replication of human individuals is ethically unacceptable and contrary to human integrity and morality.

[31] By somatic cell nuclear transfer (SCNT).

[32] Cloning of a human being (referred to as 'reproductive cloning') has been condemned universally.

[33] See R. Brownsword, 'Bioethics Today, Bioethics Tomorrow, Stem Cell Research and the Dignitarian Alliance', p.15; see also 'Human Cloning and Human Dignity: An Ethical Inquiry', Washington, DC, July 2002.

to human dignity, such as reproductive cloning of human beings shall not be permitted. States and competent international organizations are invited to cooperate in identifying such practices and in determining, nationally or internationally, appropriate measures to be taken to ensure that the principles set out in this Declaration are respected.'[34] The UNESCO International Bioethics Committee has developed a *Declaration on Universal Norms in Bioethics*. This *Declaration* also refers to the principle of human dignity, declaring, 'any decision or practice shall be made...with full respect for the inherent dignity of the human person, human rights and fundamental freedoms' (Article 4a). There is also the overriding principle that nothing in the *Declaration* may be interpreted as 'implying for any State...or person any claim to engage in...any act contrary to human rights, fundamental freedoms and human dignity' (Article 31).

In 1997, the Council of Europe released its *Convention on Human Rights and Biomedicine*.[35] The Preamble states, *inter alia,* 'that conscious that the misuse of biology and medicine may lead to acts endangering human dignity' and requires signatories to 'take such measures as are necessary to safeguard human dignity and the fundamental rights and freedoms of the individual with regard to the application of biology and medicine'. The *Convention* provides in Article 1 'that the purpose and object is to protect the dignity and identity of all human beings...with regard to the application of biology and medicine'. The Council added an *Additional Protocol* to this Convention to address the widespread concerns with human cloning. The *Protocol on Prohibition on Cloning of Human Beings* states that: 'Any intervention seeking to create a human being genetically identical to another human being, whether living or dead, is prohibited.'[36] Council of Europe Secretary said at the signing ceremony to the Protocol prohibiting human cloning, that 'at a time when occasional voices are being raised to assert the acceptability of human cloning and even to put it more rapidly into practice, it is important for Europe solemnly to declare its determination to defend *human dignity* against the abuse of scientific techniques.'[37] Many European countries reacted to this Convention and introduced specific legislation prohibiting cloning intended to produce genetically identical individuals, although others had already done so.[38] In the USA, the National Bioethics

---

[34] The Declaration was proclaimed at the 29th Session of the General Conference of UNESCO on 11 November 1997.

[35] The Convention for the Protection of Human Rights and Dignity with regard to the application of Biology and Medicine was approved by the Council of Europe in November 1996 and has been signed by some 20 of the 40 member-states.

[36] The Draft Additional Protocol on the Prohibition of Cloning Beings was adopted by the Parliamentary Assembly of the Council of Europe on 22 September 1997 and has been signed most member-states.

[37] Australian Health Ethics Committee Papers, Item 3.1, 23 January 1998.

[38] For example: Denmark: *Scientific Ethical Committee System and the Handling of Biomedical Research Projects,* Act No. 503 (1992) and *Medically Assisted Procreation*, Act No. 4060 (1997); Germany: *Federal Embryo Protection Act*, (1990); Norway: *Medical Use of Biotechnology*, Law No. 56 (1994); Spain: *Assisted Reproduction Procedures*, Law No. 35 (1988); Sweden: Law No. 115 (1991).

Advisory Commission, the forerunner of the current President's Council on Bioethics, handed down their Report, *Cloning Human Beings* and recommended legislation dealing with human cloning combined with a moratorium.[39]

The cloning debate was also conducted vigorously at the national level. It is hardly likely that it will ever be feasible to harmonize law and policy in stem cell research although there is a clear international consensus in prohibitions on so-called reproductive cloning.[40]

Most recently, the United Nations passed a non-binding resolution, originally proposed by Costa Rica, opposing reproductive cloning after some two years of debate. Agreement had been difficult to reach, on a form of words that would not impact on stem cell work in member nations.[41] Again the United Nations recognizing that 'reproductive cloning...poses a particularly serious problem' invoked the idea of human dignity in its draft resolution proposing that the rapid development of the life sciences...may pose dangers to the integrity and dignity of the individual.

The Report cautioned, 'any regulatory or legislative actions undertaken to effect the foregoing prohibition on creating a child by somatic cell nuclear transfer should be carefully written so as not to interfere with other important areas of scientific research'.[42] Similar sentiments were expressed in British[43] and Australian[44] reports. The debate about whether cloning procedures should be banned entirely or whether 'therapeutic' applications of cloning should be carefully regulated.[45]By contrast,

---

[39] See National Bioethics Advisory Commission Report, *Cloning Human Beings, Recommendation II* (June 1997).

[40] D. Chalmers and D. Nicol, 'Embryonic Stem Cell Research: Can the Law Balance Ethical, Scientific and Economic Values', *Law and the Human Genome Review*, Parts 1 and 2, 18 (2003) pp.43–53 and pp.91–108; see also S. Halliday, 'A Comparative Approach to the Regulation of Human Embryonic Stem Cell Research in Europe', *Medical Literature Review*, 12 (2004), pp.40–69.

[41] See S. Mayor, 'United Nations Committee Approves Declaration on Human Cloning', *British Medical Journal*, 330 (2005), p.496; and, 'United Nations Calls for Ban on All Forms of Human Cloning', *BioEdge*, 149 (8 March 2005), p.3. The resolution also stated the United Nations was 'Determined to Prevent Such an Attack on the Dignity of the Individual'.

[42] Ibid., Recommendation III.

[43] See Department of Health, UK, *Stem Cell Research: Medical Progress with Responsibility* (June 2000); A Report from the Chief Medical Officer's Expert Group Reviewing the Potential of Developments in Stem Cell Research and Cell Nuclear Replacement to Benefit Human Health and Government Response to the Recommendations Made in the Chief Medical Officer's Expert Group Report, CM 4833 (August 2000). See also A Joint Committee of the Human Genetics Advisory Commission and the Human Fertilization and Embryology Authority, Cloning Issues in Reproduction Science and Medicine (December 1998).

[44] Australian Health Ethics Committee, *Scientific, Ethical and Regulatory Considerations Relevant to Cloning of Human Beings* (16 December 1998). A Report to the Commonwealth Minister for Health and Aged Care recommended that the Commonwealth Government should reaffirm the UNESCO Declaration on the Human Genome and Human Rights, in particular Article 11, which states that '... reproductive cloning of human beings, shall not be permitted'.

[45] J. Robertson, 'Human Cloning and the Challenge of Regulation', *New England Journal of Medicine*, 339, No. 2 (1998), p.119; G. Annas, 'Why We Should Ban Human Cloning?' *New England Journal of Medicine*, 339, No. 2 (1998), p.122.

arguments based on human dignity have been less prominent in the international debates on stem cell technology and its regulation. Stem cell technology involves extracting developing cells from a human embryo (or some other adult cells) and efforts are made to dedifferentiate developing cell lines into human organs for transplantation and other therapeutic purposes. The technology can involve transferring somatic cells into an enucleated egg and then extracting the cells at the blastocyst stage. This is often referred to as 'therapeutic cloning'. An Australian Ministerial Report[46] recommended that there should be community discussion '…on the possible therapeutic benefits and possible risks of the development of cloning techniques.'[47] This Recommendation was consistent with Reports from the UK,[48] the USA and Japan. There has been less public discussion and controversy over stem cell research in Japan as compared to these countries. Japan introduced a *Law for the Prohibition of Reproductive Human Cloning* in 2000 but preferred only broad based guidelines dealing with human embryonic stem cell research.[49] It has been argued that this division of regulation may indicate some ambiguity in the sense that

> [w]hile Japan's legislative openness to stem cell and [therapeutic] cloning research is consistent with the country's cultural perceptions regarding the benefits of biotechnology, Japan's legislative regime arguably runs counter to the objectives of preserving human health and dignity, objectives that purportedly underlie Japan's human cloning law.[50]

Human dignity has been invoked as one of the arguments against the patenting of human DNA.[51] References to dignity have extended beyond cloning to patenting of human material. So, the EC Directive on the *Legal Protection of Biotechnological Inventions* (98/44) that stated that 'patent law must be applied so as to respect the fundamental principles safeguarding the dignity and integrity of the person (Recital 16).'[52] The argument runs that human DNA is unique and it is not legally possible to own body parts.[53] The general position in law is that the human body cannot be owned (see). This has not prevented claims for the patenting of DNA sequences rather than entire genomes. The human dignity arguments are generally phrased in terms of a limit on the commodification of the human body.

---

[46]Australian Health Ethics Committee, Scientific, Ethical and Regulatory Considerations Relevant to Cloning of Human Beings (16 December 1998).

[47] Ibid., Recommendation IV.

[48] A joint committee of the Human Genetics Advisory Commission and the Human Fertilization and Embryology Authority, Cloning Issues in Reproduction Science and Medicine, (December 1998).

[49] T. Morisaki, 'Human ES Cell Research', in: R. Ida. *Final Report on the Project Dialogue and Promotion of Bioethics in Asia* (Kyoto: Kyoto University, 2004), pp.540–544.

[50] A. Campbell, 'Ethos and Economics: Examining the Rationale Underlying Stem Cell and Cloning Research Policies in the United States, Germany and Japan' 31 (2005), *American Journal of Law and Medicine*, p.85.

[51] P. Ossorio, 'Legal and Ethical Issues in Biotechnology Patenting', in: J. Burley and J. Harris (eds.), *A Companion to Genetics* (Ames, Iowa: Blackwell, 2002), pp.414–416.

[52] R. Brownsword, *Human Dignity in Bioethics and Bio-Law*, pp.25–26.

[53] D. Meyers, *The Human Body and the Law* (Edinburgh: Edinburgh Press, 2nd edn., 1990), Chapter 7.

The debates on human reproductive cloning and patenting of human DNA have drawn heavily on references to human dignity. In contradistinction to empowering aspect of human dignity when used in relation to human rights, the references in relation to cloning express human dignity in terms of a *constraint*.[54] Human dignity, in these contexts is the reason for *not* pursuing a line of research inquiry; human dignity sets limits in biotechnology, limits that may not exist if arguments based on individual autonomy prevailed.

Conclusion: Human Dignity and the Law—Individual Empowerment and Societal Restraint

The critics of the 'dignitarian alliance' may consider the term 'human dignity' vague and indeterminate and reflecting a particular religious approach. Human dignity may be an elusive concept but it has entered moral and political debate. The term has some currency in national legal systems but is used increasingly in international instruments. Beyleveld and Brownsword have identified two meanings[55]:

1. Human dignity as empowerment
2. Human dignity as constraint[56]

This is consistent with traditional distinction in law between *positive* and *negative* rights. For example, in medical law there is no enforceable right to demand medical treatment. However, once there is a *medical* decision to administer treatment, that treatment must be delivered according to accepted standards of medical care and without discrimination. A good example of a *negative* right is the right not to be involuntarily detained for mental health under the mental health legislation where treatment is not available and not provided by the patient.[57] A complaint by a person detained results in the release of a person *not* in an order to administer the treatment.

Human dignity as empowerment is closely related to the ideas of autonomy and informed choice. However, such an approach may not provide a complete account of human dignity as underlying human rights. First, some humans (the young and

[54] D. Beyleveld and R. Brownsword, *Human Dignity in Bioethics and Biolaw*, pp.29–47.

[55] D. Beyleveld and R. Brownsword, *Human Dignity in Bioethics and Biolaw*.

[56] In the French Conseil d'état October 27 1995 local laws on dwarf-throwing were upheld. The dwarfs argued that they consented to the throwing, were exercising their free choice as adults and were employed. Nevertheless the Conseil d'état ruled that the practice was not entertainment as it compromised human dignity and was contrary to ordre public. This illustrates both the human rights as autonomy and empowerment and human rights as constraint. See D. Beyleveld and R. Brownsword, *Human Dignity in Bioethics and Bio-law*, Chapter 1, pp.25–27.

[57] L. Skene, *Law and Medical Practice* (Sydney: Butterworths, 2004), at para.2.110–2.114.

old) may be excluded from this account. They have rights but they may have to be enjoyed only in a secondary sense. Second, human dignity as justifying human rights must also be limited by the decision-making capacity of others that must be respected.[58] There is an argument whether *negative* rights are also based on autonomy or dignity. Human rights and the right of self-determination (autonomy) usually activate some action by another party. In this respect they give rise to positive duties or rights. On the other hand, it is difficult to argue that autonomy is the basis of a *negative* right. Human dignity gives a reasonable explanation for some of these *negative* rights. For example, the right not to be involuntarily detained may be based upon the essential dignity of the individual—it is the dignity of the individual that is being protected. Similarly, in an argument on euthanasia, the individual patient cannot direct the doctor to administer the treatment. The patient does not have an *autonomous* and *positive* right to die. The doctor's ethical duty to do no harm and to act beneficently to the patient is more likely based upon the essential dignity of the individual. In this respect, humans have dignity not because of any human right arising from law or international treaty or intrinsic autonomy but because of the fact that they are human. In this respect, autonomy and human rights is an insufficient explanation of the law's response and explanation particularly of *negative* rights.[59]

Brownsword[60] has argued persuasively that the term human dignity, despite criticisms, has a core of accepted meaning. Human dignity is generally used in a conservative sense and to human and human actions. The term may well underpin human rights and autonomy but it goes further and recognizes not only individual rights but also societal interests. Human dignity does not reduce embryo research to the rights of the gamete providers but can include areas outside of traditional human rights arguments. As a prominent example, during the human reproductive cloning debates, the human dignity arguments went beyond the rights of gamete donors' embryos to a wider social consideration of public research standards and the treatment of embryos. As Brownsword has observed, human dignity will still be relevant even if human cloning was proven to be a safe procedure.

Human dignity is not only established in international instruments, it is also a term that speaks across national boundaries.

---

[58] R. Brownsword,'Regulating Human Genetics: New Dilemmas for a New Millennium', *Medical Literature Review*, 12 (2004), p.24.

[59] E. Pellegrino and D. Thomasma, *The Christian Virtues in Legal Practice* (Ann Arbor, MI: Georgetown University Press, 1996), passim.

[60] R. Brownsword, 'Regulating Human Genetics: New Dilemmas for a New Millennium', pp.14–39.

16
Doing Justice to Dignity in the Criminal Law

Julia Davis

An important task for any community is to find a source of principled limits on the criminal law. This search is frustrated by the fact that the concept of wrongdoing, just like the contested concept of a crime itself, is open and empty of factual content. The ordinary definitions of wrongdoing, as conduct that deviates from a rule, standard or norm of conduct that is thought to be right, and of a crime as 'a legal wrong that can be followed by criminal proceedings which may result in punishment'[1] both leave undone the hard work of identifying in precise factual terms the conduct that ought to be forbidden by the criminal law and providing acceptable reasons why it is thought to be right to punish offenders who are responsible for that conduct.

Legislators who have found that the meaning of these terms does not yield a universally accepted test for recognizing criminal wrongdoing have sought assistance from other sources including religious teachings, moral and legal philosophy, and criminology. Despite our continuing community conversations about crime, wrongdoing, and punishment, however, we have not agreed upon a clear test that can neatly divide the conduct that we feel compelled to act against from the conduct that we feel we must tolerate or deal with in other ways. Whenever a likely candidate is put forward by one camp, opposition from another points up its weaknesses. Consequently, legislators, whose allegiance to John Stuart Mill's harm principle is challenged by the Kantian principle of autonomy, adopt compromises that open the law up to criticism that it is illogical, inconsistent, and unprincipled. Legal theorists, pulled by opposing values, respond in different ways: some hail the collapse of the harm principle and call for a new critical principle[2]; some smuggle aspects of one theory into another to bolster its perceived shortcomings[3]; others craft hybrid

[1] G. Williams, *Textbook of Criminal Law* (London: Stevens & Sons, 1983), pp.27–28.

[2] B.E. Harcourt, 'The Collapse of the Harm Principle', *Journal of Criminal Law and Criminology*, 90 (1999), p.109.

[3] For example, Joel Feinberg adopts an extended normative definition of harm as an indefensible and wrongful setback to interest, done with fault, and in violation of a person's rights in *Harm to Others* (Oxford: Oxford University Press, 1984), pp.105–106, 36, 214–215, 186; *Harmless Wrongdoing* (Oxford: Oxford University Press, 1988), p.26.

J. Malpas and N. Lickiss (eds.), Perspectives on Human Dignity: A Conversation, 169–182.

theories that use different principles at different stages[4]; while sceptics argue that the law is hopelessly ambiguous, fatally contradictory, and fundamentally incapable of delivering justice.[5]

In the last half of the 20th century legislators and legal philosophers began to use the idea of human dignity to supplement, and at times to displace, a reliance on the traditional concepts of harm and autonomy as the source of principled controls over the state's entitlement to forbid conduct on the pain of criminal punishment.[6] The emergence of the notion of human dignity forces us once again to think about the nature of the good life for human beings, to clarify the role that the criminal law should play in securing that vision and to reconsider the relative value that the state should place on our welfare and autonomy interests and our shared desire to be respected by others as persons of equal dignity and worth.

This chapter presents a model of criminal wrongdoing that does justice to the elements of welfare, autonomy, and dignity and explains how the notion of human dignity can be used to fill out our understanding of the duties that the criminal law imposes upon us. The first section examines the relative merits of the three suggested candidates for keeping the criminal law within principled boundaries, namely, the harm principle, the principle of autonomy, and the idea of human dignity. The second presents an account of a crime as conduct that threatens the foundations of the good life for human beings living together as a community. I argue that our criminal law contains a distinctive conception of justice that is based on our vision of ourselves as equals in dignity, worth and value, and which imposes a duty on each of us to respect others by treating their interests in welfare and autonomy as carrying a value equal to our own. I suggest that we cannot justify criminalizing any conduct unless it breaches both the harm principle, which sets the factual boundaries of the criminal law, and the equal dignity principle, which provides the criminal law with its moral heart. The chapter concludes by explaining why our allegiance to the principle that all human beings are equal in dignity will sometimes require us to refrain from criminalizing certain controversial kinds of conduct that may appear to be supremely undignified.

---

[4] See, for example, H.L.A. Hart, *Punishment and Responsibility* (Oxford: Clarendon Press, 1984).

[5] A. Norrie, *Crime, Reason and History* (London: Weidenfeld & Nicolson, 1993); 'Simulacra of Morality? Beyond the Ideal/Actual Antinomies of Criminal Justice', in: R.A. Duff (ed.), *Philosophy and the Criminal Law* (Cambridge: Cambridge University Press, 1998), p.101; A. Norrie, *Punishment, Responsibility and Justice: A Relational Critique* (Oxford: Oxford University Press, 2000).

[6] J. Hampton, 'Correcting Harms Versus Righting Wrongs', *University of California at Los Angeles Law Review*, 39 (1992), p.1659; M. Dan-Cohen, 'Basic Values and the Victim's State of Mind', *California Law Review*, 88 (2000), p.759.

The Search for the Moral Limits of the Criminal Law

The Harm Principle

John Stuart Mill argued that the state should be entitled to restrict our liberty only when our conduct risks doing harm to others.[7] This 'very simple' principle has strong initial appeal because the essentially factual notion of harm-doing, as conduct that makes someone or something worse off, appears to provide a straightforward test that can give content to the moral, but factually empty, concepts of wrongdoing and crime. Furthermore, the utilitarian concern with harm and human welfare sits well with the state's duty to govern for the health, safety, and well-being of its citizens. Three problems arise however, when we put the notion of harm into place as the critical principle that determines the contours of the criminal law.

The first problem is that a harm-based test would push the criminal law far beyond its current boundaries because, although it is relatively easy to identify, harm is ubiquitous. If we track the consequences far enough, almost any conduct can lead to harm and so theoretically attract the criminal sanction. Certainly, the harm principle's perceived strength (in liberal eyes at least) in ruling out the criminalization of conduct that is essentially objected to on the grounds of offence or moralism has been weakened by politicians who use 'broken windows' arguments to extend the criminal law by finding remote harms in conduct traditionally considered to be harmless to others like prostitution, begging, selling alcohol, using drugs, and engaging in homosexual activity.[8]

The next problem arises because equating harm-doing with wrongdoing (and reducing the moral problem to a purely factual question) leaves out something important; specifically, it does not take account of the characteristic attitude of contempt for the value of others that we read into conduct commonly seen as criminal. To solve this problem Jerome Hall posited the existence of a special kind of 'penal', 'social', or 'criminal' harm 'the essential determination of which is the moral culpability of the actor',[9] and Joel Feinberg adopted an extended normative definition of 'harm' that includes notions of fault, moral wrongdoing, and the idea of violations of rights.[10] Unfortunately, these manoeuvers lead to a third problem—the struggle over the meaning of harm. Once the stronger moral notions of culpability and wrongdoing are added into these extended definitions of 'harm',

---

[7] J.S. Mill, *On Liberty and Other Essays* (Oxford: Oxford University Press, 1998), pp.13–14.

[8] See B.E. Harcourt, 'The Collapse of the Harm Principle', *Journal of Criminal Law and Criminology*, 90 (1999), p.109; J. Feinberg, 'Harm to Others—A Rejoinder', *Criminal Justice Ethics*, 5 (1986), p.27.

[9] J. Hall, *General Principles of Criminal Law*, 2nd edn. (Indianapolis: Bobbs-Merrill, 1960), pp.215, 242.

[10] See Feinberg, *Harm to Others*, as cited in note 3 above.

they overpower it and harm's usefulness as a factual test is lost. In a frustrating twist, these definitional tactics, which were designed to enhance harm's limiting function, destroy its original meaning and we are forced back to the debates about the nature of moral wrongdoing that divided us in the first place. Adopting a definition of a crime as the culpable choice to harm another may improve upon our understanding of a crime as mere harm-doing, but it means that the harm principle ceases to be the critical principle that we had hoped for. So, although the concept of harm does appear to offer a usefully factual source of limits on the criminal law, its own limitations and our struggles over its meaning and role have led philosophers and lawyers to put forward the concept of autonomy as a necessary supplement to the harm principle.

The Autonomy Principle

Immanuel Kant's theory of autonomy and treating persons as ends in themselves has been very influential in Anglo-American justifications of punishment. Arguments over the relative importance of human welfare and autonomy have persisted, however, not only between consequentialists and deontologists, but also between unaligned theorists who attempt to find a place for both the harm principle and the autonomy principle in the criminal law. Furthermore, recent debates over autonomy's role have moved away from Kant's account, which grants us equal moral worth insofar as we are rational and autonomous,[11] in favour of a more factual account of autonomy's significance. Autonomy, defined as the exercise of control over the conduct of one's own life by defining, choosing, and pursuing a good life on one's own terms (regardless of whether those decisions are based in morality or in rationality[12]) is seen simply as another object of desire that may deserve legal protection. So conceived, it is no longer the key moral attribute shared by human beings that justifies our duties to others. Theorists following this approach disagree not only over the meaning of autonomy and its relation to the harm principle and the matter of human welfare, but also over the priority that these aspects should have in structuring the criminal law.

Andrew Ashworth and Nicola Lacey argue that autonomy and welfare represent competing values.[13] They suggest that the criminal law does not (and cannot) rank

---

[11] See chapters by Jeff Malpas, Rosalind Hursthouse and Andrew Brennan, and Y.S. Lo in this volume for extended discussions on autonomy.

[12] On Joseph Raz's account 'a man is autonomous even if he chooses the bad'; J. Raz, *The Morality of Freedom* (Oxford: Clarendon Press, 1986), p.411.

[13] N. Lacey, *State Punishment: Political Principles and Community Values* (London: Routledge, 1988), pp.103–105; A. Ashworth, *Principles of Criminal Law* (Oxford: Clarendon Press, 2nd edn., 1996), p.24.

one consistently over the other and argue that we must negotiate compromises between the two on a case by case basis.[14] By contrast, John Gardner and Joseph Raz maintain that autonomy as the 'key ideal of human well-being for our age' is the true source of the value that we place on our welfare interests.[15] When defining autonomy, however, they also give primacy to the notion of capacity or functioning, and they resolve the dilemma over autonomy's relationship to the concept of harm by classing as harmful only the adverse effects upon welfare that will reduce the prospective exercise of a person's autonomy.[16] Like Feinberg, who also links interferences with autonomy to the harm principle, Gardner and Raz agree that conduct causing only transitory pain, disfigurement, grief, and distress, which are disliked states that 'come to us, are suffered for a time, and then go, leaving us whole and undamaged as we were before'[17] cannot count either as harmful or as an interference with autonomy.

The insistence that adverse effects upon welfare are harmful only when they impair future capacity for chosen action seems not only to put an artificial limit upon the meaning of harm but also to underrate the importance we place on our welfare. We do appear to value an intact, unblemished body and the absence of pain, grief, and distress as important aspects of the existence that we aim to secure for ourselves, and, whether these effects disable us from action or not, we do regard ourselves as being worse off or harmed if we are blighted in such ways even if it is only for a short time.

---

[14] A. Ashworth, *Principles of Criminal Law* (Oxford: Oxford University Press, 4th edn., 2003), pp.323–329; Lacey suggests in *State Punishment*, above note 13 (p.117) that 'it would be foolish to imagine that one always acts as an absolute constraint on the pursuit of the other'. She argues (p.187) that trade-offs between the two must be made when a community considers the aim and the distribution of punishment. Recently, however, she has argued that the values of autonomy and welfare are not necessarily in opposition: *Unspeakable Subjects* (Oxford: Hart Publishing, 1998), p.52.

[15] J. Gardner, 'On the General Part of the Criminal Law', in: R. A. Duff (ed.), *Philosophy and the Criminal Law* (Cambridge: Cambridge University Press, 1998), pp.205, 242–243. See also J. Raz, 'Autonomy, Toleration and the Harm Principle', in: R. Gavison (ed.), *Issues in Contemporary Legal Philosophy* (Oxford: Clarendon Press, 1987), pp.313, 327–320; *The Morality of Freedom* (Oxford: Clarendon Press, 1986), pp.413–441.

[16] Joseph Raz argues that harm has a 'forward looking aspect' that is linked directly to autonomy and that we can classify as harmful only consequences that 'affect options or projects' either by depriving 'a person of opportunities or of the ability to use them' or by reducing the 'ability to act in ways that he might desire'; J. Raz, *The Morality of Freedom*, above note 15, pp.413–414. John Gardner emphasizes that harm is 'not the pain or lost limb or shock in itself' but is instead the consequent 'attenuation of capacity or opportunity for action, reducing the range of alternative actions and activities that are available to the person who is harmed'; J. Gardner, 'On the General Part of the Criminal Law', above, note 15, p.243.

[17] Feinberg, *Harm to Others*, above note 3, p.45. A. P. Simester and Andrew von Hirsch also limit the scope of harm to those effects that impair a person's 'opportunities to engage in worthwhile activities and relationships and to pursue valuable, self-chosen goals' in: A. P. Simester and A. von Hirsch, 'Rethinking the Offense Principle', *Legal Theory*, 8 (2002), p.269, 281.

Another troubling example is the case of a 'harmless rape', described by John Gardner and Stephen Shute, where an unconscious victim is secretly violated by another without any physical damage resulting and where the event is never discovered.[18] Gardner and Shute classify it as harmless because they insist that harm must have a prospective dimension that will affect the victim's future exercise of her autonomy. Again, it is difficult to agree with their assertion that the rape does no harm simply because the victim's future capacity for autonomy is unaffected. The victim's control over access to her body was diminished, and I suggest that, viewed objectively, this factual setback to her opportunity to exercise her autonomy must be seen as making her worse off and classified as harmful.[19]

Giving autonomy a controlling role within the harm principle also leads to a second set of problems that arise partly because our welfare interests and our autonomy interests often conflict and partly because giving primacy to one over the other unbalances the law by leaving out something we value. Our welfare interests, defined as comprising all the things both internal and external to the person that are important for human existence, cover what we might call the *passive* aspects of well-being. Our interests in autonomy comprise the *active* aspects of our well-being or, as Mill called it, well-doing.[20] Even though our desires to improve our welfare and to pursue our autonomy may sometimes conflict, reinforcing links do exist between the two; an adequate welfare-base lays the foundation for the exercise of our autonomy and exercising our autonomy can often improve our welfare. However, if one of these aspects is missing, no improvement or increase in the other can make up the loss. The pampered slave, whose welfare interests are completely satisfied, but whose entitlement to the free exercise of his will is denied, cannot be said to live well. Equally, the woman, whose entitlement to exercise her autonomy is guaranteed, but whose living conditions of deprivation and poverty mean that her choices are limited to deciding which of her children gets enough to eat, does not have a good life.[21]

---

[18] J. Gardner and S. Shute, 'The Wrongness of Rape', in: J. Horder (ed), *Oxford Essays in Jurisprudence*, 4th Series (Oxford: Oxford University Press, 2000), p.193.

[19] The criminal law exists not simply to respond to subjectively experienced wrongs or the subjectively experienced harms that flow from those wrongs, but to make an objective, public, assessment of conduct. Criminal law is the external view, and consequently we are entitled to make external assessments of harm just as Gardner and Shute go on to make an external assessment of wrongdoing in this case.

[20] John Stuart Mill saw the good life as composed of 'well-being' and 'well-doing': see *On Liberty*, above note 7, p.84. The useful notions of 'passive well-being' and 'active well-being' used by John Gardner neatly match Mill's two elements; see 'On the General Part of the Criminal Law' above, note 15.

[21] Partha Dasgupta, explains how destitution creates both physical pain as well as the moral pain of having to make tragic choices over the allocation of food and health care in *Human Well-being and the Natural Environment* (Oxford: Oxford University Press, 2001), p.37.

If we view welfare and autonomy as incommensurable elements of the good life and as equally worthy of the law's protection, then neither can take priority in shaping the criminal law. Because we do commonly see ourselves as worse-off in a factual sense when these interests are set back, it follows that conduct that sets back either our welfare or our autonomy should be covered by the harm principle. While this move improves our theory of harm and settles the relationship between harm, welfare, and autonomy (in its modern factual sense), however, it does not bring us any closer to resolving the other problems that arise if the harm principle sets the limits of the criminal law. Even in its modified form, it still fails to capture the message about the value of others that we object to in conduct that is commonly called criminal, and if any conduct that risks a setback either to another's autonomy interests or to their welfare interests qualifies as harmful, the boundaries of the criminal law would extend even further than they do now.

One solution to these dilemmas might be to return to Kant's account of our moral worth as being grounded in our rationality and our capacity to will that our maxims become universal law. Unfortunately, this vision of autonomy's special moral significance is open to the objection that it may lead us to ignore non-human animals and any non-rational or incapacitated humans,[22] and so, to salvage what is valuable in Kant's account of our moral worth, we must turn to the idea that has dominated modern legal thinking and examine the role that human dignity can play in the criminal law.

Human Dignity

After World War II, the idea that state authorities have a fundamental duty to respect the equal dignity of all human beings began to feature in both International Human Rights Law and the domestic constitutions of states like Germany and Israel.[23] Even in France and the USA where there is no express legislative recognition of human dignity (but where the concept of equality has strong constitutional support) the idea has been used to limit the law right through the criminal justice process. Courts have struck down laws criminalizing homosexual sodomy,[24] upheld

---

[22] See Rosalind Hursthouse, 'Human Dignity and Charity', Chapter 7 in this volume.

[23] See, I. Englard, 'Human Dignity: From Antiquity to Modern Israel's Constitutional Framework', *Cardozo Law Review*, 21 (2000), p.1903; T. Hörnle, 'Offensive Behaviour and German Penal Law', *Buffalo Criminal Law Review*, 5 (2001), p.255; J. Resnick and J. C. Suk, 'Adding Insult to Injury: Questioning the Role of Dignity in Conceptions of Sovereignty', *Stanford Law Review*, 55 (2003), p.1921. Courts in both Israel and Germany are empowered to strike down legislation that conflicts with this duty.

[24] In *Lawrence v. Texas*, 123 S Ct 2472 (2003), the US Supreme Court declared unconstitutional a Texas law forbidding homosexual sodomy on the grounds that by criminalizing only homosexual sodomy and unjustifiably creating a class of 'second-class citizens', the Texas legislature had failed in its duty to respect equally the dignity of those persons subject to the law.

laws banning dwarf tossing events,[25] outlawed punishments like castration,[26] prohibited routine strip searches[27] and forbidden race or gender-based discrimination in jury selection,[28] all on the grounds that the law must recognize our equal dignity. The emphasis on the special moral dignity of persons traces back to Aristotle and Cicero[29] and features in the theories of utilitarians like Mill and Bentham and deontologists like Kant and Hegel.[30] This solid core of agreement between philosophers whose views are often opposed suggests that the equal dignity principle may be well suited to the task of justifying principled limits on the criminal law. Before we can give dignity this crucial role, however, we must resolve three difficulties emerging from the dignity jurisprudence that cloud its meaning, use, and significance.

The first problem is the blurring of the boundaries between dignity and harm. Just as legal philosophers have smuggled moral elements into their accounts of harm, so have lawyers fused harm with dignity as American courts use the idea of 'dignitary harms' to justify overturning legislation. 'Dignitary' or 'expressive' harms are said to be imposed on individuals by the improper messages about individual value that state laws express; they result from the attitudes expressed through government actions rather than the material consequences they cause.[31]

---

[25] A French dwarf, who lost before the Conseil d'État (27 October 1995) req nos (Commune de Morsang-sur-Orge) and 143–578 (Ville d'Aix-en-Provence) took his case to the United Nations Human Rights Committee on the grounds that the French regulations banning the organization of dwarf throwing contests violated his rights under the International Covenant on Civil and Political Rights. The case was not successful: *Mr Manuel Wackenheim v. France*, Communication No. 854/1999, United Nations Document CCPR/C/75/D/8541999 (13 November 1996), United Nations Document A/57/40 at 179 (2002) Decision of the Human Rights Committee, 75th Session, 26 September 2002.

[26] See Meir Dan-Cohen's discussion of *State v. Braxton*, 326 SE 2d 410 (SC 1985), where the appellate court withdrew the option that the lower court had given to offenders between choosing 30 years imprisonment or being surgically castrated; M. Dan-Cohen, 'Basic Values and the Victim's State of Mind', *California Law Review*, 88 (2000), p.759, text at footnote 13.

[27] See the ruling by the US District Court for the Eastern District of New York in *Augustin v. Jablonsky*, 99-CV-3126 (DRH) (ARL) 2001 US Dist LEXIS 10276 forbidding routine strip searches upon arrest for minor offences.

[28] The US Supreme Court prohibited discrimination on the basis of race or gender in jury selection in: *Batson v. Kentucky*, 476 US 79, 90 L Ed 2d 69 (1986) gender; and *J.E.B. v. Alabama ex rel T.B.*, 511 US 127, 114 L Ed 2d 89 (1994) race.

[29] R.W. Wright, 'The Principles of Justice', *Notre Dame Law Review*, 75 (2000), p.1859. Nicola Lacey, in State Punishment, above, note 13, p.144–148, traces the liberal themes of equality and 'taking persons seriously as moral agents worthy of equal respect and concern' from Kant, Bentham, and Mill, to the work of H. L. A. Hart, Ronald Dworkin, John Rawls, and Peter Singer.

[30] See Mill's discussion of Bentham's famous aphorism 'Each is to count for one and no-one more than one' in *On Liberty*, above, note 7, p.198–199; and I. Kant, *The Metaphysics of Morals* (Cambridge: Cambridge University Press, 1991), pp.434–435.

[31] R. H. Pildes and R. G. Niemi, 'Expressive Harms, "Bizarre Districts", and Voting Rights', *Michigan Law Review*, 92 (1993), pp.483, 506–507; see also E. S. Anderson and R. H. Pildes, 'Expressive Theories of Law: A General Restatement', *University of Pennsylvania Law Review*, 148 (2000), p.1503.

These harms are a fiction designed to give legal standing to people who are not themselves threatened by the impugned laws, but who, because they wish to overturn them, must prove injury to comply with rules-governing procedure. This usage should be resisted because the source of these complaints is located in the normative realm of value and not in the factual world of welfare or autonomy interests. They tell us nothing new about harm. Rather, they remind us that we see ourselves as being equal in dignity and that we feel morally outraged when the law does not do justice to that value.

The second problem arises because dignity has two senses. Dignity in the first sense refers to the inherent worth that attaches to all human beings simply because they are human beings, and in our times this worth is seen as equal worth. In its second sense dignity refers to a state of existence or conduct that is characterized by the absence of perceived indignity, humiliation, or degradation. It is linked to our feelings, experiential well-being and self-esteem. Because dignity is not simply the opposite of perceived indignity, however, there is an asymmetry between the two senses that creates problems in legal debates. Dignity as equal worth is a normative quality. It exists in the moral sphere and remains untouched by events or experience; we cannot differ in equality, nor have more or less of it. Conversely, dignity in the second sense is a quantitative and factual matter; we can progressively lose our dignity as more and more indignities are heaped upon us. Dignity in this factual sense cannot advance our search for moral limits. If we want protection from perceived indignities we can simply appeal to the harm principle that defends our welfare and autonomy, but this kind of dignity is too weak to do the moral work of justifying the duties to others that the criminal law imposes upon us.[32] However, dignity in its normative sense offers more hope, precisely because it focuses upon the moral worth of human beings and because it is now welded to the powerful idea of equality.

The third problem casting doubt on dignity's usefulness as a limiting principle arises because dignity-based arguments work both ways. This is illustrated by the 'dwarf tossing' case, *France v. Wackenheim*,[33] where both parties invoked the notion of human dignity to justify opposing arguments. France (using dignity in the second sense), argued that using human beings as projectiles create an undignified public spectacle. Mr Wackenheim, whose welfare and autonomy interests were not harmed by his participation, claimed that dignity consists in having a job and being treated without discrimination based on size (thereby using both senses). This case suggests that, on its own, the concept of human dignity does not give us enough guidance. Dignity is not an open concept like wrongdoing, but we struggle over its significance in the law because it has different senses and often points us in opposite directions. It is morally important, but factually imprecise. So, while dignity

[32] This may account for a recent editorial doubting the usefulness of the concept of dignity by R. Macklin, 'Dignity is a Useless Concept', *British Medical Journal*, 327 (2003), p.1419.

[33] See *France v. Wackenheim*, above, note 25.

may offer us a moral justification for our criminal laws, it cannot determine their factual content.

It seems that the search for a single controlling principle must fail. A harm-based assessment offers us a usefully factual test that protects our welfare and autonomy, but it is too broad in scope and leaves out the moral dimensions of a crime. On the other hand, the normative claim that human beings are equal in dignity or worth may offer us a usefully moral justification for our criminal law, but it cannot tell us what kinds of conduct those laws should forbid. The challenge then, is to place these key elements into some kind of harmony by creating a model of the criminal law that not only reflects and protects the lives that we want to live and the kind of community that we want to be, but can also ensure that our criminal laws do justice to all those living within our community of equals.

The Good Life Model of Criminal Wrongdoing

My model of the criminal law aims to reflect the value we place both on protecting ourselves from conduct that may harm us and on responding to conduct that does not respect us as persons of equal dignity. It is based on the assumption that there is a logical connection between our vision of the fundamental elements of the good life for human beings and our understanding of the nature of a crime, seen as conduct which threatens those elements. I suggest that we can identify three incommensurate elements of the good life that the criminal law should protect. They are our welfare interests, our autonomy interests, and our shared desire to be respected by others as persons of equal dignity and worth. The two factual elements of welfare and autonomy represent the things that we want *for ourselves* from life in general. By contrast, the third element is normative and relational; being respected as a person of equal worth is something that we want *from others* because it confirms our vision of ourselves as members of a community of equals who have recognized in each other a reciprocal entitlement to be treated as equals. These elements were discussed in Section 1 and appear in Table 1, below.

In Table 2, below, the positive elements in the model of the good life are transposed into the negative elements contained in the model of a crime. Just like the good life that it reflects and protects, therefore, a crime has two dimensions: a normative or moral dimension governed by a principle that requires each person to respect others as persons of equal dignity, worth, and value; and a factual dimension that protects our interests in welfare and autonomy, which is governed by the harm to others principle. Because our demand that others respect us as equals contains two sub-aspects that include both the attitudes that others take towards us as well as their actual conduct towards us, the notion of equal respect can be linked both to the definition of fault and the definition of wrongdoing.

Table 1 The two dimensions of the Good Life

The factual dimension		The normative dimension
WELFARE Having and Being	AUTONOMY Choosing, Doing and Achieving	RESPECT Counting as an Equal
1. Definition		
The welfare factors include all those things, both internal and external to the person, that are important to human existence.	Autonomy is the exercise of control over the conduct of one's own life by defining, choosing and pursuing the good life on one's own terms.	Respect is an attitude which recognizes that each human being is entitled to be treated as a person of equal dignity, worth, and value.
2. Focus		
Passive states of well-being.	Active states of well-being or 'well-doing'.	A relational state of being treated right by others.
3. Basis		
Our common needs for: • Physical, emotional, and mental health; • Possessions and wealth; • Reputation; • Community services and institutions; • Social support; and • A safe and secure physical environment.	Our common desires to: • Define the good life for ourselves; to choose when, where and how to pursue it; and to succeed in that pursuit. • This depends on both—our capacity, and—our factual opportunities for decisions and action.	Our shared beliefs in: • The equality of all human beings; • The ideas of justice, reciprocity, rationality, and the principle that we should treat: like cases alike, equal cases equally, and different cases differently.

Table 2 The two dimensions of a crime

The factual dimension		The normative dimension	
The 'Harm to Others' Principle		The 'Respect Others as Equals' Principle	
Harm to welfare	Harm to autonomy	Wrongdoing	Fault
Setbacks to welfare (i.e. our passive states of well-being) that make us worse off.	Setbacks to autonomy (i.e. our active states of well-being) that reduce either our capacity or our opportunities for chosen action.	Conduct towards others. Conduct that deviates from the norm requiring each person to respect others by treating them as persons of equal dignity, worth, and value.	Responses to others. An attitude which fails, in the circumstances, to recognize or to respond properly to the equal dignity, worth, and value of others.

The key to understanding how this model justifies transforming our reciprocal desires for respect into rules requiring respectful conduct lies in the crucial connection between our vision of ourselves as equals in dignity and our allegiance to the principle of justice that directs that like cases should be treated alike, and equal cases, equally.[34] Once we recognize that we are all equal, the direction to treat equal cases equally requires more from us than a mere attitude of respect. In fact, the principle of justice is directed not to our attitudes at all, but to our conduct itself; given that we are equals, it requires us—whatever we might think of others—to treat them as equals. This connection between justice and our equal worth enables us to make laws mandating respectful conduct that apply to all within the community of equals and it suggests that the critical message is not that we see ourselves simply as persons possessing dignity, but that we see ourselves as possessing dignity in equal measure.

At its moral heart, the criminal law contains a distinctive conception of justice that requires equal treatment of equals by equals. However, before we can give factual content to our moral norm of equal respect, we must return to the good life model and recognize that we are equal not only in a moral sense, but in two essential factual ways as well. As equal human beings and equal members of a community we also share a wide range of factual interests in welfare and autonomy. It follows that if our common interests in welfare and autonomy are of equal value, then no one-person's interests can take priority over those of any others, because equality mandates a stand-off. This means that the criminal law, as the law of equal justice, imposes a reciprocal duty on each of us to respect others by treating their fundamental interests in welfare and autonomy as carrying a value that is equal to our own and so, whenever the desires of two or more persons conflict, any use of fraud, force, or coercion is ruled out and the only acceptable way to resolve the issue is to resort to persuasion or to let the status quo prevail. It also imposes a limited, unilateral duty on each human animal to respect the interests that we share equally with other non-human animals. Our recognition that we share interests in welfare and existence as a species with other animals, but not interests in autonomy, explains why it is lawful to kill an animal humanely and eat it, but not to torture it or neglect its welfare.[35]

The law of equal justice also explains why the criminal law imposes an extended duty on able-bodied adults of full capacity to make special efforts to equalizse the position of any children, or non-rational, incapacitated humans who are disadvantaged by their circumstances of factual inequality. This comes about because equality is an abstract concept, which, when applied to human beings, makes sense only in circumstances of factual difference. If we must treat equal cases equally we must also treat different cases differently. Consequently, we are not entitled to ignore the weak, whose identity and intrinsic worth as human beings remains unchanged by their factual incapacity. Rather our duty is to make extra efforts to compensate for their reduced capacity for autonomy. So, in our encounters with other beings, there is first a moment of recognition when we realize that we are equal both in our inherent worth and in our factual interests in autonomy and welfare. This is followed by a

[34] This principle of justice can be traced back to Aristotle's account of justice in Book V, *The Nichomachean Ethics* (Oxford: Oxford University Press, 1998), pp.106–136.

[35] It appears that some animals may share our passion for equal justice: S.F. Brosnan and F.B.M. de Waal, 'Monkeys Reject Unequal Pay', *Nature*, 425 (2003), p.279.

moment of acknowledgement of the consequent duty to respect that equal dignity and those equally shared interests, and finally, each time we are faced with choosing our path through life, with a moment of choice to accept or reject that duty. This takes us back to Aristotle, who said that 'if a man harms another by choice, he acts unjustly ... provided that the act violates proportion or equality.'[36]

Conclusion: The Paradox of Dignity

The good life model of the criminal law indicates that we are not justified in criminalizing any conduct unless it breaches not only the 'harm to others' principle which gives factual content to this concept of a crime, but also the 'equal respect for others' principle which provides the criminal law with its moral justification. Under the good life model of the criminal law, the primary moral principle requiring us to respect the equal dignity, worth, and value of others explains why we also need the harm principle to give factual content to the criminal law, because we cannot treat others as equals until we can identify the ways in which we are factually equal. Furthermore, the model's combination of the two principles also helps us to limit the spread of the criminal law that would occur if we used only the harm principle as our source of limits. The good life model, because it contains the equal-respect principle that focuses on both the attitude of disrespect and the wrongful conduct that evidences that disrespect, defines a crime as conduct that is animated by a failure to recognize or to respond properly to the equal dignity, worth, and value of others and their equal entitlement to pursue and enjoy their welfare and exercise their autonomy within the boundaries provided for by the state. This means that we cannot classify any conduct that risks harm as criminal, but only conduct that risks harm to others, which is also read as a conscious failure of respect.

The good life model places the duty of equal justice on each of us within the community as individual persons. It also put limits on the most dangerous of legal persons: the state itself. It justifies the state's punitive responses to those who have failed in their conduct to do equal justice to others and limits the state to criminalizing only conduct that both threatens harm to the equally shared welfare or autonomy interests of others and is read as a failure to respect the equal value of others. This account of the limits on the criminal law points up an interesting paradox that results from the asymmetry feature of the meaning of dignity discussed in Section 2. The paradox of dignity requires the state, in the name of our equal dignity, to refrain from criminalizing certain controversial or upsetting kinds of conduct, for example, dwarf tossing events, that may appear to be supremely undignified.

It arises because our vision of ourselves as equals in dignity and worth, which gives the criminal law its moral justification, grounds our duty to respect others as

---

[36] Aristotle, This principle of justice can be traced back to Aristotle's account of justice in Book V of the *Nichomachean Ethics*, 1136a 1–4.

sovereign equals, entitled to exercise their capacity for autonomy in ways that are antithetical to their own welfare interests as objectively viewed by others or in ways that appear to others to be offensively undignified, provided their conduct does not itself risk harm to the welfare or autonomy of others. This means that we must respect both the choices of a dwarf, who enjoys being paid to fly through the air in a safe, regulated dwarf tossing event, and the choices of those who wish to test their strength by hurling the dwarf through the air. So, under the good life model, the state can insist that dwarf tossing is carried out in safety, but it cannot criminalize those events within a legal system that is itself justified because it must stand up for our equal dignity.

17
Human Dignity: The New Phase in International Law

Michael Tate

I should like to sound an optimistic note concerning the recognition of human dignity in the present era. In fact, I believe we are witnessing a turning point in world civilization. Long-standing legal doctrines and the consigning to oblivion the fate of women in times of war have, in the last decade or so, been superseded by the institution of legal processes designed to require individuals to assume personal responsibility for violations of International Humanitarian Law.

The subjection of Agostino Pinochet and Slobodan Milosevic to legal process of a trans-or supra-national kind represents a most significant advance in the protection of human dignity.

The doctrine of 'Sovereign Immunity' had served the interests of relationships between nation states for several centuries. Among other aspects, a *serving* head of state was assured of comprehensive immunity from the criminal law process of a foreign State, and a *former* head of state obtained immunity from such processes in regard to official activities while holding such office.

It will be recalled that the UK Lords of Appeal permitted extradition proceedings, instituted by a Spanish magistrate against the former head of state of Chile, to proceed on the allegation that he had organized and authorized the commission of torture whilst holding that high office.[1]

While the case turned on the fact that the UK, Chile, and Spain had each ratified the Torture Convention of 1984, nevertheless the ruling indicated that judicial benches were prepared to put high office holders of foreign states in jeopardy of individual prosecution and punishment for criminal activities which grievously violated human dignity.

Judicial activism of this sort coincided with even more important (because more representative of global opinion) activity by the UN Security Council. By a 1993 Resolution of that body establishing the International War Crimes Tribunal on the Former Yugoslavia (hereafter 'the Tribunal'), the doctrine of Sovereign Immunity was emptied of its protective power. Thus article 7.2 of the Tribunal Statute provides:

[1] *R. v. Bow Street Metropolitan Stipendiary Magistrate* and others ex parte Pinochet Ugarte (Amnesty International and others intervening) No. 3 [1999] 2 All E R 97.

J. Malpas and N. Lickiss (eds.), Perspectives on Human Dignity: A Conversation, 183–186.

> The official position of any accused person, whether as head of state or government or as a responsible government official, shall not relieve such person of criminal responsibility or mitigate punishment.

That article enabled the Tribunal to confirm an indictment against, and issue an arrest warrant for, the then *serving* president of the Federal Republic of Yugoslavia.

The allegations or such serious violations of the human dignity of individuals as constitute crimes against humanity are now being tested in The Hague. But, whatever the outcome, the mere subjection of the (now) former head of state to trial for widespread or systematic attacks on civilian populations (whose protection in times of armed conflict is of the essence of International Humanitarian Law), is of enormous significance.

The Tribunal has also been particularly effective in inaugurating a new era in prosecuting gross violations of the human dignity of women committed during the course of armed conflict. Hitherto, such violations have been barely acknowledged let alone punished. Thus, whilst at the Tokyo War Crime Trials, several Japanese officers were held criminally responsible for the systematic sexual violation of women in a particular area of conflict (the 'rape of Nanking') no such prosecutions were attempted at Nuremberg.

By contrast, the Tribunal has tried and punished various commanders, requiring them to accept immediate or command responsibility for the rape, sexual torture, and slavery of numerous women caught up in the Yugoslav conflict. It quickly became apparent that such crimes were not isolated instances of the personal dominance of a man over a woman but part of the systematic terrorizing of the civilian population of a particular city or region designed in many instances to aid the project of 'ethnic cleansing' by frightening whole populations into moving out of vulnerable areas to protect their womenfolk.

The sister tribunal dealing with the horrendous conflict in Rwanda (where 800,000 Tutsis were slaughtered by Hutus in the course of three months), has held a local mayor criminally responsible for permitting and encouraging the public rape of Tutsi women in his mayoral compound. It found that this sexual violence was part of the process aimed at the destruction of the Tutsi people as such, and was therefore genocidal in intent. Paul Akayesu was found guilty of genocide.[2] This is a truly remarkable advance in the judicial vindication in the human dignity of women.

My conclusion even from such a brief survey is that this security council sponsored jurisdiction over war crimes, crimes against humanity and genocide, and the jurisprudence emerging from the trials constitutes a secular corpus of natural law (at least in its prohibitory aspect).

The highest political organ of the world community has agreed that some activities are inherently evil because they radically attack what it is to be a human community. Their detection, prosecution, and punishment, takes precedence over

---

[2] *The Prosecutor v. Jean Paul Akayesu*. Case No: ICTR 96–4-T.

the interests of nation states (such as represented by the doctrine of sovereign immunity), and their scope extends to the fate of women whose dignity had hitherto been violated by men with impunity.

Crimes against *Humanity* are well named. This naming requires a certain sense of solidarity which goes beyond seeing such crimes as numerous instances of attacks on individuals. As Trial Chamber 1 has said of certain such crimes: 'they transcend the individual, since, through the assault on the latter, humanity is negated.'[3]

The coming into force of the Treaty of Rome of July 1998 establishing the International Criminal Court augers well for the future. Australia has ratified that Treaty. This has already had the beneficial effect of the Australian Parliament's passing of legislation providing for the prosecution of war crimes, crimes against humanity, and genocide.

This is to enable Australia to exercise primacy of jurisdiction where it is alleged, for example, that a member of the Australian Armed Forces has committed such a crime whilst on overseas duty. (The ICC only picks up jurisdiction where a nation state is unable or unwilling to carry out an effective prosecution). This is an important advance in the protection of human dignity under Australian domestic law and is a direct consequence of the international movement, which I have outlined earlier.

It may be objected that I am overly optimistic and that I have not given sufficient weight to the fact that some nation states are not willing to subject themselves to such international structures as the International Criminal Court. And it is indeed unfortunate that the USA has not ratified the Rome Treaty. After all it too could exercise primacy of jurisdiction in the same way as provided for by Australia.

But I would not focus on the USA. At least that nation has relatively strong intermediate social organizations which can, with varying degrees of success, hold US authorities accountable for gross violations of human dignity. The free media's publicizing of the Abu Graihb degradations, and the increasing restiveness of the federal judiciary in the face of claims of untrammelled executive power over Guatanamo Bay detainees, are both helpful signs.

A nation such as North Korea is of greater concern. It simply juxtaposes the all-powerful state against the atomized individual with no comparable social bodies capable of advocating the claims of human dignity. In fact, totalitarian or authoritarian regimes invariably destroy the independent voices of the media, the judiciary, faith groups, and trade unions simultaneously with the subjection of individuals to torture, sexual violence, 'disappearance', and other violations of human dignity.

Our task worldwide should be to foster the building of such intermediate social structures in societies where the risk is great of such violations. Let internal political evolution play its role and then the beneficial expressions of globalization as represented by the ICC will be more naturally adopted as appropriate means to protect human dignity.

[3] War Crimes Tribunal, Judgment of 29 November 1996.

I am confident that we are witnessing the emergence of structures which, because they go beyond moral outrage or political reaction (such as economic sanctions against a regime) to the ascription of personal responsibility to individuals for crimes, will have a profound impact on the decision–makers involved in armed conflict. International Humanitarian Law has moved from aspirational to practically effective law, and that is excellent for the protection of human dignity.

18
Dignity and Health

Martin Tattersall

Dignity is a property of an individual, and of the ways others react to him or her. Dignity is closely linked to, even if not identical with, an individual's autonomy. Health professionals can influence a patient's perspective on his or her dignity or worth through their consultation and communication style. The orientation of heath professionals towards treating people with disease rather than simply treating disease (in people) requires not only consideration of research evidence relating to the effectiveness of different interventions in groups of people with a particular health problem but also consideration of individual health factors and patient 'values' in reaching a management recommendation.

Shared Decision-Making

Shared decision-making (SDM) describes a partnership between health professional and patient, in which each contributes to decisions about treatment or care. Respect for patient autonomy underpins the current trend to SDM in health care. Charles, Gafni, and Whelan defined four components of SDM, namely the simultaneous involvement of doctor and patient in all phases of decision-making, information exchange in both directions and by both parties, mutual deliberation on treatment options, and agreement on the treatment to implement.[1] Doctors are increasingly urged to practice SDM. When the aim is to include patients in decision-making, it is the process of involvement rather than its outcome which is relevant.

We have investigated whether a successful tailoring of patient participation confers benefits to patients, and whether patients who jointly decided on treatment with their oncologist experienced better outcomes.[2] A match between preferred and perceived

[1] C. Charles, A. Gafni, T. Whelan, 'Shared Decision Making in the Medical Encounter. What Does it Mean? (Or it Takes Two to Tango)', *Social Science and Medicine*, 44 (1997), pp.681–692, and 'Decision-making in the Physician-patient Encounter: Revisiting the Shared Treatment Decision-making Model', *Social Science and Medicine*, 49 (1999), pp.651–656.

[2] M. Gattellari, P.N. Butow, and M. Tattersall, 'Sharing Decisions in Cancer Care', *Social Science and Medicine*, 52 (2001), pp.1865–1878.

J. Malpas and N. Lickiss (eds.), Perspectives on Human Dignity: A Conversation, 187–191.

roles in decision-making was found for just over one-third of patients, with 29% more active than preferred, and 37% participating to a lesser degree than preferred. Patients whose level of participation was less than desired wanted more information about treatment options and side effects, and expressed a greater need for assurance as well as a chance to talk about their fears. Patients less active in decision-making than desired were also significantly less satisfied. Irrespective of preference, patients who reported a shared role in decision-making were most satisfied with their consultation, with their doctor and with information about treatments and emotional support. Patient reports of their levels of participation in decision-making were correlated with oncologist but not their own behaviour. This finding suggests that the consultation itself and the doctors' behaviour in particular may be pivotal in generating the discrepancy between preferred and actual roles in treatment decisions.

Taking a History

'Taking a history' is a crucial medical skill: it is an important means not only of learning what symptoms exist, but also of establishing rapport with the patient. Every patient is unique in the story that they tell. The use of open-ended questions encourages patients to describe their medical history 'in their own words'. Their story, however, will commonly fit into a pattern which will suggest a particular illness or diagnosis. In one sense that is the purpose of telling the story, in order to make sense of it and to help with the medical problem. The skilful clinician will listen to the story carefully, then introduce clarifying questions and formulate the key aspects, and check their interpretation of the history by summarizing the story and seeking additional input/comments from the patient. Listening forms a key part of taking a history, but it is also an important means of demonstrating how the doctor values the patient. The doctor has to be seen to listen. There are skills to be developed in active listening. This is more than just nodding the head at intervals; it involves giving time and space to another person. The taking of a family and 'social' history is an important component of a medical consultation. Formally these aspects explore the context of the patient's medical history, and lead to an understanding of the consequences of the patient's symptoms and of possible treatment approaches on their way of life. Patient fears, concerns, and values can be explored. Humour may also find a place in the medical consultation, in part as a means of reducing tension, but also as a 'humanizing' influence on what otherwise may be a very 'clinical' experience.

Prompting Patients to Ask Questions

We have studied the effects of providing patients with question-prompt lists before consultation with cancer specialists. This simple intervention has been found in several studies to increase patient asking question during the consultation, particularly about the future.[3] Moreover, when the oncologist endorsed use of the question-prompt list during the consultation, this improved patient recall and satisfaction with the consultation, and reduced the consultation time.[4] Perhaps this intervention not only prompts patients to think about issues which are important for them to mention during a medical consultation, but also indicates how much the doctor values the patient's contribution to the consultation.

Decision aids have been developed to assist patients and their doctors to weigh up differences between 'reasonable' treatment options. These interventions include a 'values clarification' exercise enabling patients and their doctors' to consider together issues which influence choice between treatment options in a way which 'values' the patient input. Decision aids are increasingly used to enhance the 'quality' of medical decisions when treatment options are preference sensitive.

Within Australia and elsewhere, 'patient-centred care' is increasingly promoted as the optimal approach by health authorities. Surveys of groups of doctors in Canada and in Australia have documented that at least in cancer care, there is considerable professional support for SDM.[5] 'Paternalism' while still supported, particularly in contexts where 'reasonable' treatment options do not exist, is recognized increasingly as inappropriate for better-informed and younger patients.

Conflicts of Interest are an Increasing Reality in the Conduct of Medical Practice

The community expectation that doctors act in the best interests of patients is challenged by reports of 'rationing' of health care, and by wide variations in practice influenced by doctor 'vested' interest. 'Evidence-based medicine', and the preparation of treatment guidelines by a variety of bodies including those funded by government, the 'For Profit' as well as 'Not for Profit' Health Industry raise concerns that factors other than optimal patient outcomes do not always underpin medical practice. Community understanding of these developments is limited, though in Australia, 'consumer versions' of practice guidelines have been developed for some cancer types and contexts. The increase in new medical interventions and health-care products over the past few years has been funded largely by the For Profit Industry, and the power of this Industry to influence doctors and the health

---

[3] R.F. Brown, P.N. Butow, S.M. Dunn, and M.H.N. Tattersall, 'Promoting Patient Participation and Shortening Cancer Consultations; a Randomised Trial', *British Journal of Cancer*, 85 (2001), pp.1273–1279; P. Butow, R. Devine, M. Boyer, S. Pendlebury, M. Jackson, and M.H.N. Tattersall, 'Cancer Consultation Preparation Package: Changing Patients but not Physicians is Not Enough', *Journal of Clinical Oncology*, 22 (2004), pp.4401–4409.

[4] Brown, Butow, Dunn, and Tattersall, 'Promoting Patient Participation and Shortening Cancer Consultations; a Randomised Trial'.

[5] C.A. Charles et al., 'Shared Treatment Decision Making: What Does it Mean to Physicians?', *Journal of Clinical Oncology*, 21 (2003), pp.932–936.

bureaucracy has been discussed widely in the medical and general media.[6] Many professional bodies including the Australian Medical Association and the Royal Australasian College of Physicians have prepared Ethical Guidelines for their members relating to interactions with the For Profit Health Care Industry, and the possibility of regulation in this area has been raised.

Surprisingly there has been little attention to giving doctors guidance on how to disclose to patients their relationship with the For Profit Industry. I suspect that many patients would be disturbed to learn that the pharmaceutical industry spends much more of their 'research' budget on marketing to doctors (and to 'consumers' in the USA and New Zealand) than on research to develop new products. They might also be disturbed to know that their doctor had financial ties with a particular drug manufacturer, one of whose products had been recommended and prescribed by their doctor. These developments have the potential to undermine the basis of trust in health professionals, a trend which has been evident in surveys over the past decades.

Direct to consumer marketing of pharmaceuticals, and media reports of cancer 'breakthroughs' unrealistically raise patient expectations and threatens patient dignity. Patients increasingly expect to access information about their health status. The creation of a multitude of health information sources accessed by patients mean that an individual's doctor is rarely the only information source available to patients. Nevertheless, patients report that their doctor is commonly the source of most information relevant to their status. The possibility that their doctor's information or treatment recommendation is biased by undisclosed 'competing interests' is an important and increasing concern which has the potential to further erode patient trust in the medical profession.

Considerations of Dignity are Commonly Raised in Reference to the Care of Patients Who Have a Life Limiting Illness

Recognition of the inevitability of death, and respect for the value of human life are important qualities for health-care professionals. There is more to life than the number of years lived and subjective well-being. When the treatment goal is not cure, quality of life issues assume greater importance in management recommendations. When the preservation of dignity becomes the primary goal of care, treatment options expand beyond the symptom management paradigm and encompass the physical, psychological, social, and existential aspects of the patient's experience. Patients ascribe their own meaning or importance to the notion of dying with dignity.

---

[6] R. Moynihan and M. Sweet, 'Medicine, the Media and Monetary Interests: The Need for Transparency and Professionalism', *Medical Journal of Australia*, 17 (2000), pp.631–634; R. Moynihan, 'Who Pays for the Pizza? Redefining the Relationships Between Doctors and Drug Companies 2: Disentanglement', *British Medical Journal*, 326 (2003), pp.1193–1196.

Chochinov's 'Dignity–conserving' model of palliative care targets the maintenance of dignity as a therapeutic objective, and identifies a series of interventions grouped under 'Illness related concerns, Dignity conserving repertoire and Social dignity inventory'.[7] These perspectives provide health professionals with a therapeutic map. The identification of dignity-conserving perspectives and practices within the repertoire is particularly helpful as means of recognizing individual qualities and approaches to maintenance of dignity.

The Competing Obligations of Health Professionals to Individual Patients and Within the Global Society

The relief of suffering is a worthy goal of health care globally and at the level of the individual. Doctors doing their best for individuals in the developed world, however, contribute to the growth of disparity in health care around the world. Inequalities in care are increasing and escalating health-care costs contribute to a growing disparity between life expectancy and the perceived quality of life in the developed and developing world. The health 'benefits' flowing from biotechnology contribute to inequality in health care, suffering, and indignity. Individual and societal income is not a major contributor to happiness and human dignity. The proposal that human dignity should be at the centre of global health appeals to me as a clinician and as a citizen.[8] This proposal makes the link between poverty, excessive inequality, and lack of dignity.

---

[7] H. M. Chochinov, 'Dignity and the Eye of the Beholder', *Journal of Clinical Oncology*, 22 (2004), pp.1336–1340.

[8] R. Horton, 'Rediscovering Human Dignity', *The Lancet*, 364 (2004), pp.1081–1085.

19
Human Dignity: The Perspective of a Gynaecological Oncologist

Neville F. Hacker

When I was first asked to give a 20-minute talk to a colloquium at the University of Tasmania on the topic of Human Dignity, I was initially somewhat ambivalent! On the one hand, I felt certain it would be a very interesting meeting, but on the other hand, I wondered what I would have to contribute, being much more pragmatic than philosophical. I was told there would be a wide range of disciplines represented, and that it was my professional experience, rather than any background in philosophy, that I was expected to bring to the meeting.

Feeling appropriately reassured, I then had to start to think more seriously about the subject. Human Dignity is a term we bandy about frequently in medical circles, but what do we really mean?

I remembered reading a chapter entitled, 'The Dignity of Man' by a German Professor of Philosophy, Franz Josef Wetz in a recent anatomy book.[1] In this chapter, Wetz indicates that to the ancient Greeks and Romans, dignity was considered to be the result of individual achievement and social recognition. A dignified person observed the correct moderation, and lived according to reason.

The Roman philosopher and politician Cicero was the first to espouse the idea of innate human dignity, but it was Christianity that saw his ideas generally accepted. In this concept, human dignity was based on the biblical God creating human beings in His Own image. As God's special creation, humans were accorded an absolute value, as a result of which they differed from all other creatures. Hence, human dignity was an essential characteristic, possessed by each of us, regardless of our origins or lifestyle. It must be respected by every individual and all social institutions, up to the State itself.

In today's secular, pluralistic society, Christian beliefs have become incomprehensible for many people. Many are no longer willing to accept human superiority over the animal and plant world, so the concept of innate human dignity based on our being created in God's image, cannot exist.

[1] F.J. Wetz, 'The Dignity of Man', in: G. von Hagens and A. Whalley (eds.), *Body Worlds–The Anatomical Exhibition of Real Human Bodies* (Heidelberg: Institute for Plastination, 2002), pp.235–253.

J. Malpas and N. Lickiss (eds.), Perspectives on Human Dignity: A Conversation, 193–197.

So where does all this leave me personally in my conceptualization of human dignity. I believe that human dignity is not an innate quality, but rather an acquired asset. I believe it is acquired throughout life, from childhood to the time of death, and may vary in any individual from time to time, depending on personal experiences. It is initially acquired from parents, and other relatives and close family friends, who endeavour to instill self-confidence in the child, and to impart a code of behaviour, consistent with their own values. Subsequently, teachers, peers, and role models in the workplace or in the wider community, including religious leaders, may also be very influential in shaping one's dignity.

What is this asset or personal quality known as human dignity? I believe it is basically self-respect, believing in one's own self-worth. As such, it is really a state of mind. In practice it means behaving, and interacting with others with integrity, and in such a manner as to gain the respect of one's peers. A dignified person would be courteous and respectful of others, and would act with moderation at all times.

As a gynaecological oncologist, I see women with cancer every day. Almost without exception, patients with cancer say that their experience of a life-threatening illness has made them a better person. They have been forced to confront their own mortality and to reassess their priorities. They find out who their friends are, and what the really important issues in life are. Not infrequently, they acquire more dignity over time.

I well remember a young woman, 26 years of age, whom I saw with cancer of the cervix in 1987. She had experienced abuse as a child and had left home and school at an early age. She was withdrawn and dishevelled whenever she saw me for the first couple of years, and felt that the cancer was yet another cruel twist of fate for her. She was on welfare, had no self-worth, and no trust in anybody. The entire team treated her with their usual respect and compassion, and following her surgery and radiation, I explained to her that we were hopeful she would be cured. After about 3–4 years of follow-up, when it was obvious even to the patient herself that she was doing well, her demeanour began to change. She started to take more pride in her appearance, and to develop some trust in the health-care professionals. She went on to complete her high school education, obtained a university degree, and has been able to hold down a well-paid job ever since.

I believe that this young woman's experience with cancer at an early age taught her a new set of values, and she acquired much more dignity as a result of this experience. Although this is a fairly extreme example, I have seen many other patients progressively acquire dignity as they confront their own mortality through an experience with cancer.

What are the implications for the medical profession? How should we respect a person's dignity? Probably the most important aspect of respect for human dignity is to treat the person as a whole being, not as an organ, such as a uterus or an ovary (in the case of my specialty). This implies asking the patient about her psychosocial, spiritual, and existential needs, not just about her physical symptoms. It means giving adequate information about the diagnosis and the treatment options, and taking the time to answer all of her questions. Patients increasingly want to share in decision-making, but some, particularly older patients, still prefer to leave the decision-making to their doctor. This right should be respected, as should the patient's right to a second opinion, at the other extreme.

It is less than 50 years ago that patients, even in the USA, were not told they had a diagnosis of cancer, because of the stigma associated with the diagnosis, and the desire to 'protect' the patient from psychological trauma. Even today, I see elderly women patients from many European, Middle Eastern, and Latin American countries, whose adult children ask me to withhold the diagnosis of cancer from them. If palliative care is appropriate for the woman concerned, I will sometimes accede to their request, but if anti-cancer treatment with surgery, radiation, or chemotherapy is involved, I will tell the family that I cannot treat their mother unless we have an honest doctor–patient relationship. No one has ever taken their mother elsewhere when informed of this approach, and on breaking the news of the diagnosis to the patient, I find the usual reaction is one of relief. The veil of secrecy has finally been lifted, and all members of the family and the health-care team can talk openly and honestly with the patient about her situation. There is no longer any whispering in the corridors, and the patient's dignity has been restored.

Human dignity is strongly influenced by culture. For example, some Moslems teach their daughters from a young age that dignity for a woman is maintained only if she dresses in such a manner that is totally unprovocative to men. On the other hand, women of Western cultures can dress in a much more revealing way, yet bring no condemnation from their peers, and have no loss of dignity in the eyes of fellow Westerners.

From a medical point of view, one aspect of treating women with dignity is having respect for their modesty and privacy during a physical examination, regardless of their cultural background. This means providing an appropriate screen or curtain behind which they can get dressed, having a female nurse present during a pelvic examination, and draping the torso and legs appropriately in a gown and/or sheet. Even in our Western culture, most women expect such treatment, but an occasional patient will insist on throwing off any drapes, lying naked or semi-naked on the couch, and getting dressed in full view of the doctor. This suggests that personal concepts of dignity also vary with the individual.

We have a fellow training in our cancer centre at present who comes from a large Eastern European city. He gave us a talk recently about the current status of gynaecological cancer care at his hospital, which is the major centre for gynaecological oncology in his country. I was rather appalled at his description of their weekly Tumour Board meeting. The meeting is usually attended by about 15 doctors, mainly male, and there are usually about a dozen patients presented. After the patient's history has been given, the patient herself is brought in before the meeting, asked to remove all her clothes, and lie on an examination couch. She then has a pelvic examination performed by four or five perfect strangers, without any gowns or sheets, and in full view of the entire group.

After she dresses and leaves the room, her management is discussed. The group determines whether she needs surgery or radiation, for example, and also who will perform the surgery. The patient is not told her diagnosis, and is given no options or explanations regarding her management. The surgeon may well not even introduce himself to the patient preoperatively, while the final indignity is that post-operatively, she is managed in a different ward, by a different group of doctors and nurses, so that there is absolutely no continuity of care.

Basically, the women are treated as unintelligent objects who are incapable of dealing psychologically with a diagnosis of cancer, and unable to comprehend the intricacies of cancer management. The surgeons too are treated as technicians or robots. They are told to perform a particular operation on a particular patient, but without any responsibility for the initial diagnosis, the decision-making regarding best practice, or the post-operative outcome.

The whole 'cancer experience,' at least for women in this Eastern European country, is a very impersonal one. No meaningful doctor–patient relationship is ever established, because not only is the inpatient care fragmented, but also there is very little follow-up after discharge from hospital.

Most women in our country expect an opportunity to discuss not only the diagnosis and treatment, but also multiple related issues including hormone replacement therapy, psychosocial concerns, resumption of sexual activity, diet, exercise, and any lifestyle constraints, and these can only be discussed in a meaningful way during follow-up visits. The impact of the initial diagnosis is so overwhelming that the immediate concern for the patient is survival. Many women who have fully recovered physically from their cancer treatment will take several months to even consider resumption of sexual activity, for example, and even then will often need a lot of support and encouragement from the health-care team.

When I spoke to our Fellow after the talk, I asked if he considered this approach a serious affront to human dignity. He said that after seeing how the system worked in Australia, he could now appreciate this, and could also understand how these women were completely disempowered by the medical profession. He said that it had always been this way, however, and the women themselves had no greater expectations. It is hoped that after completing his training in Australia, he will be able to return to his native country and progressively change the system to foster greater respect for the dignity of both patients and staff.

It is not possible to talk about human dignity as an oncologist without saying a few words about dying with dignity. As I have indicated that I believe human dignity is basically a state of mind, it follows that the medical profession cannot confer death with dignity on a patient. However, we can certainly ensure that a patient's dignity is not affronted at this most vulnerable time.

In order to maintain a patient's dignity, it is clearly important to control symptoms adequately, particularly pain. Equally important however, is to place intrinsic value on the terminal phase of life, and to treat the person as though she still has unique worth as an individual. It is important that the medical team prepare a patient adequately for death, while allowing her to continue to function autonomously for as long as possible. Patients should be kept informed of any new developments in their condition, but some simply want to 'switch off' at various stages along the way. This right should be respected, if their dignity is not to be affronted.

A lot is taught in medical schools about preparation for birth, yet very little is taught about preparation for death.[2] Births and deaths obviously occur in equal numbers, and I feel that this is a serious deficiency in our medical education. Most doctors feel impotent in the presence of a dying patient, so the usual response is to tell the patient there is nothing more that can be done. This is absolutely devastating news for a patient because clearly there is much more that needs to be done, albeit in a palliative sense, before the patient departs this life. Patients hate being abandoned by doctors and nurses with whom they have developed a meaningful relationship, and I believe a dignified death demands as much continuity of care as possible.

Much has been written about voluntary euthanasia, with protagonists suggesting it will ensure a dignified death. In my experience, good palliative care and a team of dedicated health-care professionals make requests for voluntary euthanasia rare, and I would personally be opposed to the legalization of euthanasia.

This is not to suggest that heavy sedation may not sometimes be appropriate, or that active management of such things as pneumonia may not be inappropriate. It is also not to suggest that life should be unnecessarily prolonged, particularly if symptoms cannot be adequately controlled or meaningful communication with close family members no longer achieved. The recent case in the USA of Terri Schiavo highlights this point.[3] This unfortunate patient suffered irreversible brain damage in 1990, and had lived in a 'persistent vegetative state' ever since, being kept alive with a feeding tube. Having nursed his wife for the first seven years hoping for some reversal of the brain damage, her husband had to seek permission via the law courts to remove the feeding tube so that his wife could finally die naturally and with dignity.

A common concern of dying patients is that they are being a burden to others, including the health-care professionals, and this concern is occasionally associated with requests for euthanasia. Women are used to looking after everyone else in the family, yet they often have great difficulty in reversing roles, and letting others look after them when they are sick. I often try to stress to women that they must change this mindset, and accept the fact that those close to them are very grateful for the nurturing they have received in the past, and are only too willing to return the favour. This is particularly so during the terminal phase of life, when remaining time is short, and the last opportunities exist to reflect on those things which are most important to the patient.

Focusing one's mind on human dignity for this discussion has been both rewarding and enlightening. There are so many facets to the subject that it is difficult to encompass them all in a single definition. I am reminded of what a judge once said of pornography: 'It's difficult to define, but you know it when you see it.' I think the same could be said of human dignity.

---

[2] C.Y. Muller, 'The Miracle of Life and the Privilege of Death', *Obstetrics and Gynecology*, 103 (2004), pp.1314–1316.

[3] Report in *Sydney Daily Telegraph*, 23 March 2005.

20
The Social Origins of Dignity in Medical Care at the End of Life

Nicholas Christakis

How do social forces constrain or foster dignity at the end of an individual's life? Such a question rightly concerns individual patients, their families, and decision-makers beyond the circle of immediately affected people. A society in which people die in an undignified fashion must surely be concerned with this state of affairs. And a key measure of the credibility of any health-care system is surely the respect and dignity it accords to its most vulnerable patients, those who are dying.

Unfortunately, numerous studies in the US document that many patients die prolonged and painful deaths, receiving unwanted, invasive, and impersonal care in the process. Surely this is undignified however dignity is defined. What is more, this type of care is not consistent with the care people themselves desire. Table 1 illustrates the discrepancy between people's desires regarding their terminal care,[1] and the outcomes that are actually observed. This is a sorry report card indeed. The gap between the care that is desired and the care that is provided is substantial and, at least in most cases, needless. For example, 40–70% of Americans die in pain, yet effective treatment for pain is widely available.

This discrepancy threatens patient dignity in at least two ways. First, it is undignified in itself to die in pain or otherwise endure a bad death. Second, it is undignified to give patients a kind of care at the end of life that is inconsistent with their wishes. In a comprehensive, grounds-up study of how Americans define a 'good death,' involving the identification and assessment of 44 relevant attributes, one study found that patients identify a heterogeneous set of objectives, as shown in Table 2.[2] The items on this list are noteworthy for their explicit statement of the importance of dignity, for their emphasis on metaphysical concerns near the end of life, and for their emphasis on specifically social aspects of good death—all of which are key elements of dignity.

---

[1] K.E. Steinhauser et al., 'Factors Considered Important at the End of Life by Patients, Family, Physicians, and Other Care Providers,' *Journal of the American Medical Association*, 284 (2000), pp.2476–2482.

[2] Ibid.

J. Malpas and N. Lickiss (eds.), Perspectives on Human Dignity: A Conversation, 199–207.

Table 1 The contrast between ideal, desired deaths, and reality (K.E. Steinhauser, N.A. Christakis, E.C. Clipp, M. McNeilly, L. McIntyre, and J.A. Tulsky, 'Factors Considered Important at the End of Life by Patients, Family, Physicians, and Other Care Providers,' *JAMA*, 284 (2000), pp.2476–2482.)

Attribute	% of patients agreeing 'very important'	% of Americans achieving objective
Be free of pain	93	30–50
Not be a burden to family	89	45
Have a doctor who listens	95	30–45
Die at home	70	15
Know what to expect	96	15

Table 2 Patient-identified attributes of a good death (K.E. Steinhauser, N.A. Christakis, E.C. Clipp, M. McNeilly, L. McIntyre, and J.A. Tulsky, 'Factors Considered Important at the End of Life by Patients, Family, Physicians, and Other Care Providers,' *JAMA*, 284 (2000), pp.2476–2482.)

Attribute	% of patients agreeing 'very important'
Be kept clean	99
Name a decision-maker*	98
Have a nurse one likes*	97
Know what to expect	96
Have someone who will listen*	95
Maintain one's dignity	95
Trust/like one's physician*	94
Have finances in order	94
Be free of pain	93
Be mentally aware	92
Say goodbye to important people*	90
Be at peace with God	89
Not burden family*	89
Resolve unfinished business	86
Share time with close friends*	85
Believe family is prepared*	85
Feel prepared to die	84
Presence of family*	81
Not burden society*	81
Not die alone*	75

* These attributes of a good death, deemed by patients to be very important, all contain explicitly or implicitly social elements.

Unfortunately, not only do physicians appear to be ill-equipped to provide the kind of care that patients desire, but also, they often do not even realize that such features are important to patients. For example, while the great majority of patients identify important aspects of a good death as including being mentally aware, being at peace with God, retaining the ability to help others, and not burdening family or society, only roughly half of physicians are aware that such features are important to patients at the end of life.

Though the two are not necessarily the same thing, a good death is clearly related to a dignified death. One empirically derived conceptual model of dignity in dying patients, based on interviews with terminally ill people, is worth examining in this regard since the items identified in this model as being part of dignity are closely related to attributes of a good death. This work highlighted three aspects of dignified care at the end of life: (1) bodily concerns (such as cognitive acuity, functional capacity, physical and psychological distress); (2) 'dignity practices' (such as the ability to help others, being hopeful, maintaining a sense of normalcy), and (3) social features (such as not burdening others, being concerned about the aftermath of one's death, and having social support).[3] Interestingly—and worrisomely—many of these items are also the ones that patients think are important aspects of a good death but doctors relatively less so. This itself may help to explain why so many sick people find modern medical care undignified.

Most generally, the lack of dignity in care at the end of life appears to arise from a more widespread misdirection of the efforts of the health-care system in the care of seriously ill patients. Psychiatrist Leon Eisenberg drew a classic distinction between 'disease' and 'illness,' wherein the former is the biological expression and the latter is the 'lived experience' of disease, including its social and moral aspects.[4] When doctors treat disease and not illness, they contribute to a decrement in the patient's dignity. Indeed, routinized forms of care that are increasingly prevalent in medicine, such as 'clinical practice guidelines,' while very advantageous in several ways, also run the risk of effacing the salience of the individual and his unique circumstances and hence, in treating a person like a mere object, compromising his dignity.

Dignity and Its Social Origins

The way the health-care system treats a vulnerable, terminally ill patient is thus instrumental to whether a patient ultimately has a dignified death. This is related to the classic argument, advanced by psychologist B.F. Skinner in *Beyond Freedom and Dignity*, that dignity is not an inherent attribute of individuals, originating within them, but rather is a product of their physical and social environment.[5] The circumstances surrounding the seriously ill should be objects of inquiry if we want to

[3] H.M. Cochinov, T. Hack, S. McClement, L. Kristjanson, and M. Harlos, 'Dignity in the Terminally Ill: A Developing Empirical Model', *Social Science and Medicine*, 54 (2002), pp.433–443.

[4] L. Eisenberg, 'Disease and Illness: Distinctions Between Professional and Popular Ideas of Sickness', *Culture, Medicine, and Psychiatry*, 1 (1977), pp.9–23.

[5] B.F. Skinner, *Beyond Freedom and Dignity* (Indianapolis: Hackett Publishing, 2002 [1971]).

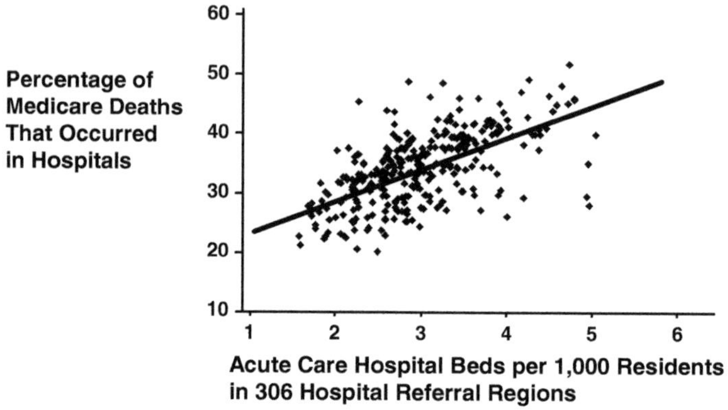

Fig. 1 Relationship between regional hospital bed supply and occurrence of death in institutions (Dartmouth Medical School, *The Dartmouth Atlas of Health Care*, 1998 (Chicago: American Hospital Association, 1998), http://www.dartmouthatlas.org/)

understand the dignity afforded by the health-care system and should be objects of our intervention if we want to enhance human dignity, especially at the end of life.

For example, much could be said of the importance of reforming medical institutions or medical procedures so that care at the end of life could become more dignified. Two external aspects of our care system that impinge on the ability of individuals to have a good death, a death in keeping with their preferences and comporting with their dignity, illustrate this point.

Figure 1 shows the association between the percent of deaths occurring in hospitals and the regional supply of hospital beds, based on data from the *Dartmouth Atlas of Health Care in the U.S.*[6] The data suggest that as much as 38% of the variation in whether death occurs in a hospital can be attributed to the local availability of hospital beds. That is, if you are a patient who wants to die at home and you happen to live in an area with lots of hospital beds, you are especially unlikely to have your wishes fulfilled, for reasons having nothing to do with your preferences. On the bright side, these results suggest that public policy (e.g. as it pertains to the placement of hospital beds) matters, and can affect what happens, both in the sense of increasing the likelihood of a particular outcome, and also in the sense of enabling people to realize their own objectives.

Figure 2 documents the substantial inability of physicians to formulate accurate prognoses. In this study, doctors made predictions about how long 505 of their patients would live. The objective was to quantify the magnitude and nature of the error in the prognoses physicians formulate (and not necessarily communicate). This study found that doctors overestimate survival by a factor of about five.[7] That

[6] Dartmouth Medical School, *The Dartmouth Atlas of Health Care*, 1998 (Chicago: American Hospital Association, 1998).

[7] N.A. Christakis and E.B. Lamont, "Extent and Determinants of Error in Doctors' Prognoses for Terminally Ill Patients: Prospective Cohort Study', *British Medical Journal*, 320 (2000), pp.469–473.

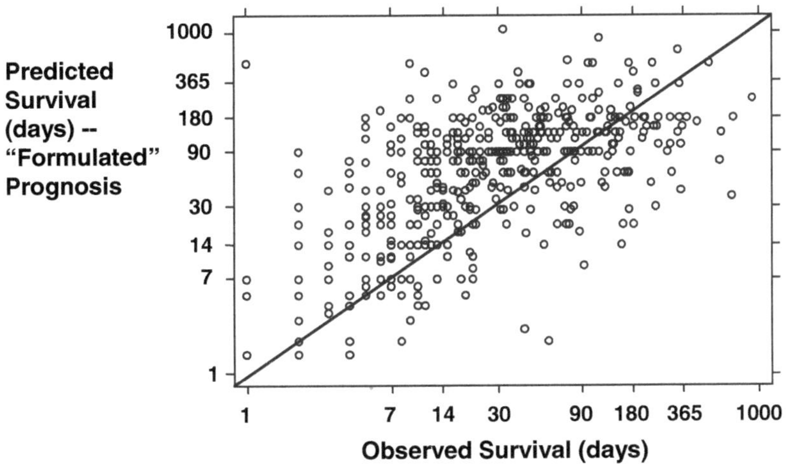

Fig. 2 Relationship of prognoses formulated by physicians and actual patient survival (N.A. Christakis and E.B. Lamont, 'Extent and Determinants of Error in Doctors' Prognoses for Terminally Ill Patients: Prospective Cohort Study,' *British Medical Journal*, 320 (2000), pp.469–473.)

is, for the typical patient in the last year of their life, the doctor thinks that they may have, say, six months to live, but actually they can expect to live only a month. This kind of prognostic mis-calibration can seriously undermine high-quality care near the end of life in various ways.[8] For example, another study found that patients' generally optimistic and incorrect prognostic estimates were associated with an aversion to palliative care. That is, patients' false understanding of their situation can interfere with their ability to realize the kind of end-of-life care they themselves also say they want.[9]

These two rather technical examples of how structural features of the medical system affect patient experience highlight not only the larger debate about internally held versus externally bestowed dignity, but they also raise the classic sociological concern of the 'collective constraints on individual opportunities,' or how individual experience is shaped by the social setting. Other examples with respect to the care of the terminally ill abound, such as how a lack of training in end-of-life care or in opioid use, or structural features affecting the availability of drugs used in end-of-life care, or rules governing access to hospice care, affect patient experience and patient dignity. If we are to increase dignity at the end of life, our efforts ought necessarily to be directed at the health-care system.

[8] N.A. Christakis, *Death Foretold: Prophecy and Prognosis in Medical Care* (Chicago: University of Chicago Press, 1999).

[9] J. Weeks, et al., 'Relationship Between Cancer Patients' Predictions of Prognosis and Their Treatment Preferences,' *Journal of the American Medical Association*, 279 (1988), pp.1709–1714.

Death with Dignity and Euthanasia

Despite the recognition of the extent to which dignity depends on the environment surrounding an individual, dignity also appears related to traits within an individual. For example, dignity is typically felt to contain a notion of personal self-governance. Consequently, 'death with dignity' has become, sadly, a euphemism for certain kinds of physician-assisted suicide and euthanasia. Support for euthanasia is often driven not only by a desire to avoid what is seen as the 'torture' of patients by the health-care system, but also by arguments about a 'respect for persons' or a 'respect for a person's dignity'.

Indeed, modern modes of death and dying have become so problematic that euthanasia is achieving new legitimacy such that a 'death with dignity' movement emerged in the USA beginning in the 1990s. The most fundamental reason for this is that modern medicine—whatever else it does—often increases suffering when it prolongs life. Moreover, this increase in suffering takes place in a setting wherein patients see front-page newspaper headlines asserting that 'doctors are lax in easing pain' and that 'doctors admit ignoring dying patients wishes'. Patients appear to want not just the 'right to die', but also the right to be killed. People are dissatisfied with the technicalization, medicalization, professionalization, and institutionalization of death in modern American society. Euthanasia—in many ways paradoxically—is seen as standing in opposition to these developments.[10]

Hospitals are becoming increasingly viewed as singularly unsuited not only to a 'natural', but also to a painless and dignified death. The juxtaposition in a hospital of high technology, bureaucracy, and professionalization on the one hand and the most fundamental and unchanging of human experiences—such as birth, death, and pain—on the other hand, is increasingly viewed as inauspicious. Hospitals are coming to be construed as a necessary evil for the curable, but as an unnecessary evil for the incurable.

In fact, one of the assumptions underlying the increasing acceptability of euthanasia in American society is that dying is a private, individual, self-directed, and intimate event. Dying in modern contexts connotes a fear of losing control, which loss is antithetical to a core American value. The option to be killed is thus somehow seen as restoring dignity to a process that has become undignified.

This is disquieting. Whatever the policy, clinical, or ethical justifications for it, there is nothing dignified about euthanasia. The problem with euthanasia is that it eradicates the pain by eradicating the patient. It solves the problem by eliminating the victim. And it addresses what might rightly be seen as an external threat to human dignity by internalizing it within the suffering patient.

---

[10] N.A. Christakis, 'Managing Death: The Growing Acceptance of Euthanasia in Contemporary American Society', in: R. P. Hamel and E.R. DuBose (eds.), *Must We Suffer Our Way to Death? Cultural and Theological Perspectives on Death by Choice* (Dallas, Texas: Southern Methodist University Press, 1996), pp.15–44.

Table 3 'Ideal Types' and the historical evolution of perceptions of death (T. Walter, The Revival of Death (London: Routledge, 1994), p. 48)

Context	Traditional	Modern	Neo-modern
Bodily context	Quick and frequent	Hidden	Prolonged
Social context	Community	Public/private	Private = public
Authority	Religion	Medicine	Self

This shift in the appeal of euthanasia can also be traced, in part, to the observation that a person is seen as dignified (and gets credit from others) when he does something that is volitional, that is neither motivated by biological impulses nor by the external threat or reward of others. We grant maximal dignity when there is no obvious reason for a behavior. Hence, we regard the acceptance of death—and some regard the euthanistic embrace of death—as especially dignified. 'We recognise a person's dignity or worth when we give him credit for what he has done. The amount we give is inversely proportional to the conspicuousness of the causes of his behavior.'[11] Indeed, we give the most credit when there are evident reasons for behaving differently.

But does dignity really arise in proportion to resisting some kind of temptation? And does dignity demand that doctors and patients practice euthanasia? When people fashion their own way of dying, *sui generis*, we nowadays accord them tremendous dignity. Is having a wholly individual or 'original' or self-imposed death what is dignified? Is complying with prevalent norms about a good death dignified? Or does dignity have altogether different origins?

This example of the dignity in accepting pain and suffering or, paradoxically, in rejecting these features at the end of life, and hurrying death on, highlight sociologist Tony Waters' observation that notions of a good death have changed across time, as illustrated in Table 3.[12] At present, death typically involves prolonged illness, occurs in a social context that melds the personal and the public, and invokes as an ultimate authority (one that properly exercising the most control over the process) the self. In 'neo-modern death,' the split between public and private domains is effaced when a private experience is publicly celebrated.

The Social Origins of Dignity at the End of Life

Something about dying alone, apart from others and hence socially disconnected, appears especially undignified—dying 'like an animal' in the parlance of many patients. This may be part of the origin of suspicions that hospital deaths are undignified because the deaths occur in an institutionalized and sequestered way, apart

[11] B.F. Skinner, *Beyond Freedom and Dignity* (Indianapolis: Hackett Publishing, 2002 [1971]), p.58.

[12] T. Walter, *The Revival of Death* (London: Routledge, 1994).

from relevant others, or with inauthentic interactions with others—that is, not 'real' others, but instead with people inhabiting social *roles*, such as a 'doctor' or a 'nurse.' This may also explain why patients so often want to have truly personal interactions with their caregivers, as this in part helps restore their dignity. Earlier, we noted the salience in patients' perceptions of a good death of having a doctor who listens. Here is one physician's description of such an attempt by a patient at social connection:

> The last day I saw him in the emergency room, he was looking at me with those roving eyes and gasping for breath. I leaned over him and stroked his hair. He looked at me and said, 'how's that new house of yours?' I said, 'I'm not really moved in.' And he said, 'You make sure you decorate it nicely.' It was a very personal interchange. He was dying, and his last interaction with me was as a person, not as a doctor.[13]

Dignity for the patient here, in part, means being known as a person rather than as a diseased individual, and interacting with the doctor in a personal way.

There is, moreover, something dignified about making social connections even when one is about to lose all of them. And people seem to crave this. Here is one example of a family member's description:

> He got home, and they got him out of the ambulance. I remember him saying, "Oh, can I wait just a minute, to remember the sunshine." This for somebody who hadn't seen the sun in so long. It was almost like we had a party that evening. Everybody was there, and we sang songs. He died that night, at home, and everybody was there.[14]

Another patient explicitly makes the connection between dignity and social connections:

> [What gives my life dignity is] having a family. Having the little fellow that lives next door. That give me a lot of cheer. Well, it doesn't matter how bad things get. I always know that my family is there and I'm very lucky. Not everybody's family is supportive. But I know that they love me. Yeah, because I belong to somebody and they belong to me.[15]

This recognition that social connections are a key part of a dignified death is supported as well by the frequency with which items related to social connections make it onto the list of important attributes of a good death in Table 2. There are strong social components in patients' definition of a good death.

In short, a key way that dignity is 'social' is that people incorporate social elements into their perceptions of a good or dignified death. As we have seen, a second key respect in which dignity has social origins is the observation that institutional structures affect patient dignity. Finally, the social environment impinging

---

[13] K. E. Steinhauser, E. C. Clipp, M. McNeilly, N.A. Christakis, L. McIntyre, and J.A. Tulsky, 'In Search of a Good Death: Observations of Patients, Families, and Providers', *Annals of Internal Medicine*, 132 (2000), pp.825–832.

[14] Ibid.

[15] H.M. Cochinov, T. Hack, S. McClement, L. Kristjanson, and M. Harlos, 'Dignity in the Terminally Ill: A Developing Empirical Model', pp.433–443.

Table 4 Additional features of idealized types of death (T. Walter, The Revival of Death, (London: Routledge, 1994), p. 48)

	Traditional	Modern	Neo-modern
L	Plague	Cancer/CD	Cancer/AIDS
Trajectory	Fast	Hidden	Prolonged
Life expectancy	40	70	80
Typical death	Child	Elderly	Elderly
Atypical death	Old (venerated)	Young (senseless)	Young(senseless)
Others seen dying	Frequently	Rarely	'Witnessing'
Authority	God	Medicine	Self
Know through	Clergy (male)	Doctors (male)	Counselors (female)
Good death	Conscious ready to meet God	Unconscious/sudden no bother to others	Aware/precious finish business

on dignity at the end of life is of substantial relevance for another reason: social factors contribute to the very definition of a dignified death and, consequently, perceptions may vary across social and cultural groups. There is a social construction of notions of dignity, a strictly social ontology.

Indignity originates in the treatment of one person by others. And, conversely and just as assuredly, dignity can depend upon the treatment of one person by others. While this is a general observation, it is especially relevant in end-of-life care. If we are serious about dignity, we should revise the way we care about the dying—not only for the sake of patients—but also for the sake of doctors; for it is undignified for the doctor, and for our society, to provide undignified care.

21
Dying with Dignity: The Story Reveals Its Meaning

Jack Coulehan

The concept of 'dying with dignity' appears frequently in public discourse about aggressive medical intervention near the end of life. Stripped to the level of sound bite, 'death with dignity' represents a rallying cry for groups that favor legalization of measures like physician assisted suicide (PAS) and euthanasia. More frequently, though, 'death with dignity' has multiple meanings; and because of that, conversations about dignity among patients, families, and health-care professionals often result in miscommunication, and may enhance distress, rather than decreasing it. In this essay I want to explore in some detail what people mean when they say 'I want to die with dignity' or when they claim that a deceased loved one did or did not die with dignity.

I begin with the story of a patient who expressed on many occasions during the last months of her life her desire to die with dignity, but in the long run was not able to achieve that goal. I then suggest distinctions between external and intrinsic dignity, and experiential and 'real' intrinsic dignity. To investigate intrinsic dignity, I explore—with broad strokes and not at all deeply—two candidates for the 'real'meaning of human dignity: autonomy or self-determination; and dignity as relationship. In so doing, I add grist to the mill by presenting a second narrative about a dying patient, much different from the first. In conclusion, I present a brief differential diagnosis of dying without dignity and suggest the outlines of an appropriate 'treatment' for alienation and disrespect at the end of life.

Death Without Dignity: The Story of Joyce Evans

> She just wanted to die with a little dignity. That's all she asked for, to die with dignity. But in the end she suffered so terribly. The pain was unbearable. It was so awful, so ... unnecessary. If only we could have given her the death she wanted. ...

Not long ago an acquaintance told me how angry and distressed she was about the manner in which her mother had died. When Joyce Evans first learned that she had pancreatic cancer, she had made her intentions clear. She knew there was no possibility of a cure. Nonetheless, the doctor told her about various treatment

J. Malpas and N. Lickiss (eds.), Perspectives on Human Dignity: A Conversation, 209–223.

options—a 'debulking' surgical procedure to prevent bile-duct obstruction, several types of standard chemotherapy, and possible opportunities to enroll in clinical trials of new chemotherapeutic agents. Mrs. Evans, a retired accountant, explained that her primary goals for the remainder of her life were to remain as active as possible, spend time with her children and grandchildren, put her affairs in order, and enjoy the blessings each day would bring. Her oncologist paid lip service to these goals, but suggested that aggressive interventions might help her attain them: a surgery consult regarding a palliative 'debulking' procedure and a referral to a world-class cancer center, just in case 'something new' was available to help her.

In a matter of days, Mrs. Evans mounted a medical treadmill that she found more and more difficult to control. First, she underwent surgery. This was followed by a series of complications, then chemotherapy, tube feeding, more chemotherapy, additional infections, all of which were accompanied by intractable pain. One disaster led to another. Mrs. Evans suffered not only from her physical symptoms (many of which resulted from her treatment, rather than the disease), but also emotionally and spiritually. This medical treadmill continued for six months.

None of the medical specialists or other health professionals expressed opposition to Mrs. Evans' original goal of supportive and palliative care at the end of life. For example, they agreed that a hospice referral would be ideal, but they kept postponing it. 'It's not time yet' they would tell the patient and her daughter. And when speaking to the daughter alone, they would explain, 'We don't want her to lose hope. That will only make her more depressed.' At long last at her daughter's insistence, Mrs. Evans found herself enrolled in a local hospice program, but only nine days before she took her last breath. 'It was awful' the daughter said. 'My mother was in agony. It kept getting worse and worse, but no one ever slowed down enough to listen to what she was saying. They wouldn't pay attention.'

This is a far-too-frequent narrative about dying in the USA today.[1] According to her daughter's story, Mrs. Evans began the process with a clear idea of what she wanted. She expressed her wishes, but in the conversations that ensued she evidently chose to accept advice regarding 'palliative' measures that were, in fact, destructive and demoralizing, rather than beneficial. She wound up after six months a desperate, battered, despondent patient who had not experienced the 'few good months' she hoped for.

This story is open to many interpretations. The medical specialists might argue that Mrs. Evans was ambivalent about her goals. She knew the risks of aggressive therapy and chose to take them because there was a small chance of a good remission.

---

[1] See, for instance, I. Byock, *Dying Well: The Prospect for Growth at the End of Life* (New York: Riverhead Books, 1997); D. Callahan, *What Kind of Life: The Limits of Medical Progress* (New York: Simon & Schuster, 1990); J. Coulehan, 'Death with Dignity: Images, Stories, and Reflections', in: Harvey, R. (ed.), *Joyous Wakes, Dignified Deaths: Issues in Death and Dying* (Albany: State University of New York Press), pp.19–58; S.B. Nuland, *How We Die. Reflections on Life's Final Chapter* (New York: Alfred A. Knopf, 1994); M.J. Field and C.K. Cassel (eds.), *Approaching Death: Improving Care at the End of Life* (Institute of Medicine, Washington, DC: National Academy Press, 1997).

A psychologist might wonder about the role of denial and magical thinking in her decision-making. A skeptic might point to my acquaintance, the savvy, articulate daughter: why did not she speak up more forcibly to insist that her mother's wishes be honored? I have little doubt that if Mrs. Evans and her daughter had been considerably more assertive and consistent; she would have received a prompt hospice referral and suffered much less during her final months. Nonetheless, Mrs. Evans' story is typical of the American way of dying. This narrative encapsulates and validates popular beliefs and anxieties about the way we die in the USA today. Such 'horror stories' constitute a reservoir of images, fears, expectations, anger, and desperation that, in the aggregate, form our prevalent cultural narrative of dying.[2]

This cultural narrative stipulates dichotomy and antagonism. Physician versus patient, institution versus individual, law versus medicine, public interest versus private interest, health insurer versus insured person, and strong versus weak. Like many features of contemporary culture, our prevailing ethos of dying is often visualized as a conflict between aggressor and victim. Doctors and the medical-care system are aggressors; suffering patients and their families are victims. Victimization implies violence. And certainly this précis of dying is violent—bodily invasion, kidnapping, psychological battering, and economic rape. The scenario describes, in essence, a hostile takeover of the dying person's body.

I am primarily concerned here with the central concept that Mrs. Evans invoked and her daughter elaborated; that is, dignity. What did they mean by dying with dignity? Clearly, in this case we do not need to reflect very much. Mrs. Evans' goals—functionality, happiness, closure, social support, and self-determination—are consistent with (even if not essential for) any reasonable notion of human dignity. Alternatively, her experience—uncontrolled symptoms, separation from family, progressive debility, lack of support, and loss of autonomy—convey a vivid image of indignity. When we look at the details of Mrs. Evans' story, for example, the nights she spent in the hospital raving in delirium so that her arms and legs had to be tied down, the loss of dignity becomes so evident we need no definition. We want to say, 'It is pointless to argue over the precise meaning of dignity in Mrs. Evans' case. Her experience is surely an abomination to the human heart. Anyone can see that she lost every shred (or at least most of the shreds) of human dignity.' Mrs. Evans cries out to us from the depths of our own hearts.

What Does It Mean to Die with Dignity?

The term 'death with dignity' evokes a broad plethora of meanings—theological, philosophical, social, political, and personal—many of which are suggested in one way or another by Mrs. Evans' story.[3] I want to analyze several conceptions and

[2] Something also exemplified in the sources referred to in the preceding note.

[3] For some of these meanings see M.D.M. Fowler, 'Suffering', in: J.F. Kilmer, A.B. Miller, and E.D. Pellegrino (eds.), *Dignity and Dying. A Christian Appraisal* (Grand Rapids, MI: William

permutations of human dignity as they are represented in this narrative because Mrs. Evans' dilemma is in fact so typical. Those of us who are caregivers may be most familiar with the physical and emotional indignities that characterize Mrs. Evan's story. Philosophers and chaplains, medical administrators and health care activists, legislators and economists may encounter aspects of this patient's narrative that relate to their own professions and, in so doing, perhaps find additional understandings of dignity or the loss thereof.

On the outside looking in: Let me begin with the external features of Joyce Evans' dying. She experienced sustained and apparently intractable abdominal pain. Almost continually nauseated, she vomited every time she tried to eat. However, when fed through a percutaneous gastric tube, she developed abdominal distension and fluid overload. She was generally too weak to interact with friends and family, and when she did interact she was irritable and unpleasant. She was reduced to 'carping and whining' when awake and hence made her friends and family feel progressively more uncomfortable, as her daughter later confessed. At the outset, Joyce Evans was a strong, independent woman who stated explicitly that she wanted to maintain her independence; by the time she died, however, she had become a tortured, disagreeable, and physically offensive old woman. Clearly, this is a *real* sense in which Joyce Evans lost her dignity in the process of dying. This *external dignity* (i.e. visible to others) is the aggregate of at least three components. First, the cancer changed her body and diminished its ability to function; it gradually stripped her of most of the 'dignified' aspects of adult life; e.g. personal independence, mobility, intellectual, and emotional interests; and so forth. This process was largely inevitable.

Second, her indignity was compounded by the medical and cultural milieu in which she found herself. Had she entered a hospice program at an earlier stage, for example, she may have experienced significantly less suffering. Certainly, she would not have been subjected to the added insult of surgery and chemotherapy. While her independence would just as surely have melted away, although perhaps at a slower rate, Mrs. Evans may have been able to develop emotional and spiritual resources that would have—at least, in part—compensated for the loss.[4] With these new resources, she may have been able to ameliorate the external loss of dignity; for example, by appearing to be brave, by transmitting family stories or wisdom; or by maintaining a more lively interest in her loved ones.

B. Eerdmans, 1996); S. Hauerwas, *Suffering Presence. Theological Reflections on Medicine, the Mentally Handicapped, and the Church* (Edinburgh: T & T Clark, 1986); H. Kung, and J. Walter, *Dying with Dignity. A Plea for Personal Responsibility* (New York: Continuum, 1998); D. W. Moller, *On Death Without Dignity. The Human Impact of Technical Dying* (Amityville, New York: Baywood, 1990); D.P. Sulmasy, 'Death and Human Dignity', *Linacre Quarterly*, 61 (1994), pp.27–36; H.M. Chochinov, 'Dignity and the Eye of the Beholder', *Journal of Clinical Oncology*, 22 (2004), pp.1336–1340; R. Horton, 'Rediscovering Human Dignity', *The Lancet*, 364 (2004), pp.1081–1085.

[4] See D. S. Davis and L. Zoloth, *Notes from a Narrow Ridge: Religion and Bioethics* (Hagerstown, MD: University Publishing Group, 1999).

Her immediate personal and social milieu—her daughter, family, close friends, and emotional and spiritual advisors also contributed to indignity. I consider this a separate factor (in tension with the larger social milieu) because those with whom she had her most intimate relationships failed to affirm her *right to live* while she was dying. *The clutter and clang of the world was so invasive and noisy, these persons were unable to listen to the still small voice of Mrs. Evans' needs.* Perhaps if they had been more exceptional people, if they were willing to fight city hall, so to speak, they would have been able to better safeguard Mrs. Evans' external dignity.[5] But the requirement that dying persons be 'conferred' dignity by being surrounded by truly exceptional friends is inhumane, because it discounts the value of the ordinariness we share as human beings.

On the inside looking out: Now I want to consider *intrinsic* human dignity, which is quite a different kettle of fish. By the term 'intrinsic' I mean dignity that is irrevocably bound up with being a person; that is, essential to being human. In a later section of this chapter, I want to look at two conceptions of intrinsic dignity and their implications. Here I want to stick closely to Mrs. Evans' own story and ask, 'In the process of dying, did she, in fact, lose her intrinsic dignity?' To answer this question, I need to make a further distinction. Let us stipulate that intrinsic human dignity exists independent of experience; whether it be an immortal soul, a spark of divine light, a social construct, or even a stable epiphenomenon that arises from neural complexity. No matter what the source, the mere fact of possessing dignity need not imply that a person experience herself as possessing it. Mrs. Evans, for example, may have become so demoralized that she believed she was despicable, even if, in fact, at another level she retained a belief in her immortal soul. Clearly, dying people can and do sometimes experience themselves as unworthy wretches, despite contemporaneously holding the belief that life is sacred and the soul immortal. We do not know what Mrs. Evans' specific beliefs were in these matters, but we do know that she cried out in agony.

Dying in the World of Joyce Evans

To a large extent, Joyce Evans lived (and died) in the contemporary world described by Philippe Aries in *The Hour of Our Death*, his cultural history of dying that spans Western society from the beginning of the Christian (Common) era to the present.[6] He argues that human beings are forced to create social conventions that give some measure of control over the savage beast of death (i.e. the frightening knowledge that I will, in fact, die). Aries delineated five sequential

[5] S. Hauerwas, *Suffering Presence: Theological Reflections on Medicine, the Mentally Handicapped and the Church* (Edinburgh: T & T Clark, 1986); H. Kung and J. Walter, *Dying with Dignity: A Plea for Personal Responsibility* (New York: Continuum, 1998).

[6] P. Aries, *The Hour of Our Death* (New York: Oxford University Press, 1982).

models that have developed in European culture over the last 2,000 years. The first was the early Christian 'tame death' grounded in a belief that any individual person's death constituted an event that affected the whole community. Other features of this model included belief in an afterlife (something like prolonged sleep in anticipation of bodily resurrection at the end of the world); acknowledgment of evil in this world and the next; and community prayer and ritual to insure the dying person's safe passage into 'eternal rest'. In essence, dying occurred in the context of community solidarity.

Aries contrasts 'tame death' with the model prevalent today, which he terms 'invisible death'.[7] Nowadays, the individual rather than the community is the locus of life experience; communal relationships are secondary and optional; and dying means personal extinction. Since in our secular culture, we no longer believe in evil or afterlife, death is meaningless. By relocating dying to the hospital, we cope with death by splitting the acknowledged fact of extinction from its emotional impact, which we blunt or avoid because death has been sanitized and removed from everyday experience. Aries writes, 'A heavy silence has fallen over the subject of death. When this silence is broken … it is to reduce death to the insignificance of an ordinary event that is mentioned with feigned indifference.'[8]

The sanitized 'invisible death' eschews preparation for encountering the beast. The beast emerges from its lair in many guises, among which is the alluring face of medical technology. Closely bound up with the reclusion of death from social life is the embarrassment that we feel in the presence of dying people. Even when we acknowledge a private need for 'getting my head into the right place' before death, we avoid public ritual. If we are afraid of dependency, we agonize over asking others to support us, terrified that we will become a burden (and be *seen* as a burden) on them.

We consider personal or public preparation for death to be morbid. When asked in what manner they would choose to die, contemporaries often answer, 'I'd like to die in my sleep. Just drift away. No fuss, no bother, no pain.' Others reply, 'I'll take a sudden, massive heart attack. One minute I'm playing tennis. The next minute. … Wham! I'm gone.' The odds, however, are against such a preferred departure since 90% of Americans and Europeans die of chronic medical conditions that progress in an episodic downward spiral for months or years. Given this denial of death, it is understandable that preparation for death is looked upon as strange or pathological behavior. Culturally, we prefer the fighter, the optimist, and the person willing to take risks in order to survive, as compared to the passive person who appears to have lost hope.

This, then, is the world in which Joyce Evans lived. Her dying was indeed invisible because it lurked behind a façade of frenetic activity, and insofar as was possible her suffering went on behind closed doors. Every time her personal experience (that still small voice) spoke up for dignity, in one way or another the militant

---

[7] Ibid.

[8] Ibid.

structures of medical care deflected the question by luring her with more machines and additional options. Paradoxically, embedded in this context of inadequate information, displaced feelings, questionable relationships, and seeming inability to make clear-headed decisions, is a major candidate for the meaning of intrinsic human dignity; that is, dignity as choice, self-determination, or the right to die.

Dignity as Choice: The Right to Die

Most contemporary bioethicists do not explicitly discuss dignity, but the high value they place on the principle of autonomy or self-determination suggests that they would consider an attack on autonomy to be the same as an attack on dignity.[9] Secular bioethics is often admittedly 'thin' because it sees itself more as a set of processes and procedures for decision-making, than a theory of morality (i.e. a 'thick' ethics).[10] Generally, a watered-down version of Kantian autonomy trumps all. A few medical ethicists ground their thinking in virtue theory, which of course predicates a theory of the Good, but their works rarely serve as the meat-and-potatoes of clinical ethics.[11] In fact, Daniel Sulmasy concludes that freedom of choice serves as the philosophical basis for secular American biomedical ethics, and also for today's death with dignity movement; for example, the right of PAS or euthanasia.[12] Dignity as choice has two attractive features as a foundational concept. First, it honors self-determination as the building block of morality. Thus, it is consistent with the American emphasis on liberty, rights, and autonomy. From this perspective, a legal right to PAS or euthanasia seems to be a reasonable, almost inevitable, extension of currently accepted inalienable rights and liberties.

The second attractive feature of dignity as choice is that the medium is the message—it is entirely process, requiring no substantive criterion. The content of one's choice is irrelevant to dignity; as long as the 'chooser' is judged intact. Thus, if a person considers himself a fighter determined to spit in the face of death and hang on as long as possible, his version of death with dignity would involve highly aggressive technological intervention, even if the intervention entails very large burden and promises only marginal, if any, benefit. Mrs. Evans, under this rubric, would qualify as dying with dignity, except for her (evidently misplaced) conviction that this was

---

[9] T.L. Beauchamp and T.L. Childress, *Principles of Biomedical Ethics* (New York: Oxford University Press, 5th edn., 2001); R. Veatch, *The Basics of Bioethics* (New York: Prentice-Hall, 2nd edn., 2002); J. Harris (ed.), *Bioethics* (New York: Oxford University Press, 2001).

[10] Engelhardt, H.T., *The Foundations of Bioethics* (New York: Oxford University Press, 2nd edn., 1996).

[11] E.D. Pellegrino and D.C. Thomasma, *The Virtues in Medical Practice* (New York: Oxford University Press, 1993); J.F. Drane, *Becoming a Good Doctor* (Kansas City: Sheed & Ward, 1995).

[12] D.P. Sulmasy, 'Death and Human Dignity', *Linacre Quarterly*, 61 (1994), pp.27–36.

not, in fact, what she wanted. Alternatively, if a person believes in a quiet death, refusing, rather than accepting, treatment would exemplify dignity. Furthermore, if she prefers to avoid useless suffering and becoming a burden during the *natural* process of dying, dignity for her might include suicide, PAS, or euthanasia.[13]

Timothy Quill's *Death and Dignity: Making Choices and Taking Charge* is a good illustration of dignity as autonomous choice.[14] Although Quill states that 'the patient's quest for a dignified death should be a fundamental part of the equation for end-of-life medical decisions' he assumes that human dignity either cannot or need not be explicitly defined.[15] This is because dignity is utterly idiosyncratic: 'Dignity involves the integration of a person's physical, emotional, intellectual, and spiritual aspects; it is complex and unique to each individual.'[16] It is clear from the book's subtitle however, that 'making choices and taking charge' are crucial features. Presumably, having no choice in the matter, or not being able to take charge, constitutes loss of dignity.

Problems with Dignity as Choice

Although dignity as self-determination is prima facie appealing, it is also troublesome. The first problem is that choice (as conceptualized here) is historically and culturally specific. Most people throughout most of human history have died in

---

[13] A.L. Caplan, L. Snyder and K. Faber-Langendoen, 'The Role of Guidelines in the Practice of Physician-assisted Suicide', *Annals of Internal Medicine*, 132 (0000), pp.476–481; A.E. Chin, K. Hedberg, G.K. Higginson, and D.W. Fleming, 'Legalized Physician-assisted Suicide in Oregon—The First Year's Experience', *New England Journal of Medicine*, 340 (1999), pp.577–583; J. Coulehan, 'The Man with Stars Inside', *Annals of Internal Medicine*, 126 (1997), pp.799–802; K.M. Dixon, 'The Quality of Mercy: Reflections on Provider-assisted Suicide', *Journal of Clinical Ethics*, 8 (1997), pp.290–302; E.J. Emanuel, D.L. Fairclough and L.I. Emanuel, 'Attitudes and Desires Related to Euthanasia and Physician-assisted Suicide Among Terminally Ill Patients and Their Caregivers', *Journal of the American Medical Association*, 284 (2001), pp.2460–2468; D.E. Meier, C.A. Emmons, S. Wallenstein, T. Quill, R.S. Morrison, and C.K. Cassel, 'A National Survey of Physician-assisted Suicide and Euthanasia in the United States', *New England Journal of Medicine*, 338 (1998), pp.1193–1201; *Oregon's Death with Dignity Act: Three Years of Legalized Physician-assisted Suicide* (Portland, Oregon: Oregon Health Division, 22 February 2001); T.E. Quill, D.E. Meier, S.D. Block, and J.A. Billings, 'The Debate over Physician-assisted Suicide: Empirical Data and Convergent Views', *Annals of Internal Medicine*, 128 (1998), pp.552–558; L. Snyder, L. and D.P. Sulmasy (For the Ethics and Human Rights Committee, American College of Physicians) 'Physician-assisted Suicide', *Annals of Internal Medicine*, 135 (2001), pp.209–216; A.D. Sullivan, K. Hedberg, and D.W. Fleming, 'Legalized Physician-assisted Suicide in Oregon: The Second Year's Experience', *New England Journal of Medicine*, 342 (2000), pp.598–604.

[14] T.E. Quill, *Death and Dignity: Making Choices and Taking Charge* (New York: W.W. Norton, 1993).

[15] Ibid.

[16] Ibid.

ways and under circumstances that allowed them no choice. They died of accidents, wars, and plagues. The physical aspects of their deaths were often mean and revolting. Hundreds of millions of people in the third world today face similar conditions. Millions die of malnutrition and preventable disease. Certainly if 'taking charge' were a sine qua non for death with dignity, most human beings alive in the world today will die undignified deaths, as have the vast majority of their ancestors.

Dignity-as-choice also leaves out people who simply have no capacity to choose, or are unable to choose in a rational manner. Obviously, infants and children lack this sort of dignity. Those who suffer from developmental disability or serious mental disorder also lack this sort of dignity. Finally, persons who labor under the burden of progressive dementia must, at some point during the course of their condition, lose the ability to make autonomous choices. Much of contemporary biomedical ethics struggles with these questions, but once again almost entirely from the perspective of process (who should be assigned to make choices for such people?) and decisional standards (what standards should they use to make the decisions?). The question of whether compromised adults actually *have* intrinsic human dignity (specifically since they cannot choose) is largely unaddressed. If it is addressed, dignity may simply be denied (as I take Peter Singer's position to be in *Writings on the Ethical Life*[17]), or they may be granted a trace or penumbra of dignity that derives from their relationships (see later).[18]

A final worrisome feature of the dignity-as-choice proposition is that it discounts relational and social dimensions of personhood since autonomy is the sine qua non. Yet, if, in fact, human experience is fundamentally relational, there may be multiple constraints on choice and, moreover, some choices may be better or more dignified than others. While the claim that self-determination has primacy over relational values like community, solidarity, compassion, and fellow feeling, is a defining aspect of 'thin' American culture, millions of Americans—perhaps most of us—believe that these values must be given significant weight[19]; and that, in particular, human dignity involves such values at a deeper level than it involves the naked ability to make rational choices.

---

[17] P. Singer, *Writings on the Ethical Life* (New York: The Ecco Press, 2000), pp.170–185.

[18] A.E. Buchanan and D.W. Brock, *Deciding for Others. The Ethics of Surrogate Decision Making* (Cambridge: Cambridge University Press, 1990); C.E. Schneider, *The Practice of Autonomy. Patients, Doctors, and Medical Decisions* (New York: Oxford University Press, 1998); M. R. Wicclair, *Ethics and the Elderly* (New York: Oxford University Press, 1993).

[19] D. Callahan, *Setting Limits: Medical Goals in an Aging Society* (New York: Simon & Schuster, 1987); S. Hauerwas, *God, Medicine, and Suffering* (Grand Rapids, MI: William B. Eerdmans, 1990); J.V.M. Welie, *In the Face of Suffering: The Philosophical-Anthropological Foundations of Clinical Ethics* (Omaha: Creighton University Press, 1998).

Dignity as Relational: The Right to Live: The Story of Grace Navarro

Grace Navarro was an avuncular and independent woman who sold her farm in New Hampshire after her husband died and she settled on Long Island to be close to a favorite granddaughter and her family. I remember Mrs. Navarro as a tall, angular woman wearing a purple print dress, her white hair worn in a bun. I see her sitting beside my desk, purse in lap, explaining her gratitude that the Lord had spared her to a biblical age of three score and ten. I took care of her for several years, but never learned much about her private life because she was fiercely reserved, albeit quite eccentric when it came to wearing the purple print dresses. However, she usually brought a *zing* of wry humor to the office, usually at the expense of the Democrats, or her own aging process. 'It's all downhill from here,' she would say. 'And what's worse, we don't even *have* hills on Long Island!'

When I told Mrs. Navarro about the large mass in her right lung, she took out a small white handkerchief, dabbed her eyes a couple of times, and said, 'Well, that explains it.' After we confirmed the diagnosis, she underwent a short course of palliative radiotherapy. During the four months before she died, I saw Mrs. Navarro a couple more times in the office and made several home visits. She moved in with her granddaughter and enrolled in a home hospice program. I communicated frequently with the hospice nurse, primarily regarding management of pain, shortness of breath, and other symptoms. At my first house call Mrs. Navarro was still on her feet, meticulously dressed in a flowered housecoat, but she had lost weight. She greeted me at the door using a walker, an implement that she had dubbed 'my sick frame'. By the time of my second visit, she was in bed. Her voice was weak, her face and white hair almost invisible against a crisp pillow. Later, she developed brain metastases and became confused and incontinent. Then one day the nurse phoned to say that Mrs. Navarro had died.

I attended the funeral service at the Unitarian Universalist Church where Mrs. Navarro had *not* actually been active, although her granddaughter and husband were congregants. These folks talked a lot about virtue and nature, but avoided the word God like the plague. They appeared to be a flinty, straightforward group of people, consistent with my impression of Mrs. Navarro herself, and they had evidently provided a lot of support for her during the final weeks by simply *being there*. The Unitarians I met did not say much, but they had connected with her. *The New Shorter Oxford English Dictionary* gives as its first definition of dignity, 'the quality of being worthy or honorable; true worth; excellence'.[20] Mrs. Navarro fitted that definition, although, of course, Mrs. Evans did as well. Mrs. Navarro also demonstrated a 'dignified' set of behaviors and interactions as she approached death. Unlike Joyce Evans, she appeared to accept and relish each day as it came, and seemed not to be overwhelmed by the process that consumed her.

---

[20] L. Brown (ed.), *The New Shorter Oxford English Dictionary*, Vol. 1 (Oxford: Clarendon Press, 1993), p.671.

The Story Reveals Its Meaning

I chose Grace Navarro's story to introduce the second concept of intrinsic dignity—dignity as relational—even though it appears to present a paradox. Mrs. Navarro not only placed high value on self-determination, she consistently acted upon her choices and to a large extent wrote the final chapter of her life story. Alternatively, Joyce Evans, whom I have discussed in detail, did not live her last months as she had said she wanted to. Even though she often reiterated her wish to be left alone, at times she also expressed apparently conflicting desires, and as she became sicker, a widening gap developed between (a) her desire for a dignified death and (b) the way her story actually unfolded. In essence, although neither woman had the legal 'right to die' by PAS or euthanasia that epitomizes dignity-as-choice, they both had the potential to enjoy the 'right to live' that a relational conception of dignity confers. While Grace Navarro engaged fully in her right to live, Joyce Evans largely gave up this right, or allowed it to slip away, because of ambivalence, intimidation, and confusion.

Concepts of intrinsic human dignity that have *content* in addition to *process* (choice) are 'relational' because they presume that dignity inheres in one's relationship to a bigger picture, a *telos*, or some locus of meaning in the universe. For example, if one has a soul, the soul implies a relationship with God. Or, if the universe is analogous to a living organism striving toward perfection, this implies that one has a role to play (a relationship) in the vast scheme of things, or the music of the spheres. Relational concepts of human dignity predicate content; dignity means something. In particular, it means communication, narrative, and responsibility.

Communication

Relationship places primary emphasis on the human ability to communicate; in fact, it predicates a fundamental *need* to communicate. Human flourishing requires a vast network of connections, most of which take place at levels at once more personal (emotional, spiritual) and more detached (social, cultural, economic) than our imagined ideal of communication; that is, the free choice of rational decision-makers. We need to touch one another. We need to experience the pain of others, and also to feel their elation and joy. Hence, there is no human dignity without empathy.[21]

The greatest challenge to dignity is the attempt to close ourselves off, to disconnect from others. To some extent human beings have achieved spiritual growth by

[21] E.J. Cassell, *The Nature of Suffering and the Goals of Medicine* (New York: Oxford University Press, 1991); J. Coulehan, 'An Alternative View: Listening to Patients', *The Lancet* 354 (1999), pp.1467–1468; J. Coulehan, 'Attention Must be Paid!' *Journal of the American Medical Association*, 283 (2000), p.976; E.S. More and M.A. Milligan (eds.), *The Empathic Practitioner. Empathy, Gender, and Medicine* (New Brunswick, NJ: Rutgers University Press, 1994).

developing greater empathy and, thereby, increasing their willingness to interact with people from other clans or tribes or religions.[22] 'How do we live with moral differences and yet sustain an overarching community?' asks Jonathan Sacks in *The Dignity of Difference*. The answer, he maintains, 'is conversation—not mere debate but the disciplined act of communicating…and listening'.[23] As Isaiah Berlin wrote, 'It is a terrible and dangerous arrogance to believe that you alone are right. … '[24]

We communicate within networks of relationships. We understand that 'those who cope best with tragedy befalling loved ones are those who are involved in healthy personal relationships that are deeply intimate, even though it is (precisely) this kind of intimacy that made tragedy possible in the first place.'[25] Paradoxically, the closer we get to others in a way that facilitates true human understanding, or empathy, the better able we are to cope with their eventual loss and, I believe, with the prospect of our own deaths.

Narrative

The second implication of relational dignity is that it is not only grounded in relationship, but also in story. For human beings to find a belief or value meaningful in their lives, it has to be expressed in the form of a story.[26] This is certainly true of dignity. To say that the source of human dignity is that we are made in God's image means nothing, unless 'made in God's image' presupposes a rich and complex tradition of stories. But, of course, meaningful stories do not have to include God among their characters. Take Camus' novel *The Plague*, for example, which tells a compelling story of human dignity, most notably in the character of Dr. Rieux, who devotes his entire being to fighting the plague and encouraging others with his dedication and kindness, even though he believes that life is absurd and there is no one out there

---

[22] J. Sacks, *The Dignity of Difference. How to Avoid the Clash of Civilizations* (London: Continuum, 2002).

[23] Ibid., p.83.

[24] I. Berlin, *Liberty* (Oxford: Oxford University Press, 2002), p.345.

[25] G. W. Harris, *Dignity and Vulnerability. Strength and Quality of Character* (Berkeley, CA: University of California Press, 1997), p.131.

[26] H. Brody, 'My Story is Broken; Can You Help Me Fix It? Medical Ethics and the Joint Construction of Narrative', *Literature and Medicine*, 13 (1994), pp.79–92; R. Charon, 'Narrative Medicine: A Model for Empathy, Reflection, Profession, and Trust', *Journal of the American Medical Association*, 286 (2001), pp.1897–1902; R. Charon, 'Narrative Medicine: Form, Function, and Ethics', *Annals of Internal Medicine*, 134 (2001), pp.83–87; K. Montgomery, *Doctors' Stories: The Narrative Structure of Medical Knowledge* (Princeton, NJ: Princeton University Press, 1991); D.B. Morris, 'Narrative, Ethics, and Thinking with Stories', *Narrative*, 9 (2001), pp.55–77; H.L. Nelson (ed.), *Stories and Their Limits: Narrative Approaches to Bioethics* (New York: Routledge, 1997); M. Nussbaum, 'Love's Knowledge', *Essays on Philosophy and Literature* (New York: Oxford University Press, 1990).

listening to our prayers.[27] In essence, the fact that we can respond emotionally to Rieux's story, that it may stir us to act in more virtuous ways, in some sense *creates* the virtue and dignity that his fictional actions portray. Or consider Mother Teresa. 'The salient point is that her love revealed—taught—what it is to be a human being' because of the way in which her actions forced us to look upon the afflicted as possessing human dignity. Our amazement 'in response to her is not a wonder at [Mother Teresa], but a wonder *that human life could be as her love revealed it to be*'.[28] There is a sense in which our personal and collective responses to Mother Teresa's story both reveals the dignity of the dying poor of Calcutta *and also* our own dignity in being able to respond with compassion to the story. The story is not about Mother Theresa, but about the possibility of human dignity.[29]

Responsibility

Finally, dignity as relationship implies responsibility.[30] This concept is embodied in the fictional Dr. Rieux, as well in as our responses to stories like those of Mother Theresa or Mohandas Gandhi or Nelson Mandela. 'What morality restores to an increasingly uncertain world is the idea of responsibility—that what we do, severally and collectively, makes a difference, and that the future lies in our hands.'[31] Virtually everyone would agree that as human beings we have a responsibility to care for the dying. However, a relational conception of dignity also suggests that dying persons continue to have responsibilities toward other people (or perhaps toward the Other), even though they may of necessity be very limited during the final stages of illness.

The Hospice Way of Dying

Hospice's first objective is to alleviate, in so far as is possible, the patient's physical, emotional, and spiritual suffering.[32] One could visualize the patient as remaining passive, as layers of pain and conflict are removed. However, hospice has a

[27] A. Camus, *The Plague* (New York: Vintage International, 1947, reissued 1991).

[28] R. Gaita, *Good and Evil: An Absolute Conception* (London: Routledge, 1991), p.205.

[29] Ibid., p.205.

[30] N. Elias, *The Loneliness of Dying* (Oxford: Basil Blackwell, 1985); K. Kramer, *The Sacred Art of Dying* (New York: Paulist Press, 1988); D.P. Sulmasy, *The Healer's Calling: A Spirituality for Physicians and Other Health Care Professionals* (New York: The Paulist Press, 1997); T.E. Hill, *Respect, Pluralism, and Justice*. Kantian Perspectives (Oxford: Oxford University Press, 2000).

[31] J. Sacks, *The Dignity of Difference. How to Avoid the Clash of Civilizations* (London: Continuum, 2002), p.84.

[32] I. Byock, *Dying Well: The Prospect for Growth at the End of Life* (New York: Riverhead Books, 1997).

second, and in a sense deeper, objective as well; that is, to provide circumstances in which dying persons may actively participate in their last phase of life, a phase that involves the integration, connection, and meaning of their lives.[33] I will not describe the philosophy of hospice, or its clinical and programmatic implementation; this material is readily accessible in numerous lay publications.

I do want to point out, however, that hospice (and the palliative medicine movement, which is closely related to hospice) derive largely from a *relational conception of human dignity*. While there is certainly some overlap, *the conception of dignity as choice or self-determination* generally has less affinity for the philosophy of hospice. In particular, while a 'right to die' believer may embrace the first objective of hospice (relief of suffering), he or she may have little use for the second objective (existential growth). Miller, for example, contrasts arguments advanced by advocates of euthanasia with beliefs embedded in the 'hospice model' of dying. Miller acknowledges that hospice philosophy arguably presents 'the best approach to dying', yet contends that hospice can be 'tendentious, presumptuous, paternalistic, and intolerant'.[34] Even though the hospice model may be more virtuous than suicide, Miller argues that it is paternalistic to demand that people be virtuous in their dying. Instead, they should be allowed to choose.[35]

Conclusion

Let me return at last to what Joyce Evan's daughter told me not long after her mother died, 'She just wanted to die with a little dignity. That's all she asked for, to die with dignity. But in the end she suffered so terribly. ... It was so awful, so unnecessary.'

I agree. It was awful and unnecessary. From the perspective of people around her, Mrs. Evans's human dignity withered away as her disease progressed. As I have argued, she found herself living in the world of 'invisible death, which (para-

---

[33] I. Byock, *Dying Well*; D. Barnard, A. Towers, P. Boston, and Y. Lambrinidou, *Crossing Over. Narratives of Palliative Care* (New York: Oxford University Press, 2000); MM. Mendiola, 'Overworked, But Uncritically Tested: Human Dignity and the Aid-in-Dying Debate', in: E.E. Shelp (ed.), *Secular Bioethics in Theological Perspective* (Dordrecht: Kluwer Academic Publishers, 1996), pp.129–143; K.E. Steinhausen, E.C. Clipp, M. McNeilly, N.A. Christakis, L. M. McIntyre, and J.A. Tulsky, 'In Search of a Good Death: Observations of Patients, Families, and Providers', *Annals of Internal Medicine*, 132(10) (2000), pp.825–832; D. Tataryn and H.M. Chochinov, 'Predicting the Trajectory of the Will to Live in Terminally Ill Patients', *Psychosomatics*, 43 (2002), pp.370–377; H.M. Chochinov, T. Hack, T. Hassard, L.J. Kristjanson, S. McClement, and M. Harlos, 'Dignity in the Terminally Ill: A Cross-sectional, Cohort Study', *The Lancet*, 360 (2002), pp.2026–2030.

[34] F.G. Miller, 'The Good Death, Virtue, and Physician-assisted Death: An Examination of the Hospice Way of Death', *Cambridge Quarterly of Healthcare Ethics*, 5 (1996), pp.92–97.

[35] Ibid.

doxically) prevented her from having life-affirming relationships with her health care professionals, and to a large extent with her friends and family as well.' This world was characterized by dysfunctional communication, loneliness, and an experiential loss of dignity. Respect for autonomy was a key concept used by Mrs. Evans and her caregivers, but it is unclear how much personal impact the idea of self-determination had, or how it guided her decisions, during the months of her final illness.

If indeed there is a more fundamental and universal concept of human dignity that is based on relationships, Mrs. Evans fared little better. Once again, she experienced alienation and loss of dignity, even if, in some cosmic sense, she remained an untainted child of God. If indeed a substantive basis for human dignity exists, it surely takes more than natural phenomena like illness and incapacity to 'lose' it. If dignity involves communication, narrative, and responsibility, then one would have to do severe violence to these human qualities—perhaps by inverting them and using them for evil—to forego the right to be respected as a person. In any case, the story of Mrs. Evans remains ambiguous, because her experience may have included glimpses of redemption. (I use the word 'redemption' here to signify a sense of being worthy of respect, or being a part of a larger meaningful whole, not in its more specifically religious connotation.)

Alternatively, it is easy for us say that Grace Navarro died with dignity. While her physical devastation was very similar to that of Mrs. Evans, she carried herself with such an aura of external dignity that people around her never considered her undignified, even though she eventually became incontinent and completely helpless. Moreover, she appeared truly autonomous in her decision-making, but the choosing itself was grounded in a broader sense of connection and community. In her case it was quite clear that she was living with dignity; and her story reveals its meaning.

Bibliography

'A Conversation with Habib Malik', http://usinfo.state.gov/journals/itdhr/1098/ijdp/habib.htm

Abdul, Aziz S., 'Human Rights in Islamic Perspectives', in: A. Pollis and P. Schwab (eds.), *Human Rights: Cultural and Ideological Perspectives* (New York: Praeger, 1979).

Abrams, M. H. et al. (eds.), *The Norton Anthology of English Literature*, II (New York: W.W. Norton, 1962).

Adshead, S. A. M., *The End of the Chinese Empire* (Auckland: Heinemann, 1973).

Alexander, L., 'Medical Science Under Dictatorship', *New England Journal of Medicine*, 241 (1949), pp.39–47.

American Declaration of the Rights and Duties of Man, Final Act of the Ninth International Conference of American States, 1948.

Ammicht-Quinn, R., 'Whose Dignity is Inviolable? Human Beings, Machines and the Discourse of Dignity', in: R. Ammicht-Quinn, M. Junker-Kenny, and E. Tamez (eds.), *The Discourse of Human Dignity* (London: SCM Press, 2003).

Ammicht-Quinn, R., M. Junker-Kenny, and E. Tamez (eds.), *The Discourse of Human Dignity* (London: SCM Press, 2003).

Amnesty International, Female Genital Mutilation: A Human Rights Information Pack (AI Index: ACT 77/05/97) http://web.amnesty.org/actforwomen/index-eng#a7

Anderson, E. S. and R. H. Pildes, 'Expressive Theories of Law: A General Restatement', *University of Pennsylvania Law Review*, 148 (2000), pp.1503–1576.

An-Na'im, A. A. (ed.), *Human Rights in Cross-Cultural Perspective: A Request for Consensus* (Philadelphia, PA: University of Pennsylvania Press, 1992).

Annas, G., 'Why We Should Ban Human Cloning?', *New England Journal of Medicine* 339(2) (1998), pp.122–125.

Antonovsky, A., *Health Stress and Coping* (San Francisco, CA: Jossey-Bass, 1979).

Antonovsky, A., *Unravelling the Mystery of Health: How People Manage to Stay Well* (San Francisco, CA: Jossey-Bass, 1987).

Arieli, Y., 'On the Necessary and Sufficient Conditions for the Emergence of the Doctrine of the Dignity of Man and His Rights', in: D. Kretzmer and E. Klein (eds.), *The Concept of Human Dignity in Human Rights Discourse* (The Hague: Kluwer Law International, 2002), pp.11–17.

Aries, P., *The Hour of Our Death* (New York: Oxford University Press, 1982).

Aristotle, *Eudemian Ethics*, 2nd edn., trans. Michael Woods (New York: Oxford University Press, 1991).

Aristotle, *The Nichomachean Ethics* (Oxford: Oxford University Press, 1998).

Arlington, K., 'Fury Over Term for Girl Killers', *Mercury* (Hobart, Tasmania, 5 May 2007), p.27.

Ashworth, A., *Principles of Criminal Law* (Oxford: Clarendon Press, 2nd edn., 1996).

Ashworth, A., *Principles of Criminal Law* (Oxford: Oxford University Press, 4th edn., 2003).

Australian Health Ethics Committee, *Scientific, Ethical and Regulatory Considerations Relevant to Cloning of Human Beings* (16 December 1998). A Report to the Commonwealth Minister for Health and Aged Care, http://www.nhmrc.gov.au/ethics/human/ahec/history/_files/e4res.pdf

Bacon, F., *Novum Organum* (1620).

Baker-Fletcher, G., *Somebodyness: Martin Luther King, Jr. and the Theory of Dignity*, Harvard Dissertations in Divinity, No. 31 (Minneapolis, MN: Fortress Press, 1993).

Barnard, D. et al., *Crossing Over: Narratives of Palliative Care* (New York: Oxford University Press, 2000).

Baumeister, Roy F., 'Violent Pride', *Scientific American*, 284 (2001), pp.96–101.

Beauchamp, T. L. and T. L. Childress, *Principles of Biomedical Ethics* (New York: Oxford University Press, 5th edn., 2001).

Benjamin, M., *Splitting the Difference: Compromise and Integrity in Ethics and Politics* (Kansas: University Press of Kansas, 1990).

Berlin, I., *Liberty* (Oxford: Oxford University Press, 2002).

Betzanos, B. J., 'Wilhelm Dilthey: An Introduction', in: W Dilthey, *Introduction to the Human Sciences*, trans. R. J. Betzanos (Detroit, MI: Wayne University Press, 1988).

Beyleveld, D. and R. Brownsword, *Human Dignity in Bioethics and Biolaw* (Oxford: Oxford University Press, 2001).

Bowlby, J., *Attachment* (London: Hogarth, 1969).

Bowlby, J., *Separation* (London: Hogarth, 1973).

Bowlby, J., *Loss Sadness and Depression* (London: Hogarth, 1980).

Brady, I., *The Time at Darwin's Reef: Poetic Explorations in Anthropology and History* (Walnut Creek, CA: Rowman & Littlefield, 2003).

Brody, H., 'My Story Is Broken: Can You Help Me Fix It? Medical Ethics and the Joint Construction of Narrative', *Literature and Medicine*, 13 (1994), pp.79–92.

Brooke, C., *Queries: Past, Present and Future* (London: The Planet Office, 1907).

Brosnan, S. F. and F. B. M. de Waal, 'Monkeys Reject Unequal Pay', *Nature*, 425, (2003).

Brown, L. (ed.), *The New Shorter Oxford English Dictionary*, Vol. 1 (Oxford: Clarendon Press, 1993).

Brown, R. F. et al., 'Promoting Patient Participation and Shortening Cancer Consultations: A Randomized Trial', *British Journal of Cancer*, 85 (2001), pp.1273–1279.

Brownlie, I. (ed.), *Basic Documents on Human Rights* (Oxford: Clarendon Press, 1994).

Brownsword, R., 'Bioethics Today, Bioethics Tomorrow, Stem Cell Research and the Dignitarian Alliance', *Notre Dame Journal of Law Ethics and Public Policy*, 17 (2003), pp.15–52.

Brownsword, R. 'Regulating Human Genetics: New Dilemmas for a New Millennium', *Medical Literature Review*, 12 (2004), pp.14–39.

Bryder, T., 'Patterns for Future Research on Self-esteem and Human Dignity in Mass Society', *Political Psychology*, 15(3) (1994), pp.401–414.

Buchanan, A. E. and D. W. Brock, *Deciding for Others: The Ethics of Surrogate Decision Making* (Cambridge: Cambridge University Press, 1990).

Burkhardt, J., *The Civilization of the Renaissance in Italy* (Oxford: Phaidon, 1945).

Burley, J. and J. Harris, *A Companion to Genetics* (London: Blackwell, 2002).

Bush, George W., *State of the Union Address*, 29 January 2002, http://www.whitehouse.gov/news/releases/2002/01/20020129–11.html

Butow, P. et al., 'Cancer Consultation Preparation Package: Changing Patients but not Physicians Is not Enough', *Journal of Clinical Oncology*, 22 (2004), pp.4401–4409.

Byock, I., *Dying Well: The Prospect for Growth at the End of Life* (New York: Riverhead Books, 1997).

Callaghan, D., *The Troubled Dream of Life: In Search of a Peaceful Death* (New York: Touchstone, 1993).

Callahan, D., *Setting Limits: Medical Goals in an Aging Society* (New York: Simon & Schuster, 1987).

Callahan, D., *What Kind of Life: The Limits of Medical Progress* (New York: Simon & Schuster, 1990).

Campbell, A., *Rediscovering Palliative Care* (London: Darton, Longman & Todd, 1981).

Campbell, A., 'Ethos and Economics: Examining the Rationale Underlying Stem Cell and Cloning Research Policies in the United States, Germany and Japan', *American Journal of Law and Medicine*, 31 (2005), pp.47–86.

Camus, A., *The Plague* (New York: Vintage International, 1947, reissued 1991).
Caplan, A. L., L. Snyder, and K. Faber-Langendoen, 'The Role of Guidelines in the Practice of Physician-assisted Suicide', *Annals of Internal Medicine*, 132 (2000), pp.476–481.
Carson R. A. and C. R. Burns (eds.), *Philosophy of Medicine and Bioethics* (Dordrecht, The Netherlands: Kluwer, 1997).
Casement, P., *On Learning from the Patient* (London: Routledge, 1985).
Cassell, E., 'The Goal of Medicine and the Relief of Suffering', *New England Journal of Medicine*, 306 (1982), pp.639–636.
Cassell, E. J., *The Nature of Suffering and the Goals of Medicine* (New York: Oxford University Press, 1991).
Cassirer, E., P. O. Kristeller, and H. H. Randall, Jr., *The Renaissance Philosophy of Man* (Chicago, IL: Universitry of Chicago Press, 1948).
Chalmers, D. and D. Nicol, 'Embryonic Stem Cell Research: Can the Law Balance Ethical, Scientific and Economic Values', *Law and the Human Genome Review*, Parts 1 and 2, 18 (2003), pp.43–53 & pp.91–108.
Chaloupka, G., *Journey in Time* (Sydney: New Holland Publishers, 1999).
Charles, C., A. Gafni, and T. Whelan, 'Shared Decision Making in the Medical Encounter. What Does It Mean? (or It Takes Two to Tango)', *Social Science and Medicine*, 44 (1997), pp.681–692.
Charles, C., A. Gafni, and T. Whelan, 'Decision-making in the Physician-Patient Encounter: Revisiting the Shared Treatment Decision-making Model', *Social Science and Medicine*, 49 (1999), pp.651–656.
Charles, C. A. et al., 'Shared Treatment Decision Making: What Does It Mean to Physicians?', *Journal of Clinical Oncology*, 21 (2003), pp.932–936.
Charon, R., 'Narrative Medicine: A Model for Empathy, Reflection, Profession, and Trust', *Journal of the American Medical Association*, 286 (2001), pp.862–864.
Charon, R., 'Narrative Medicine: Form, Function, and Ethics', *Annals of Internal Medicine*, 134 (2001), pp.83–87.
Chaskalson, A., 'Human Dignity as a Constitutional Value', in: D. Kretzmer and E. Klein (eds.), *The Concept of Human Dignity in Human Rights Discourse* (The Hague: Kluwer Law International, 2002), pp.135–136.
Chauvel, R. 'Papua and Indonesia' in: D. Kingsbury and H. Aveling (eds.), *Autonomy and Disintegration in Indonesia* (London/New York: Routledge Curzon, 2003).
Cherny, N. I., 'The Problem of Suffering', in: D. Doyle et al. (eds.), *Oxford Textbook of Palliative Medicine* (Oxford: Oxford University Press, 3rd edn., 2004), pp.7–14.
Chin, A. E. et al., 'Legalized Physician-assisted Suicide in Oregon—The First Year's Experience', *New England Journal of Medicine*, 340 (1999).
Chochinov, H. M., 'Dignity and the Eye of the Beholder', *Journal of Clinical Oncology*, 22 (2004), pp.1336–1340.
Chochinov, H. M. et al., 'Dignity in the Terminally Ill: A Cross-sectional, Cohort Study', *The Lancet*, 360 (2002).
Chochinov, H. M., 'Dignity and the essence of Medicine: the ABC and D of dignity conserving care', *British Medical Journal* 335 (2007), pp.184–187.
Christakis, N. A., 'Managing Death: The Growing Acceptance of Euthanasia in Contemporary American Society', in: R. P. Hamel and E. R. DuBose (eds.), *Must We Suffer Our Way to Death? Cultural and Theological Perspectives on Death by Choice* (Dallas, TX: Southern Methodist University Press, 1996).
Christakis, N. A., *Death Foretold: Prophecy and Prognosis in Medical Care* (Chicago, IL: University of Chicago Press, 1999).
Christakis, N. A. and E. B. Lamont, '"Extent and Determinants of Error in Doctors" Prognoses for Terminally Ill Patients: Prospective Cohort Study', *British Medical Journal* (2000), pp.469–473.
Cohn, H., 'On the Meaning of Human Dignity', *Israel Yearbook on Human Rights*, 13 (1981), pp.231–232.
Conference on Security and Co-operation in Europe, Final Act, Helsinki, 1975, http://www.hri.org/docs/Helsinki75.html Convention on Human Rights and Biomedicine
Cookson, C. et al., *Genetic Engineering: The New Challenge* (European Union Patent Office, 1993).

Cooley, C., *Human Nature and the Social Order* (New York: Scribner's, 1902).
Copley S. and A. Edgar (eds.), *David Hume—Selected Essays* (Oxford: Oxford University Press, 1996).
Coulehan, J., 'An Alternative View: Listening to Patients', *The Lancet*, 354 (1999), pp.1467–1468.
Coulehan, J., 'Attention Must be Paid!', *Journal of the American Medical Association*, 283 (2000), p.976.
Coulehan, J., 'Death with Dignity: Images, Stories, and Reflections', in: R. Harvey, (ed.), *Joyous Wakes, Dignified Deaths: Issues in Death and Dying* (Albany, NY: State University of New York Press, 2001).
Coulehan, J., 'The Man with Stars Inside', *Annals of Internal Medicine*, 126 (1997), pp.799–802.
Cupitt, D., *Radicals and the Future of the Church* (London: SCM Press, 1989).
Cupitt, D., *The Revelation of Being* (London: SCM Press, 1998).
Cutcliffe, J. R. and K. Herth, 'The Concept of Hope in Nursing 1: Its Origins, Background and Nature', *British Journal of Nursing*, 11 (2002), pp.832–840.
Damasio, A., *Descartes' Error: Emotion, Reason and the Human Brain* (New York: Harper Perennial, 1995).
Dan-Cohen, M., 'Basic Values and the Victim's State of Mind', *California Law Review*, 88 (2000), pp.759–778.
Dan-Cohen, M., *Harmful Thoughts* (Princeton, NJ: Princeton University Press, 2002).
Dante, A., *The Divine Comedy*, trans. Allen Mandelbaum (New York: Bantam Books, 1984).
Dartmouth Medical School, *The Dartmouth Atlas of Health Care* (Chicago, IL: American Hospital Association, 1998).
Dasgupta, P., *Human Well-being and the Natural Environment* (Oxford: Oxford University Press, 2001).
Davidson, D., 'The Folly of Trying to Define Truth', *Truth, Language and History* (Oxford: Clarendon Press, 2005).
Davidson, D., *Subjective, Intersubjective, Objective* (Oxford: Clarendon Press, 2001).
Davis, D. S. and L. Zoloth, *Notes from a Narrow Ridge: Religion and Bioethics* (Hagerstown, MD: University Publishing Group, 1999).
de Certeau, M., *The Practice of Everyday Life* (Berkeley, CA: University of California Press, 1988).
de Schweinitz, K., *The Rise and Fall of British India* (London: Methuen, 1983).
de Tocqueville, A., *Democracy in America*. Edited and abridged by Richard Heffner (New York: Mentor Books, Times Mirror, 1956).
della Mirandola, Giovanni P., 'Oration on the Dignity of Man', trans. Elizabeth L. Forbes, in: E. Cassirer (ed.), *The Renaissance Philosophy of Man* (Chicago, IL: University of Chicago Press, 1948), pp.224–225.
della Mirandola, Giovanni P., *Oration on the Dignity of Man*, http://www.wsu.edu:8080/~dee/REN/ORATION.HTM
Dening, G., *Islands and Beaches: Discourse on a Silent Land, Marquesas 1774–1880* (Honolulu, HI: University Press of Hawaii, 1980).
Dening, G., *Performances* (Chicago, IL: University of Chicago Press, 1996).
Dening, G., *Beach Crossings. Voyaging Across Times, Cultures and Self* (Philadelphia, PA: University of Pennsylvania Press, 2004).
Dicke, K., 'The Founding Function of Human Dignity in the Universal Declaration of Human Rights', in: D. Kretzmer and E. Klein (eds.), *The Concept of Human Dignity in Human Rights Discourse* (The Hague: Kluwer Law International, 2002), pp.111–112.
Dillon, Robin S., 'Respect', in: E. Zalta (ed.), *Stanford Encyclopedia of Philosophy*, 2003 (http://plato.stanford.edu/entries/respect/).
Dilthey, W., *Introduction to the Human Sciences* (1923), trans. R. J. Betzanos (Detroit, MI: Wayne University Press, 1988).
Dixon, K. M., 'The Quality of Mercy: Reflections on Provider-assisted Suicide', *Journal of Clinical Ethics*, 8 (1997), pp.290–302.
Donnelly, J., 'Human Rights and Human Dignity: An Analytic Critique of Non-Western Conceptions of Human Rights', *American Political Science Review*, 76(2) (1982), pp.303–16.

Doyle, D. et al. (eds.), *Oxford Textbook of Palliative Medicine* (Oxford: Oxford University Press, 3rd edn., 2004).
Drane, J. F., *Becoming a Good Doctor* (Kansas City, MO: Sheed & Ward, 1995).
Duff, R. A. (ed.), *Philosophy and the Criminal Law* (Cambridge: Cambridge University Press, 1998).
Dworkin, R., *Taking Rights Seriously* (Cambridge, MA: Harvard University Press, 1977).
Erikson, E. H., *The Life Cycle Completed: A Review* (New York: W.W. Norton, 1982).
Eisenberg, L., 'Disease and Illness: Distinctions Between Professional and Popular Ideas of Sickness', *Culture, Medicine, and Psychiatry*, 1 (1977), pp.9–23.
Eliade, M., *The Myth of the Eternal Return: Or Cosmos and History* (Princeton, NJ: Princeton University Press, 1974).
Elias, N., *The Loneliness of Dying* (Oxford: Basil Blackwell, 1985).
Emanuel, E. J., D. L. Fairclough, and L. I. Emanuel, 'Attitudes and Desires Related to Euthanasia and Physician-assisted Suicide Among Terminally Ill Patients and Their Caregivers', *Journal of the American Medical Association*, 284 (2001), pp.2460–2468.
Engelhardt, H. T., *The Foundations of Bioethics* (New York: Oxford University Press, 2nd edn., 1996).
Englard, I., 'Human Dignity: From Antiquity to Modern Israel's Constitutional Framework', *Cardozo Law Review*, 21 (2000), pp.1903–1928.
Erikson, E. H., *Identity and the Life Cycle*, Psychological Issues Monograph (New York: International Universities Press, 1969).
Evans, T. (ed.), *Human Rights Fifty Years On: A Reappraisal* (Manchester: Manchester University Press, 1998).
Evans, T., 'Introduction: Power, Hegemony and the Universalization of Human Rights', in: T. Evans (ed.), *Human Rights Fifty Years On: A Reappraisal* (Manchester: Manchester University Press, 1998).
Falconer, Alan D., 'Human Dignity', in: J. Macquarrie and J. Childers (eds.), *A New Dictionary of Christian Ethics* (London: SCM Press 1986), pp.278–279.
Fanon, F., *The Wretched of the Earth* (Harmondsworth: Penguin, 1963).
Farberman, R., 'A Stain on Medical Ethics', *The Lancet*, 366 (2005), p.712.
Feinberg, J., *Harm to Others* (Oxford: Oxford University Press, 1984).
Feinberg, J., 'Harm to Others: A Rejoinder', *Criminal Justice Ethics*, 5 (1986), pp.16–29.
Feinberg, J., *Harmless Wrongdoing* (Oxford: Oxford University Press, 1988).
Field, M. J. and Cassel C. K. (eds.), *Approaching Death: Improving Care at the End of Life* (Institute of Medicine, Washington, DC: National Academy Press, 1997).
Flannery, A. (ed.), *The Church in the Modern World* (1965),Vatican Council II: The Conciliar and Post Conciliar Documents (Dublin: Dominican Publications, 1975).
Fonte, J., 'Democracy's Trojan Horse', *The National Interest*, Summer 2004, http://findarticles.com/p/articles/mi_m2751/is_76/ai_n6127318
Foot, P., 'Euthanasia', *Philosophy and Public Affairs*, 6 (Winter 1977), pp.85–112.
Forster, E. M., *A Passage to India* (London: Penguin, 1979) and *Howard's End* (London: Penguin, 1910).
Foucault, M., *The Birth of the Clinic: The Archaeology of Medical Practice* (New York: Vintage, 1993).
Fowler, M. D. M., 'Suffering', in: J. F. Kilmer, A. B. Miller, and E. D. Pellegrino (eds.), *Dignity and Dying. A Christian Appraisal* (Grand Rapids, MI: William B. Eerdmans, 1996).
Frankl, V., *Man's Search for Meaning* (New York: Simon & Schuster, 1984).
Frowein, J., 'Human Dignity in International Law', in: D. Kretzmer and E. Klein (eds.), *The Concept of Human Dignity in Human Rights Discourse* (Hague: Kluwer Law International, 2002).
Fulford, K. W. M., 'The Potential of Medicine as a Resource for Philosophy', *Theoretical Medicine*, 12 (1991), pp.81–85.
Gaita, R., *Good and Evil. An Absolute Conception* (London: Routledge, 1991).
Gardner, J., 'On the General Part of the Criminal Law', in: R. A. Duff (ed.), *Philosophy and the Criminal Law* (Cambridge: Cambridge University Press, 1998), pp.205, 242–243.
Gardner, J. and S. Shute, 'The Wrongness of Rape', in: J. Horder (ed.), *Oxford Essays in Jurisprudence*, 4th Series (Oxford: Oxford University Press, 2000), p.193.

Gattellari, M., Butow, P. N., and Tattersall M., 'Sharing Decisions in Cancer Care', *Social Science and Medicine*, 52 (2001), pp.1865–1878.

General Medical Council, *Tomorrow's Doctors: Recommendations on Undergraduate Medical Education* (London: General Medical Council, 1993).

Gillman, N., *Sacred Fragments: Recovering Theology for the Modern Jew*, (Philadelphia, PA: The Jewish Publication Society, 1990), pp.18–24.

Glendon, M. A., *A World Made New. Eleanor Roosevelt and the Universal Declaration of Human Rights* (New York: Random House, 2001).

Gopinath, Aruna Manuel, L., *Quezon: The Tutelary Democrat* (Quezon City: New Day Publishers, 1987).

Gordon, D., *Times Literary Supplement*, 13 August 2004, summarising James Q. Whitman.

Gormally, L., *Euthanasia, Clinical Practice and the Law* (London: Linacre Centre, 1994).

Gotesky R. and Laszlo E. (eds.), *Human Dignity: This Century and the Next* (New York: Gordon & Breach, 1970).

Grant, M. (trans.), *Cicero: Selected Works* (Harmondsworth, Middlesex: Penguin 1960).

Greenhalgh, T. and Hurwitz, B. (eds.), *Narrative Medicine* (London: British Medical Journal Books, 1998).

Griffin, M. T. and Atkins E. M., 'Notes on Translation,' in: *Cicero: On Duties* (New York: Cambridge University Press, 1991), pp.xlvi–xlvii.

Gruenwald, D. A. and White, E. J., 'The Illness Experience of Older Adults Near the End of Life: A Systematic Review', *Anaesthesiology Clinics of North America*, 24 (2006), pp.163–180.

Gullick, J., *Indigenous Political Systems of Western Malaya* (London: Athlone, 1958), p.98.

Hack, T. F. et al., 'Defining Dignity in Terminally Ill Cancer Patients: A Factor Analytic Approach', *Psycho-Oncology*, 13 (2004), pp.700–708.

Hall, J., *General Principles of Criminal Law*, 2nd edn. (Indianapolis, IN: Bobbs-Merrill, 1960).

Hall, R., *The Island in the Mind* (Sydney: Pan Macmillan, 1996).

Halliday, S., 'A Comparative Approach to the Regulation of Human Embryonic Stem Cell Research in Europe', *Medical Literature Review*, 12 (2004), pp.40–69.

Hamel, R. P. and DuBose, E. R. (eds.), *Must We Suffer Our Way to Death? Cultural and Theological Perspectives on Death by Choice* (Dallas, TX: Southern Methodist University Press, 1996).

Hampton, J., 'Correcting Harms Versus Righting Wrongs', *University of California at Los Angeles Law Review*, 39 (1992), p.1659.

Hand, S. (ed.), *The Levinas Reader* (Oxford: Blackwell, 1993).

Harcourt, B. E., 'The Collapse of the Harm Principle', *Journal of Criminal Law and Criminology*, 90 (1999), pp.109–194.

Hardt, M. and Negri, A., *Empire* (Cambridge, MA: Harvard University Press, 2000).

Hare, R. M., *Moral Thinking: Its Levels, Methods, and Point* (New York: Oxford University Press, 1981).

Harman, G. and Donald, D. (eds.), *Semantics of Natural Language* (Dordrecht, The Netherlands: D. Reidel, 1972).

Harris, G. W., *Dignity and Vulnerability: Strength and Quality of Character* (Berkeley, CA: University of California Press, 1997).

Harris, J., 'Goodbye Dolly? The Ethics of Human Cloning', *Journal of Medical Ethics*, 23 (1997), pp.353–360.

Harris, J. (ed.), *Bioethics* (New York: Oxford University Press, 2001).

Harris, J. and John, S., 'Genetic Equity', *Nature Reviews Genetics*, 5 (2004), pp.796–800.

Hart, H. L. A., *Punishment and Responsibility* (Oxford: Clarendon Press, 1984).

Harvey, R. (ed.), *Joyous Wakes, Dignified Deaths: Issues in Death and Dying* (Albany, NY: State University of New York Press).

Hauerwas, S., 'Suffering Presence', *Theological Reflections on Medicine, the Mentally Handicapped, and the Church* (Edinburgh: T & T Clark, 1986).

Hauerwas, S., *God, Medicine, and Suffering* (Grand Rapids, MI: William B. Eerdmans, 1990).

Hayakawa, S. I., *Language in Thought and Action* (New York: Harcourt Brace Jovanovich, 1978).

Heaney, S., *The Redress of Poetry* (London: Faber & Faber, 1995).

Heidegger, M., 'Building Dwelling Thinking', in: *Poetry, Language, Thought* (New York: Harper Colophon Books, 1975).
Heidegger, M., 'Letter on Humanism', in *Martin Heidegger: Basic Writings*, ed. David Farrell Krell (New York: Harper Collins, 1993), pp. 213–266.
Henkin, L., 'International Human Rights as "Rights"', in: M. Winston (ed.), *The Philosophy of Human Rights* (Belmont, CA: Wadsworth, 1989), pp.134–135.
Henkin, L., 'Human Dignity and Constitutional Rights', in: M. J. Meyer and W. A. Parent (eds.), *The Constitution of Rights: Human Dignity and American Values* (Ithaca, NY: Cornell University Press, 1992).
Hetherington, J., *Forty-Two Faces* (Melbourne, Cheshire, 1962).
Hill, T. E., *Respect, Pluralism, and Justice: Kantian Perspectives* (Oxford: Oxford University Press, 2000).
Hobbes, T., Leviathan, R. Tuck (ed.) (Cambridge: Cambridge University Press, 1996).
Hobson, R., *Forms of Feeling: The Heart of Psychotherapy* (London: Routledge, 1985).
Hockett, Charles F., *A Course in Modern Linguistics* (New York: Macmillan, 1958).
Hockley, J., 'The Concept of Hope and the Will to Live', *Palliative Medicine*, 7 (1993), pp.181–186.
Holloway, R., *Doubts and Loves: What Is Left of Christianity* (Edinburgh: Canongate Books, 2002).
Hopkins, G. M., 'That Nature is a Heraclitean Fire and of the Comfort of the Resurrection', in: Robert Bridges (ed.), *Poems of Gerard Manley Hopkins* (London: Humphrey Milford, 1918).
Horder, J. (ed.), *Oxford Essays in Jurisprudence*, 4th Series (Oxford: Oxford University Press, 2000).
Hörnle, T., 'Offensive Behaviour and German Penal Law', *Buffalo Criminal Law Review*, 5 (2001), pp.255–278.
Horton, R., 'Rediscovering Human Dignity', *The Lancet*, 364 (2004), pp.1081–1085.
House of Lords, United Kingdom, Select Committee on the Assisted Dying for the Terminally Ill Bill Report House of Lords Paper 86-I discussed in: 'Assisted Dying for the Terminally Ill: House of Lords Select Committee', *Bulletin of Medical Ethics*, 206 (2005), pp.9–11.
Howard, R. and Donnelly, J., 'Human Dignity, Human Rights and Political Regimes', *American Political Science Review*, 80 (1986), pp.801–817.
Howard, R., 'Dignity, Community, and Human Rights', in: A. A. An-Na'im (ed.), *Human Rights in Cross-Cultural Perspective: A Request for Consensus* (Philadelphia, PA: University of Pennsylvania Press, 1992).
Hume, D., 'On the Dignity or Meanness of Human Nature', in: S. Copley and A. Edgar (eds.), *David Hume—Selected Essays* (Oxford: Oxford University Press, 1996).
Hunter, W., *Introductory Lectures to Students*, St. Thomas' Hospital Manuscript, 55, 182, (ca. 1780).
Hurwitz, B., 'Narrative and the Practice of Medicine', *The Lancet*, 356 (2000), pp.2086–2089.
Iglesias, T., 'Bedrock Truths and the Dignity of the Individual', *Logos* 4 (2001), pp.114–134.
Inoue, K., *Individual Dignity in Modern Japanese Thought: The Evolution of the Concept of Jinkaku in Moral and Educational Discourse*, Michigan Monograph Series in Japanese Studies, 35 (Ann Arbor, MI: University of Michigan, 2001).
Ionesco, Eugène quoted in George Steiner, 'The Retreat from the Word', in: *Language and Silence: Essays on Language, Literature, and the Inhuman* (New York: Atheneum, 1977).
Ishay, M. R., *The History of Human Rights: From Ancient Times to the Globalization Era* (Berkeley, CA: University of California Press, 2004).
Ishiguro, K., *The Remains of the Day* (London: Faber & Faber, 1996).
Ishiguro, K., *Never Let Me Go* (London: Faber & Faber, 2003).
Israel Democracy Institute, *Human Dignity in the Israel Defence Forces* (Israel: Israel Democracy Institute, 2001).
Ivanhoe, P. J and van Norden B., *Readings in Classical Chinese Philosophy* (Indianapolis, IN: Hackett, 2001).
James, W., *Varieties of Religious Experience* (New York: Random House Modern Library, 1957).
Kahn, M., *Between Therapist and Client: The New Relationship* (New York: Freeman, 1997).
Kaku, M., *Visions* (Oxford: Oxford University Press, 1998).

Kant, I., *Grounding for the Metaphysics of Morals* (1785), trans. James W. Ellington (Indianapolis, IN: Hackett, 1981).

Kant, I., *Groundwork of the Metaphysics of Morals* (1785), trans. H. J. Paton (New York: Harper, 1964).

Kant, I., *The Metaphysics of Morals* (1797), trans. M. Gregor (Cambridge: Cambridge University Press, 1991).

Kaplan, O., 'The Development of the Informed Consent Doctrine in the Israeli Courts', 15th World Congress on Medical Law Sydney, 2 August 2004.

Karpin, 'Book Review', *Medical Literature Review*, 12 (2004), pp.323–327.

Kerr, F., *Immortal Longings* (London: SPCK, 1997).

Kilmer, J. F., Miller, A. B., and Pellegrino, E. D. (eds.), *Dignity and Dying: A Christian Appraisal* (Grand Rapids, MI: William B. Eerdmans, 1996).

Kilner, J. F., 'Human Dignity', *Encyclopaedia of Bioethics* (New York: Macmillan Reference USA, 3rd edn., 2004).

Kilner, J. F., 'Human Dignity', *Encyclopaedia of Bioethics* (New York: Macmillan Reference USA, 3rd edn., 2004).

King, Martin, L. Jr., 'Letter from Birmingham Jail', 1963, http://www.africa.upenn.edu/Articles_Gen/Letter_Birmingham.html

Kingsbury, D. and Harry, A. (eds.), *Autonomy and Disintegration in Indonesia* (London/New York: Routledge Curzon, 2003).

Kirklin, D. and Richardson R. (eds.), *Medical Humanities: A Practical Introduction* (London: Royal College of Physicians, 2001).

Klastersky, J., Schimpff, S. and Senn, H. J. (eds.), *Supportive Care for Oncologists: A Handbook for Oncologists* (New York: Dekker, 2nd edn., 1999), pp.677–692.

Kmir, O., 'Honor and Dignity Cultures: The Case of Kavod and Kvod Ha-Adam in Israeli Society and Law', in: D. Kretzmer and E. Klein (eds.), *The Concept of Human Dignity in Human Rights Discourse* (The Hague: Kluwer Law International, 2002).

Korsgaard, C. M., *Creating the Kingdom of Ends* (Cambridge: Cambridge University Press, 1996).

Korsgaard, C. M., *The Sources of Normativity* (Cambridge: Cambridge University Press, 1996).

Kramer, K., *The Sacred Art of Dying* (New York: Paulist Press, 1988).

Kretzmer, D. and E. Klein (eds.), *The Concept of Human Dignity in Human Rights Discourse* (The Hague: Kluwer Law International, 2002).

Kripke, S., 'Identity and Necessity', in: Milton K. Munitz (ed.), *Identity and Individuation* (New York: New York University Press, 1971), pp.135–164.

Kripke, S., 'Naming and Necessity', in: G. Harman and D. Davidson (eds.), *Semantics of Natural Language* (Dordrecht, The Netherlands: D. Reidel, 1972), pp.253–355.

Kroeke, C. H. et al., 'Social Networks, Social Support, and Survival After Breast Cancer Diagnosis', *Journal of Clinical Oncology*, 24 (2006), p.1105.

Kung, H. and Walter, J., *Dying with Dignity: A Plea for Personal Responsibility* (New York: Continuum, 1998).

Kymlicka, W., *Contemporary Political Philosophy: An Introduction* (Oxford: Oxford University Press, 1990).

Lacey, N., *State Punishment: Political Principles and Community Values* (London: Routledge, 1988).

Lacey, N., *Unspeakable Subjects: Feminist Essays in Legal and Social Theory* (Oxford: Hart, 1998).

Lau, D. C., *Confucius: The Analects* (Hong Kong: The Chinese University Press, 1992).

Levinas, E., *Basic Philosophical Writings*, edited by A. Peperzak, S. Critchley, and R. Bernasconi (Bloomington, IN: Indiana University Press, 1996).

Lewis, B., *The Political Language of Islam* (Chicago, IL: University of Chicago Press, 1988).

Lewis-Williams, D., *The Mind in the Cave* (London: Thames & Hudson, 2002).

Lickiss, J. N., *The Aboriginal People of Sydney: A Study of Human Ecology,* M.D. thesis (Sydney: University of Sydney, 1972).

Lickiss, J. N., 'Speech and Community', *Proceedings of Annual Convention of Australian Association for Speech and Hearing* (1978), pp.4–12.

Lickiss, J. N., 'On the Care of Our Aged: Privilege and Responsibility', *Australian Rehabilitation Review*, 2 (6) (1982), pp.51–57.
Lickiss, J. N., 'Care of the Patient Close to Death', in: J. Klastersky, S. Schimpff, and H. J. Senn (eds.), *Supportive Care for Oncologists: A Handbook for Oncologists* (New York: Dekker, 2nd edn., 1999), pp.677–692.
Lickiss, J. N., 'Late Lessons from Auschwitz: Is There Anything More to Learn for the 21st Century?', letter, *Journal of Medical Ethics*, 27 (2001), pp.137–138.
Lively, P., *Perfect Happiness* (London: Heinemann, 1983).
Lo, Y. S., 'Natural and Artifactual: Restored Nature as Subject', *Environmental Ethics* 21 (1999), pp.247–266.
Luria, Y., 'A Matter of Dignity', in: A. Nemdar (ed.), *Virtues and Feelings* (Ramat Gan: Hoshen Le Mishpat, 1994).
Lyotard, Jean F., *Rudiments Païens* quoted in Michel de Certeau, *The Practice of Everyday Life* (Berkeley, CA: University of California Press, 1988).
M. Winston (ed.), *The Philosophy of Human Rights* (Belmont, CA: Wadsworth, 1989), pp.134–135.
Mackler, A. L., *Jewish and Catholic Bioethics: A Comparative Analysis* (Washington, DC: Georgetown University Press, 2003).
Macklin, R., 'Cloning and Public Policy', in: J. Burley and J. Harris (eds.), *A Companion to Genetics* (Oxford: Blackwell, 2002).
Macklin, R., 'Dignity is a Useless Concept', *British Medical Journal*, 327 (2003), pp.1419–1420.
Macklin, R., 'Reflections on the Human Dignity Symposium: Is Dignity a Useless Concept?', *Journal of Palliative Care*, 20 (2004), pp.212–216.
Macquarrie, J., *In Search of Humanity* (London: SCM Press, 1982).
Malpas, J., *Place and Experience: A Philosophical Topography* (Cambridge: Cambridge University Press, 1999).
Manderson, D., 'Philosophical Basis of the Duty of Care', unpublished lecture, Annual Symposium, Sydney Institute of Palliative Medicine (2001).
Manuel Wackenheim v. France, Communication No. 854/1999, United Nations Document CCPR/C/75/D/8541999 (13 November 1996), United Nations Document A/57/40 at 179 (2002) Decision of the Human Rights Committee, 75th Session, 26 September 2002.
Markhan, Edwin, *The Shoes of Happiness and Other Poems* (New York: Doubleday, 1916).
Maslow, A. H., *Motivation and Personality* (New York: Harper & Row, 1970).
Mason, C. (ed.), *Journeys Into Palliative Care: Roots and Reflections* (London: Jessica Kingsley, 2002).
Mayer, J. D. and Cobb, C. D., 'Educational Policy on Emotional Intelligence: Does It Make Sense?', *Educational Psychology Review*, 12 (2000), pp.163–183.
Mayor, S., 'United Nations Calls for Ban on All Forms of Human Cloning', *BioEdge*, 149 (8 March 2005), p.3.
Mayor, S., 'United Nations Committee Approves Declaration on Human Cloning', *British Medical Journal*, 330 (2005), p.496.
McGrew, A. G., 'Human Rights in a Global Age: Coming to Terms with Globalization', in: T. Evans (ed.), *Human Rights Fifty Years On: A Reappraisal* (Manchester: Manchester University Press, 1998).
Meier, D. E. et al., 'A National Survey of Physician-assisted Suicide and Euthanasia in the United States', *New England Journal of Medicine*, 338 (1998), pp.1193–1201.
Meier, D. E., Back A. L., and Morrison S., 'The Inner Life of Physicians and the Care of the Seriously Ill', *Journal of the American Medical Association*, 286 (2001), pp.3007–3014.
Mendiola, M. M., 'Overworked, but Uncritically Tested: Human Dignity and the Aid-in-dying Debate', in: E. E. Shelp (ed.), *Secular Bioethics in Theological Perspective* (Dordrecht, The Netherlands: Kluwer, 1996).
Meyer, M. J. and Parent, W. A. (eds.), *The Constitution of Rights: Human Dignity and American Values* (Ithaca, NY: Cornell University Press, 1992).
Meyer, M. J., 'Dignity as a (Modern) Virtue', in: D. Kretzmer and E. Klein, E. (eds.), *The Concept of Human Dignity in Human Rights Discourse* (The Hague: Kluwer Law International, 2002).
Meyer, M. J., 'Dignity, Rights and Self-control', *Ethics*, 99 (1989), p.524.

Meyers, D. W., *The Human Body and the Law: A Medico-legal Study* (1970) (Edinburgh: Edinburgh University Press, 2nd edn., 1990).
Miguel, C. R., 'Human Dignity: History of an Idea', http://search.netscape.com/ns/boomframe.jsp?query=human+dignity=history=idea=miguel&page=1&0ffset=0&, 20 January 2005.
Mill, J. S., *On Liberty and Other Essays* (Oxford: Oxford University Press, 1998).
Miller, F. G., 'The Good Death, Virtue, and Physician-assisted Death: An Examination of the Hospice Way of Death', *Cambridge Quarterly of Healthcare Ethics*, 5 (1996), pp.92–97.
Milosz, C., *The Captive Mind,* trans. Jane Zielonko from the Polish (Ringwood: Penguin, 1980).
Mollenkott, Virginia R., 'Reproductive Choice: Basic to Justice for Women', *Christian Scholar's Review* 17 (March 1988), pp.286–293.
Moller, D. W., *On Death Without Dignity: The Human Impact of Technical Dying* (Amityville, New York: Baywood, 1990).
Montgomery, K., *Doctors' Stories: The Narrative Structure of Medical Knowledge* (Princeton, NJ: Princeton University Press, 1991).
More, E. S. and M. A. Milligan (eds.), *The Empathic Practitioner: Empathy, Gender, and Medicine* (New Brunswick, NJ: Rutgers University Press, 1994).
Morisaki, T., 'Human ES Cell Research', in: R. Ida (ed.), *Final Report on the Project Dialogue and Promotion of Bioethics in Asia* (Kyoto: Kyoto University, 2004).
Morris, D. B., 'Narrative, Ethics, and Thinking with Stories', *Narrative*, 9 (2001), pp.55–77.
Morse, J. M. and Doberneck, B., 'Delineating the Concept of Hope', *Sigma Theta Tau International*, 27 (1995), pp.277–285.
Morse, J. M., 'Toward a Praxis Theory of Suffering', *Advances in Nursing Science*, 24 (2001), pp.47–59.
Mortimer, K., 'The Impossible Profession: The Doctor–Priest Relationship', *Proceedings of the Australian Association of Gerontology*, 2 (1974), pp.81–82.
Moynihan, R., 'Who Pays for the Pizza? Redefining the Relationships Between Doctors and Drug Companies 2: Disentanglement', *British Medical Journal*, 326 (2003), pp.1193–1196.
Moynihan, R. and Sweet, M., 'Medicine, the Media and Monetary Interests: The Need for Transparency and Professionalism', *Medical Journal of Australia*, 17 (2000), pp.631–634.
Muller, C. Y., 'The Miracle of Life and the Privilege of Death', *Obstetrics and Gynecology*, 103 (2004), pp.1314–1316.
Munzer, S., 'Property, Patents and Genetic Material', in: J. Burley and J. Harris (eds.), *A Companion to Genetics* (Ames, IA: Blackwell, 2002).
Needleman, J., 'The Perception of Mortality', *Annals of the New York Academy of Sciences*, 164 (3) (1969), pp.733–738.
Nekolaichuk, C. L. and Bruera, E., 'On the Nature of Hope in Palliative Care', *Journal of Palliative Care*, 14 (1998), pp.36–42.
Nelson, H. L. (ed.), *Stories and Their Limits: Narrative Approaches to Bioethics* (New York: Routledge, 1997).
Nemdar, A. (ed.), *Virtues and Feelings* (Ramat Gan: Hoshen Le Mishpat, 1994).
Nordenfeldt, L., 'Dignity and the Care of the Elderly', *Medicine, Health Care and Philosophy*, 6 (2003), pp.103–106.
Norrie, A., *Crime, Reason and History* (London: Weidenfeld & Nicolson, 1993).
Norrie, A., 'Simulacra of Morality? Beyond the Ideal/Actual Antinomies of Criminal Justice', in: R. A. Duff (ed.), *Philosophy and the Criminal Law* (Cambridge: Cambridge University Press, 1998).
Norrie, A., *Punishment, Responsibility and Justice: A Relational Critique* (Oxford: Oxford University Press, 2000).
Novak, M., 'The Judeo-Christian Foundation of Human Dignity, Personal Liberty, and the Concept of the Person', *Journal of Markets and Morality*, 1 (1998), pp.107–121.
Novak, M., 'Human Dignity, Human Rights', *First Things*, 97 (1999), pp.39–42.
Nuland, S. B., *How We Die: Reflections on Life's Final Chapter* (New York: Alfred A. Knopf, 1994).
Nussbaum, M., 'Love's Knowledge', *Essays on Philosophy and Literature* (New York: Oxford University Press, 1990).

Nussbaum, M., *Upheavals of Thought: The Intelligence of the Emotions* (Cambridge: Cambridge University Press, 2001).
O'Rourke, K. and P. Boyle, *Medical Ethics*, 2nd edn. (Washington, DC: Georgetown University Press, 1993).
Oades, Rizalino, A., *The Social and Economic Background of Philippine Nationalism*, 1830–1892 (Ph.D. thesis, University of Hawaii, 1972, [microfilm]. University of Hawaii, 1974).
Oregon Health Division, *Oregon's Death with Dignity Act: Three Years of Legalized Physician-assisted Suicide* (Portland, OR: Oregon Health Division, 22 February 2001).
Osler, W., *The Principles and Practice of Medicine* (New York: Appleton, 1892).
Ossorio, P., 'Legal and Ethical Issues in Biotechnology Patenting', in: J. Burley and J. Harris (eds.), *A Companion to Genetics* (Ames, IA: Blackwell, 2002), pp.414–416.
Pannenberg, W., *Anthropology in Theological Perspective*, trans. M. O'Connell (Edinburgh: T & T Clark, 1985).
Paul, R., *The Symbolism of Evil* (Boston, MA: Beacon Books, 1969).
Pellegrino, E. D. and Thomasma, D. C., *The Virtues in Medical Practice* (New York: Oxford University Press, 1993).
Pellegrino, E. and Thomasma, D., *The Christian Virtues in Legal Practice*, (Ann Arbor, MI: Georgetown University Press, 1996).
Peters, F. E., *Greek Philosophical Terms: A Historical Lexicon* (New York: New York University Press, 1967).
Pildes, R. H. and Niemi, R. G., 'Expressive Harms, "Bizarre Districts", and Voting Rights', *Michigan Law Review*, 92 (1993).
Pintos, G. D and David, N. Weisstub (eds.), *Human Rights and Health Care*, (Dordrecht, The Netherlands: Springer, 2006).
Pollis, A. and Schwab P. (eds.), *Human Rights: Cultural and Ideological Perspectives* (New York: Praeger, 1979).
Pope Benedict XVI, *The Human Person, The Heart of Peace: Message for the Celebration of the World Day of Peace*, 1 January 2007, para. 2, http://www.vatican.va/holy_father/benedict_xvi/messages/peace/documents/hf_ben-xvi_mes_20061208_xl-world-day-peace_en.html
Pope John Paul II, Papal Encyclical 1993, *Veritatis Splendor*, http://www.vatican.va/holy_father/john_paul_ii/encyclicals/documents/hf_jp-ii_enc_06081993_veritatis-splendor_en.html
Pope John Paul II, Papal Encyclical 1991, *Centesimus Annus*, http://www.vatican.va/holy_father/john_paul_ii/encyclicals/documents/hf_jp-ii_enc_01051991_centesimus-annus_en.html
Pope Leo XIII, Papal Encyclical, *Rerum Novarum, On Capital and Labor Encyclical*, 15 May 1891, http://www.papalencyclicals.net/Leo13/l13rerum.htm
Pope Leo XIII, Papal Encyclical, *Libertas*: *On the Nature of Human Liberty*, 20 June 1888, http://www.papalencyclicals.net/Leo13/l13liber.htm
President's Council on Bioethics, *Human Cloning and Human Dignity: An Ethical Inquiry*, Washington D. C., July 2002, http://www.bioethics.gov/reports/cloningreport/index.html
Pritchard M., 'Human Dignity and Justice', *Ethics*, 82 (1972), pp.299–213.
Quill, T. E., *Death and Dignity. Making Choices and Taking Charge* (New York: W.W. Norton, 1993).
Quill, T. E. et al., 'The Debate Over Physician-assisted Suicide: Empirical Data and Convergent Views', *Annals of Internal Medicine*, 128 (1998), pp.552–558.
Rachels, J., *The End of Life: Euthanasia and Morality* (Oxford: Oxford University Press, 1986).
Raz, J., *The Morality of Freedom* (Oxford: Clarendon Press, 1986).
Raz, J., 'Autonomy, Toleration and the Harm Principle', in: R. Gavison (ed.), *Issues in Contemporary Legal Philosophy* (Oxford: Clarendon Press, 1987).
Reid, A. (ed.), *Slavery, Bondage and Dependency in Southeast Asia* (Brisbane: University of Queensland Press, 1983).
Remen, R., *Kitchen Table Wisdom* (New York: Riverhead Books, 1996).
Resnick, J. and J. C. Suk, 'Adding Insult to Injury: Questioning the Role of Dignity in Conceptions of Sovereignty', *Stanford Law Review*, 55 (2003), pp.1921–1962.

Rhinelander, P. H., *Is Man Comprehensible to Man?* (Stanford, CA: Stanford University Press, 1973).

Rich, A., 'The Demon Lover', in: *Leaflets* (New York: W. W. Norton, 1981).

Rich, B., 'A Prescription for the Pain: The Emerging Standard of Care for Pain Management', *William Mitchell Law Review*, 26 (1999), pp.1–92.

Richards, I. A., *The Philosophy of Rhetoric* (New York: Oxford University Press, 1965, ca. 1936).

Robertson, J., 'Human Cloning and the Challenge of Regulation', *New England Journal of Medicine*, 339 (1998), pp.119–121.

Robinson, R., *An Atheist's Values* (Oxford: Basil Blackwell, 1975).

Rogers, C., *On Becoming a Person: The Therapist's View of Psychotherapy* (London: Constable, 1967).

Rolston, H., III, *Environmental Ethics* (Philadelphia, PA: Temple University Press, 1988).

Rotenstreich, N., *Man and His Dignity* (Jerusalem: Magnes Press, 1983).

Sacks, J., *The Dignity of Difference: How to Avoid the Clash of Civilizations* (London: Continuum, 2002).

Scarry, E., *The Body in Pain: The Making and Unmaking of the World* (New York: Oxford University Press, 1985).

Schachter, O., 'Human Dignity as a Normative Concept', *American Journal of International Law*, 77 (4) (1983), pp.848–854.

Schneider, C. E., *The Practice of Autonomy: Patients, Doctors, and Medical Decisions* (New York: Oxford University Press, 1998).

Schopenhauer, A., O*n the Basis of Morality*, trans. E. F. J. Payne (Providence: Berghahn Books, 1995).

Schotsmans, P. and Meulenbergs, T. (eds.), *Euthanasia and Palliative Care in the Low Countries* (Leuven, Belgium: Peeters, 2005).

Shelp, E. E. (ed.), *Secular Bioethics in Theological Perspective* (Dordrecht, The Netherlands: Kluwer, 1996).

Shorey v. PT Ltd (2003) *197 ALR 410*; Re by Gardner Public Advocate (2003) Unreported Victorian Supreme Court, BC200302640.

Shultziner, D., 'Human Dignity–Functions and Meanings', *Global Jurist Topics*, 3 (2003), pp.1–21.

Silver, L., *Re-making Eden* (London: Weidenfeld & Nicolson, 1998).

Simester, A. P. and von Hirsch, A., 'Rethinking the Offense Principle', *Legal Theory*, 8 (2002), pp.269–295.

Singer, P., *Writings on the Ethical Life* (New York: The Ecco Press, 2000).

Skene, L., *Law and Medical Practice* (Sydney: Butterworths, 2004).

Skinner, B. F., *Beyond Freedom and Dignity* (Indianapolis, IN: Hackett, 2002 [1971]).

Snyder, L. and Sulmasy, D. P. (For the Ethics and Human Rights Committee, American College of Physicians) 'Physician-assisted Suicide', *Annals of Internal Medicine*, 135 (2001), pp.209–216.

Sokalska, M. E., *Review European Journal of Health Law*, 9 (2002), pp.413–421.

Spencer, H., *The Principles of Ethics*, 1, Part 2, Chapter 8 (1879).

Spiegelberg, H., 'Human Dignity: A Challenge to Contemporary Philosophy', in: R. Gotesky and E. Laszlo (eds.), *Human Dignity. This Century and the Next* (New York: Gordon & Breach, 1970).

St Joseph's Hospice, *Mission Statement* (ca. 1980).

Stanley, H. E. J. (trans.), *The Philippine Islands* (London: Hakluyt Society, 1868).

Statman, D., 'Two Concepts of Dignity', *Iyyuney Mishpat*, 24 (2001), pp.541–603.

Statman, D., 'Humiliation, Dignity and Self-Respect', in: D. Kretzmer and E. Klein (eds.), *The Concept of Human Dignity in Human Rights Discourse* (The Hague: Kluwer Law International, 2002).

Steiner, G., *After Babel: Aspects of Language and Translation* (Oxford: Oxford University Press, 1992).

Steiner, G., *Language and Silence: Essays on Language, Literature, and the Inhuman* (New York: Atheneum, 1977).

Steinhauser, K. E. et al., 'In Search of a Good Death: Observations of Patients, Families, and Providers', *Annals of Internal Medicine*, 132 (2000), pp.825–832.
Steinhauser, K. E. et al., 'Factors Considered Important at the End of Life by Patients, Family, Physicians, and Other Care Providers', *Journal of the American Medical Association*, 284 (2000), pp.2476–2482.
Stern, D., *The Interpersonal World of the Human Infant* (New York: Basic Books, 1984).
Steve, F., *Syncretism in the West*, http://www.safarmer.com/pico/oration.html
Street, A. and Kissane, D., 'Constructions of Dignity in End-of-Life Care', *Journal of Palliative Care*, 17 (2001), pp.93–101.
Sullivan, A. D. K. Hedberg, and Fleming D. W., 'Legalized Physician-assisted Suicide in Oregon: The Second Year's Experience', *New England Journal of Medicine*, 342 (2000), pp.598–604.
Sullivan, P., *Social Relations of Dependence in a Malay State: Nineteenth-Century Perak* (The Malaysian Branch of the Royal Asiatic Society, monograph no. 10. Kuala Lumpur: MBRAS., 1982), p.63
Sulmasy, D. P., 'Death and Human Dignity', *Linacre Quarterly*, 61 (4) (1994), p.27–36.
Sulmasy, D. P., *The Healer's Calling. A Spirituality for Physicians and Other Health Care Professionals* (New York: The Paulist Press, 1997).
Sulmasy, D. P., 'Death With Dignity: What Does It Mean?', *Josephinum Journal of Theology*, 4 (1997), pp.13–23.
Sulmasy, D. P., 'Death, Dignity, and the Theory of Value', *Ethical Perspectives*, 9 (2003), pp.103–118.
Sulmasy, D. P., 'Dignity and the Human as a Natural Kind', in: C. R. Taylor and R. Dell'Oro. (eds.), *Health and Human Flourishing* (Washington, DC: Georgetown University Press, 2006).
Sulmasy, D. P., 'Dignity, Rights, Health Care, and Human Flourishing', in: G. Diaz Pintos and David N. Weisstub (eds.), *Human Rights and Health Care* (Dordrecht, The Netherlands: Springer, 2006).
Sulston, J. and Ferry, G., *The Common Thread* (London: Corgi Books, 2004).
Supplementary Convention on the Abolition of Slavery, the Slave Trade and Institutions and Practices Similar to Slavery, adopted on 7 September 1956.
Susin, L. C., 'A Critique of the Identity Paradigm', *Concilium* (2000/2), pp.78–90.
Svensson, M., 'Review of Confucianism and Human Rights', *Journal of Asian Studies*, 58 (1999), pp.1–2.
Tarnas, R., *The Passion of the Western Mind: Understanding the Ideas that have Shaped Our World View* (New York: Ballantyne Books, 1991).
Tataryn, D. and Chochinov, H. M., 'Predicting the Trajectory of the Will to Live in Terminally Ill Patients', *Psychosomatics*, 43 (2002), pp.370–377.
Taussig, M. T., *The Devil and Commodity Fetishism in South America* (Chapel Hill, NC: University of North Carolina Press, 1980).
Taylor, C., *The Sources of the Self: The Making of Modern Identity* (Cambridge, MA: Harvard University Press, 1989).
Taylor, C., 'The Politics of Recognition', in: A. Gutmann (ed.), *Multiculturalism and "the Politics of Recognition": An Essay* (Princeton, NJ: Princeton University Press, 1992).
Taylor, C. R. and Dell'Oro, R., *Health and Human Flourishing* (Washington, DC: Georgetown University Press, 2006).
ten Have, Henk, 'From Synthesis and System to Morals and Procedure: The Development of Philosophy of Medicine', in: R. A. Carson and C. R. Burns (eds.), *Philosophy of Medicine and Bioethics* (Dordrecht, The Netherlands: Kluwer, 1997), pp.105–123.
ten Have, Henk, 'Images of Man in Philosophy of Medicine', *Advances in Bioethics*, 4 (1998), pp.173–193.
The African Charter on Human and People's Rights, 17 June 1981, http://www1.umn.edu/humanrts/instree/z1afchar.htm
The American Declaration of the Rights and Duties of Man, 1948.
The Basic Law of Federal Republic of Germany, 1949, http://www.iuscomp.org/gla/statutes/GG.htm
The Basic Law of Spain, 1945, http://www.servat.unibe.ch/law/icl/sp00000_.html

The Constitution of China, adopted 4 December 1982, http://english.people.com.cn/constitution/constitution.html

The Constitution of Hungary, 20 August 1949, http://www.constitution.org/cons/hungary.txt

The Constitution of India, 1949, http://indiacode.nic.in/coiweb/welcome.html

The Constitution of Iran, adopted 24 October 1979, http://www.iranonline.com/iran/iran-info/Government/constitution.html

The Constitution of Ireland, 1937, http://www.taoiseach.gov.ie/attached_files/html%20files/Constitution%20of%20Ireland%20(Eng)Nov2004.htm

The Constitution of Portugal, 2 April 1976, http://www.servat.unibe.ch/law/icl/po00000_.html

The Constitution of South Africa, 1996, http://www.info.gov.za/documents/constitution/index.htm

The Constitution of Thailand, 1997, http://www.parliament.go.th/files/library/b05-b.htm

The Israeli Basic Law: Human Dignity and Liberty, 25 March 1992 (revised at 10 March 1994), http://www.jewishvirtuallibrary.org/jsource/Politics/Basic_Law_Human_Dignity_and_Liberty.html

The Lambeth Conference, *Resolutions from 1998*, http://www.lambethconference.org/resolutions/1998/1998–1–14.cfm

The Universal Declaration of Human Rights, http://www.un.org/Overview/rights.html

Thomasma, D. C., Weisstub D. N. and Herve, C. (eds.), *Personhood and Health Care* (Dordrecht, The Netherlands: Kluwer, 2001).

Tomasi, J., *Liberalism Beyond Justice: Citizens, Society, and the Boundaries of Political Theory* (Princeton, NJ: Princeton University Press, 2001).

Tooley, M., *Abortion and Infanticide* (Oxford: Clarendon Press, 1983).

Trinkaus, C., 'The Renaissance Idea of the Dignity of Man', in: Philip P. Weiner (ed.), *Dictionary of the History of Ideas*, Vol. IV (New York: Charles Scribners' Sons, 1973), pp.136–147, http://etext.lib.virginia.edu/cgi-local/DHI/dhi.cgi?id=dv4–20

Turner, K. R. et al., 'Dignity in Dying: A Preliminary Study of Patients in the Last Three Days of Life', *Journal of Palliative Care*, 12 (1996), pp.7–13.

UK, Department of Health A Joint Committee of the Human Genetics Advisory Commission and the Human Fertilisation and Embryology Authority, *Cloning Issues in Reproduction Science and Medicine* (December 1998), http://www.advisorybodies.doh.gov.uk/hgac/papers/papers_c.htm

UK, Department of Health, Stem Cell Research: Medical Progress with Responsibility (June 2000); A Report from the Chief Medical Officer's Expert Group Reviewing the Potential of Developments in Stem Cell Research and Cell Nuclear Replacement to Benefit Human Health and Government Response to the Recommendations Made in the Chief Medical Officer's Expert Group Report, CM 4833 (August 2000), http://www.dh.gov.uk/prod_consum_dh/groups/dh_digitalassets/@dh/@en/documents/digitalasset/dh_4065085.pdf

UNESCO, Declaration on Bioethics and Human Rights, 2005.

United Nations Covenant on Civil and Political Rights, adopted by GA Res. 2200A of 16 December 1966, http://www.unhchr.ch/html/menu3/b/a_ccpr.htm

United Nations Covenant on Economic, Social and Cultural Rights, adopted by GA Res. 2200A (XXI) of 16 December 1966, http://www.arabhumanrights.org/cbased/ga/covenant-escr66e.html

Universal Declaration of Human Rights, http://www.un.org/Overview/rights.html

Vacco v. Quill 521 US 793 (1997)

Vatican Council II, 'Pastoral Constitution on the Church in the Modern World', 7 December 1965, http://www.vatican.va/archive/hist_councils/ii_vatican_council/documents/vat-ii_cons_19651207_gaudium-et-spes_en.html

Veatch, R., Th*e Basics of Bioethics* (New York: Prentice-Hall, 2nd edn., 2002).

Victoria, Parliament of, Social Development Committee, *Report on Inquiry into Options for Dying with Dignity: Incorporating a Discussion Paper on a Range of Views on Options for Dying with Dignity* VGPO, Melbourne (1986).

von Hagens, G. and Whalley A. (eds.*), Body Worlds—The Anatomical Exhibition of Real Human Bodies*, (Germany: Institute for Plastination, 2002).

Walter, T., *The Revival of Death* (London: Routledge, 1994).
Walzer, M., *Thick and Thin: Moral Argument at Home and Abroad* (Notre Dame: University of Notre Dame Press, 1994).
Warnock, M., 'Philosophy and Ethics', in: C. Cookson et al., *Genetic Engineering: The New Challenge* (European Union Patent Office, 1993).
Warren, J. F., *The Sulu Zone* (Singapore: Singapore UP, 1981).
Warren, Mary, A., 'On the Moral and Legal Status of Abortion', in: *Biomedical Ethics*, pp.417–423.
Weeks, J. et al., 'Relationship Between Cancer Patients' Predictions of Prognosis and Their Treatment Preferences,' *Journal of the American Medical Association*, 279 (1988), pp.1709–1714.
Welie, J. V. M., *In the Face of Suffering: The Philosophical Foundations of Clinical Ethics* (Omaha, NE: Creighton University Press, 1998).on University Press.
Wetz, F. J., 'The Dignity of Man', in: G. von Hagens and A. Whalley (eds.), *Body Worlds—The Anatomical Exhibition of Real Human Bodies*(Germany: Institute for Plastination, 2002).
White, P., *The Aunt's Story* (London, Eyre & Spottiswoode, 1948).
White, P., 'The Prodigal Son', *Australian Letters*, I, 1 (1958).
White, P., *The Tree of Man* (Ringwood: Penguin, 1963).
White, P., *Voss* (Ringwood: Penguin, 1971).
Whitman, W., 'Song of Myself', 7, *Leaves of Grass* (London: G.P. Putnam's sons, 1897).
Wicclair, M. R., *Ethics and the Elderly* (New York: Oxford University Press, 1993).
Wiggins, D., *Sameness and Substance* (Cambridge, MA: Harvard University Press, 1980).
Wiggins, D., *Sameness and Substance Renewed* (Cambridge: Cambridge University Press, 2001).
Williams, G., *Textbook of Criminal Law* (London: Stevens & Sons, 1983).
Winnicott, D., *The Family and Individual Development* (London: Tavistock, 1965).
Wittgenstein, L., *Philosophical Investigations*, trans. G.E.M. Anscombe, 3rd edn. (Oxford: Blackwell, 2001).
Wright, R. W., 'The Principles of Justice', *Notre Dame Law Review*, 75 (2000), pp.1859–1892.
Yalom, I., *Existential Psychotherapy* (New York: Basic Books, 1980).
Yates, K., 'The Nursing Perspective: Pain is the Breaking of the Shell that Encases your Understanding', in: C. Mason (ed.), *Journeys Into Palliative Care: Roots and Reflections* (London: Jessica Kingsley, 2002).
Zhang, Q., 'The Idea of Human Dignity in Classical Chinese Philosophy: A Reconstruction of Confucianism', *Journal of Chinese Philosophy*, 27 (2000), pp.299–323.

MIX
Papier aus verantwortungsvollen Quellen
Paper from responsible sources
FSC® C105338

If you have any concerns about our products,
you can contact us on
ProductSafety@springernature.com

In case Publisher is established outside the EU,
the EU authorized representative is:
Springer Nature Customer Service Center GmbH
Europaplatz 3, 69115 Heidelberg, Germany

Printed by Libri Plureos GmbH
in Hamburg, Germany